DEFINING AND APPLYING HRM IN THE WORKPLACE

DEFINING AND APPLYING HRM IN THE WORKPLACE
Essentials for the Real World

Richard Heiser

LANGDON STREET PRESS | MINNEAPOLIS, MN

Copyright © 2015 by Richard Heiser, Workforce HRM, LLC

Langdon Street Press
322 First Avenue N, 5th floor
Minneapolis, MN 55401
612.455.2293
www.langdonstreetpress.com

All rights reserved. No part of this publication may be reproduced, stored in a retrieval system, or transmitted, in any form or by any means, electronic, mechanical, photocopying, recording, or otherwise, without the prior written permission of the author.

The advice and strategies contained herein may not be suitable for every situation. This work is sold with the understanding that the publisher and author are not engaged in rendering legal, accounting or other professional services. If professional assistance is required, the services of a competent professional should be sought. Neither the publisher nor the author shall be liable for damages arising herein. The fact that an organization or website is referred to in this work as a citation and/or a potential source of further information does not mean that the author or the publisher endorses the information that the organization or website may provide or recommendations it may make. Further, readers should be aware that websites listed in this work may have changed or disappeared between when this work was written and when it is read.

ISBN-13: 978-1-63413-549-8
LCCN: 2015908073

Distributed by Itasca Books

Cover Design by Sophie Chi
Typeset by B. Cook

Printed in the United States of America

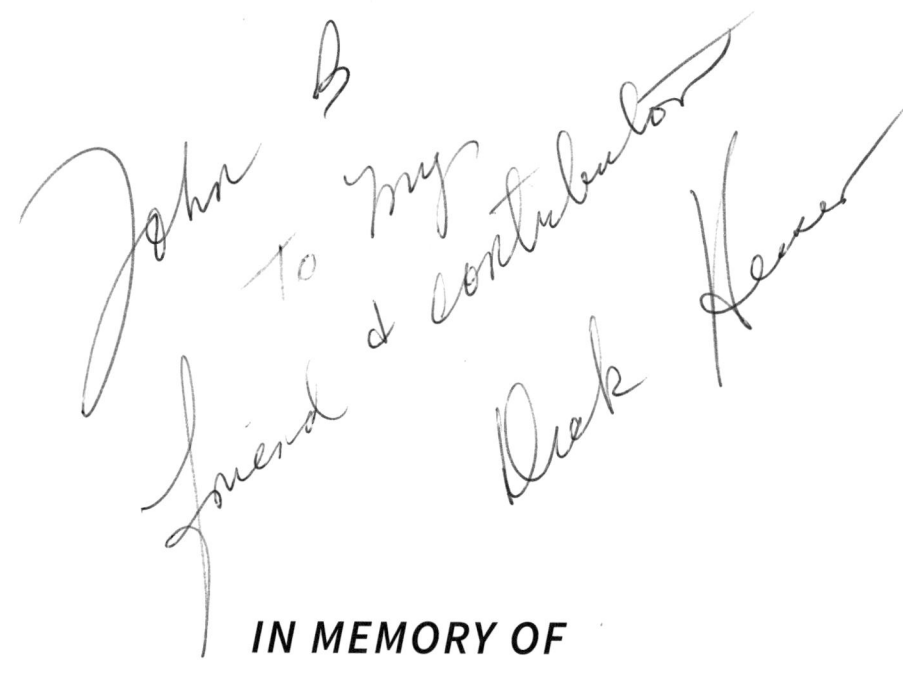

IN MEMORY OF
THESE GIANTS AMONG MEN

R. N. Hoerner, Sr.

M. P. MacDougall

Ermon Boyd

Charles E. Heiser

ACKNOWLEDGMENTS

One of my blessings has been an interesting and challenging career. In the first decade of my work life, several people were influential and/or connected with others to my benefit. I'd like to acknowledge J. C. Morgan, Meredith Whicker, Merrill Sealey, my parents and my wife, Joann.

I will be forever grateful for the technical assistance of Mary Foote Morris and Linda Wolf, as well as the years of patience and effort by Angie Herron and Nancy Maragioglio, without whom this project would not have been completed.

CONTENTS

INTRODUCTION xv
Workplace History xv
Defining Human Resource Management xvii
About the Presentation xviii

UNIT I: STAFFING PRACTICES AND OVERSIGHT

CHAPTER 1: BEGIN WITH THE WORK 1
Chapter Objectives 1
Learning about Work 1
Common Categories of Work and Workers 2
Using Work Knowledge 8
Studying Work 9
The Formation of a Position 13
Writing Job Descriptions 13
Ancillary Information 18
Program Administration 21
Summary Remarks 23
Review Materials 24

CHAPTER 2: STAFFING METHODS AND CHOICES 27
Chapter Objectives 27
Staffing Organizations 27
Preparation and Tools 34
The Process 40
Choosing Among Candidates 49
Uncommon Situations 55
Offers 58
Enrollment 59
Easing Integration 62
Summary Remarks 62
Review Materials 64

CHAPTER 3: DELIVER LEARNING OPPORTUNITIES 67
Chapter Objectives 67

Workplace Education..67
Newcomer Training (Orientation)...........................70
The Supervisor: A Central Figure.............................75
Training Supervisors..79
Occupational Education..82
Management Development....................................82
Tools and Instruments...83
Summary Remarks...85
Review Materials..86

UNIT II: PROVIDE FOR PERFORMANCE

CHAPTER 4: WORKPLACE ORGANIZATIONS..............91
Chapter Objectives..91
A View of Different Economic Sectors...................91
A Framework..97
Elements of an Organization.................................100
The Rights and Roles of Workers and Managers....107
A Variety of HRM Priorities...................................107
Summary Remarks...111
Review Materials..112

CHAPTER 5: ENABLE WORKER PERFORMANCE........115
Chapter Objectives..115
On Being a Good Place to Work...........................115
Employee-Employer Relationships: A Mix of Elements....115
Influential Researchers..121
The Conditions of Influence..................................122
The Manner of Management................................128
The Role of Employee Communications.............132
Action Programming...138
Conditions and Standards for Adoption.............139
Summary Remarks...140
Review Materials..141

UNIT III: SUSTAIN AN ABLE WORKFORCE

CHAPTER 6: DELIVER PAY..................................145
Chapter Objectives..145
Providing Employment Income............................145
Planning for Pay...145
Common Methods of Pay.....................................147
Organizing Pay Practices.......................................150
Developing Pay Levels..152
Learning the Pay Market.......................................156
Constructing Pay Guidelines................................157
Pay Decisions...160

Administration..161
Summary Remarks...163
Review Materials..165

CHAPTER 7: BENEFITS FOR RECRUITING AND RETENTION...169
Chapter Objectives..169
Considerations in Planning..................................169
Flexible and Free Time..173
Health Care..180
Survivors Insurance...182
Retirement and Deferred Income Plans....................182
Ancillary Benefits..184
Non-financial Benefits..186
Communicating Benefit Value...............................186
Administration..187
Summary Remarks...188
Review Materials..189

CHAPTER 8: SAFEGUARD THE HUMAN RESOURCE...........191
Chapter Objectives..191
Workplace Health Threats...................................191
Other Resources...200
Regulations...200
OSHA Administration...208
Summary Remarks...211
Review Materials..212

UNIT IV: MANAGE LEGAL MATTERS
CHAPTER 9: ENDING THE RELATIONSHIP....................219
Chapter Objectives..219
An Overview of Separations.................................219
Voluntary Separations..219
Administrative (Without Fault) Separations..............220
Involuntary Terminations....................................222
Dismissals...223
Monitoring Discharges..231
Managing the Meeting..232
Helping Employees Recover.................................234
Summary Remarks...235
Review Materials..236

CHAPTER 10: RECORDS, PRIVACY AND REPORTS..........239
Chapter Objectives..239
Contents of Records..239
Protecting Privacy...241

Administration..........244
Reports..........251
Summary Remarks..........252
Review Materials..........255

CHAPTER 11: LEGAL COMPLIANCE AND RISKS..........257
Chapter Objectives..........257
The Role of Laws and Regulations..........257
Illegal Discrimination..........260
Notifications to Employees..........263
Unions and Collective Action..........264
Compensation Matters..........265
Accommodations..........266
Subjects of State Law..........267
Legal Landmines..........268
Risk Reduction Actions..........269
Summary Remarks..........274
Review Materials..........275

LIST OF ACRONYMS..........279

GLOSSARY..........283

INDEX..........305

INTRODUCTION

Workplace History

Workforce management in the U.S. has an inglorious history. In the first decades of our nation, commerce and public organizations operated without any meaningful oversight by law and only a rare sense of concern for their employees, who were commonly *hired preferentially* on the basis of the candidate's national origin, religion, gender, physical ability, race, and in government, politics. Conversely, there was flagrant (and legal) adverse discrimination in dismissals on the basis of those same factors. For example, a firm might employ only white, male, evangelical Christians. People with disabilities were simply ignored. Teenage children were commonly employed in unsafe conditions. Authoritarian, arbitrary and frequently ruthless supervision was normal. Employees were dismissed on a whim, and the fear of job loss was the principal motivator in the workplace, where workers were often viewed as a commodity.

In the federal government, after a century of hiring based on ability, a spoils system evolved in which the political party that had won the most recent election filled job vacancies with supporters. In 1881 President Garfield was shot and killed by a disgruntled job seeker and attention was focused on the patronage practices. In 1883 the Pendleton Civil Service Reform Act was enacted to require that federal hiring be based on merit, in the form of test results. The act reaffirmed a previous commitment stating that the federal government provide for the preferential hiring of veterans, which still remains and extends to public employment in many states. In ensuing years legislation limited the political activity of federal employees, mandated a method of ranking jobs for pay purposes and permitted dismissals only on the basis of just cause.

What few social systems we had to protect employees in these early years were of little import: "In the early part of the 20th century, 10% of all girls and 20% of all boys aged 10 to 15 were working 12-hour days in the factories or fields."[1] Regulations that did exist were unknown or ignored. In 1907, 3,000 coal miners died on the job. Despite the massive number of deaths, however, employers wielded enough power, and government enforcers so little, that coal mine inspectors were denied access to the mines. Retirement, medical and employment insurance plans were nonexistent, and the ill and elderly relied on family support.

Unions were viewed as un-American and were violently resisted. One union-organizing confrontation at the Republic Steel Company in Chicago resulted in ten strikers shot dead and eighty-four others wounded by police gunfire. In Minneapolis, police gunfire killed two union demonstrators and wounded sixty-five. The Ludlow (Colorado) Massacre resulted in the death of sixty-six, including women and children, as the result of military action. In just one year following World War I, there were 3,600 strikes in the U.S., and workplace injustices and violence unsettled the population.

---

[1] Linda Leuzzi, *Industry and Business* (New York: Chelsea House Publishers, 1997), 66.

In the 1930s the nation was engulfed in the Great Depression. Between 1929 and 1932, the gross national product dropped more than 50 percent. The stock market fell 90 percent. Nine thousand banks failed between 1930 and 1932, and Federal Deposit Insurance, created to protect deposits, didn't yet exist. Unemployment reached 25 percent. Such conditions readied the public for change and stirred cries for government action.

Newly elected President Franklin D. Roosevelt's administration began a controversial enlargement of authority under the constitutional mandate of "providing for the general welfare" to *include workplaces.* Among outcries of socialism, the government enacted three pieces of economic safety net legislation to relieve suffering in down cycles of business and injustices by some employers. These social welfare programs and curbs to management power firmly established the federal government as a participant in the management of workplaces.

Today those who employ human resources in the millions of workplaces in the U.S. must maintain certain conditions and follow established standards. The following three laws, as well as the early Civil Service law, remain cornerstones of human resource management in this country.

- The Social Security Act of 1935 initiated federal old-age benefits, included financial assistance for dependent children and provided help for the states to develop unemployment compensation programs.

- Also enacted in 1935, the National Labor Relations Act endorsed the formation of labor unions and provided that private sector management must bargain in good faith about wages, hours and working conditions with duly formed unions. In 1933 there were 3 million union members in a variety of unions; in 1939 there were 8.2 million and in 1947, 15.4 million. In 1955, 35 percent of the non-agricultural workforce was organized. As a result of changes in the nature of work and improved conditions, however, that percentage has declined to about 11 percent in this twenty-first century.

- In 1938 the Fair Labor Standards Act provided a minimum wage for those involved in interstate commerce. The act also established the forty-hour workweek as a national standard by requiring premium pay for hours worked beyond those forty. In addition, excessive hours and unsafe work for child laborers were prohibited.

In the mid-century, international conflicts were of paramount concern, and production for military purposes revived the economy. Even during this period, married or pregnant women were denied employment or discharged, and absence for family matters rarely received consideration. Racial discrimination was common across the country. Following World War II, there were instances of unions and managements plundering pension funds, union strikes were common and hundreds still died in coal mine explosions. These conditions prompted additional federal laws.

The functional management of people during this period was male dominated and often referred to as *labor relations* or *personnel administration.* In the predominantly industrial economy, the personnel management function was often responsible for the hiring of hourly personnel, administering labor contracts and controlling injury costs.

During the last fifty years, government action and workplace psychology studies have shaped human resource management into its present form. Laws were enacted providing workplace safety standards in 1970, and equality and justice in employment grew primarily through Title VII of the 1964 Civil Rights Act (CRA). Legislation requiring extensive benefit plan protocols and mandated family leave rights have since been enacted, and today there are about ten federal enactments that are foundational to human resource management.

Over the years, court decisions have tempered management power in favor of the public's interest and employee rights. This combination of government and court actions continues to curb management latitude and increase costs for employers. On the other hand, many of the deplorable workplace practices listed above have been irrevocably reformed.

In the 1960s and '70s, workplace studies of employee motivation by Maslow and Herzberg were accepted as a popular psychological basis for understanding and influencing the human element in organizations. During these years of enlightened management theorists (such as Drucker and McGregor), principles were being formed and adopted, manufacturing industries began to decline and commercial services increased. This was also the period when the predominant gender of HR specialists was changing from male to female. This foundation of law and workplace psychology helps define contemporary human resource management. In this twenty-first century the purposes and components of HRM are increasingly defined.

Readers should keep in mind that most workers in the private sector are employed in businesses with fewer than twenty employees, and that a high percentage of small employers are not subject to many laws because of their size or because they are not engaged in interstate commerce. Nevertheless, fair employment practices are a common standard held by the general public and to ignore them is unwise. The practices of large employers are prominent in this manual because their practices are more definitive and comprehensive.

Defining Human Resource Management

Human resources, like financial and physical resources, require management for effective acquisition and utilization. As with other assets, workers are *acquired, sustained and applied*. *Human resource management* is a common element among private, government and nonprofit sectors in this country, but is differentiated by the intended output of the people and the sources of authority and financing. Readers will quickly grasp that HRM is management of a *function* (i.e., a combination of activities that embrace, but do not direct, individual workers).

The terms *human resource management* and *personnel management* are used interchangeably, although the scope of the former is generally viewed as broader than the latter. The term *worker* (vs. employee) is frequently used in recognition of the different status of people engaged in performing work for an employer. *Specialist* is used to indicate a position devoted particularly to HR matters or one aspect of the total function, while *generalist* applies to a position or person that deals with a wide scope of personnel management matters. A *practitioner* is an HR specialist practitioner or a supervisor practitioner of personnel management.

The terms *hire* and *employ,* and additionally, *job* and *position,* are exchanged. More frequently, the terms *firm, enterprise, company* and *employer* are interchanged, but use of the term *organization* suggests inclusion of public sector institutions. Sometimes the word *function* is applied to the total subject of HRM but also to a major component thereof, such as compensation.

About the Presentation

This book is an instrument through which learning about personnel management can be realized either through individual or group study. Eleven chapters are arranged into four major aspects of HRM: staffing, enabling performance, sustaining an able workforce and managing legal matters. Definitions, illustrations and bibliographic citations offer additional information. Chapters include checklists with which to accomplish practical projects, and instructions on how to draft job descriptions, choose personnel, provide fair pay and train supervisors. Each chapter is summarized and provides suggestions on means of measuring functional effectiveness. An extensive glossary, list of acronyms and index serve as additional learning aids.

Chapters often reference the necessary steps in preparation for organization *start-ups*,[2] and toward the end, they highlight personal attributes useful for accomplishing the different aspects of the function. The book emphasizes the role of communication with workers and the value of job knowledge.

The pursuit of functional objectives involves developing, adopting and managing suitable policies and applying the programs, procedures and practices to accomplish them. Readers will become familiar with *principles* of equity and due process, *policies* for fair employment and employee injury protection, *programs* for compensation and training, *procedures* in employment and termination, and uniform and consistent *practices* to promote positive relationships in employment.

This manual is designed for practical application by general management "doers," those who are more directly involved in personnel matters on a daily basis than theoretical and academic "thinkers."

Legal matters are pervasive in twenty-first-century HRM, and there are legal considerations to every aspect of personnel management. Law continuously changes by jurisdiction; consider the current health care issues as an example. Readers should rely on current and local legal resources when addressing specific issues.

---

[2] The author served as the principal HR director in starting new organizations, several of which had first-day workforces of more than 1,000 personnel.

UNIT I

STAFFING PRACTICES AND OVERSIGHT

To understand the work, determine desirable worker attributes, recruit and choose able workers of sound character for work satisfying to them, prompt workplace integration and do so within cost and time parameters.

CHAPTER 1: BEGIN WITH THE WORK

CHAPTER 2: STAFFING METHODS AND CHOICES

CHAPTER 3: DELIVER LEARNING OPPORTUNITIES

CHAPTER 1
BEGIN WITH THE WORK

Chapter Objectives

- The application of job knowledge in HRM
- Collecting job information
- The content of a job description
- How to express job content
- Identifying worker requirements
- Developing performance standards

Learning about Work

Before staffing, those responsible for hiring must clearly understand the work to be done. Whatever its nature, the type of work determines the type of people who are interested in the job and who can do the job, the equipment necessary to perform the job, the nature of the workstation in which the job is to be accomplished, as well as necessary pay, training and safety needs. Knowledge of the work to be done is core information in personnel staffing, training, compensation and performance evaluation. Those interested in the history of work analysis should read about the time-and-motion studies of Frank and Lillian Gilbreth.

There are more than a million different types of jobs in the U.S. for which people are compensated. These jobs have evolved from *private sector* commercialism or *public service* activity. Twenty-three million workers are in civilian *government* jobs; the private sector has about 110 million. The largest single segment of workers is in service occupations, such as retail, administration and finance. Millions of *self-employed* people and millions more in *nonprofit* organizations carry out family, health and human services.

Work involves a group of *tasks* to be accomplished that are formed into a *position* and, if there are others like it, a *job.* A collection of related jobs comprise an *occupation,* such as sales or accounting. There are some principal occupations common to organizations of all economic groups, such as general management, finance and human resource management. Other very common occupations include administration services, information processing, marketing, purchasing and legal services.[3]

Informal and broad categories of work used in public discourse include "white or blue collar" and "information workers." As could be expected, more definitive terms, such as "regular," "shift" or "telecommuting," are used by those involved with workplace occupations. Specific categories of jobs, such as those eligible under law for overtime pay and those subject to drug and alcohol testing in the interest of public safety, are formed to accomplish regulatory needs. For greater understanding of the scope of human resource applications, some common categories follow.

> **The nature of the work to be done and the conditions of the workstation must be established before a suitable worker can be selected.**

Common Categories of Work and Workers

Time-Sensitive Positions

A common characteristic that distinguishes positions is the amount of *time spent* on the job. *Full-time* positions are those normally scheduled in accord with a designated schedule, typically thirty-five to forty hours a week. *Part-time* jobs, common in the retail industry, are scheduled for some number of hours fewer than full time. *Regular* jobs are those with activity that is anticipated to last for an indefinite period, and *temporary* positions are those anticipated to be necessary for a limited period of time. Seasonal businesses, such as those related to agriculture, have many temporary and part-time jobs.

Supervisor Positions

The purpose of these positions is to direct people and the use of equipment and other resources as part of a process devoted to the production of a product or service. The position of supervisor is the first level of management and represents direction of at least two full-time subordinates, as per the federal definition. Team leader positions are normally work facilitators, but without sufficient authority to be considered supervisory.

Internship Positions

These positions exist for the education and experience of the intern and are unpaid or provide only a minimum source of income. Interns are most often college students not added to the employer's payroll and are *not to replace* a payroll worker. One Wage and Hour official believes that inappropriate use of intern workers as cheap labor is "a vexing problem" but is "not at the top of our priority

---

[3] W. David Patton et al., *Human Resource Management: The Public Service Perspective* (New York: Houghton Mifflin, 2002), 47.

list."[4] A judge recently expressed that interns must do work primarily for their own education as they would in an educational facility, not for the benefit of the employer. Further, the Fair Labor Standards Act "does not allow employees to waive their entitlement to wages."[5] A suggestion offered by the National Association of Colleges and Employers to relieve the "problem" is to have qualifying criteria include a *structured* learning experience that serves as a classroom extension for a defined period of time, under professional supervision and with feedback provided to the intern.

The Self-Employed

One in nine workers in the U.S. works for himself or herself. Typical of their work is law, real estate, technical services, insurance and independent sales. Many of these fifteen million people provide services to a variety of clients.[6] *Independent contractors* (often "consultants") frequently serve in a temporary, adjunctive role to an organization; their daily presence at the workplace is typically unnecessary.

The government takes a keen interest in whether work performed by independent contractors is indeed adjunct or so integrated within a firm's operations that the worker is actually an employee. One reason for this interest is that employers must deduct federal tax monies from their employees but *not* for those considered independent contractors, who are responsible for their own tax returns. The IRS publishes differentiating guidelines on the differences between contractors and employees.

As with overtime eligibility issues, gray areas exist in determining employee or contractor status, and investigations are common. Some firms use contracts to document the relationship, but

---

Sample phrases from a typical independent contractor agreement:

"The company desires to protect and ensure the non-disclosure of trade secrets, confidential and other valuable or proprietary information . . ."

"The contractor enters this temporary working agreement with the company with the understanding that either party can terminate the relationship at any time . . ."

"The contractor, for additional consideration, is willing to devote time and energy toward the efforts of the company on the following basis . . ."

---

[4] Remarks by Michael Hancock of the DOL as printed in "Intern Nation," *Time Magazine,* September 12, 2011.
[5] *Glatt v. Fox Searchlight Pictures, Inc.*, No. 11-067841 (S.D.N.Y. June 11, 2013).
[6] U.S. Census Bureau.

it's *the actual situation,* including the degree of management control, that determines status. An employer may desire a written agreement to demonstrate a legitimate intent, to specify the relationship and/or to formally prevent the "outsider" from inappropriately using the client organization's name.

A legitimate independent contractor typically[7]:
- performs work for several firms simultaneously, or has a history of doing so
- has freedom from workplace controls, such as scheduled hours, to which other workers are subject
- determines how the contracted work is to be done and often trains others
- has personal responsibility for health insurance and profit or loss
- receives general direction but not supervision
- performs work that is not an ongoing activity of the enterprise
- has a relationship of limited duration
- has a method of pay different from that of employees

An employee typically:
- is subject to direction about what, where and when to perform work
- participates in an ongoing relationship with the client firm for an indefinite period
- has all resources and supplies provided by the client firm
- is constrained with procedures and a schedule imposed by the client firm
- participates in client firm's employee programs and benefits

Bargaining Unit Work

Some work is performed under the provisions of a labor contract, much of it in government employment. The titles of the positions subject to the agreements are specifically listed in contracts and have pay, benefit and grievance provisions that differ from circumstances of non-union employees. Management and security personnel are excluded from bargaining units under law.

Safety-Sensitive Positions

A number of public transportation jobs have the potential to put the public at risk and so require drug and alcohol testing, to be administered by employers. Pilots, commercial drivers and railroad engineers are subject to Department of Transportation requirements.

---

[7] Steven Hipple, "Self-Employment in the United States," *Monthly Labor Review* 133, no. 9 (September 2010): 35-39.

Equal-Opportunity Occupational Classifications

Affirmative action and equal employment opportunity (EEO) reports establish the following classifications of work into which employers must slot their employees for annual equal-opportunity occupational classifications (EEOC) reporting purposes:

- Executives and senior-level officials
- First/Mid-level officials and managers
- Professional staff
- Technical staff
- Sales workers
- Administrative support workers
- Operators
- Craft workers
- Laborers and helpers
- Service workers

The federal government requires employers with more than 100 workers to submit reports that cross-reference these classifications with an employee's race category. Making inquiries of people on a racial matter is an affront to many of non-white heritage who consider themselves simply Americans. The report perpetuates distinctions between us on the basis of race and any value of the data is obscure.

Telecommuting Employees

Working off-site and communicating with supervisors via telecommunications equipment is common practice in many occupations. In making such arrangements, management must deal with the loss of some control of the work performed. Many personnel prize the opportunity of remote work because of the possibility of integrating it with other life activities, as well as for the reduced commuting time and independence it affords. Some workers may not have the discipline, home resources, or desire for such an arrangement. Others, though the work might permit such a status, prefer a workplace condition that provides social opportunities and affiliation with colleagues.

An estimated 16 million workers telecommute, and in some occupations it is becoming a normal arrangement. In the U.S. Patent and Trademark Office, 4,000 employees work from home at least part of the week.

Agreements are preferable in order to spell out the hours of work, ownership of equipment, and information security, and should include an employment-at-will condition that establishes the employer's right to terminate a worker at any time and the worker's right to quit at any time. The Wage and Hour Division law regarding overtime applies to remote work, but to date, Occupational

Safety and Health Administration (OSHA) enforcers acknowledge an employer's limited ability to control remote conditions and are not routinely visiting home workplaces.

Dual Occupation Workers

A significant number of our workforce have two employers or personally generate a second source of income. The job titles of custodian/delivery person or beautician/home care worker are examples of "slasher" workers. These situations are often prompted by income needs, occupational transition or self-employment.

Technical Workers

This term includes a broad scope of work, including data utilization, miniaturization, and equipment development and repair. In this twenty-first century it frequently involves high levels of engineering, science and math knowledge. There is a growing need around the world for those with the ability to understand, develop and apply technical communications and production tools. The use of robots, computers and personal communication equipment is increasing, and nurses and other medical specialists remain in high demand.

Shift Employees

While most work is performed during daylight hours, there is massive work activity in the afternoon (second shift), or evening (third, or graveyard, shift). Night work is common in law enforcement, food preparation, maintenance, entertainment, factory production and medical services. About 20 percent of all workers leave home for jobs that begin after midnight. Some industrial work units rotate through three shift periods, such as 7:00 a.m. to 3:00 p.m., 3:00 p.m. to 11:00 p.m., and 11:00 p.m. to 7:00 a.m. Work performed at night presents special concerns because there is often less supervision and thus a greater possibility of lower productivity and quality, illegal drug use, sexual activity and theft.

Overtime-Eligible Positions

Management is expected to determine whether the nature of work in a position necessitates the payment of time-and-a-half the regular rate for the hours of work greater than forty in a designated workweek (defined as any fixed period of 168 consecutive hours). These determinations are necessary for legal compliance, and violations by employers are common. The Fair Labor Standards Act (FLSA) provides the basis for classifications that apply to employers who account for $500,000 of revenue during the year and whose work involves interstate commerce. The law does not apply to babysitters, seasonal workers or employees of entertainment venues. It does apply to 80 million other working Americans in the public and private sectors. There are also state laws that require overtime pay by smaller employers in intrastate commerce; these state laws may have more stringent requirements for exemption from paying premium pay than do federal laws.

The type of work subject to overtime, *nonexempt* pay is generally hourly-paid clerical and production work as performed by receptionists, assemblers, laborers, accounting clerks, machine operators, police, firefighters, paramedics, caregivers and inside salespeople. The most common jobs in the U.S. and their average 2012 pay as reported by the U.S. Bureau of Labor Statistics (BLS) are retail salespeople ($25,310), cashiers ($20,370) and food preparation workers ($18,720). The federal law does not list all the work subject to the overtime premium, but does provide that positions paying less than $23,660 a year are eligible for premium pay hours. This federal "one size fits all" number is at the pay level of custodians in our large metropolitan areas and of supervisors in Wyoming, Alabama, and much of Mid-America; pay levels differ across our land.

Exempt work, that which is not specified in the law as overtime eligible, comprises most of the positions that pay more than $23,660. People occupying these jobs needn't be paid the premium, are generally paid a fixed salary and are not subject to have their pay docked for most absences. Exempt work (meaning exempt from overtime premium pay) is not a matter of pay, job title or arbitrary management decisions, but depends on *the activity* and *pay level.* The government has listed executives, computer experts, professionals, administrators, and outside salespeople (defined hereafter) as generally exempted from the overtime pay regulations. Brief definitions of exempted positions follow, but government definitions by the Department of Labor should always be used for determinations.

Management work involves decision making, directing a recognizable unit, and supervising at least two full-time employees. This exempted group generally includes managers and supervisors who make or recommend hiring and firing decisions.

Administrative work involves special expertise or process knowledge, making judgments within their role, and requiring little supervision. Only a minimum of time can be spent on routine clerical activity. Common administrative positions, which involve only limited management activities, would be purchasing agent, claims adjuster and human resources support.

Computer expert exemption includes highly specialized work of system analysis, design, and consultation with a pay level of at least $27.63 per hour (as defined by government standards). Positions such as computer or software engineers are examples, while users and technical help desk positions won't meet the test.

Professional work involves creative and learned intellectual skills as might be developed through higher education. Sample positions are teacher, chemist, artist, registered nurse and degreed accountant.

Sales work requires some travel or attending meetings outside the facility (e.g., soliciting orders or contracts for products or services). Those who conduct scripted telephone sales are subject to overtime regulations.

In the public sector there are categories of work designated by legislative edict or reference. Temporary political appointees as well as career executives occupy many federal management positions. Within the levels of government there will be lower-level jobs subject to historical *civil-*

service provisions (see glossary). At state and local levels there are usually essential employees such as police and firefighters who are without the right to withhold their services (in other words, go on strike) in economic conflicts.

Using Work Knowledge

The effective direction of workers requires a general understanding of workplace conditions and activity. Work knowledge contributes to the understanding of:

- the flow of processes that results in the product or service
- the role of individual positions in the process and hierarchy
- valid skill and knowledge requirements to accomplish the work
- physical and environmental conditions and demands
- components of job and workstation design that affect process efficiency
- tools and equipment necessary to accomplish the tasks
- characteristics that will result in pay differentials
- job hazards related to the work
- standards with which to measure worker competency
- accurate data for use in reducing legal exposure

The practice of studying work has a long history in management and is a cornerstone of managing personnel. The Classification Act of 1923 was enacted to compare jobs and bring reason to a confused mix of pay and political patronage in federal employment. Under the act, federal agencies were required to classify jobs in the "ascending order of responsibility," thereby initiating the study of work in management as a government policy.[8] A half century later, James W. Walker[9] reaffirmed and defined the practice: "Work analysis is a process of gathering and examining information on the principal work activities in a position and the qualifications . . . necessary to perform these activities. It may be variously referred to as job analysis, activity analysis, task analysis, or work analysis."

In large organizations like the federal government, the need and investment in job study is massive and requires burdensome documentation. In very small firms, an owner normally has performed each task and knows the job well. The time and dollars devoted to work study and documentation corresponds generally to the size of an organization, its need for disseminating job information and the vulnerability to issues about pay equity.

---

[8] W. David Patton et al., *Human Resource Management: The Public Service Perspective* (New York: Houghton Mifflin, 2002), 55.
[9] James W. Walker, *Human Resource Planning* (New York: McGraw-Hill, 1980), 144–5.

Understanding the work and conditions of a position is necessary to match the knowledge and skills of the worker assigned to perform it. The success of that marriage plays a role in achieving employee satisfaction and the full utility of the worker.

Studying Work

A Production (Input/Output) Scheme

Employers arrange work into a strategy that will achieve desired results in an effective and efficient manner. Constructs of work systems involve linking work, facilities, equipment, methods and users of the product or service to achieve predictable results and minimal dysfunctions. Industrial and sometimes safety engineers are frequent contributors to system design.

Process in Organization

Management Initiatives → Applied Materials and Supplies, Human Resources Work → Product or Services

Planning and implementing the manner, relationships and methods of work is *work analysis*. Inputs, tasks and elements are identified, clustered and combined into a *position* that fits the flow of the process. This formation is subject to *job analysis,* which is studying the duties and responsibilities that define a given position. The results of job analysis are summarized in a *job description*.

Job Study Techniques

The activities and tasks involved in a position or job are collected in different ways. Specialists most commonly use observation, checklists, questionnaires, technical manuals, task lists and interviews of the workers and supervisors. White-collar jobs are often studied through incumbent interviews and questionnaires. In repetitive production systems, time records and, sometimes, time-and-motion studies (i.e., stopwatch timing of identified work elements) are used to break down and record the job into a sequential list of activities. These records are used to arrive at a normal amount of time for completion of the task being studied, thus serving as a way to measure performance.

Work methods should be adjusted and practiced for a period of time before study. The safest and most efficient methods should be fixed before documentation. The employees and their supervisors who know the job best should be interviewed. Some employees tend to understate their contribution to the system while others exaggerate. Occasionally the employee has developed shortcuts that are not disclosed. The employee and supervisor should verify the documented material.

Collecting Information

The amount of information collected for documentation varies widely. Government entities are typically very thorough and might complete a dozen pages of information, but the private sector, subject to competitive forces, cost considerations and less oversight are more likely to have two or three pages of notes. One consideration in determining the extent of the detail is the level of legal exposure to which an organization is subject. Government contractors have a level of exposure far greater than does a local landscaper. In the interest of efficiency and order, data is recorded systematically on forms standard to an organization. Inquiries are generally about what, why, where, when and how regarding the work. There should be several different means of work information input used and *several observations at different times*. There are scores of questions and notable points of interest in studies, but those highlighted in the following sample questionnaire are common.[10]

The process of analyzing and relating the components of a job is most often done by experienced practitioners involved in employment or pay administration but sometimes by outside specialists. Job analysis assignments might include recording and studying the activities of loggers in the predawn mists of Montana, conducting time-and-motion studies in a deafening Iowa machine shop, reviewing questionnaires completed by Minnesota casino gaming dealers or interviewing cattle buyers about their activities in a Nebraska feedlot. Documented work preferably applies to activity in the normal workstation at a point in time, without historical or speculative considerations. Typically an analyst is a guest in someone else's abode. After prior notice the analyst should arrive in a timely manner, explain the task to be performed and indicate the source of authority that approved this suspicious and inconvenient intrusion.

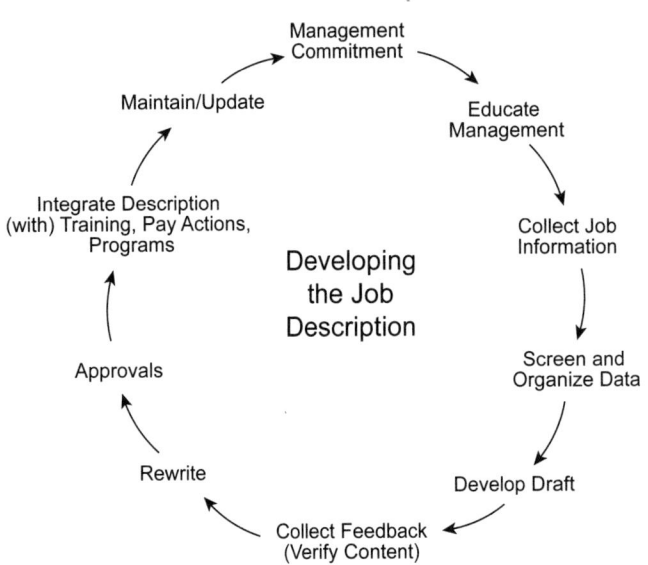

---

[10] A historical view of early job evaluation and classification construct can be found in *A Manual of Job Evaluation*, Eugene Benke, Burk and Hay, 1941, Harper and Brothers, pg. 41.

Job Study Interview Pattern

1. Put the worker at ease. ("It's all about the work.")

2. Explain the study's purpose, procedure and time frames.

3. Use open-ended, non-threatening questions. ("Tell me about...," "What happens when...")

4. Ask one question at a time. Demonstrate interest. Don't hurry.

5. Be a good listener and take notes of answers and observations.

6. At the completion of the study period, review the input and observation notes with the employee.

7. Review the outcome with the supervisor.

8. Prepare a description draft of the duties, and collect and list related information and additional questions.

9. Collect feedback and further information from the supervisor and redraft the document. Review the collected information with the person on the job at the time of the interview.

The information collected and organized must reflect an understanding of how the activity fits in the productive process. The desired *outcomes* of the work must be evident. An analyst must understand the necessity of the tasks under study; they must clearly contribute to the purposes of the unit or at least support the desired outcome. If the need for the position or activity isn't clear, it should be tested. Justification for the position should be expressed in the initial summary statement. An effective analyst will not let inefficiency or waste be adopted in a description lest it be perpetuated.[11]

Law requires the use of valid selection criteria in personnel assignments, which demands an understanding of the activities and the competencies to perform them. Disability law requires knowing the difference between important versus incidental job duties as a means of focusing on essential job criteria. As pay studies are based on the comparison of scope, responsibility and

---

[11] Sandeep Arora, *Business Process Management: Process Is the Enterprise* (Lulu, 2005), 47.

the position in hierarchy, almost anything about a job and its performance is useful or necessary information in staffing, pay decisions, and training. The best time to collect and record the information for so many future needs is at the point of a primary job study.

> ## Sample Job Study Questionnaire Content
>
> This questionnaire is designed to gather information that will be used along with other material to describe this position's purpose, responsibilities and role in the organization. The questions refer to position requirements and the way it is performed—not your personal qualifications or how well you perform. There is no need to complete any question that does not apply to your position. Similarly, you should include any information that you think is important but is not specifically requested. Base your responses on the position as it is now. Don't worry about your writing style. Most important is that the basic information is recorded in order to prepare a position description.
>
> - Why is this work performed? What is the intended outcome?
> - How does this work contribute to the production process and the desired results of the organization?
> - Is this job and all of its activity necessary?
> - What communication or collaboration with others is necessary?
> - What are key responsibilities and the risks of unnecessary costs?
> - Relate the sequence of activity.
> - Are there optional methods? If so, specify.
> - What equipment, supplies and tools are used?
> - What types of decisions or difficulties are encountered?
> - Under what conditions (e.g., heat, dust, noise) is the work performed?
> - Where is the work performed?
> - What knowledge and skills are necessary to perform the work?
> - What might interrupt the work sequence?
> - What physical demands (e.g., lifting, hearing) are necessary?
> - What hazards exist?
> - Which activities are crucial and which are of minor import?

The Formation of a Position

Work and job studies can involve more than rote data collection. Combining and arranging tasks into a productive position demands understanding of the desired outputs and formative logic. A study is expected to result in an effective, efficient and logical body of work. The array of job tasks in a position normally focus on a common *purpose,* are *congruent,* related in terms of *sequence* and *difficulty* and fit into a suitable *role* in a larger process.

The design of a job affects personnel placement as well as productivity. An observer may see a possible improvement in methods more readily than a worker because of a wider view of the company as a whole. The arrangement and provisions of the *workstation,* like the environment and access to necessities, impact potential productivity, too. The following characteristics make a position challenging and interesting and should be considered in design.

- Does this combination of duties permit some personal autonomy?
- Is there a means of measuring accomplishment?
- Can the employee be fully accountable?
- Is the work viewed as important?
- Is there potential to demonstrate particular skills and knowledge?
- Are the requirements of this position balanced relative to related jobs?

Regardless of the depth of study, the initial methods of accomplishing the studied tasks can be expected to change within a few weeks of the study. Shortcuts and efficiencies will be found. It's common, too, that workers with duties that can be completed in six hours will stretch the activity into eight. For that reason, methods and output must be carefully expressed and occasionally audited.

Writing Job Descriptions

Purpose and Scope

Job descriptions express a factual makeup of a position in a manner understandable to a reader. Their use can reduce uncertainty and conflict and provide definition and order. A job description should provide:

- A basis for comparison with other jobs in ranking, pay surveys and other studies
- Duties, roles and responsibilities
- Categorization of positions for administrative and regulatory purposes
- Desirable and valid hiring qualifications
- Basis for performance standards

ABBREVIATED JOB CONTENT RECORDING FORM

Title of Position _____   Date _____

In the right column estimate the percentage of time devoted to the task.

		% of Time
Summary Description Describe purpose and function of job, why it is necessary	_____ _____ _____	
Major Areas of Accountability Identify peripheral functions	_____ _____ _____	
Important Duties List in order of importance	_____ _____ _____	
Conditions List uncommon physical, mental, hazardous elements	_____ _____ _____	

Recorder _____   Sources _____

Date _____

Written descriptions are common in larger organizations and are primary tools in staffing and pay administration. Many firms don't use descriptions because management has never seen any need for them, trusting to sufficient recall, or believes they aren't worth the time and cost. Job descriptions can also be viewed as confining to an employee when management seeks creativity, and have frequently been used as an excuse by workers to limit cooperation (e.g., "That work is not in my job description").

> **Job descriptions are about the work, not the people.**

Developing original position descriptions is time-consuming; each requires several drafts and hours of work. A comprehensive writing project, if undertaken, could begin with entry-level jobs, which most often need staffing, and other jobs most often vacant. Descriptions require periodic updating. While drafts of many positions can be found online, they will inevitably be incomplete and/or inaccurate. The substantial and accurate content of the actual position must be collected on-site.

Law doesn't require job descriptions in the private sector, but these summaries can impact employee-employer conflicts. A current and accurate description can be useful, but one that belies management claims can be damaging, as they are subject to subpoena by courts. Most employment lawyers recommend writing job descriptions to validate management's reliance on essential job aspects and hiring qualifications. However, position descriptions should be 1) used and kept current, 2) never developed at all, or 3) destroyed if inaccurate. Relying on personal recall is more desirable than using inaccurate documents.

Content

Descriptions normally include:

- Position title
- Management approval and date
- Purpose of the position (or summary, objective, function)
- Scope of responsibilities
- Indication of the output (e.g., meets a sales quota)
- Primary and important duties
- Necessary interactions with others
- Accountabilities
- Physical demands
- Emotional circumstances (e.g., stress, danger)
- Mental demands (e.g., reading, writing, calculating)

- Qualifications for selection
- A final statement that the incumbent is expected to report for work as expected and to perform assigned business-related duties

Language and Form

Different formats and writing styles are used in descriptions. However, a single construct is typically used within any single organization; doing so will foster completeness, clarity and ease of compiling information for surveys.

> **The purpose and expectations for every position should be clear and understood by both supervisor and worker.**

Formatting

1. There are several common choices for displaying information.
    i. Chronological sequence of activities (job flow): "Selects earliest dated job order."
    ii. Frequency of duties beginning with the most common: "Responds to frequent telephone inquiries."
    iii. Relative importance of the duties beginning with the paramount duty: "Identifies symptoms."
    iv. Groupings in aspects of several major functions: "A) Prepares agenda, B) Prepares meeting materials, C) Makes presentation."

2. Consider the ease of entering information in a database and efficient retrieval when constructing a form.

Writing Style

The length of the document doesn't relate to the position's difficulty; "responsible and accountable for the success of our billion-dollar company" is an appropriate description for a CEO, but cashier duties can take several pages of detail. In general, routine jobs tend to provide detail and management positions express responsibilities more broadly. Some common principles of documentation include:

1. Record the approximate percentage of estimated time devoted to major elements to add perspective.
2. Use short, simple, clear, impersonal and precise statements.
3. Begin each statement with an active verb.
4. Use present tense.

5. Use unsophisticated terms (e.g., "city" rather than "urban area") and only common abbreviations to make the description understandable.

6. Condense an item to its essence (e.g., "feeds power saw").

7. Eliminate all unnecessary words.

8. Express "why" things are done when it is helpful to understanding.

9. Avoid expansive adjectives (e.g., "complex" or "far-reaching").

10. Avoid names; use titles.

11. Avoid negative statements (e.g., "does not have to prepare coffee").

Action Word Examples

PRODUCTION POSITIONS

keys, adjusts, counts, feeds, inspects, loads, lubricates, marks, measures, stacks, removes, calculates, drives, pours, pushes, carries, assembles, cleans, wipes, operates, positions, records, weighs, writes, lifts, observes, cuts

ADMINISTRATIVE AND MANAGEMENT POSITIONS

analyzes, creates, advises, enforces, assigns, negotiates, recommends, inspects, purchases, reports, originates, interviews, supervises, contracts, approves, prepares, represents, trains, monitors, sells, diagnoses, authorizes, implements, investigates, directs, interprets, communicates, plans, organizes, resolves, initiates, schedules, responds

CLERICAL POSITIONS

bills, lists, records, posts, compiles, computes, enters, mails, schedules, inventories, copies, inspects, composes, codes, sorts, operates, receives, registers, informs, credits, compares, collects, expedites, obtains, submits, corresponds, deletes, adds, replaces, collates, follows up, arranges, charts, files

---

Titling Principles

Proper job titles contribute to order and understanding in an organization and focus on the nature of the job and its relationship among others. A title helps form an identity or concept in the mind. Misleading titles can have adverse consequences by causing confusion in matching with jobs for pay comparison and can be an embarrassment to management. Several such notorious job titles are "Graffiti Removal Trainee," "Director of Direct Reporting," and "Semi-Senior Auditor."

Executives can assign an exaggerated title in lieu of money—after all, a fancy title doesn't cost anything—and employees can lobby for an inflated (or more descriptive) title. Sewer cleaners are often "plumbers" and janitors "maintenance engineers." Management sometimes minimizes title issues (or seeks equalitarianism) with a general "associate" title. Regardless of title practices, there will be a recognizable pecking order among a unit of workers.

A simple titling program requires selecting some options from among patterns. Common practices applied include maintaining gender neutrality, using descriptive terms, minding brevity, using a level indicator, and corresponding with other titles. For example, unless defined, middle-management terms like "superintendent," "supervisor" and "department head" might be used interchangeably. At a higher level, having a distinctive level of "manager" and "director" will help clarify status. A general pattern can be established for the sequence of terms in a title. For example:

Corporate Technical Director   Division Sales Manager
  (1)   (2)   (3)   (1)   (2)   (3)

(1) Organizational indicator (corporate, division)
(2) Functional identification term (technical, sales)
(3) Level (director, manager)

In smaller organizations, a unit indicator is unnecessary, hence *surgical* nurse, or *warehouse* manager. A reverse system is sometimes used, such as Director of Marketing, which is inconsistent with how people normally express a title. In very large organizations, job-coding numbers may be used, which will electronically convert to position title, location and department. Monitoring for uniformity of titles can be accomplished without bureaucratic mandates, but some executive should be in charge of titling issues and challenges because ego, bias or self-interest can become involved.

Ancillary Information

The initial study of a job is an opportune time to record supplemental information. The purpose and importance of *working condition* specifications and the segregation of important *job duties* increased with the Americans with Disabilities legislation. Identifying valid job-related *qualifications* is the professional standard in fair employment practices. In subsequent reading, the value of having *standards of performance* with which to evaluate personnel and justify dismissals becomes evident.

Documenting Conditions

Environmental conditions and the equipment used should be recorded. If the work is under the ground or in a more traditional office setting, knowing those conditions is necessary to comprehend the work activity. Listing all of these elements in detail can be tedious and at some point becomes excessive. Public-sector analysts tend toward comprehensive lists, as is necessary in that regulatory environment. Private-sector analysts tend to identify and record only the uncommon requirements that are likely to be considerations. The following checklists reflect private sector practices rather than the more extensive public sector practices.

Essential vs. Peripheral Activities

When evaluating applicants with disabilities, the Americans with Disabilities Act (ADA) expects the identification and use of legitimate physical and mental requirements. People aren't to be automatically disqualified on the basis of inability to perform incidental duties that can be dealt with in another way. Management is to discern between important job duties and other duties. On a description it's relatively simple to asterisk the duties that are peripheral. Those are the activities unnecessary for satisfactory accomplishment of the job and completion of the task sequence. Key considerations in differentiating among the functions follow.

> **PHYSICAL REQUIREMENTS:**
> (AS PERFORMED)
> ❑ Normal office activity
> ❑ Light work (e.g., lift 10 lbs.)
> ❑ Heavier/constant work
> ❑ Other strenuous activity (note)
>
> **MENTAL REQUIREMENTS:**
> (AS PERFORMED)
> ❑ Reading, writing, calculating
> ❑ Social skills
> ❑ Stress control
> ❑ Creative responses
> ❑ Other (note)

Essential Functions:

- Does this position exist to perform this activity?
- Are there critical times in the flow of work when this duty is vital?
- Is this function critically related to the process of work?
- Does this function require a substantial (15–20 percent) amount of time?

Nonessential Functions:

- Does this work require general abilities rather than expertise?
- Can this work be put off until another time?
- Is this function basically stand-alone work rather than integrated with a related sequence of activities?
- Are other people or methods available to perform this work?

Determining Qualifications

A job analysis generates the information from which job qualifications can be developed. A basic question is: What competencies are necessary to accomplish these tasks? The array of knowledge, skills and abilities necessary or desirable to fulfill work demands are endless. Necessary abili-

> **Qualifications are determined by the skills, knowledge and abilities necessary to perform a task effectively and efficiently.**

ties may not be observable but identified only through a full understanding of the process and probing questions of the worker and supervisor. Particularly helpful is quantitative data that determines the potential *success or failure* of an incumbent, what competencies are *different* from those on related jobs and what *training* needs are normally necessary.

Don't be seduced by impressive attributes of the incumbent on the job being studied; these qualities might be unnecessary or in excess. Remember, it's about the work. The quality of the study result, like much work in a human resource function, depends on objectivity and a resistance to unrelated influences.

Productivity Standards

An analysis of a job will reveal what can be reasonably expected in terms of results. Workers and their supervisor should always share a clear understanding of the normal output expected from the position or workstation. This is true throughout an organization. A performance standard must be sufficiently clear *that it can be expressed and definitively determined* if the output is, or is not, sufficiently accomplished.

There are general standards for employees about tardiness, absences and conduct, but job outputs require customized study. Expectations of a position may mean, on the negative side, avoiding any errors, budget deviations, complaints or failures in relationships. On the positive side, these expectations could include meeting cost and time objectives. Standards might set quantities of the number of assemblies to be completed, customer inquiries or sales quota satisfied within a period of time. Are patrons greeted in a timely manner? Are customers satisfied with the product? However, conditions change (such as output specifications) and are affected by uncontrollable influences (e.g., supplies are unavailable). These changes must be anticipated and accommodated appropriately.

To determine the *performance standards* for each job, consider three to four important functions to target with the following questions: If this task is performed suitably, what is the outcome and time frame? How can it be known this job was completed satisfactorily?

> **A work standard is based on the desired results.**

Samples of Standards

1. Sales clerks are to be fully occupied helping a customer, refolding or cleaning during work time.
2. Vehicles are inspected, serviced and tested in accord with the checklist at the beginning of each shift.
3. Necessary supplies and materials for workers are always timely and properly positioned.

Sometimes whether a job is being performed satisfactorily is subject to question, or the removal of an employee from a particular job must be justified. In those situations, typically in the public sector or when the worker is covered by a union contract, accepted *standards* can serve as a sound basis for the decision. In routine work, numbers are often used as points of measurement, such as 10,000 keystrokes an hour from data entry clerks, eight patients per shift for nurses, and a thirteen-second maximum allowance before answering calls for city service operators. Such specificity is effective in stable and predictable conditions.[12]

> *"Objecting to numerical quotas, noted Quality Management proponent W. Edwards Deming believed that specific standards throttle worker potential, and that "once workers have completed their quotas for the day, they quit working."*
>
> —From Mary Walton, *The Deming Management Method*
> (New York: Putnam Publishing Group, 1988), 78.
>
> **In deference to this thinking, and because the vast number of workers do their best in any circumstance, definitive output requirements might be counterproductive in certain cultures or with certain groups and individuals.**

Job Ranking Considerations

About a dozen common elements have been recognized, adopted and used for ranking jobs for almost one hundred years. Readers should understand that all jobs require some level of necessary knowledge, physical effort, responsibility, decision making and stress. Recording work and job data should include information with which to make comparative judgments of one job to another on the basis of these elements. The ranking of jobs is primarily for pay purposes, and how it is done will be addressed in the chapter dealing with wages and salaries.

Program Administration

An introductory statement to a job description program should express top management's endorsement. The program should outline format, the frequency of audits, rules of accessibility and the use for which they are intended. How work is accomplished is constantly changing, and keeping information current and uniform is time-consuming.

---

[12] Elizabeth Bennett, "Productivity: Metrics That Have Mattered, Over Time," *Baseline*, May 2004.

Sample Position Description

Title: Human Resource Manager
Department: Administration
Approving Supervisor:
Reports to: Executive Vice President

Date: January 1, 2014
Revised:
Executive Approval:

Summary Statement: Directs a human resource function in support of management. Develops, manages and monitors policies, programs and procedures through which a desirable complement of human resources are acquired and maintained. Develops and provides HRM training for management. Provides advice and counsel on management methods, workplace conditions and legal compliance.

Scope: A technical organization of about 500 employees. Provides direction to a payroll/record administrator.

Major Accountabilities:

20%	1. Administers established staffing and employment procedures in support of operating management.
	  a. Assists in drafting job descriptions and qualifications.
	  b. Recruits for inside and outside job candidates for vacancies as requested.
	  c. Interviews and evaluates applicants as requested.
	  d. Conducts background investigations on all new personnel.

5%	2. Develops and administers employment, job assignment and termination procedures.
10%	3. Manages orientation, employee assistance, complaints, basic supervisory training and other programs.
5%	4. Ensures employee communications fulfill government requirements with filed knowledgments.
5%	5. Initiates communications materials such as handbooks and announcements in the interest of positive employee relations and legal risk reduction.

10%	6. Maintains desirable wage-and-salary program.
	  a. Provides suitable description and titling of benchmark jobs.
	  b. Applies job ranking methods.
	  c. Develops competitive wage-and-salary data.
	  d. Prepares pay guidelines and recommends adjustments.
	  e. Monitors pay changes for compliance with guidelines.
	  f. Rules on overtime eligibility status.

5%	7. Provides and coordinates management training as requested and approved.

5%	8. Recommends benefit program design and changes.
	  a. Conducts new-employee enrollments in programs.
	  b. Administers time-off and absence records and controls.
	  c. Monitors insurance administration and savings plan administration with Finance Management.

10%	9. Develops and maintains personnel files and functional records applying electronic methods as suitable.
	  a. Provides for compliance with government records regulations and employee information privacy.
	  b. Maintains an efficient system for additions, changes and deletions.
	  c. Develops informational reports, surveys or feedback for management.

10%	10. Recommends policies and programs to advance positive employee relationships.
5%	11. Promotes and monitors the safety program.*
10%	12. Remains current with HR trends and regulations and updates management. 13. Monitors the legal compliance of human resource management activities in employment, records, training, safety and related matters. 14. Monitors HR function expenses and recommends suitable allocations and cost control measures. 15. Monitors workers' compensation, unemployment and other benefit costs.* 16. May serve as a designated EEO or privacy data official. 17. Performs other business-related duties as requested.[13]

NOTE: Candidates can expect fair employment practices, employment history verification and drug and alcohol testing.

*Peripheral functions (not essential)

---

[13] This phrase is noteworthy, as supervisors have been known to ask subordinates for loans, to shop for gifts or groceries, or to financially help a family member.

Work Environment Conditions: Normal office conditions with occasional need for travel to attend local meetings.

Equipment Used (Office Equipment, Machinery, Tools, Software, Etc.): Normal office equipment, HRIS software, visual aid equipment.

Mental Requirements (As Presently Performed): Requires good reading, writing, research, speaking and mathematical skills. Understanding the essentials of the business/agency. Must analyze situations, make decisions and be a student of human nature.

Physical Requirements (As Presently Performed): Light lifting (10 lbs.).
Ability to see, hear and communicate with others via telephone, computer and in person.

Employment/Selection Criteria (Skill, Experience, and Education Requirements; See Performance Standards): A favorable employment and performance record, appropriate aptitude, interest, earnings and other indicators of compatibility. Qualifications include three years of work and training with personnel record maintenance, employment, computer use, benefits enrollment, and fair employment compliance. Possess skills to comprehend and apply management and regulatory knowledge and conduct interviews and meetings. Must exercise discretion.

Expectations and Performance Standards:

- Provides timely and quality employment assistance to management
- Provides sound counsel on legal and functional matters to management
- Monitors compliance with policies, rules and expectations
- Initiates and administers approved programs and procedures for the maintenance of the function
- Fulfills required employee communications in a timely manner
- Maintains records that are complete, accurate, orderly, secure and in compliance
- Represents management thinking with pay and benefit actions
- Brings significant employee issues to management's attention
- Demonstrates exemplary conduct and respect for others
- Maintains respectful and effective working relationships

Summary Remarks

The work performed in an organization is a foundation for much of management's decision making, initially in qualifying job candidates. In large organizations, job information is usually documented, but in smaller organizations, individual managers function on the basis of sufficiently understanding the work without written materials.

This chapter provided some perspective on the nation's work activity and explained how to collect, express and display information about work being performed, all skills that are commonly used in the management of personnel. The presentation also explained how to determine qualifications and performance standards, how jobs are categorized for overtime and other purposes, and the construct of titles.

The satisfaction of safety, equal opportunity, and pay laws requires knowledge of the work performed. Appropriate use of work information is most often evidenced by its use in determining job qualifications, pay and job equity. Employee motivation, retention and the degree to which a worker is utilized are also affected by the design of the job. Work studies can contribute to the efficiency and effectiveness of processes, organization analysis and training.

Applicable Competencies

Interviewing, research and writing skills, interest in the work and process, skill in complete and accurate recording of information.

Applicable Resources

Job analysis checklist, standard job description format and relevant regulations.

Review Materials

Content Exercises

1. List three uses for position analysis or a job description.
2. List three sources used to generate job content.
3. Define *incumbent* and *essential activity*.
4. Starting with an action verb, draft a phrase describing an essential activity of a movie ticket taker, dental surgeon and a supervisor.
5. Consider your most recent or present position and draft one statement of purpose and three job duty phrases based on chronology, importance or the time devoted to each activity.
6. Be prepared to list five classifications of *exempt* work as defined by the federal government, with an example of each.

Practical Applications

1. Consider the workstation and process in which you work. Identify the primary inputs and outputs.
2. Compare an authentic position description to the content recommendations of this chapter.
3. Note differences and any details such as the overtime status recorded on some forms.
4. How are essential functions and job qualifications determined, recorded and applied by your employer?
5. Visit a state Wage and Hour department website and research two regulations such as child labor, mealtime or overtime regulations in your state.
6. If you have access to a union contract, describe the bargaining unit (i.e., the list of positions included or excluded from membership).
7. Review newspaper or website advertisements and report on one position title that might be improved or is inconsistent with suggestions of the author.
8. Make a draft of your position description. If your present position is documented, make corrections or improvements. Explain difficulties or alternative methods of construct.

Case-Study Discussions

Case 1.1

A Job Analysis

You are a student aspiring to a career in public administration. You have previously worked summers in landscaping and fast-food businesses. Before your senior year in college, you have secured summer work as an intern for the county.

When you report to work, you are told you are the first employee assigned to write job descriptions. The initial description is to be that of the courthouse janitors, one of which works during the day and the other at night. Your supervisor says she doesn't know how to do it, nor does anyone else; you are to have a draft by the end of the week, and "By the way, the night janitor hardly speaks English." You decide to form a plan to review with your supervisor.

- How do you expect to proceed?
- How will you collect and organize information?
- What resources of information might be available?
- How will you format the information in the description? Why?

Case 1.2

Work, Qualifications and Standards

The duties of a job are crucial in determining the criteria to be used in selecting someone to adequately perform a job and satisfy the standards of performance. Work through each step completely in the order listed below.

Put in mind *one* of the three following jobs: apparel retail clerk, grocery cashier or a post office delivery position. Use your present view of the job, without further research.

1. List at least three *duties* of the job.
2. List three or more *skills, points of knowledge,* or *abilities* you expect would be valid hiring criteria.
3. Suggest three *standards* for successfully performing the job.
4. Speculate on any hazards associated with the selected job.
5. Suggest some training that most candidates for the selected job would require.

Case 1.3

Employee or Contractor?

Lisa is the owner of a small machining company. She decided that her company would benefit if it had a quality certification. She initiated the certification process, which requires the critical analysis and documentation of each task used in machining. Her uncle Jake had been an industrial engineer prior to his retirement five years ago and seemed capable of carrying out that aspect of the certifying procedure. Uncle Jake would be an able and reliable resource, and would enjoy some income. Lisa agreed to pay Jake a daily rate for each workday. They signed an agreement stipulating an independent contractor status, pay rate and a monthly pay date. Jake understood that he would pay any resulting taxes.

Family members were a little concerned about Jake's physical ability to undertake this project, which was expected to take at least a full year to complete. As a result, Lisa had Jake enrolled in the company health plan. Lest he get injured on the job, she also added him to the workers' compensation insurance list as a technician.

Jake and Lisa examined the methodology required by the certification system, agreed to its requirements, and Jake set off to work. Jake wasn't accomplished with a keyboard so Lisa assigned a data input person to convert Jake's notes. The analytical work and documentation proceeded well. Jake did exercise some flexible scheduling to accommodate an occasional "sleep in." The only interruption in progress was a period of two weeks when Lisa had Jake oversee a night-shift crew while the normal supervisor was on vacation.

1. Are there any reasons why the IRS would question Jake's independent contractor status?
2. What elements support that status?
3. What are key swing factors that could establish Jake's status one way or another?

CHAPTER 2
STAFFING METHODS AND CHOICES

Chapter Objectives

- Objectives of staffing
- Options and practices
- Generating applicants
- The value of standard process
- The application form as a tool
- Interviewing techniques
- Compliance and defensive measures
- Choosing quality employees
- Compatibility with aptitudes and interests
- The reality test of the background investigation

Staffing Organizations

A Definition

In thinking about employment activity, most minds leap to the idea of a personnel practitioner adding a newcomer to a payroll. Actually, many assignments to new jobs involve present employees, and not new hires. Then, too, supervisors most often make new-hire decisions and a hiring specialist may have a role in only certain units or levels of an organization. Further, in contemporary management fewer and fewer workers are actually employees of the firm for whom they perform work. By using the term *staffing*, this chapter addresses filling job vacancies from whatever source is deemed the wisest, including work that can be accomplished with contracted, temporary or leased workers, none of which are added to the payroll as employees. Regardless of the source of the worker, and before taking any hiring action, the hiring party must understand the *qualifications and attributes*, addressed in the first chapter, that are necessary for a person to succeed on the assignment, thus justifying the investment in dollars.

Most readers probably started their employment experience with babysitting, mowing lawns or doing chores for neighbors or relatives. We graduated to an unfamiliar workplace among strangers, being told to perform work that was sometimes unpleasant and with which we were totally unfamiliar. The idea of discriminating among employment possibilities became important. Confidence in our abilities to perform, pay level, interests, aptitudes, expectations, opportunity and surroundings all became considerations. Employers in turn discriminate on the basis of applicant work histories, skills and knowledge, and so arriving at an understanding that suggests a successful match for both parties becomes complex.

An employer's challenge is to promptly identify and *choose people for vacancies* that have the necessary *ability to perform the work* (chapter 1) *under conditions that the candidate will find acceptable* (chapters 5 and 6) and that is *satisfying* or at least comfortable for the worker. Needless to say, the worker must be able to reach the point of competency within a reasonable period of time. To that end, it's common for employment practitioners to collaborate with supervisors and help personnel new to a unit or a position with some basic education and transitional effort (chapter 3).

Acquiring and assigning proper and able personnel is a time-consuming and crucially important activity of organizations. In contrast, a vacant position impairs and stresses an organization; the element of *urgency* in filling vacancies is integral to the efficiency, effectiveness and outcome of a staffing project. In that regard, many organizations find it cost-effective to develop lists of contingency personnel.

The impact of the costs of necessary personnel and their recruitment to an organization depends on the nature of activity, but is always a consideration. Some economic activity is labor intensive, requiring many people relative to output, while other industries rely heavily on other resources (e.g., railroad tracks and cars) to generate output. Robots make automobile assembly lines less labor intensive, and earthmoving equipment has replaced millions of workers in labor-intensive construction projects. Often the financial function of an organization will establish budgets for staffing complements that drive staffing activity. If the number of employees drops below the normal number, a staffing initiative may be automatic. If an addition is requested above the predetermined complement, the approval of a top executive is likely necessary. Other managements require top management authorization for any hiring action.

Distinctions

There is no "one size fits all" in staffing methods. The method and positions involved in the process often differ in each unit. The employee selection process is a maze of considerations. An employer is generally concerned with the timely *availability* of applicants, their *industriousness, compatibility with the situation, abilities* and hopefully some *passion* for the opportunity. Fundamentally, a worker that evidences a positive inclination for performance is preferable to a passive candidate "looking for a job." An applicant is concerned with *his or her personal interests, comfort, adequate conditions, opportunity* and most of all, with the related *income*. Each of the parties is exchanging information and examining what the other has to offer in a maze of possible points of connection.

An effective staffing project explores recruiting options and moves quickly through a well-designed sequence of actions comparing an applicant with specific *selection criteria* for the targeted position(s). In the end, the organization wants effective work performed in each of its positions (otherwise known as performance management, a strategy addressed in chapter 4) as soon as practicable.

Fairness in Choices

While there are many considerations in matching people and work, there is one overriding commonality in staffing methods and objectives. The United States government has adopted a standard of fairness and *equal opportunity to which employers are obligated to follow*. Not only is staffing difficult and time-consuming, it must be accomplished in a manner that follows a legal protocol and provides equal opportunity to candidates. The standard of fairness applies to all employee personnel placements and assignments, including training, hiring and promotion opportunities in all but rare exceptions. Federal law prohibits discrimination on the basis of union activity, race, religion, age, national origin and gender.

Several principal federal enactments defining contemporary staffing practices are the Civil Rights Act (Title VII), the Civil Service Reform Act, the Americans with Disabilities Act, and the Immigration Reform and Control Act (IRCA). These laws are monitored primarily by the U.S. Equal Employment Opportunity Commission (EEOC) and, for government contractors, the Office of Federal Contract Compliance Programs (OFCCP). Such laws demand staffing decisions based on *essential job-related considerations*. This requires a study of vacancies in order to determine and apply only valid and essential job-related requirements for candidates that are to be assessed in an unbiased manner.[14]

A *standard employment process* is a framework for providing uniform and consistent consideration of applicants for opportunities, which helps to assure the fairness just discussed by filtering candidates through a standard pattern of qualifying steps designed to identify the best candidates. Comparing people against the same criteria and under the same circumstances makes it easier for the evaluator, provides a foundation of fairness, and minimizes allegations of preferential consideration.

The vast majority of job opportunities are to be available to the populace in general, so a broadcast isn't to be too specifically targeted. Employment laws create an expectation of a "level playing field" standard that is expected to result in workplaces reflecting the diversity of the geographical area. While doing so, however, IRCA limits opportunities only to those with a *legal right* to work in the United States. Other laws impose, or logically demand, the exclusion of candidates on the basis of their undesirable background.

> **One objective of the federal government is expressed in the Civil Service Reform Act (PL 29-454) sec. 2301: "[T]o achieve a workforce from all segments of society" in terms of age, gender, religion, national origin and race.**

Twenty-first-century demographics, social climate and law require that employers be "ready, willing and able" to accept the individual differences and diversity among the working population. The Census Bureau reports that most babies being born are members of minority groups. In large cities there may be 100 different foreign languages spoken. A minority ethnic group of the nation

---

[14] For a study of the technical regulations, see section 60.3 Uniform Guidelines on Employee Selection Procedure (1978); 43 FR 38295 (August 25, 1978).

may represent a majority of the population in one geographical area. After centuries of flagrant workplace discrimination,[15] a massive cultural change of minimizing racial bias in the workplace was substantially accomplished during a span of one generation late in the previous century.

In addition to federal law, states and municipalities often have fair employment laws. These laws are enforced by agencies with names including Office of State Employee Relations, Division of Human Resources, or the Division of Personnel. Management must be aware of protections of people from *unacceptable discrimination* as legislated in their state based on:

- Marital status (Montana)
- Same-sex civil unions (Hawaii)
- Unemployment status (New Jersey)
- Political affiliation (District of Columbia)
- Sexual orientation (Connecticut)
- Diagnosis of sickle-cell anemia (Louisiana)
- Smoking habits off-site (Minnesota)
- Genetic information (Arkansas)
- Public assistance status (North Dakota)
- Height and weight (Michigan)
- Physical appearance (District of Columbia)
- Female attire on males (California)

An organization's total staffing program normally establishes fair and functional procedures for use by all the hiring managers as well as to provide assistance, training and tools with which to achieve the desired ends. Nevertheless, readers should recognize that good intentions are still subject to human failures. There are studies that indicate sometimes an ethnic or female name on an application will more often be screened out, while attractive, taller men or those who have the same interests and background as the interviewer are disproportionately advanced in a selection process.[16]

Methods of Staffing

Work can be completed within an organization or outsourced. A specific job vacancy is also satisfied from within or without. Job vacancies from within are filled through the *transfer, promotion* or a*ssignment* of available personnel.

In the event a staff reduction creates a vacancy under a union contract, union members may be able to "bump" into the vacant job on the basis of years of service. Employees that have

---

[15] The term "discrimination" means to choose one in preference to another, such as choosing one ice cream flavor over another, a very normal act. However, *illegal* discrimination in employment is to select one person in preference to another because of a factor the public has deemed unfair and illegal (such as race or religion).
[16] Don Peck, "They're Watching You at Work," *The Atlantic*, December 2013, 66–67.

temporary impairments as the result of workplace injury or illness may be able to fulfill the essential factors of a vacant position. Under state workers' compensation (reference Vermont and New York), the Family and Medical Leave Act or the Americans with Disabilities Act, such employees are to be considered for the work with or without an accommodation by the employer. In the absence of a clear and reasonable cause, not using an available and able employee can open exposure to legal action.[17] Conversely, it's not uncommon that an appointment or promotion of a deserving internal candidate is thwarted and expediency foiled because equal opportunity requires that the opportunity be publicized.

Internal candidates are more of a known quantity with greater chance of success than those from outside the organization. Vacant positions are typically first communicated to present employees while outside broadcasting gets underway.

Filling vacancies from outside the organization involves different techniques. At some private-sector workplaces a supervisor simply selects someone from a congregation of hopefuls at the door or street corner. In some industries a union card is a ticket for work. In small firms, friends and relatives may constitute the workforce. In many organizations a vice president may walk into an orientation meeting with a niece or other relative and give notice that she or he starts work in his department that day. This latter circumstance, known as nepotism, compromises fair employment practices and is prohibited in federal or state government;[18] it is also a dysfunction in that it is normally contrary to desired practice. Nevertheless, it is not uncommon in the private sector.

To lease workers is to acquire and supervise workers who are on the payroll, and actually employees of record, with another entity. Organizations such as professional employer associations will hire, compensate and place employees with a remote contracted business for what is expected to be a long-term, not temporary, relationship. Such arrangements relieve an employer of the distraction and costs of employment activity, but may result in a loss of worker allegiance. The supervising organization remains subject to fair employment and safety regulations and therefore should have a legal representative examine contracts. Kelly Services and Walmart are heavy users of temporary workers. A notable percentage of assemblers and manual labor work is provided through temporary agencies. Temporary staffing is used to meet surges in need and normally provides modest compensation to workers.

Specific occupations tend to have distinctive approaches. For example, research or sales units will often skip initial general recruiting and sourcing steps in a selection process because of their special circumstances (i.e., because those unfamiliar with their "unique" work aren't believed suited to evaluate qualifications for their occupation). First responders and volunteers have unique tests and background investigation procedures that depart from the norm. Methods used for executive and political position selection are sometimes obscure, and often involve personal relationships.

---

[17] EEOC Press Release 3-16-2009 reported a class-action settlement of $850,000 with an airline for denying an employee only because he was on a light duty status.
[18] Nevertheless, in 2012 the U.S. Inspector General reported that some individuals in the Justice Department were "insufficiently impressed with the principles of fair and open" hiring competition and were guilty of nepotism. Relatives hired included five daughters, three sons, a cousin, a nephew, a niece and two granddaughters. The Justice Department was guilty of similar violations of "applicable statutes and regulations" in 2004 and 2008.

The size of the federal government presents a colossal staffing challenge. When job vacancies go empty for some time, public managers are likely to reduce qualifications, hire to a temporary job, redesign a job, skip a job posting or do some creative description writing in order to fit in a worker that is immediately available.[19] Those expedient steps can compromise procedures, process and management control. Competitive testing is commonly used as a sole winnowing method in federal and state government processes. Government invests heavily in tests to ensure "merit" and to avoid allegations of political favoritism.[20]

Public personnel selection systems come in an assortment of shapes, sizes and operating philosophies.[21] Several states, such as Florida and Georgia, have adopted some private sector practices wherein responsibility for personnel decisions is granted to the department head.[22] In the federal government, many agencies apply centralized testing and screening of applicants through the Office of Personnel Management. Others, such as Homeland Security, the Postal Service, the Foreign Service, and the Department of Defense, have internal personnel services; less emphasis is placed on the historical practice of *pre-tested banks of applicants*.[23] Many municipalities, because of the influence of local business, have altered their procedures to grant greater supervisor control. If one considers the collection of differences among federal government agencies, our 50 states, more than 3,000 counties (some larger than a few states), 13,000 school districts and about 19,000 municipalities (defined by the Census Bureau as "political subdivisions . . . to provide general local government"), the mix of policies and proceedings in the public sector is overwhelming. Speculation is that among the *total* of public units, one-third have employment choices controlled by a central personnel office, one-third resemble the private sector and another third have elements of both.

Top management normally recruits and hires the top-level personnel. They have an advantage of social and industry acquaintances and often have relationships with industry-specific search professionals. These search professionals, sometimes referred to as headhunters, are normally contracted to act as representatives of the company because they have expertise in knowing how to surface quality candidates. The higher the position in a hierarchy, the more time and study is devoted to selection.

International Staffing

Organizations often begin exploring overseas activity gradually by partnering with others or investing in a firm in a related undertaking. Subsequent options are to select an agent to represent their

---

[19] Stephen E. Condrey, ed., *Handbook of Human Resource Management in Government*, 2nd ed. (San Francisco: Jossey-Bass, 2010), 109.
[20] President Garfield was murdered because of a political patronage issue.
[21] W. David Patton et al., *Human Resource Management: The Public Service Perspective* (New York: Houghton Mifflin, 2002), 46.
[22] Sally Coleman Selden, Ingraham, Jacobson, "Human Resource Practices in State Government," *Public Administration Review* 61, no. 5 (September/October 2001): 599.
[23] Vestiges of the historic civil-service system exist in some state and local jurisdictions. Provisions exercise varying degrees of control, such as staff providing a predetermined number of previously approved job candidates, often between three and six, from which the department can choose. See Patricia Wallace Ingraham, *The Foundation of Merit* (Boston: Johns Hopkins University Press, 1995), 55.

interests or find someone, either a host country or expatriated U.S. manager, to manage activities on-site. Some form of a *base position* is often defined with which to launch subsequent action.

Providing for nonprofit and commercial management in foreign locations involves more difficult circumstances than in the U.S., as the workforce ethics, sourcing and compensation will be different. Familiar U.S. positions, policy and practices must be sidelined and a reconfigured scheme of work and life developed in order to function within the social order that exists in the country where the position will be located. The chosen representative or manager must be compatible with the host country or have the ability to adapt to functioning in that environment by changing his or her manner of work. If a national of the host country occupies the position, he or she must, in turn, adapt to the manner of the American institution. In international employment the personal attributes of *adapting*, *self- sufficiency* and *interest in additional learning* are primary qualifications.

Soliciting people for international work is typically ongoing because retention is frequently poor. About one-third of expatriates leave their positions after only a few years, most often because of the inability of someone in the family to adapt, due to inadequate training or their detour from a chosen career path.[24] If family is involved, the likelihood of significant tenure is reduced.

Trying to function in a foreign land may be difficult, but is easiest for Americans in locations where English is spoken, as in the Western cultures of North America, Europe and Australia. Language competency is frequently an issue, however, and interpreters are commonly used when there are language differences. These interpreters should be selected through professional sources such as universities. Adaptability is even difficult in societies where American churches and the earlier Colonial powers had major influence (Africa, South America), though less so in the larger areas of population. However, the physical conditions in large sections of most continents have, by our standards, deficiencies with sanitation, refrigeration, transportation, medical care and communication systems. Currency is yet another difference to overcome.

The manner of societal functioning can also be significantly different. In some countries political disruption is not uncommon, while values, beliefs and law are, and in some places they are frightening by our standards (e.g., limbs cut off for thievery, death for adultery).

In the commercial setting, there are general tendencies for slow and centralized decision making, complex tax and financing systems, inefficient systems that require extraordinary maintenance that is not always available, and cultures where employees write their own contracts and are employed for their lifetime. What is common among foreign nationals and expatriates is their self-interest and allegiance to homeland.

Employing a professional or manager overseas, whether from the U.S. or the host country, involves particular emphasis on several matters. The *motivation* for an American to undertake overseas work should be explored thoroughly. Is the candidate in pursuit of an opportunity or escaping from something? In some firms, overseas assignments are a career path necessity, but not so in most circumstances.

---

[24] Dr. Sonja Treven, "Human Resources Management in the Global Environment," *The Journal of American Academy of Business, Cambridge* 8, no. 1 (March 2006).

There are international training service providers through business schools, consulting firms and programmed Internet learning experiences. The federal government, with its State and Defense Department needs, is by far the greatest single provider of education on matters affecting an international workforce, such as:

- Geography and currency
- Laws, values and regulations
- Language
- Workforce culture
- Social and government differences
- Business practices

Staffing with people from the host country has a score of advantages, including less cost, ready assimilation into the culture, established relationships, knowledge of economic, legal, political and social conditions, language fluency, and the ability to source technical and other resources. These advantages result in fewer errors, lower total costs, greater efficiencies and expedient decisions.[25]

Preparation and Tools

Documents and Materials

A number of forms, documents and decisions are necessary before initiating employment activity. Tax forms, benefit enrollment cards and other forms to be completed must be in inventory. *Educational materials* about policies, pay levels and benefit offerings must be prepared. A proper *application form* is necessary as well as an *information transmittal form* (e.g., personnel change notification forms) with which to route information about employees to payroll and benefits units. Job content, preferably in the form of a *description*, identifying any job *hazards* and *essential functions* of those jobs to be initially filled, should also be prepared.

Authorization

The control of staffing and related expenses of employment actions requires some manner of approval by top management. Whatever the level and method of staffing authorization, consistent practices within and between units must be established.

Standard Application Form

The standard application form is a key document in employment. It transmits relevant information from and about applicants in a methodical manner. Information is typically collected in anticipation

---

[25] "We believe very strongly that our China business has to be run mainly by the people who speak Mandarin and grew up in China and understand the culture. It's the same in other countries." Christopher O'Leary, Executive Vice President, General Mills, quoted in the *Minneapolis Star Tribune*, January 22, 2012.

of payroll record needs, so "short forms" can be used that minimize extensive information collection and provide only for regulatory needs. Be cautious of off-the-shelf forms, as they may ask information considered unsuitable in your state. Résumés are convenient, but for anyone being interviewed or seriously considered, an approved standard application form should be completed and used in the process in order to prevent inappropriate information, such as religious affiliation, from getting into personnel files.

There is typically a section of small print on the back of most application forms that authorizes background inquiries and includes notices and disclaimers that can be useful in legal controversies; every candidate should sign it as a defensive measure against legal actions.

Authorization for Inquiries

Read the following statements carefully and sign the application.

I understand that omitting requested information or giving false information on my application, in my interview(s), or in the process of my pre-employment evaluation might result in rejection of my application or, as an employee, discipline. I hereby give (<u>employer</u>) the right to investigate my past employment, schools and activities without limitation. I release from all liability all persons and employers who supply such information. I indemnify this employer and its agents or others against any liability that might result from an investigation and related statements or information sought related to my application for work.

Signature:_____ Date:_____

It seems that most personnel specialists believe they are the only ones who can design a proper application form, so thousands of "perfect" forms exist for reference. The form should provide ample space for responses to readily understood questions. Online applications will not be comfortable for, or stimulate responses from, everyone so optional methods of submission will increase the number of applications. Someone with knowledge of the federal and applicable state law should review any such form.

Qualifications

In order to select suitable employees it's necessary to first know *what they are expected to do* and what competencies will help them do it. Starter jobs often only require a basic education, such as reading and simple calculations, along with personal reliability and industriousness that have hopefully developed through school. Not so incidentally, about four million youngsters ages fifteen to seventeen are hired and earn paychecks in the summer months, which is considerable hiring activity. Staffers who hire these youngsters come to know the positive and negative characteristics of candidates for these jobs very well.

The qualifications for an employee can be segregated into those attributes that will make a good employee, such as reliability and industriousness, and the knowledge and skills necessary to perform the job.[26] A candidate may be a rare find with a unique skill set, but if the employee is a "job jumper" or seeks flexible hours or telecommuting that the employer is not able to provide, there is no "fit." Though there is no certainty in personnel selection, successful personnel choices most often focus on what is known about the candidate and the job, what is to be done and what the candidate will be able to do.

Interviewers

Not everyone can, or should, represent the organization in an employment interview. Some people have difficulty overcoming years of environmental conditioning toward a religious or racial bias or are uncomfortable in an interview and give a lecture to use their allotted time. Training is absolutely necessary, at least for legal concerns, but also to identify a lack of communication skills or other issues.[27] Executives and others in management can be a surprise with their lack of skills; don't assume competency.

An interviewer can quell or stimulate the exchange of information as well as subsequent legal action. Anyone in an interviewer role should understand the legal landmines involved, though this caution should not impair the use of technical specialists or potential teammates participating in sections of an interview to share their knowledge or perspective.

> **Use thoughtful questions and minimize casual, undisciplined remarks.**
>
> **Interviewers who don't talk very much but listen well will learn more.**

Public sector interviewers normally are well schooled in potential missteps and use preplanned interview questions, consider the questions a verbal standard test and conduct the process in a consistent and uniform manner.[28] Generally, private sector interviewers are less well disciplined due to a less structured environment and less training and are more subject to error and legal exposure.

Sourcing Applicants

Knowing where potential applicants can be found and how to get a message to them is called *sourcing*. Knowing how to access distinct populations is a key factor in recruiting success. The more technical and rare the skill set desired, the greater the difficulty in reaching that particular talent pool.

---

[26] Sunil Ramlall, "A Review of Employee Motivation Theories and Their Implications for Employee Retention within Organizations," *Journal of American Academy of Business, Cambridge* 5, no. 1/2 (September 2004): 59.
[27] Interviewers normally develop a "safe" routine after some stumbling.
[28] "Unstructured interviews should not be used for evaluating job candidates." Cynthia Fisher, *Human Resource Management* (New York: Houghton Mifflin, 1999), 362.

While the advertising of a vacancy is most often directed to the general population, connecting with those with the particular required talent is most effective and efficient in terms of cost and time. Moreover, when there is an obligation for affirmative action, the targeting of minority groups is required.

The federal government, federal contractors, and some cities, states and firms in the private sector are committed to affirmative action plans in hiring minorities and veterans. Such efforts are devoted to proactive and focused sourcing and broadcasting to targeted groups. Many states and municipalities grant preferences for veterans. However, affirmative action programs can be a political football, with some contending that affirmative action and preference results in reverse discrimination that unfairly denies opportunity to qualified people who happen to be young, white males. Several states, such as Michigan and Arizona, have taken political action to prohibit preferential hiring in public institutions.

Difficult sourcing situations may require that temporary or full-time employment agencies[29] or leasing firms be contracted. Notifications of vacancies posted in community centers and associations, or advertising placed in different news media, are also common techniques. Large organizations search electronic job boards and social media[30] and develop their own websites to solicit applicants.

Another source used is foreign professionals or other specialists with unique skills that aren't available in the United States. Two-thirds of the visa requests are in science, technology, engineering and mathematics disciplines (STEM). To secure college-educated workers from overseas, the H-1B visa is used and permits work for up to six years. Because such searches involve the government, quotas, and trade agreements, immigration lawyers are generally necessary and even then, management may suffer uncertainty and long waiting periods.

There are prominent and general patterns too in sourcing personnel within each of the public, private and nonprofit sectors. Different types of people are attracted to work in each of the sectors. Private firms broadcast in their industry and through sources reaching the general public, nonprofits have local and national publication networks, and the public sector normally emphasizes recruiting sites known to and followed by public employees. To counter that ingrained tendency, Esmeralda County, Nevada, requires that their vacancies be advertised at least once in a public newspaper.

> **Responses to many employer websites are limited because the sites are too difficult to navigate and repetitive inquiries frustrate applicants.**

---

[29] Provisions of an agreement with an employment agency could well address the following: fees, refunds, time frames, indemnity from law violations of the agency, tenure of anyone hired, and expectations of qualifications and their verification. John Remington et al, *Human Resources Law*, 5th ed. (Upper Saddle River: Prentice Hall, 2011).

[30] H. Kristl. Davison, Maraist, Bing, "Friend or Foe? The Promise and Pitfalls of Using Social Networking Sites for HR Decisions," *Journal of Business and Psychology* 26, no. 2, (June 2011): 153–159.

Broadcasting Techniques

Broadcasting a job vacancy involves casting a lure toward the target in order to generate desirable responses. The manner of contact varies by the type of worker sought. Labor and physical workers don't use electronic media as much as white-collar workers, so *traditional newspaper and employment services* remain effective contact tools for certain populations.

Internet postings by job seekers are perhaps the most popular source of finding administrative, managerial, technical and professional people. Internet job boards, such as Monster.com, are heavily used and the only strategy employed by some job seekers. There are indications that female applicants have a more favorable reaction to using the Internet.[31] Employer websites are also used to solicit applications, and their success is related significantly to the degree the web design is applicant friendly.

Applications in massive numbers that flow through websites of large institutions are often mechanically screened and are subject to finite qualifications and screening terms that can disqualify able people. A few firms require the review of every electronic application by a real person. In most private sector firms, digital applications constitute a major source of applicants for professional and technical jobs, but equate to only a modest percentage of all new employees.

Personal networking searches by employees among friends and acquaintances are also productive. A healthy percentage of job seekers find work through *personal contacts* with someone in the employer's present workforce. An employee referring someone knows something of the individual, the job and the organization. Such referrals are a source to be utilized and not discouraged. However, as with limits in using only electronic posting, using only internal job posting and word-of-mouth advertising tends to limit diversity. Hence, broadcasting through internal and external personal, print and electronic channels for the same position casts a wider net.

Professional and technical *recruiters* are distinctive in that they search through personal networks to locate and entice potential candidates that are employed and don't respond to advertisements. Recruiters tend to learn the characteristics of certain occupations and cultivate a web of sources that reach beyond normal advertising. It's advantageous to develop relationships with services and people who are attached to, or know of, pools of talent, such as people in the occupation or instructors in schools. Professional recruiters or agencies in pursuit of executives may purchase access to screened Internet sources, but primarily use the telephone.

If sources of potential applicants are known, the message to which they are exposed must be enticing in order to generate an interest and a reply. Very often, broadcasting an opportunity involves simply notifying present employees via a hard copy or electronic job posting. Federal jobs are announced on USAJobs.[32] Government agency or business websites can be effective for broadcasting job openings and are even used for completing pre-qualification tests. LinkedIn is a popular international website used heavily for connecting professional people and opportunities. Elec-

---

[31] For research on the subject of corporate websites, see Brigitte Pfieffelmann, Wagner and Libkuman, "Recruiting on Corporate Web Sites: Perception of Fit and Attraction," *International Journal of Selection and Assessment* 18, no. 1 (March 2010).

[32] An extensive discussion of state and federal electronic recruiting activity can be found at "State and Federal E-Recruiting Effectiveness," by Sally Coleman Selden and Joe Orenstein, *International Journal of Selection and Assessment* 19, no. 1 (March 2011): 31–40.

tronic media has the advantages of low cost and quick response, but using it exclusively limits outreach. Firms with government contracts who use the Internet as a primary tool for recruiting are monitored by the OFCCP to determine if its exclusive use results in an adverse impact on minority populations. This effort suggests that at some point the exclusive use of electronic media by an employer may not satisfy the equal opportunity test. This is another reason why using multiple broadcasting methods is so important.

Recruiting Options

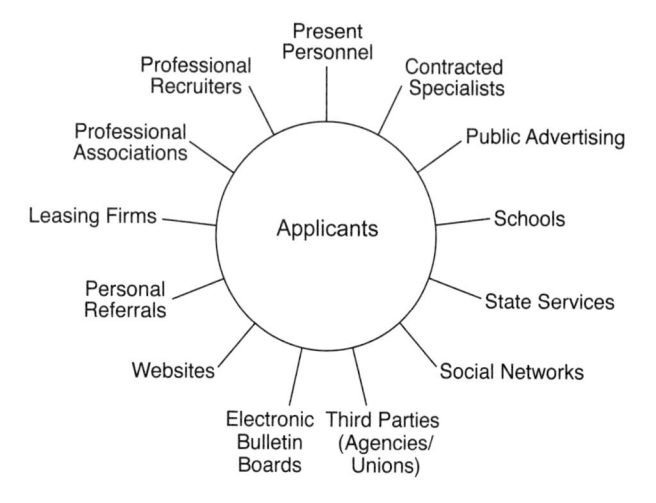

Applicants:
- Present Personnel
- Contracted Specialists
- Public Advertising
- Schools
- State Services
- Social Networks
- Third Parties (Agencies/Unions)
- Electronic Bulletin Boards
- Websites
- Personal Referrals
- Leasing Firms
- Professional Associations
- Professional Recruiters

Beyond a simple notification, advertising messages are normally designed to attract a high number of responses from a wide population of potential applicants, including minority groups. As an example of numbers that can be generated, in 2011, Xcel Energy advertised 1,900 job vacancies in eight states and received 40,000 applications.

Recruiting results vary with economic and industry conditions. Knowing the best means of messaging to potential candidates contributes mightily to cost-effectiveness. People are frequently attentive to one particular media and not to another. Advertising expenditures are more willingly underwritten when the message is known to reach suitable people, when a high number of replies are desired and when affirmative action effort is a consideration.

Job broadcasts should include 1) a headline with broad appeal, 2) a targeted reach to the most likely sources of applicants, 3) a display that makes a positive impression, 4) the use of different media, 5) a description of basic duties and necessary qualifications, 6) an honest representation of conditions, 7) an ease of reply and 8) the identification of the employer.

AN ADVERTISEMENT FORMAT

A prominent, descriptive, meaningful headline

Primary duties of the position

The necessary qualifications

Desirable feature(s) of the employer

Convenient methods of replying

Name of employer

Job bulletins issued by the state for the public arena, a website (professional or the employer's), radio, billboards, an open house, job fairs, postings on vehicles, window or building signage, or a booth at professional meetings can all be effective media in a particular situation. A management commitment to partner with a particular school (to yield internships or other relationships) or professional association could prove a worthwhile long-term strategy.

Applicants react to different bait.[33] Some will react to a location advantage because they are suffering a long commute;[34] others may appreciate a firm's social responsibility or "sustaining" commitment,[35] flexible hours, a faith focus or attractive benefits.[36] In the case of volunteers, the altruistic opportunity is a primary appeal, while still others volunteer for social interactions, excitement or learning.

Different readers of a notice or advertisement will react to any presentation as appealing, neutral or a turnoff. The content should limit the qualification demands to the essentials, and offer several convenient ways to reply. Requiring that replies be only through fax or e-mail in clerical or laboring occupations will limit the number of responses. It's counterproductive to spark the interest of someone only to frustrate him or her with roadblocks to replying. Use an 800 number for immediate and personal contact. An internal job posting form is typically a bulletin board or online announcement without any extraneous content. These postings typically include dates of posting and removal, job title, qualifications, department, supervisor, pay, the person to contact with questions and a list on which to express interest. As an example of a successful internal posting, in 2011, Allianz Insurance (MN) filled 25 percent of their vacancies with referrals from internal personnel while using extensive electronic media.

The Process

The process organizations use for personnel selection requires preparation. Applicants enter the process after forms have been completed and interview and testing routines established. At the Mayo Clinic in Rochester, Minnesota, outside applicants create an online account, including a job preference, for the firm's "Talent Community." If there is a matching opportunity, a position description of the job is transmitted. An applicant's response may generate the scheduling of an interview. Preliminary steps include fixing qualifications, compensation decisions, job descriptions and reading interviews.

The staffing process displayed below is applied generally in the selection of both internal and external people in any workplace for any assignment. There are additional required procedures for applicants with disabilities, including providing access to a building in order to engage the process,[37] and language interpreters if necessary. If the site is one that provides telephone access to the general public, there must also be telephone communication devices for the deaf.

---

[33] Child care, flextime, telecommuting and eldercare are identified as particularly appealing to women in recruiting. Lori Foster Thompson and Kimberly R. Aspinwall, "The Recruitment Value of Work/Life Benefits," *Personnel Review* 38, no. 2 (2009).
[34] The Census Bureau reports the average commute is twenty-five minutes.
[35] T. S. Behrend, Baker, Thompson, "Effects of Pro-Environmental Recruiting Messages: The Role of Organization Reputation," *Journal of Business and Psychology* 24, no. 3 (September 2009): 341–350.
[36] To encourage contract renewal in a dire nurse-recruiting situation in the Czech Republic, a clinic offered five weeks of vacation, complimentary German lessons, free liposuction and silicone breast implants. *The New York Times* (6/14/09).
[37] ADA Accessibility Guidelines for Buildings and Facilities (ADAAG), September 2007.

General Staffing Process

Step	Action
Acquire approval	Document authorization for the project*
Establish qualifications	Confirm the desired characteristics of candidates
Advertise/post the vacancy	Broadcast to targeted sources and general population
Receive and evaluate replies	Identify replies that match specifications
Legitimize applicants	Make initial inquiries and address questions
Explore qualifications	Generate additional information through tests/interviews
Coordinate with hiring unit	Report project status and verify criteria
Select final candidates	Evaluate and prioritize
Investigate backgrounds	Verify and add to information
Final interviews and offer	Answer questions, resolve issues, commit in writing
Employment eligibility verification	Collect right-to-work evidence
Enrollment	Complete payroll, records and benefit documents
Ease the integration	Provide "head start" help for the first workday

* Hiring steps in government units are often specified in regulations.

Evaluating Replies

The Screening Process

A broadcasting effort can generate replies in the form of résumés, electronic messages, letters, e-mails or telephone inquiries. An initial screening often begins by eliminating applications of those who don't follow instructions in their application. Any materials submitted by the applicants beyond those specifically requested are disposed of—they may reveal undesired information (pictures, religious references) that represents legal exposure for the employer. Some screeners exercise zero tolerance of applicants' failure to provide their present pay level or other informational inquiries. Such rejections may be based on the inconvenience caused the screener or an expectation that any candidate must be able to follow simple directions. This lack of tolerance may also suggest arrogance on the part of the employer with the expectation that there will be an ample number of candidates. Hiring supervisors usually want to see the most qualified applicants and don't care how candidates accessed the process.

The content of a reply to broadcasting efforts is compared to the qualifications to ensure the response constitutes that of a qualified candidate. The process will proceed with either all or a select few of the candidates to the point of final selection. Typically, before the time and effort of personal interviews with candidates is committed, there are confirming telephone discussions by the screener to avoid unnecessary time and costs.

The role of the screener/evaluator will vary but can be expected to discern at least those applicants who are likely to be *good employees*. In lower-skilled jobs where skill and knowledge requirements are modest, the initial screener may have full hiring authority. Most jobs, however, because of the occupational skills and knowledge involved, require a decision by a supervisor or someone familiar with the necessary worker competencies. Sometimes screening of executives involves advanced education in psychology in order to evaluate abstract competencies.

> **A completed and signed application form with only relevant information is a cornerstone of a successful employment procedure.**

The pursuit of identifying characteristics of applicants that might predict success on a job has a long history. It was natural that when employment criteria was limited by government action to only specific job-related factors, employment practitioners leaped to demonstrate that tenure in previous employment, physical size, commute time and previous earnings were valid job-related considerations for certain positions. Simple validation studies were used to validate these factors and apply them as initial evaluation items on weighted application blanks.[38]

It turns out that there are a number of fickle factors in prediction. Previous experience is not always a plus, and though academic success is a very common selection assumption, the senior vice president of People Operations at Google has been quoted as saying that "academic environments are artificial environments" and not compatible to the world of work.[39] Transcom is abandoning academic criteria for tech support positions in favor of college dropouts "living in their parents' basement" who taught themselves about information technology.[40]

Conversely, commuting distance and participation in social networks can predict success in certain jobs. Very few organizations pursue criteria validation on many jobs, as it is a studious and costly undertaking.

The contemporary development of selection studies has been facilitated by computers and the massive amount of information about people that is available in data banks and sources such as LinkedIn. More information is available online by searching the term "people analytics."

Qualifying Candidates

An applicant's *alleged attributes* should match the desirable *qualifications* determined through the job analysis and broadcast. Sometimes an e-mail or cover letter reply will correspond to the attributes of an applicant point by point in accord with the listed qualifications in the advertising. Such replies are unusual and welcome because it's often difficult to discern the competencies of applicants.

---

[38] John Remington et al, *Human Resources Law*, 5th ed. (Upper Saddle River: Prentice Hall, 2011), 69–71.
[39] Laszlo Bock, quoted in the *New York Times* and reported in Don Peck's "They're Watching You at Work," *The Atlantic*, December 2013, 82.
[40] Ibid.

Frequently, the vocational aptitude and occupational interests of an applicant are unclear. Sometimes information is convoluted because of efforts to spin experience. A candidate may be the "brightest and best" but lack evidence of interest or aptitude for the work to be done. The announcement of qualifications for a position can benefit from listing "evidence of aptitude and interest" because accepting an applicant who fulfills other criteria without evidence of satisfying that criteria can be costly.

If an applicant is found to fit the needs of a position, they should be contacted immediately so they know they are in the game. If the credentials *may* be sound, a clarifying question or two might resolve the uncertainty. It's a matter of common courtesy and positive public relations to initiate prompt replies to all applicants. Failing to do so is often viewed negatively by unsuccessful applicants and thereby results in some degree of public relations damage. Nevertheless, most employers believe the costs and time involved in replying to a mass of replies is prohibitive. Certainly any applicants with whom the employer has had person-to-person exchanges should be kept informed of their status.

> **The staffing function is devoted to building a body of responsible and able workers who are compatible with the work to be done, the organization and its culture, and the level of career and compensation opportunity.**

Interviews and Questions

Inadvisable Inquiries of Applicants

Questions about experience, education and competencies of applicants are asked on the application form and supplemented with more detail in interviews. Some information about a person is irrelevant to work needs and should be avoided, lest it be interpreted as a basis for illegal discrimination. Inappropriate subjects include military obligations, birthplace, child care arrangements, impairments, marital status, Saturday work availability, name derivation or nationality.

There is prevailing paranoia about asking quasi-personal questions that aren't predicated on illegal bias. Nevertheless, any legal counsel and good sense suggest that *certain subjects and inquiries be avoided* on the basis of good judgment to avoid erroneous perceptions. Another legal landmine is having *notes on an application* that might be twisted in a legal action to suggest evidence of discrimination.[41]

Interview questions and exchanges should follow a pattern in order to be thorough, consistent and on point; avoid wayward inquiries that might lead to unrelated knowledge or careless inquiries. Interviewers who conduct hundreds of interviews develop a routine that should be documented in case of legal allegations. Those only occasionally engaged in the process should

---

[41] Notations on an application cost one employer $92,500. See *Ramsey v. American Air Filter Co.*, 722 F.2d 1303 (7th Cir. 1985).

also use a written plan for reference and develop a prescribed protocol. A well-designed and tested *patterned interview* will conform to appropriate subject matter and increase objectivity and reliability.[42]

After a job offer, personal questions (regarding birthdates, Social Security number) necessary for benefits enrollment are permitted because this information is not being used illegally.

Telephone Interviews

Typically, applicants who appear to be qualified on paper are telephoned in order to address lingering questions, provide an opportunity for the applicant to make inquiries, and estimate compatibility and availability before being judged a qualified candidate. (E-mail contacts are impersonal.) Sometimes knockout factors surface, such as an unwillingness to travel or work overtime, or the pay is such that the applicant loses interest. These preliminary and qualifying exchanges of employment demands result in an in-or-out decision before an additional investment in processing the candidate.

Applicant Reception

The reception of an applicant for an interview is the first personal contact of the parties; the impressions of either party can be positive or negative. An employer should provide courteous, efficient and pleasant surroundings. All those who might serve as receptionist should understand the status of the current employment situation ("only engineering applicants" or "no applications accepted") in order to deal with those who inquire. They should also understand the special considerations to be extended to the disabled. Provisions should be available for comfortably completing application forms. Indeed, an applicant may have to be convinced that completing an application form is necessary after having submitted a résumé or making an appointment. During the reception process the applicant is also under observation and can make a positive or negative impression on the gatekeeper. An arrogant manner, inappropriate attire or tardiness leave a notable impression.

> **Job candidates come in all sizes, shapes and colors but must be evaluated only on the basis of job-related characteristics.**

Personal Interviews

Generally, the first interview is conducted by an employment specialist or other screener. The initial objectives are to ensure the applicant has *appropriate qualifications*, a *compatible personality* and is *presentable* to the hiring manager. A basic question is whether indicators suggest that this would be a good employee, without a finite judgment on specific job abilities. Candidates obviously unsuitable should be courteously derailed at this point to minimize time loss. If there is any single point at

---

[42] Stephen E. Condrey, ed., *Handbook of Human Resources Management in Government*, 2nd ed. (San Francisco: Jossey-Bass, 2010), 123.

which an applicant becomes a candidate it is probably here, at the point where many aspirants are winnowed to a few for serious consideration. This is also a convenient point at which detailed *background reference contact information* can be collected.

The telephone and personal interviews are the points at which a more complete picture of the candidate can best be explored. Probes for interests, ambitions and experiences not yet exposed that relate to employment, though perhaps not the specific job being considered, help complete the candidate profile.

The interview by the supervisor focuses on the *job competencies* of the candidate. Knowing what is helpful and harmful to performance success, a supervisor can make specific and finite inquiries to discern the level of key knowledge as well as to gain a sense of how the values and characteristics of the candidate will fit with associates.

> **Able interviewers using sound procedures can usually identify potentially good *employees*, but it normally takes the supervisor to evaluate the potential for *job success*.**

Interviews are not only an exchange about essential matters, but an educational opportunity to learn the thinking and patterns of behavior of the other party. Conversation might move to management priorities, plans or something meaningful about the candidate's aspirations. In public employment, or when the position is high in the hierarchy, the number of interviews increases. Sometimes a committee of people whose work is associated with the position will interview a candidate. Sometimes interviews of key and high-potential personnel lead to psychological assessment interviews and tests, all to verify candidate attributes.

INITIAL INTERVIEW OUTLINE

A. PREPARATION
1. Know the essential functions of the job.
2. Know the necessary qualifications.
3. Prepare a quiet meeting place.
4. Notify the receptionist and other potential interviewers.
5. Examine the (standard) application and note points of inquiry to explore.
   a. Is it signed?
   b. Is it a suitable permanent record?

B. GREETING
1. Introduce yourself and welcome the visitor.
2. Provide a routine pattern of hospitality.
3. Avoid unnecessary, pointless and extemporaneous remarks to prevent stumbling into subjects with legal exposure.

C. INTERVIEW
1. Outline the agenda and intentions, and give notice of note taking.
2. Begin with low-intensity subjects.
3. Collect information.
   a. Complete work history details.
   b. Explore interests, aptitudes and preferences.
   c. Explore applicable skills and knowledge.
      i. "Tell me about your experience with _____."
      ii. "Explain how that job was performed."
   d. Make other inquiries.
      i. "Are you able to meet our work schedule?"
      ii. "Is there any reason you cannot perform the essential elements of this position?"
      iii. "Are you eligible to work in the U.S.?"
      iv. "How many days were you absent from work last year for non-medical reasons?"
      v. "What are your pay expectations?"
      vi. "In what way does this position fit your vocational pursuits?"
      vii. "What aspects of this situation are most important to you?"
4. Evaluate responses and double-check for any disqualifying responses.
5. Collect specific contact information for background inquiries.

D. PROVIDE INFORMATION
1. Tell about job characteristics, necessary agreements or union membership.
2. Answer questions.
3. Explain the remaining process steps and timetable.
4. Close the interview and walk the candidate to the exit.

E. ANALYZE AND EVALUATE THE CANDIDATE AGAINST JOB CRITERIA
F. DOCUMENT NOTABLE MATTERS AND CONCLUSIONS

Testing

Employment tests are primarily used in hiring procedures to identify the relative presence or absence of competencies, knowledge and the nature of personal mental or emotional health characteristics. Competency measures, like interviews and application forms, are tools of the total evaluation scheme. Sometimes they are administered online as part of an employment application.[43]

Some notable testing inadvertently occurs during interactions, such as one this author failed.[44] Tests in the normal process must be *applied precisely* for their purpose and in accord with the *administrative protocol* that testing instructions provide. An expert resource for the proper evaluation of results should be used. While many tests claim to be valid, or claim to satisfy equal opportunity standards of non-discrimination, "snake oil" sales efforts exist.[45] There is high probability that if there is a legal challenge, a statistical validation of the tests used in any specific application will have to be undertaken.

The public sector uses competitive tests extensively because tests embody objectivity and can also be used to efficiently reduce a huge number of applicants. Millions of tests for administrative, professional and technical candidates are administered each year. In the public sector, a probationary or trial period is often considered a performance test. Public safety applicants are tested for integrity and psychological fitness.[46] State, municipal and professional associations have access to testing instruments developed specifically for their vocations.

Performance tests are simple tests of actual or simulated physical job duties. The observation of someone performing duties on a temporary or part-time basis can be considered a test. As with other selection devices, performance tests require a standard protocol but can be constructed for important and specific aspects of many jobs. Examples are driving, repairing, assembling, keyboarding, calculating, welding, reading and following instructions. The applicant can perform, or not. Professor Peter Cappelli of the Wharton School has written, "Nothing in the science of prediction and selection beats observing actual performance in an equivalent role."[47]

Knowledge, management and administrative abilities aren't so readily measurable. Simulations are often used for non-manual jobs, and assessment centers may administer a battery of exercises involving leadership and organization. Situations that are encountered on the job are simulated and a candidate's manner of dealing with the situations is judged.

---

[43] Winfred Arthur Jr, Glaze, Villado, and Taylor, "The Magnitude and Extent of Cheating and Response Distortion Effects on Unprotored Internet-Based Tests." International Journal of Selection and Assessment 18, no. 1 (March 2010).

[44] Many years ago, when my farm-country manner was fresh and prominent, I was granted an interview in the executive offices of Neiman Marcus in Dallas. I recall a large office with wall hangings, a sofa and a coffee table. Early in the interview a silver tea set was delivered and set before me. I was asked if I would please pour. The female executive was most gracious despite the stumbling young man who was totally unfamiliar with the ritual.

[45] The veracity of online testing has been researched. Winfred Arthur Jr, Glaze, Villado, and Taylor, "The Magnitude and Extent of Cheating and Response Distortion Effects on Unprotored Internet-Based Tests." International Journal of Selection and Assessment 18, no. 1 (March 2010).

[46] In *Karraker v. Rent-A-Center, Inc.*, the popular Minnesota Multiphasic Personality Inventory was determined to be a medical examination and its use a violation of ADA. 316 F. Supp 2d 675 (C.D. Ill. 2004). In *Miller v. City of Springfield*, the MMPI was considered suitable as a test for police positions. 750 S.W. 2d 118, 120 (Mo. App. S.D. 1988).

[47] Reported in Don Peck, "They're Watching You at Work," *The Atlantic*, December 2013, 74.

Personality tests are frequently used to identify personal characteristics of applicants, based on the (sound or unsound) premise that certain thinking or behaviors are related to job success. A widely used personal-communications-style assessment is the Myers-Briggs Type Indicator, which is designed to improve conflict resolution and internal communications. It does not measure intelligence or skills. There are no scores, and the test is not intended to be used in selection or promotion.[48] The director of Myers-Briggs's business development states that the assessment is not intended for hiring or job candidate selection and that using the assessment for those purposes is "unethical. . . . It is most often used for teambuilding."[49] A like view asserts that "the goal of the MBTI [Myers-Briggs Type Indicator] is to provide self-insight . . . [N]either it, nor the Jungian principles it was based on, have been validated statistically."[50]

Employers use *honesty tests* to detect dishonesty and reduce property losses.[51] The Employee Polygraph Protection Act of 1988 (EPPA)[52] was passed by Congress "to prevent the denial of employment opportunities in the private sector by prohibiting the use of lie detectors by employers involved in, or affecting, interstate commerce" because of the unreliability of such testing. EPPA prohibits the use of mechanical or electrical testing devices, and the employer is prohibited from requiring, requesting or even suggesting that any employee or prospective employee must take any type of mechanical lie detector test. The act further prevents employers from using or threatening to use any of the results of a lie detector test. The use of tests are confined to law enforcement personnel, in the employment of those who manufacture, distribute or dispense controlled substances, and persons in sensitive positions directly involving national security. Several states, such as Massachusetts and Rhode Island, have specifically limited their use. Honesty tests should only be used upon the advice of a subject expert.

> **Tests and procedures "must be job-related and the results appropriate for the employer's purpose. [T]he employer [is] responsible for ensuring that its tests are valid under the UGESP [Uniform Guidelines on Employee Selection Procedures]."**
>
> —EEOC Fact Sheet

Job placement inventories are used to identify the degree of compatibility of a job with the applicant's aptitude and interests. These factors are largely independent of skill and knowledge. They can be determined generally through written or electronic instruments such as the Strong

---

[48] Douglas P. Shuit, "At 60, Myers-Briggs Is Still Sorting Out and Identifying People's Types," *Workforce Management* 82, no. 13 (December 2003): 72–74.
[49] Ibid.
[50] Juana Llorens, "Taking Inventory of Myers-Briggs," *Training and Development* 64, no. 4 (April 2010): 18–19.
[51] One view of testing under public merit selection systems is that it is based on two assumptions: 1) future job performance can be predicted by tests and 2) personnel staff is able to select personnel more effectively than managers. Several pages later the author expresses frankly that he believes tests as a primary selection device are unsuccessful. W. David Patton et al., *Human Resource Management: The Public Service Perspective* (New York: Houghton Mifflin, 2002), 198–200.
[52] Public Law, 100-347, 102 Stat. 646 et seq. 29 U.S.C. 01 ct. seq., CFR Pat 801 (1991).

Interest Inventory, or through other, more specific areas such as computer and technology aptitude measurement instruments.

Drug and/or alcohol testing is intended to prevent poor performance, theft, and drug dealing. An estimated 10 to 15 percent of U.S. workers use illegal drugs. Tests are common and those subject to a testing program should be *notified in advance* and results kept in a separate file. It's common practice that employees, but not applicants, who fail initial tests get re-tested, plus the opportunity to undergo treatment rather than disciplinary action. Many states permit drug testing only under certain conditions, including written employer policy, employee consent, detailed chain-of-custody protocol (ensuring correct legal procedures are followed for specimen identification and handling), and at employer cost.

Under federal law, personnel in safety-sensitive public transportation must be drug free. Any employer operating commercial or other motor vehicles of 26,000 pounds or more must maintain a testing policy and program. Before hiring a driver, an employer must acquire the applicant's testing record for the previous two years. Employers are to maintain testing records and provide supervisors with two hours of training, including how to determine "reasonable suspicion" of drug use in order to help the identification of those under the influence. Transportation trade associations can be of assistance in finding these required testing services.

Drug testing conducted for government agencies requires extensive controls and accuracy, as do many states. Public employees enjoy special considerations for privacy, so there must be a prevailing public need to overcome their protective rights. As would be expected, public safety and law enforcement workers are subject to testing.[53]

The Americans with Disabilities Act generally prohibits *pre-employment medical examinations*. However, lines of work such as performed by first responders and maintenance workers require different forms of strength and agility. Employers delay physical examinations until after a conditional offer of employment, and everyone in the job category is required to take the exam. Drug testing is not a medical examination under the ADA, and thus may be required at the time of application, assuming there is a compelling justification for the test, such as public safety, and the practice conforms to state law.

Choosing Among Candidates

The steps in the process of choosing among candidates are intended to help make a sound decision. The test information used so heavily in the public sector provides more objectivity than interviews in measuring some factors. However, tests are sometimes challenged as measuring the wrong characteristics, rendering them as invalid instruments. It's the combination of accumulated information from multiple sources and particularly information about what a person has done that increases selection success.

---

[53] Ibid., pg. 95.

Choosing Among Candidates

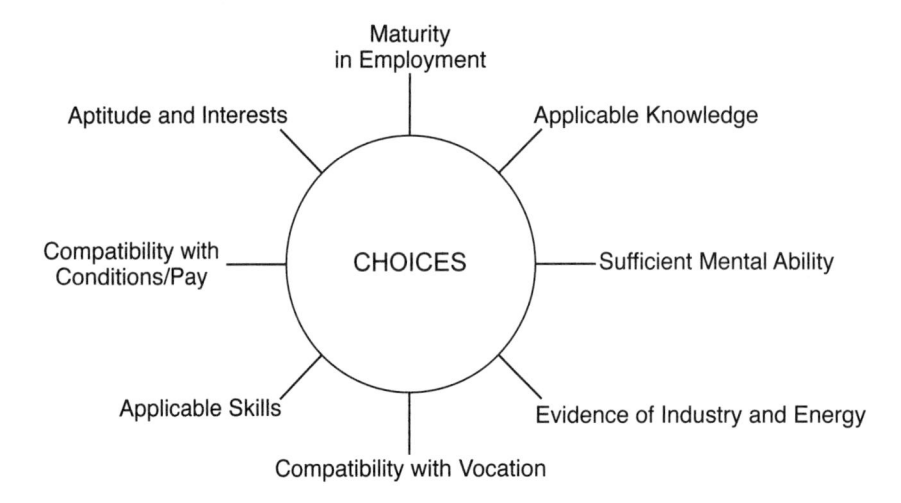

- Maturity in Employment
- Applicable Knowledge
- Sufficient Mental Ability
- Evidence of Industry and Energy
- Compatibility with Vocation
- Applicable Skills
- Compatibility with Conditions/Pay
- Aptitude and Interests

CHOICES

A process contributes to making the best choices by ensuring that final candidates *satisfy position requirements*. When finalists are determined, the final selection results from a comparison of the strengths and weaknesses of remaining candidates.

In some organizations, making the best choice for an assignment is often compromised by a historical automatic progression practice or an assumed qualification (e.g., "The best worker deserves to be supervisor"). Good workers don't necessarily make good leaders or managers, nor is requiring five or ten years of experience usually necessary. An applicant can have one year of useful experience that was repeated for ten years with no breadth of development. In many groups with a labor contract, management has agreed with the counterproductive application of seniority as the basis for promotion; knowledge, skills and ability are more useful criteria.[54]

A candidate should match the employer and the conditions in terms of the physical and mental circumstances of the position (e.g., office vs. factory), and the job in terms of the skill, knowledge requirements and the individual's interests and aptitudes. An applicant will often suppress his or her personal sense of incompatibility and ignore normal self-screening sensations in his or her eagerness for employment. To avoid job placement errors, an employer representative must be alert to an absence of evidence of compatibility and the spin of an applicant. In the end, selection choices are difficult and weighty. Good ones result in a stronger organization, and poor ones are costly.

Below is a sample selection worksheet designed to assess 1) the applicant as a desirable employee, 2) job competencies and 3) compatibility.

---

[54] W. David Patton et al., *Human Resource Management: The Public Service Perspective,* (New York: Houghton Mifflin, 2002), 211.

CANDIDATE CONSIDERATIONS

Candidate: _____   Position: _____

GENERAL FACTORS
- ❏ Suitable attire/grooming
- ❏ Maturity of conduct
- ❏ Evidence of industry and energy
- ❏ Similar experience
- ❏ Previous applicable work
- ❏ Previous employment tenure
- ❏ Candidate's views of previous employment
- ❏ Other: _____

JOB COMPETENCY INDICATORS
- ❏ Achievements in this occupational arena
- ❏ Demonstrated skills
- ❏ Demonstrated knowledge
- ❏ Appropriate electronic use skills
- ❏ Evidence of related competencies
- ❏ Communications skill adequacy
- ❏ Capacity for learning/mastering this job
- ❏ Capacity for more difficult tasks
- ❏ Social skill adequacy
- ❏ Other: _____

ORGANIZATION (UNIT) COMPATIBILTY
- ❏ Appropriate level of intellect
- ❏ Evidence of appropriate interest and aptitude
- ❏ Expectations and aspirations
- ❏ Employment likes/dislikes—culture compatibility
- ❏ Compensation compatibility
- ❏ Fit of duties with lifestyle
- ❏ Commute considerations
- ❏ Job conditions (schedule/travel/telecommute)
- ❏ Comfort with role in the hierarchy/group
- ❏ Comfort with nature of the product/service
- ❏ Other: _____

RESPONSES
- ❏ Expressions of wants, needs, job fit
- ❏ Indicators of values/beliefs/temperament
- ❏ Priorities and concerns
- ❏ Reaction to workstation/supervisor
- ❏ Points of reluctance/uncertainty
- ❏ Indicators of interest/enthusiasm
- ❏ Other: _____

NOTES:
_____
_____
_____
_____

Interviewer: _____   Date: _____

Background Verification: _____   By: _____

Supervisor Comments: _____   Date: _____

The primary considerations in choosing people are applicable skills, knowledge, aptitude, interests and abilities that are common to the position. Choosing the right people for the work is paramount in the assignment of all jobs. During the last decade, increasing electronic communication and the use of personal handheld devices have become a new consideration in worker selection. So, too, has the use of computer skills in many manufacturing jobs.

Worksite Previews

The selection process might benefit from providing a candidate with exposure to the *work area conditions* and the job being performed. Some people appreciate any work and will adapt to any conditions, but others will recognize the likelihood of incompatibility. If the job is in a freezer, foundry, horse stall, or even an office workstation, "a toe in the water" might be helpful. The working environment may be noisy or without any privacy, equipment may be antiquated, or the potential employee "won't see anybody like me" in terms of color or race. The workstation preview is a form of reality exposure that can prevent a mistake by either party.

> **An applicant's manner of *behavior and conduct in society* is a different aspect of a person than *abilities and industriousness*, which differ from *interests and aptitudes*.**

The Reality (Background) Test

Learning about an applicant's life and employment history is crucial in personnel decisions but can be difficult and frustrating for the inquirer. The record-keeping staff of previous employers will generally provide only a job title, employment dates and perhaps confirmation of an approximate pay level. To learn about a worker's skills, knowledge and conduct, it's necessary to put on the hat of a detective and talk to previous supervisors, acquaintances and others who know the person personally. Final job candidates *must* have inquiries made of their work history. Information that has been provided by the candidate must be verified and impressions confirmed or corrected. Many will find this chore time-consuming, demanding and sometimes unpleasant.

The basis for background inquiries begins with knowledge of the job and its specifications and proceeds to how the candidate's attributes relate. The application and interviews provide the means for contacting previous employers, supervisors and personal references. A *signed authorization* is necessary before the employer makes inquiries about the applicant. Typically this authorization is on the back of the application form so that it is completed automatically as part of the process. (An example is provided near the beginning of this chapter.)

Application forms and interviews represent the candidates in their own words and reflect what they want you to know. Some people spin their background and tell falsehoods in the interest of getting a job. A 2008 survey by payroll provider ADP revealed that of 5.5 million representations by applicants, 46 percent used some fabrication rather than facts. A similar survey by Résumé Doctor indicated 43 percent among 1,100 résumés were false in some manner. Consider this text taken from an Internet advertisement:

> **Diplomas from prestigious non-accredited universities based on your present knowledge and life experience.**
>
> **If you qualify, no required tests, classes, books or examinations.**
>
> **Bachelor's, Master's, MBA, Doctorate & PhD degrees available in your field.**
>
> **CALL NOW TO RECEIVE YOUR DIPLOMA WITHIN 2 WEEKS**

This issue exists at all levels. In the last few years, executives at RadioShack, Smith & Wesson, and Bausch & Lomb have been disgraced when falsehoods in their backgrounds were revealed. To prevent this from happening with new hires, seek information from a number of knowledgeable sources.

There are two general sources of information to be acquired: one from public agencies (schools/criminal records/licenses) and the other from those personally knowledgeable about the candidate. A bogus education record is not uncommon, nor is an accusation of theft in the retail sector. Criminal convictions must be evaluated thoughtfully. If a conviction took place years ago for a totally unrelated matter, its pertinence is doubtful, and an employment rejection could result in illegal discrimination exposure. However, if an accountant was convicted of embezzlement two years ago, a rejection would seem plausible in most courts.

The introduction and tone of *investigative interviews* with the applicant's previous employers should be conducted in a professional manner. If the applicant is presently employed, any inquiries with that employer should be arranged jointly. Communicating that the candidate needs "help" in qualifying for a position, or that the caller wants to be sure that the new job is a proper "fit," is truthful and sets an agreeable tone as opposed to abrupt and pointed questioning. Asking a supervisor if he or she would rehire the individual can result in a telling response. Though personal references from the application sometimes result in rehearsed information, these "friends" can be more candid than the candidate expects and can generate networking opportunities.

This intelligence gathering involves creativity and persistence that many people don't possess. If inquiries are fruitless, the candidate should be asked to stir some cooperation among references, or lose the possibility of employment. If people are especially close-mouthed about a candidate, this is greater reason to persist in pursuing information or dropping the candidate. A hiring commitment without sufficient knowledge of competency and character is incomplete and involves unwarranted risk.

For public safety occupations and positions of public trust, there are many state laws requiring thorough background investigation. Police officer records of behavior are obviously crucial, but qualifying housing managers, child service workers and private security personnel are also likely to be necessary by virtue of state regulations.

Neglect in hiring has created a common exposure to a legal charge of *negligent hiring* under common law. Indeed, some states require that an employer who has previously employed someone who demonstrated violent tendencies must assertively pass on that information to a potential employer who inquires.

> ## POINTS OF BACKGROUND INQUIRIES
>
> - What is the nature of the employee's work experience?
> - Do the employee's interests match this work?
> - Is this a quality employee?
> - What were the duties and pay?
> - Are expressed accomplishments truthful?
> - Confirm education.
> - Reason for separation?
> - Any disruptive behavior?
> - Was the employee's attendance reliable?
> - Would you reemploy the applicant?
> - Any additional information or sources?

Social media is now often used to learn about candidates. Those who carelessly remark publicly about drugs or prejudices are at the very least careless. It could be postulated that such personal information shouldn't be used in employment decisions, but the data is willingly offered to the public, and employer investments in their personnel involve serious sums of money that need to be safeguarded. Caution by an employer is necessary, however, because a site may disclose race or age information about the candidate.

There are service firms that conduct background investigations.[55] They may do a good job with the public sources and commercial driver histories, but aren't always sufficiently aggressive or prepared to pursue employment history information about the individual; in other words, they will be satisfied with a job title rather than learning the job duties.

Employers sometimes use consumer reports in investigations. If such reports are used, the employer must notify the candidate, collect an authorization, and commit to follow requirements to avoid costly legal actions. If the report is adverse, employers must provide applicants with information so they can reply.

In 2012 the National Consumer Law Center reported that because of surging demand for candidate background information, some firms have come into existence that produce invalid information and suffer no accountability for their dubious reports. Needless to say, appropriate *due diligence* is required in selecting providers for such services.

---

[55] See website BestBackgroundCheck.org.

There is a responsibility to obtain as much information as possible about potential hires, yet when receiving inquiries about your previous employees, the counsel is to provide as little information as possible. Both tactics should be adopted to best serve the employer.

> **TRUST BUT VERIFY**
>
> **To provide an element of quality control and to reduce the threat of legal vulnerability, carry out complete research on those to be employed.**

Uncommon Situations

There are occurrences and circumstances in certain occupations or states that impact employment practices, most often in the private sector. Federal and state governments typically have written directives for most personnel management contingencies. Management should be prepared to respond suitably to predictable situations.

Appearance

Interviewers and supervisors must be cautious in judging an applicant based on looks. Personal views must be subdued in favor of the organization's well-being and contemporary social and legal standards. Religious attire must be granted some latitude. If the attire is safe and not objectionable to viewing by customers or others, management should try to overcome the situation without sacrificing established principles. Documented efforts to resolve such issues, even if unsuccessful, evidence the integrity of the employer. In many courts, a consistent and reasonable uniform standard for attire and appearance based on customary business principles will stand against charges of illegal discrimination.

Young Workers

Employers are expected to verify, through a birth certificate, school-age certificate, or driver's license, the age of young people before employment. The Fair Labor Standards Act and state law prohibit minors from engaging in dangerous work such as driving, construction, and using machinery or cutting devices, and establish limits on the hours that can be worked. For example, Arkansas requires that those under age eighteen be granted thirty-minute rest breaks every five hours. Reflect also on the effect on insurance rates and consequences to image if a minor is injured on the job.

Transportation Workers

Those who employ pilots, commercial drivers, railroad personnel and others occupied in public transportation must comply with specific drug and alcohol testing and other regulations of the Department of Transportation. A written notice to prospective employees detailing the prohibitions, testing procedures and consequences of positive result testing is obligatory. Employees must acknowledge receipt of the notification in writing. Commercial vehicle operators and other directly related personnel are also subject to licensing, age, medical condition or demonstrated skill requirements. Keeping records of compliance to these requirements is imposed on employers by regulatory agencies such as the Federal Aviation Administration.

Residency Requirements[56]

In the public sector there is frequently an edict, which has been upheld by courts, that employees must live within the service area of the public unit (i.e., the state, county or city by which they are employed).

Those with a Disability[57]

There is general social view and law favoring special efforts by employers to accommodate disabled people in employment. If an individual is ruled unable to perform the essential functions of a job, the burden of proof is on the employer. Special accommodations expected of an employer include changing schedules, job demands or equipment to help accommodate the

> **Job candidates known to be disabled are to be helped getting access to facilities and engaging in the employment process. Further, it's good practice to have an exploratory conversation or performance test about competencies and possibilities.**

individual to the position. There is no expectation to impose job demands on another worker, to significantly compromise efficiency or to expend unreasonable sums of money to accomplish an accommodation.[58] However, management would be well advised not to make judgments about what a person *probably cannot do*, but instead interact with the individual about what *can* be done.[59]

Work-at-Home Arrangements

If the employee will be working at home, understand that only the location is different. The worker is subject to workers' compensation protection, and if the work is subject to overtime, accurate timekeeping and premium-pay rules apply. To date, OSHA has not pursued the routine investigation of workstations that are out of management's control.

English-Language Workplace

Twelve percent of the nation's work population is foreign born, and many employers make adjustments in that regard. Local ethnic community centers can assist in social integration and

---

[56] See *McCarthy v. Philadelphia Civil Service Commission*, 424 U.S. 96 Ct. 1154, 47 L. Ed 2nd 366 (1976).
[57] A physical or mental impairment substantially limiting a major life activity such as the performance of manual tasks, walking, seeing, hearing, speaking, breathing or learning. The corresponding law in the public sector is the Rehabilitation Act, Section 501 (1973).
[58] The EEOC maintains that 80 percent of all accommodations cost less than $500.
[59] *EEOC v. Daimler Chrysler Corp*. The employer must provide a reader for test questions to overcome a disability.

diversity efforts. If legitimately essential to job performance, speaking English can be required, but may have to be defended. Questions about the need for a language requirement swing on the "business necessity."

Previous Agreements

It is important for employers to determine if a prospective employee (typically professional or managerial) is subject to any non-compete or confidentiality agreement with a prior employer. These agreements may restrict an applicant from employment or limit his or her ability to perform services effectively.

Military Obligations

An employer should be cautious of inquiries about military obligations of a candidate. An employer cannot discriminate against anyone on that basis, and, as with other risky subjects of inquiry, the applicant might think the question will lead to illegal discrimination. When an employee returns from a military leave of absence, an employer faces reemployment obligations. Assuming an honorable discharge, veterans are entitled to reinstatement to a position of like seniority, status and pay. Their conditions of employment are to replicate those they would have had if they had not been absent. A veteran must reapply within ninety days after separation from active duty, but sooner if the service was for less than six months.

Legal Discrimination

There are positions such as restroom attendants and religious positions that legitimately justify someone of a specific gender, religion or race. Other applicants may be rejected in those circumstances on the basis that the position has a particular bona fide occupational qualification (BFOQ).[60] A second point of legitimate discrimination applies to those not eligible to work in the United States.

Religious Accommodations

Employers are to make good-faith efforts to accommodate any special religious practices that are normally observed during working time. Some employers have provided rooms for prayer, but in turn receive a negative reaction from other employees to the special treatment granted. Be guarded about granting accommodations for fear of setting an undesirable precedent.

Relocation

Staffing activity may require the relocation of a new or transferring employee. The individual could be a single technician who rents a furnished room, or an executive with a large family, two homes,

---

[60] Although *bona fide occupational qualification* (BFOQ) is a statutory term defined in Title VII, and *business necessity* was a term defined by the courts, the two items are often used interchangeably and are given the same strict interpretation.

four automobiles, two boats, three dogs and a horse. The costs of relocation in the first instance may be less than $5,000, but the second, if any agreement includes temporary housing and a "no loss on real estate" provision, could exceed half a million dollars. This wide disparity can make consistency of treatment difficult. A policy can be established outlining remuneration for common costs (travel, furniture moving) as well as a sample of the types of expenses that will *not* be paid for any employee (such as moving fees for horses, sailboats, etc.). Small employers in particular may best be served by having no policy at all and instead relying on past practice or a case-by-case approach.

Relocations rarely go smoothly, which is a reason that large employers often engage relocation service firms. If there is to be frustration and upset, it's better to have an intermediary absorb the distress. Some typical matters to be addressed in the employer's policy are:

- Moving the household goods
- Disposing of the present living accommodations and property
- Losses on property sales
- Trips to find a new home
- Temporary living expenses
- Temporary child care or eldercare
- Job search assistance for family members
- New home allowance (e.g., installation fees, drapes, etc.)

Offers

An offer of employment is often confirmed with a handshake, but at professional levels is expressed in a letter. The newcomer may want the offer in writing for verification, especially if he or she will subsequently be giving notice to a present employer.[61] The employer wants to avoid misunderstandings or any lack of clarity that can lead to future misunderstanding and allegations of misrepresentation or an "implied contract."

An offer letter should include the pay expressed as an hourly or monthly rate, the pay period, title or project, and starting date. It is sometimes necessary to make offers on a contingency basis pending additional reference or medical information. A patterned letter that has been examined for legal implications should be used.

Offer letters are often associated with professional positions or those in the hierarchy and are often used to spell out special conditions such as benefit deviations or expectations of performance. However, written forms of employment commitments are often provided, even required, in the public sector, to prevent misunderstanding about starting time, date and pay.[62]

---

[61] A coaching job offer was overruled and canceled, resulting in a finding of negligent misrepresentation after the candidate quit a $200,000 job and sold his house. *Williams v. Board of Regents of the University of Minnesota*, 763 N.W.2d 646 2008 Minn. Ct. of App. (March 31, 2009).
[62] MN Statute 181.55.

> This letter confirms your employment with the _____
> (Department Name)
>
> department on the dates specified below:
>
> Dates and schedule of employment: (subject to change)
>
> Start date:_____/_____/_____ to end date: _____/_____/_____
>   *month   day   year*   *month   day   year*
>
> COMPENSATION: Rate of pay will be $_____
>
> SUPERVISOR SIGNATURE:_____DATE:_____

Enrollment

After the acceptance of a job offer, completing paperwork will connect the new person with payroll, benefit and personnel systems and complete the employment process. The government requires forms and information; benefit participation normally requires some discussion, choices and signatures in addition to written authorization. Now that the possibility of illegal discrimination in the selection is minimized, sensitive administrative questions can be asked and answered more freely; specifically, information on age, emergency contacts, Social Security number, race and health matters. Information completed by newcomers at an enrollment meeting is routinely routed and distributed among benefit providers, payroll and personnel records for action and recording.

    A new private-sector employee is normally enrolled in an *active working status*. Sometimes, however, the association is conditional by way of a *probationary* status. Probationary periods in public organizations tend to be long. In Shelby County, Tennessee, a probationary test lasts for a period of six to nine months, whereupon there is "permanent . . . appointment to civil service." A common exception is that the favored status of veterans voids any use of a probation period. Much of the private sector has no probationary period because it is inconsistent with, and compromises, the employment-at-will condition. Further, it connotes uncertainty or doubt about the newcomer. Indeed, some who complete a probationary period in the private sector think in terms of public-sector job rights and assume they have earned proprietary job rights.[63]

    A final test is to document the *legal entitlement* of the individual to work in the United States. Once an individual is offered employment, an employer of any size is required to establish this eligibility within three days. If an employee's status is revealed to be ineligible upon completion

---
[63] League of Minnesota Cities Personnel Policies VII-4, Reference Manual.

LISTS OF ACCEPTABLE DOCUMENTS
All documents must be UNEXPIRED

Employees may present one selection from List A or a combination of one selection from List B and one selection from List C.

LIST A Documents that Establish Both Identity and Employment Authorization	LIST B Documents that Establish Identity	LIST C Documents that Establish Employment Authorization
OR	AND	
1. U.S. Passport or U.S. Passport Card	1. Driver's license or ID card issued by a State or outlying possession of the United States provided it contains a photograph or information such as name, date of birth, gender, height, eye color, and address	1. A Social Security Account Number card, unless the card includes one of the following restrictions: (1) NOT VALID FOR EMPLOYMENT (2) VALID FOR WORK ONLY WITH INS AUTHORIZATION (3) VALID FOR WORK ONLY WITH DHS AUTHORIZATION
2. Permanent Resident Card or Alien Registration Receipt Card (Form I-551)		
3. Foreign passport that contains a temporary I-551 stamp or temporary I-551 printed notation on a machine-readable immigrant visa	2. ID card issued by federal, state or local government agencies or entities, provided it contains a photograph or information such as name, date of birth, gender, height, eye color, and address	2. Certification of Birth Abroad issued by the Department of State (Form FS-545)
4. Employment Authorization Document that contains a photograph (Form I-766)		
	3. School ID card with a photograph	3. Certification of Report of Birth issued by the Department of State (Form DS-1350)
5. For a nonimmigrant alien authorized to work for a specific employer because of his or her status: a. Foreign passport; and b. Form I-94 or Form I-94A that has the following: (1) The same name as the passport; and (2) An endorsement of the alien's nonimmigrant status as long as that period of endorsement has not yet expired and the proposed employment is not in conflict with any restrictions or limitations identified on the form.	4. Voter's registration card	
	5. U.S. Military card or draft record	4. Original or certified copy of birth certificate issued by a State, county, municipal authority, or territory of the United States bearing an official seal
	6. Military dependent's ID card	
	7. U.S. Coast Guard Merchant Mariner Card	
	8. Native American tribal document	5. Native American tribal document
	9. Driver's license issued by a Canadian government authority	6. U.S. Citizen ID Card (Form I-197)
	For persons under age 18 who are unable to present a document listed above:	7. Identification Card for Use of Resident Citizen in the United States (Form I-179)
6. Passport from the Federated States of Micronesia (FSM) or the Republic of the Marshall Islands (RMI) with Form I-94 or Form I-94A indicating nonimmigrant admission under the Compact of Free Association Between the United States and the FSM or RMI	10. School record or report card	8. Employment authorization document issued by the Department of Homeland Security
	11. Clinic, doctor, or hospital record	
	12. Day-care or nursery school record	

Illustrations of many of these documents appear in Part 8 of the Handbook for Employers (M-274).

Refer to Section 2 of the instructions, titled "Employer or Authorized Representative Review and Verification," for more information about acceptable receipts.

Retrieved from www.uscis.gov/files/form/i-9.pdf.

of the form, the employer must withdraw the offer of employment immediately. The requirement of verification extends to all employees, lifetime U.S. residents as well as aliens. However, a hiring policy of *U.S. citizens only* is illegal.[64]

Law prohibits any person or entity from knowingly hiring or continuing to employ an unauthorized worker. Employers should keep a completed I-9 form of record in a distinct file. Copies of the documents proffered by the candidate do not need to be retained. Keeping copies of documents that are not authentic can prove to be disadvantageous.

The instructions to complete the form are clear and indicate the identity documents to be used. No other information for this purpose should be solicited. The Immigration and Customs Enforcement (ICE) agency can help an employer learn how to identify forged documents.

Occasionally employers will receive a "no match" letter from a government agency declaring that I-9 or tax information they receive about the employee is "no match" with their records. After the employer initially confirms internal accuracy, the employee should be contacted about the problem. They may have several months to resolve an issue, but if it is not resolved, the employee is to be terminated.

Employers may enroll and participate in E-Verify, an internal system to verify worker status through the Social Security Administration and Homeland Security. At the time of this writing, legislation has been proffered mandating its use. Federal contractors must participate, and some states[65] require participation, but at present the program is generally voluntary.

I-9 forms are to be retained for three years after the hire date or one year after termination. Keeping them longer has no advantage, and litigation could surface from careless handling, so the preferred practice is timely disposal.

The checklist shown here makes reference to understandings with individual new hires. There can be written agreement on subjects such as a non-compete or conflicts of interest. These agreements are most conveniently made at the time of employment and are discussed further in chapter 10.

New Employee Enrollment Checklist

- ❏ Application complete and signed
- ❏ Work eligibility verified
- ❏ Age evidence filed
- ❏ W-4 tax deduction form completed
- ❏ Emergency contact recorded
- ❏ Provision to report to the state's new-hire registrations
- ❏ Direct-deposit authorization
- ❏ Contracted understandings (if applicable)
- ❏ Hire date, SS number, pay rate recorded
- ❏ Group benefit enrollment completed
- ❏ Any applicable agreements between the parties
- ❏ Insurance Continuation Form (COBRA) provided

---

[64] *Sugarman v. Dougall*, 413 U.S. 634 (1973). A public employer cannot discriminate against a non-citizen.
[65] South Carolina, Arkansas, Colorado and Georgia are some of the states that have regulations.

Easing Integration

Newcomers will always suffer a measure of anxiety about the first day of a new situation. The enrollment meeting can provide information to help acclimate newcomers and avoid their suffering the unexpected. Whether presented by the supervisor or an administrator, some preparatory information will be appreciated. For example:

Communicate:
- Reporting time and place
- Supervisor's name
- Parking instructions
- Preferred point of entry
- Anticipated schedule and hours
- Provisions for lunch
- Personal gear (e.g., protective gloves, hat)
- What supplies will be provided
- Any needs for personal identification

Provide:
- Agenda for a subsequent orientation meeting
- Job description
- Building layout diagram
- Information packet
- A readied workstation

Reducing the anxiety of newcomers contributes in some measure to increased employee productivity. These efforts, following initial awareness through the selection procedures, are initial steps in the process of training and educating a workforce. Obviously, supervising job skill training is a major step, but each of the many steps in employee development is valuable.

Summary Remarks

The primary objective of HRM is to staff an organization with able and diverse personnel in a timely and legal manner. This chapter included myriad considerations involved in staffing, all directed toward enlisting workers who have a good likelihood of success. It is recommended that a variety of sources be used to locate and solicit workers with the required skill set compatible with the position.

Equal opportunity legislation centers the selection of personnel on legitimate job-related criteria. The Americans with Disabilities Act refined legitimate criteria even more clearly by requiring focus on the *essential* job-related functions of a position. Conformity to legal employment parameters applies throughout an organization, and therefore requires a manner of management oversight. Oversight of the legal standards has served to elevate the contribution of personnel management.

The identification of job demands and match to applicant attributes is at the core of filling vacancies. Deviations from the fair and equitable consideration of applicants can be justified only on the basis of substantive business necessity. The legal doctrine of fairness applies to choices made for training, promotion and work assignments.

A review of personnel choice decisions would include the following measures of good practice:

1. Valid qualifications are used in filling a vacancy.
2. Targeted recruited efforts are most cost-effective.
3. Real or perceived illegal discrimination is avoided.
4. Standard and valid forms and processes are used uniformly.
5. Advertising does not express invalid or unrelated requirements.
6. Applications are void of any unrelated inquiries.
7. Only trained personnel conduct interviews.
8. Steps, or the totality, of the process do not adversely affect minority candidates.
9. Thorough background investigations are routinely completed.
10. Every employee has his or her eligibility for work in the U.S. confirmed and recorded.

The relative success of staffing effectiveness can be measured by 1) successful ongoing audits of activity, including interviewing practices, 2) a suitable degree of diversity existing throughout the workforce, 3) department heads satisfied with the quality and timeliness of recruiting actions, 4) rational selection choices free of bias and 5) a lack of credible allegations of illegal discrimination. These accomplishments will be most readily achieved where able oversight of staffing activity is in place.

Applicable Competencies

Skills in analysis and communication, effective relationships with hiring managers, commitment to quality personnel free of undesirable characteristics, knowledge of internal jobs and external talent pools, consulting and training skills about legal considerations, ability in process management and interviewing, knowledge of applicable labor contract stipulations.

Applicable Resources

A patterned interview format, recruiting materials, standard forms that are free of undesirable content, adequate budget, and knowledge of community demographics and forms of media.

Review Materials

Content Exercises

1. List four subjects on an application form that are usually important in qualifying an applicant. List four points of inquiry that would be ill-advised.
2. Why is it important for an applicant to sign the application form?
3. What employment process capabilities should a receptionist be able to carry out?
4. Know one positive and one negative aspect of staffing a position only from within the organization.
5. Name five groups protected from prejudice under federal law and five others protected under state law.
6. Define an *applicant*, *candidate*, *expatriate*, and *headhunter*.
7. What is at least one reason for using a patterned interview?
8. What are three general areas of qualification the author suggests for selection?
9. What is the difference between equal opportunity and affirmative action?
10. Name four learning needs for overseas placement.
11. List the normal pattern of steps in staffing a vacancy.

Practical Applications

1. Examine "help wanted" advertisements on websites and in newspapers, and find four expressions or advertisement designs that you believe to be effective in attracting responses, and four that can be improved. Explain why.
2. If you were assigned to hire a mail clerk or receptionist, what are three work history qualifications a candidate should have for employment? What are three competencies that would particularly benefit a candidate for either of these positions?
3. How does an employer list a job with your state employment service?
4. Reflect on how you learned about two job opportunities for which you were eventually employed.
5. In past job searches, what were your experiences with, and views of, rejection notifications or the lack thereof?
6. Describe the employment process used in your organization. Who authorizes and interviews? What are standard procedures and training? Observations?
7. Inquire about your employer's advertising practices for applicants. Are there differences by units or occupations?

8. Analyze the application of your employer for suitable content.
9. Name common documents used to verify a right to work in the United States.

Case-Study Discussions

Case 2.1

Employment Compliance

The county HR director learned in a Monday morning meeting that a crew leader from the night shift had been sent to a maintenance shop in a remote corner of the county to establish a new worksite. The crew leader was to initiate hiring of an operating crew of three people, all of whom had to be commercially licensed truck drivers who would be performing the bulk of the work. These new employees were to service county roads and manage resources located in that area. This was an unusually expedient action resulting from the recent election of a county commissioner from that area. Office equipment, trucks and additional equipment and supplies were en route. With winter weather approaching, the crew leader was to initiate hiring and work projects as soon as possible. A permanent supervisor would be appointed and on-site within three weeks.

The HR director was surprised, and immediately recognized the employment law exposure with an untrained hiring representative. He announced in the meeting he would send someone to "help" with the hiring for a few days. The only option with such short notice was a personnel assistant who was scheduled for vacation the next week. There would be only several days to address matters at the site. He instructed the assistant to acquire the standard forms and take the necessary actions to ensure compliance with the law. Other matters could wait several weeks, but the employment and other critical compliance actions had to be addressed immediately.

Nearing the maintenance shop, Betty, the personnel assistant, observed signage for an American Indian reservation. When greeting the crew leader, she observed him handing out an off-the-shelf application form to someone inquiring about a job. Considering her assignment, what might be done in the next few days to provide for regulatory compliance in the employment process? What are the priorities? What other resources might be applied?

Case 2.2

Career Training

Kathy was selected to be the unit manager of a county maintenance facility three hours away from the county offices. She had worked on county road crews and performed some related administrative duties for several years while taking courses in pre-engineering at a vocational school. She had shown some leadership in her years with the county, but had never had supervisory responsibilities. As part of her new duties she was responsible for ensuring her unit functioned in accord with county policies, practices and employment laws. The county agreed to pay for a course in Human Resource Management and another in Supervisory Techniques offered as evening adult education through a nearby community college. It was also arranged that on those occasions when Kathy came to the county offices on business, she would spend two hours with the HR director for coaching on personnel management matters for at least a month. A priority would be employment matters because of legal vulnerabilities and Kathy's inexperience. Understanding that the county has established desirable practices, develop a list of employment practices, procedures and conditions that might be suitable subjects to be addressed in these early coaching sessions.

CHAPTER 3
DELIVER LEARNING OPPORTUNITIES

Chapter Objectives

- A head start for job training
- Mandated training and education
- The employee handbook
- The key role of the supervisor
- The skills and knowledge of supervisors
- Instructional tools and techniques

Workplace Education

When you are new to a job, you can be overwhelmed with new information. You begin a new undertaking by first "getting acclimated" to the employer and workstation, then receiving instruction on the duties of the specific job, being coached for improvement and then judged as to competency. There is often considerable pressure to achieve an adequate level of performance in the shortest possible time. In the longer term, workers continually pursue satisfaction of performance standards, keeping technically current or adapting to changing methods or demands.

The need for learning exists because of differences between a worker's present skills and knowledge and that which is desired in terms of cost, quality and output. Newcomers to an assignment must learn how to perform assigned duties and how to conduct themselves based on the preferred and prohibited behaviors. Effective personnel management must provide opportunities for newcomers to master the initial and essential matters. Schooling for a position is often conducted before getting to the workstation or even actual employment; common types of training include preparatory instruction in the use of equipment or the improvement of language skills. All of these matters relate to personnel development and effectiveness and are rudimentary elements of human resource management.

The degree of effectiveness of workers begins with *investment* devoted by top management. Vocation training has never before faced the challenges of today's technological progress. There are needs for and advantages of training activities in every organization; the needs in some technology industries are such a major aspect of the culture that they become known as "learning organizations."

> **Education and training are the differences between existing skill and knowledge and what is desired.**

The speed with which new technology and information develops requires individuals and organizations to keep current with advances. Changes in communications, electronics and robotics come quickly to mind, but advances in every discipline must be absorbed or the probability of obsolescence surfaces. In high-tech organizations, constant learning is imperative.

Helping workers learn and achieve can be *managed* in the interest of cost-effectiveness and quality or *left to random experience and chance*. Instructing and enabling employees to perform their job effectively is normally the responsibility of, and carried out by, the supervisors at every level of the hierarchy. They, in turn, must have the competency and skill to fulfill that obligation.

Given the parade of people passing through organizations, the pursuit of efficiency and effectiveness suggests that predictable needs be met through established routines and *programs*. The actual job skill training of subordinates is often delegated to a peer of the worker, who may be very able or may exhibit bad practices and impatience. The absence of structured and refined procedures in job training is a common deficiency in organization training and development. Our military is devoted to performance readiness. Their success in training demonstrates the value of clear expectations, close coaching and continuous practice. For some professionals, such as surgeons, pilots and quarterbacks, achieving performance competency can take years.

The scope of education activity can go beyond individuals or small groups and involve all the employees of the organization in order to achieve *major organizational improvement*. Refining or redirecting an entire organization by installing new computer systems or implementing customer satisfaction initiatives or total quality management (a collection of procedures to accomplish a quality improvement program) will involve top-to-bottom education under executive direction. Adjustments or redirection can be accomplished with the replacement of a key manager, a new marketing strategy or the increasing knowledge or skill of a single key employee.

Focused Effort

Efficiently moving a worker from a person of potential to a competent performer demands a clear and expressed understanding of the condition to be satisfied or corrected. The federal government[66] lists its general purpose of programs to be "designed to lead to: (A) improved ... service, (B) dollar savings, (C) the building and retention of a permanent cadre of skilled and efficient ... employees well abreast of scientific, professional, technical, and management developments ... (D) lower turnover

---

[66] The federal human resource development policy is expressed in the Government Employees Training Act (GETA).

of personnel, (E) reasonably uniform administration of training, consistent with the missions ... and (F) fair and equitable treatment of ... employees with respect to training." This comprehensive list reflects the federal culture of leaving little or nothing to chance.

Just as injuries to workers are investigated to identify dysfunctions, so too must a troublesome situation be examined to identify what must be altered. Occasionally when a production element or service is imperfect or failing, there is a rush to assume a need for training, when in fact a change in tools or equipment, the correction of a performance obstacle, adjustment of the method, or the replacement of a worker might correct the difficulty. Removing people from productive activity for developmental experiences disrupts systems and incurs extra costs. Beyond basic time costs, it is difficult to determine the full cost of training and development efforts and equally difficult to determine the value of the benefits.

> **Before training or education is initiated, the need and specific result must be sufficiently clear that it can be readily expressed to others.**

Employees value the investment an employer makes in their development. They gain new skills, grow toward their potential, and gain satisfaction. In essence, this investment "indicates that the organization values their contribution."[67] In each experience of workplace education, employees are further enabled to accomplish a functional purpose and improve their personal employment security.

Resources

Scores of methods are used to accomplish training and education needs. Some are job coaching, personal study, outside seminars and teleconferences. Unless the point of change is particularly technical, applying *in-house* expertise and materials can often be effective as well as efficient. One principal advantage of in-house efforts is that discussion and study are based on the realities of internal systems rather than theoretical circumstances. In technology firms particularly, the presence of internal knowledge and general intellectual competencies fosters obvious learning opportunities with which to "leverage the value of [internal] knowledge."[68]

In the absence of the necessary internal resources, the availability of *off-site or online training* and subject specialists for delivering supplemental education in the workplace is imperative. Walmart is one of many employers providing aid to employees who choose to undertake learning through online college courses. Technical and career schools provide practical instruction to help meet the needs of small organizations. Management development is frequently accomplished through targeted experiences, outside training seminars or job assignments.

There is an increasingly valuable relationship of secondary or high school education and two-year *post-secondary institutions* that results in improved vocational preparation. High school students can now take classes toward an associate degree at the same time they are completing

---

[67] Jeffrey Russell, Linda Russell, "Talk Me Through It," *Training and Development* 64, no. 4 (April 2010): 42–48.
[68] Sunil Ramlall, "A Review of Employee Motivation Theories and Their Implications for Employee Retention within Organizations," *Journal of American Academy of Business, Cambridge* 5, no. 1/2 (September 2004): 53.

work on their high school diploma. In January 2012, Education Secretary Arne Duncan remarked that even with many millions of people unemployed, the nation has two million technical jobs unfilled. He endorsed the concept of offering high school students advanced schooling in community colleges and vocational, technical and career schools in parallel with the latter years of their secondary education.[69]

> **Employee training and development is a process and not an event.**

Newcomer Training (Orientation)

A Process

The training and development of people new to assignments and occupations is a common process. A pattern begins with an introductory meeting for *general information* about the employer and workplace, followed by *exposure to the work area* (supplies, lunch provisions) with subsequent *instruction on job duties* and some form of *evaluation*.

The Newcomer Meeting

We have all experienced an onboarding or orientation meeting. The thrust of the meeting is to inform newcomers of general information, conditions and expectations the employer holds for employees, thus introducing a sense of order. Novice workers must be fully instructed on attendance, prompt reporting, food and restroom breaks, and paycheck deductions. The length of time devoted to an initial informational presentation can be several minutes or involve many hours over several weeks. The federal government mandates its employees receive education in ethics, privacy, diversity, computer security and more.[70] Disney World devotes several days to an introduction to the organization, with one full day devoted to its culture of courtesy and service.

Initial training and assimilation is frequently conducted for only one person, particularly among professional or managerial newcomers. Whether it be an individual or a group, devoting time to help new employees on their first day is a practical matter and a rare opportunity, as it can be difficult to take them away from their workstation later. Providing helpful early information and fundamental messages eases anxieties and accelerates the learning curve. Remember, newcomers may be experienced on job tasks, but they must still learn the location of the restroom!

---

[69] For critique on our present system of education and a look at more desirable options, the writings of Sir Ken Robinson are recommended: *The Element: How Finding Your Passion Changes Everything* (New York: Viking Press, 2009), *Out of Our Minds: Learning to Be Creative* (Chichester: Capstone Publishing, 2011) and *Finding Your Element: How to Discover Your Talents and Passions and Transform Your Life* (New York: Viking Press, 2013).
[70] Alan Clardy, "Policies for Managing the Training and Development Function: Lessons from the Federal Government," *Public Personnel Management* 37, no. 1 (Spring 2008): 37–47.

Mandated Understandings

In workplaces other than very small private and nonprofit employers, there are federal and state mandates to inform employees of specific matters. There are required posters (EEO, Safety) in every workplace, more in some states than others. It's timely and convenient to begin obligatory instruction in initial meetings. Within the health care industry, the federal government demands training related to blood-borne pathogens; in much of the transportation industry, vehicle operation training and testing is necessary. In mining, training in the use of respirators is mandated. Additional matters of employee education are:

- The prohibition of illegal discrimination and harassment
- Worksite hazards
- Workers' and unemployment compensation rights
- Facility evacuation procedures
- Eligibility for family medical leave

Failure to inform employees about these matters (or failure to have evidence of doing so) can result in costly consequences. Failure to notify staff about the prohibition of *sexual or religious bullying, stalking or harassment* may pose the greatest legal exposure, as "[leaving employees] in ignorance of the basic features of the discrimination law is an extraordinary mistake for a company to make, and such a mistake amounts to reckless indifference."[71] Illinois, Colorado and Tennessee are among states that have specifically legislated requirements for sexual harassment training. Maine requires employers of fifteen or more employees to conduct training for all new employees, including offering a description of sexual harassment and the complaint process.[72] Readers, please note that the above applies to professional and managerial personnel as well as to those workers eligible for overtime.

Training supervisors and workers to avoid and prevent abuse also includes instruction that a victim should express displeasure of the treatment, how to report abusive conduct, and the identification of a manager other than the supervisor to whom the employee may speak. It's often specified that a knowledgeable professional such as a lawyer carry out instruction on these matters.[73] Copies of the employer's policies and procedures should be provided to workers, and meetings must be conducted in a professional manner. Employers have occasionally magnified their problems when inappropriate remarks are made, or permitted by, an undisciplined instructor during a training class.[74]

---

[71] *Mathis v. Phillips Chevrolet, Inc.*, 269 F.3d 771 (7th Cir. 2001).
[72] Me. Rev. Stat. Ann. tit. 26, §807(3).
[73] *Cadena v. Pacesetter Corp.*, 224 F.3d 1203 (10th Cir. 2000).
[74] *Moller v. Dept. of Social Services*, 1995 WL 464903 (N.D. Cal. 1995) and *Caggiano v. Fontoura*, LEXIS 367 (App. Div. 2002).

Enculturation

Besides specific functional instruction and familiarization, there is often a less concrete and *higher order of perception and understanding* about the nature of the workplace that workers need to learn. Beginning with recruiting advertisements and through interviews and prepared materials, a newcomer receives exposure to employer thinking and begins to grasp not only *what* is done, but also the level of discipline, standards and manner of *how* things are accomplished. Very soon workers begin to hear what management values or favors in terms of its cultural views on aspects such as participative decisions, open communications, high energy, teamwork, social responsibility and high quality. For this reason, if no other, messages to the public and to employees should be consistent and clear.

Written Materials

Other common tools used with newcomers are an employee booklet or sheets of handout materials. Printed material has a longer educational life than the spoken word, provides clarity, uniformity and consistency, and multiplies the potential for employee readership and learning. Agendas and copies of hard-copy communication also evidence compliance with mandated communications. Still, as the handbook is normally issued at the time of employment, its greatest value is as a reference for employees. A signed receipt will prove that the employer provided the information to the employee.

While meetings with new employees are commonplace, it can't be assumed that meetings or handbooks are effective training devices. Such meetings are often so rote that extra effort to ensure understanding of the messages is neglected. Speakers should learn what they can about the nature of the audience. A presentation may have to anticipate the possibility of low reading or language

---

**Standards of Conduct
Professional and Managerial Employees**

ASSIMILATION PLAN

- Meet associates and hierarchy.
- Learn technical support availability.
- Understand workstation functions and protocols.
- Initiate related professional and industry relationships.
- Gain understanding of management priorities.
- Learn about authority, responsibilities and accountabilities.
- Gain familiarity with organizational assets and access.

DEVELOPMENTAL MATTERS

- Become familiar with suppliers/inputs.
- Learn about expectations regarding civic responsibilities, unions, political action.
- Participate in extensive product education.
- Become familiar with customer interests and preferences.
- Explore organizational, unit and personal expectations/challenges.
- Learn about competitors.
- Explore communication systems.
- Understand budgets and cost control management.
- Pursue sources of education.
- Learn the firm's decision-making protocols.

List of Subjects for Newcomers

- A management welcome
- An introduction to the company and industry
    - Size/uniqueness
    - Products or services
    - Points of pride
    - The processes for output
    - Management values, priorities
- Upward communication systems for complaints and concerns
- General compensation programs and policies
- Expectations and prohibitions (drugs, firearms, smoking)
- Personal record changes
- Transportation options
- Rules for personal use of equipment
- Lost-and-found practices
- Telephone and message protocols and policies
- The name of the supervisor

STANDARDS OF CONDUCT AND BASIC PERFORMANCE (HOURLY EMPLOYEES)

Employment Expectations

- ❑ Report to work as scheduled and on time.
- ❑ Attend to assigned tasks.
- ❑ React willingly to directions.
- ❑ Produce timely and quality work.
- ❑ Learn job standards from the supervisor.
- ❑ Be respectful of others.

Incident Alerts

- ❑ Report mistreatment.
- ❑ Treat the property of others responsibly.
- ❑ Report any threats, suspicions, fears.
- ❑ Point out any possible illegal practices by a member of management.
- ❑ Report any injuries promptly.
- ❑ Report an impending absence as directed.
- ❑ Use the prescribed complaint system.
- ❑ Follow any rules for conduct and safety.

NOTIFICATIONS AND PROHIBITIONS

- ❑ Employment is at will [if applicable].
- ❑ Overtime must be approved, and is required.
- ❑ Searches of belongings and lockers may be necessary.
- ❑ Substance abuse testing may be conducted.
- ❑ Disrespect of others is prohibited.
- ❑ Only bulletin boards can be used for the solicitation of employees.
- ❑ Distribution of non-business materials is prohibited.
- ❑ There are no absolute dates for appraisals or pay changes.
- ❑ Visitor access is limited.
- ❑ Avoid bringing valuables onto the property.
- ❑ Any weapons and illegal drugs are prohibited.
- ❑ Political activity parameters are understood (public sector).
- ❑ Residency requirements for employment are followed (public sector).
- ❑ Conflict-of-interest provision is known (public sector).

Place a check in each box to indicate that the subject has been covered.

Employee Name:_____

Date Hired:_____

Department: _____

Supervisor: _____

competency or a score of other human limitations that might require accommodation in order to achieve learning.

Materials written for the benefit of employees can create legal issues for employers. Frequently these materials are expansive, incomplete and incorrect on a technicality, or just express unnecessary matters. Group benefits are based on legal documents, so describing benefits without realizing the detailed exceptions is hazardous. Only those with expertise in such matters should communicate details.

Prescribed disciplinary practices needn't be spelled out. Expressions about *fair or competitive wages*, *promotion from within*, *job security*, or annual *pay review* commitments are restrictive and controversial, and circumstances may prevent them from being accomplished (unless committed by an act of Congress). Management still has considerable latitude under law that shouldn't be unnecessarily compromised.

Verbal remarks in an orientation meeting should be as precise as the expressions in written material. Following a statement of welcome, handouts typically address factual information about the organization, standards of conduct or rules, how to deal with complaints or concerns, and policies. Other common subjects are how to change an address, submit a complaint or grievance, and access the vacation benefit schedule.

To be most effective and conspicuous, key words of legally required written messages should be bold and in large letters.[75] The legal community advises that while disclaimers, caveats and notices (such as those below) are distractions to readers, they are desirable for the defense of the employer.

- "Programs and policies can be changed or revoked without notice."
- "Employment is at will, i.e., employees can quit or be dismissed at any time."
- "This employee-employer association or general written materials are not contractual."[76]
- "Any personal agreements must be in writing and signed by an officer."
- "These materials supersede previous statements on these subjects."
- Orientation material should include a statement that indicates understanding by an employee, such as:
    - "I am to ask a supervisor if I do not understand a policy or if I believe there has been a legal transgression by management."
    - "I have a copy of orientation materials and understand their content."
    - "I understand my employment is at the will of the parties." (NOTE: This applies mostly in the private sector.)

---

[75] *Silchia v. MCI Telecommunications Corp.*, 942 F. Supp. 1369 (D. Colo. 1996).
[76] There are many state and federal courts that rule handbooks are contracts. In Illinois, "an employee handbook or other policy statements create enforceable contractual rights if the traditional requirements for contract formation are present." *Duldulao v. St. Mary of Nazareth Hospital Center*, 115 Ill. 2nd 482, 485 (1987). Also see *Hohmeier v. Leyden Community High Schools Dist. 212*, 954 F.2d 451 (7th Cir. 1992).

Preparatory Training

Some workers, perhaps from different cultures and situations, require training and education in order to initially qualify for employment or to subsequently advance. A wide view of vocational education finds remedial skill and knowledge education common for those peripheral to the basic workforce such as the elderly, disabled, immigrants, technically disadvantaged and unemployed who need a "boost."

> **A signed receipt acknowledging the understanding of handbook content can be valuable in controversies and litigation.**

Early education is not always remedial. School curriculums offer courses that anticipate needs; elementary school youngsters are learning how to code special programming languages in summer camps. Early education is normally provided through community resources.

Supervisors, too, are sometimes motivated to pursue second-language learning for their job or for personal development. Courses are sponsored, or provided, by employers, advocate groups or career and vocational educational institutions.

The Supervisor: A Central Figure

While others in the organization can provide helpful knowledge and information, the worker's supervisor soon becomes the central figure in a workplace. The responsibility of supervisors for the training and performance of other workers magnifies their importance in organizational hierarchy. Supervisors are key players in employee relations and unit performance.

Top management isn't always as supportive of these key people as their role justifies. Most of those appointed to the position receive no training,[77] which contributes to being viewed as other than exemplary by their subordinates. Twenty-five percent of workers feel they are bullied by their supervisor,[78] which may relate to poor selection practices. A second poll of 1,000 adults indicates "half of employees work for an abusive boss."[79] Inappropriate supervisors can be detrimental to an employer.

A noteworthy management error is the historical practice of promoting the most knowledgeable or productive worker to a position of supervision. Studies at Development Dimensions International (DDI) indicate that about one-third of supervisors were promoted on the basis of technical expertise, yet personal communication, coaching and delegation skills are fundamental to their success.[80]

---

[77] In a 2011 survey by CareerBuilder of 3,910 supervisors in 2,480 firms, 58 percent of new supervisors reported no training.
[78] In a 2011 survey by CareerBuilder.
[79] "The Value of JIT Structured On-the-Job Training," *SMT Magazine* 26, no. 6 (June 2011): 50.
[80] Annamarie Lang and Bradford Thomas, "Crossing the Canyon from Technical Expert to First-Time Leader," *Training and Development* 67, no. 3 (March 2013): 36–39.

Job Training

Department management is responsible for the *job skill training* of workers to ensure they can perform the work, are provided necessary supplies and use equipment properly. Paramount to the subject of workplace education is *learning how to do a job*.[81] For more than fifty years, job instruction in many organizations has been accomplished through *Job Instruction Training (JIT)* or variations thereof. This method has the advantage of *one-on-one attention* to the trainee and *practice* of the skill being learned; results can be observed as part of the routine. Instructors follow a *documented procedure* of 1) preparing the trainee to learn, 2) presenting the task, 3) making the trainee practice ("Competence improves with experience")[82] and 4) having the monitoring instructor coach, correct and improve the trainee. JIT is an efficient and simple process for instruction but requires patient and disciplined application by the instructor.

Sometimes a checklist of considerations is used as a basis for examining a newcomer's progress. A checklist offers *an orderly basis for discussion* between trainer and trainee, and prevents overlooking an important item. The example provided is not used to judge or rank the trainee. If it is to become a report and a matter of record, it is more than a training tool, and extra care must be taken to ensure the review honestly reflects the situation.

Coaching for Improvement

People are involved with coaching their entire life. Youngsters are subject to coaching from parents, teachers and athletic coaches. In adulthood we coach offspring and others. The act of coaching is to monitor an activity and intervene in the process with a suggestion, directive or question designed to improve the performance of an individual or work team.[83]

Just as with basic job instruction, the advantages of coaching are that the trainee benefits from *one-on-one instruction*, practices the adjusted task *under guidance* and observes the *proper practice*, all within the training cycle. In contrast, group sessions, which are most often knowledge based, are more imprecise, without an opportunity for application; the results of the effort are unknown or difficult to assess. Applying the technique of role-playing does offer some practice.

Supervisors routinely monitor workplace outputs and apply coaching to advance workers to a level of satisfying standards and beyond. If there is less than adequate performance on an essential element, the supervisor and employee should collaborate to correct it. An organization's workers must meet fair and reasonable standards in order to sustain an efficient and effective work unit.

Employee Appraisals

Many organizations conduct an annual appraisal interview or performance review and file a subsequent report that identifies training needs and rates an employee in some category of effectiveness and desirability. The presence of formal appraisal programs generally relates to the size of the

---

[81] In a 2011 survey by CareerBuilder.
[82] Roger Hartley, Kinshuk, Koper, Okamoto, Spector, "The Education and Training of Learning Technologists: A Competences Approach," *Journal of Educational Technology and Society* 13, no. 2 (July 2010): 207.
[83] One published research study on the effectiveness is: Eman Salman Taie, "Coaching as an Approach to Enhance Performance," *The Journal for Quality & Participation* 34, no. 1 (April 2011): 34.

NEWCOMER PROGRESS REVIEW

Employee:_____ Date:_____ Supervisor:_____

<u>GENERAL STANDARDS</u>   <u>OK</u>   <u>OTHER</u>   <u>COMMENT</u>

Attentive to task   ____   _____   _____

Attendance/promptness   ____   _____   _____

Relationships with others   ____   _____   _____

Willing and responsive behavior   ____   _____   _____

Exercises due care with materials/equipment ____ _____ _____

Complies with rules   ____   _____   _____

Knows evacuation procedure   ____   _____   _____

Improves skills/knowledge   ____   _____   _____

Deals with hazards appropriately ____   _____   _____

Knows when to ask for assistance ____   _____   _____

Seeks to improve skills/knowledge ____   _____   _____

Adequacy of production to date   ____   _____   _____

<u>Interview Remarks:</u>

_____

_____

_____

Employee:_____   Supervisor:_____

organization, but there is an absence of any formal practices and reports among most employers. At the other extreme is the massive and complex system of the federal government, where performance management methodology requires individual employee evaluations. A word of caution: If reviews are carried out, they should be uniformly applied within a unit; otherwise there is the possibility of an allegation of illegal discrimination by someone singled out for evaluation.

Typically, supervisors are provided with a standard *appraisal report* to be completed during, or following, an interview with each subordinate worker. The performance of a worker is ongoing and could be a source of discussion at any time, but documented reports raise issues and controversy about the undertaking. Critics charge that appraisal reports are not objective or based on accepted standards—that performance is influenced by outside factors and then colored by the uncertain purpose of the exercise and by the self-interests of the supervisor.

Supervisors are responsible for the performance of the personnel in their unit. Identifying any worker needing corrective attention raises a question about the supervisor's success in training, so there is some reluctance on the part of supervisors to reveal problems.

In some federal agencies, an annual evaluation "determines pay increases."[84] One authority states "performance evaluation participation is typically disliked by supervisors and subordinates in both public and nonprofit organizations."[85] In nonprofits, formal appraisal systems often don't exist.[86]

These cautions in the use of formal appraisal programs may be better understood by realizing that the author studied under Professor Gary McLean at the University of Minnesota, who believes that "a performance appraisal is an inadequate report of an inaccurate judgment by a biased and variable judge of the extent to which a worker has attained an undefined level of mastery of an unknown proportion of an indefinite level of productivity."[87]

For the development of an effective program:

1. The purpose must be clear. Many appraisal interviews are convoluted, with a long agenda including recognition, discussions of pay and career, and news about the organization. Importantly, if a pay increase or disciplinary action is on the agenda, nothing else will be heard.

2. Performance inadequacies should have been previously addressed through coaching and meetings for that specific purpose. There should not be any serious and chronic failures to discuss.

3. An evaluation should focus on three to five essential job functions, rather than peripheral duties, plus common expectations of attendance and conduct.

4. There must be reasonable, challenging and measurable standards that indicate satisfactory performance.

---

[84] Joan E. Pynes, *Human Resources Management for Public and Nonprofit Organizations*, 3rd ed. (San Francisco: Jossey-Bass, 2009), 223.
[85] Ibid., pg. 224.
[86] Ibid.
[87] Prof. Gary McLean, University of Minnesota, "Current Practices in Performance Appraisal." An address at the Deming Forum, September 6, 1988.

5. The factors or functions used as a judgment basis must be unadulterated by adverse systemic influences, e.g., poor material, failures by other people, or economic conditions. The "management of employee performance is limited to aspects that the supervisor can influence."[88]

The *work to be done* surfaces as a tool that provides objective information for personnel management; "performance outcome expectations must be spelled out . . . in the job description."[89]

Objectivity and integrity of both the standards and judgments by the rater are necessary; bias must be minimized. *Supervisor training* must be provided that sets forth the purposes and expectations, and provides for uniformity of thinking and reporting among raters. A sufficient period of time for observation should be provided before any documented conclusions. Second opinions of evaluations, especially in the case of uncertainty or a marginal view, serve to verify judgments. Inaccurate performance records or repetitive inadequacies are legal landmines.

> **Learning is magnified when a trainee and supervisor discuss objectives, applications and results of training in pre- and post-review meetings.**

Training Supervisors

Training those who represent management should be a high priority at the highest levels of executives. Those who supervise others have a key role in the success of an organization. They can expect to reflect the methods and manner of training provided by their supervisors. Besides providing direction, a position with supervisory duties is also the most likely place for issues to surface.

Basic knowledge and skill requirements for managing employees begin with the understanding of purpose, hierarchy, production process, and the company's preferred management style and expectations. A supervisor must have understanding of policies, positions and legal pitfalls, and the programs for compensation, safety and employee relations.

Most training needs of supervisors can be carried out by internal management personnel, using small meetings and group exercises. Education of specialty subjects is often conducted by those who carry out those duties every day, such as equal opportunity or compensation administrators.[90]

New supervisors should be brought to a threshold of basic skill and knowledge. Educational activity about mandates and laws, such as safety and harassment, should be suitably documented. A list of points of learning expected of government supervisors (e.g., behaviors to be avoided) deemed important by the U.S. Office of Special Counsel are shown in the box below.

---
[88] Jeffrey Russell, Linda Russell, "Talk Me Through It," *Training and Development* 64, no. 4 (April 2010): 42–48.
[89] Ibid.
[90] Someone with sufficient responsibility to be involved in hiring and firing decisions.

Under 5 U.S.C §2302(b)(1)-(b)(12), a federal employee authorized to take, direct others to take, recommend, or approve any personnel action **may not**:

- Discriminate illegally (including discrimination based on marital status and political affiliation).
- Solicit or consider employment recommendations based on factors other than personal knowledge or records of job-related abilities or characteristics.
- Coerce the political activity of any person, or take action against any employee as reprisal for refusing to engage in political activity.
- Deceive or willfully obstruct any person from competing for employment.
- Influence any person to withdraw from competition for a position.
- Improve or injure the employment prospects of any particular employee or applicant.
- Engage in nepotism.
- Take a personnel action against an employee because of whistle-blowing.
- Take a personnel action against any employee because of the exercise of an appeal, complaint or grievance right.
- Discriminate against an employee on the basis of conduct [that] does not adversely affect the performance.
- Take or fail to take a personnel action, if such action would violate a veteran's preference requirement.
- Take a personnel action against an employee [that] violates a law, rule or regulation which implements a merit systems principle.

*From "Your Rights as a Federal Employee," https://www.osc.gov/documents/pubs

Expectations of Supervisors
(Training and Education Subjects)

MANAGEMENT EXPECTS A SUPERVISOR TO:

- Know policies, positions and values
- Support the objectives of the unit
- Follow the chain of command
- Know the business (operating) system
- Follow responsibility and authority parameters
- Set behavior expectations; set an example
- Identify substance abuse
- Provide materials and supplies
- Communicate with employees
- Prevent and analyze injuries
- Follow unit and job expectations/standards
- Know discipline and termination procedures
- Know programs (benefits, pay, security)
- Follow applicable policies and positions
- Take care of assigned assets
- Know practices applicable to minorities
- Have job instruction skills*
- Have performance coaching skills
- Know how to use/maintain assigned equipment
- Handle complaints

SUBORDINATES EXPECT A SUPERVISOR TO:

- Have training skills
- Provide cross/additional training
- Understand the unit's jobs
- Know technical matters
- Give feedback on performance/status
- Have a helpful, supportive manner
- Maintain consistency and uniformity
- Respond to appeals and concerns
- Overcome process problems
- Give personal recognition
- Listen
- Deal fairly
- Give respectful treatment
- Be able, competent and friendly
- Know "what's going on"
- Possess a measure of patience
- Match work assignments to skills
- Improve conditions
- Abate hazards
- Protect workers

* Instructing others on how to do work properly is fundamental. A time-honored procedure is Job Instruction Training (JIT). See migashco.com/cambrian/JIT.html.

Though all supervisors direct and control subordinates, there are marked differences in the skill sets required for the position among industries, economic sectors, employers and occupations. In situations with established procedures, such as accounting and testing, or in environments where the priority is to comply with regulations, supervisors might spend most of their time monitoring activity and coaching. In a for-profit environment, those who supervise personnel responsible for providing innovations to serve a multitude of customers are likely to be expected to achieve improved methods, ever higher quality, greater innovation and more expediency than their counterparts in routine process organizations.

Occupational Education

Many occupations require continual *occupational learning* as technology and changes occur. Doctors must learn about new drugs, IT staff about software developments, supervisors about new safety laws and protocols, and construction people about new products and tools. Thousands of occupations are adopting increased technology as a component for job performance to which management should react.

Department heads, through associates and associations, routinely become aware of new developments and educational needs in their occupational arena. New Internet information and electronic devices are continuously available. There are enumerable *interest groups* for professional people in engineering, finance, management and other vocations that share and dispense information of mutual interest. *Industry groups* are dedicated to hundreds of professions, including government, commercial trucking, aerospace, information technology, and law. These organizations, along with educational institutions and profit-making enterprises, sponsor educational seminars and courses dedicated to specific subjects.

In HRM, courses are readily available for training in job analysis and evaluation, interviewing and legal developments. Staff trainers may be aware of this activity, but typically department heads initiate specifically related educational opportunities for their employees.

Management Development

Providing learning opportunities for those with increased management potential receives varying degrees of attention and investment. Increased investment in selected personnel adds to the likelihood of retaining them. Some additional considerations in development investments include:

- Identifying the correct point of need
- Selecting the right candidates
- Identifying the correct skill and knowledge needs
- Establishing partnership relationships
- Providing effective coaches

Tools and Instruments

There is a body of knowledge and a number of techniques through which employee behavior is altered and learning achieved: group discussion, coaching, buddy trainers, electronic and mobile learning, and show-and-tell presentations on- and off-site.

Audiovisual devices such as PowerPoint™ are used when the delivery of materials to groups is to be repeated, but in small firms the use of group meetings are the norm. In large, dispersed organizations the use of intranet applications enables interaction with individual employees on any subject. Computers are used to present modules of subject matter and to test comprehension on product knowledge, policies, new procedures, certification studies, harassment education and insurance options. E-learning program development and application provide growing opportunity within the broad realm of HRM. Using appropriate tools and techniques effectively and applying them in a patient and disciplined manner to achieve an educational objective are valuable talents.

Group Meeting Management

A common setting for information presentation or discussion is the arena of a *group meeting*. Sometimes meetings are conducted among the operatives to coordinate the action of a production system (a production meeting); to broadcast information uniformly and efficiently and cast for answers to a problem (a brainstorming meeting); or to fulfill a group responsibility (a team or committee meeting).

Scheduling meetings well in advance will be less intrusive to a participant's order of work, and the necessary attendees are more likely to be available. Any aggregate of personnel for a period of time is expensive, and cost should always be considered in weighing the needs for a gathering. In the interest of meeting effectiveness and efficiency, managers should know when and how to conduct meetings in order to avoid criticism. The following checklists contribute to that end.

> **We can expect an increasing use of interactive electronic devices and gaming technology in training and education.**

Meeting Preparation

- Establish objectives to be met.
- Secure management endorsement.
- Set dates well in advance.
- Arrange comfortable, quiet conditions or the best site possible.
- Stir participant interest before any meeting to foster positive attitudes.
- Consider and ready materials: videos, manuals, experts.
- Form segments of learning into units of time.
- Plan repetition of the material and conduct practice exercises.
- Plan various presentation techniques.
- Prepare opening and closing remarks; make notes.
- Plan for participant comforts.
- Ask associates to critique the plan.
- Arrange other presenters or contributors.
- Provide for administrative assistance and a recorder.
- Mail out study material and agenda to stir interest and prep participants.
- Set expectations and a means of measurement.
- List the points that should be remembered.
- Practice and test for the timing of the presentation.

Meeting Management Checklist

INTRODUCTORY STEPS
- ❏ Arrive early.
- ❏ Welcome and make introductions and ease anxiety.
- ❏ Announce arrangements and ground rules (breaks, questions, cell phones).
- ❏ Express the purpose and expectations clearly.
- ❏ Define important terms or precepts.

PRESENTATION
- ❏ Engage people early and periodically.
- ❏ Speak clearly, project voice.
- ❏ Deliver one unit at a time.
- ❏ Repeat key points.
- ❏ Don't single out participants but acknowledge contributions.
- ❏ Vary methods of delivery.
- ❏ Maintain the timetable.

CLOSING
- ❏ Clear up questions.
- ❏ Secure indications of understanding or commitment.
- ❏ Summarize or state a conclusion.
- ❏ Express appreciation.
- ❏ Clean up the area.
- ❏ Follow up with participants.

Summary Remarks

Training and education in an organization is integral and continuous, and serves both the employee and employer. This chapter examined primary education for worker development, productivity and increases in the value of human assets. A commonly used series of programs begins with new-employee orientation, which provides grounding for job training and worker coaching. Educational checklists for employees and supervisors give readers a head start in understanding and/or implementing the essential learning in organizations.

The role of the supervisor as both an educator and learner is paramount. Supervisors commonly provide for job skill training, influence the working and learning environment, and, in upper management, provide for technical and occupational education of subordinates.

A number of inquiries help determine the effectiveness of education in a workplace.
- Do the people in each unit demonstrate competency?
- Does each worker satisfy output expectations of the job?
- Are process dysfunctions only rare?
- Do supervisors provide enhanced learning?
- Are performance issues unusual?
- Do records indicate that supervisors and workers have undergone basic and required training?
- Are injuries from known hazards rare?
- Do employee feedback and exit interviews report training as adequate?
- Is there open and comfortable interaction between supervisors and subordinates?

Applicable Competencies

Confidence and experience with presentations and meetings, patience with learners, facilitation skills, ability to identify training needs, and the use of different education platforms and delivery methods.

Applicable Resources

Knowledge of learning principles, industry technology, the institution, common workplace training needs, and basic communication tools and facilities.

Meeting Place Checklist

PRESENTER'S EQUIPMENT
- ❑ AV equipment
- ❑ Participant materials
- ❑ Resource materials
- ❑ Screen
- ❑ Podium
- ❑ Extension cords
- ❑ Pointer
- ❑ Wastebasket
- ❑ Markers

PARTICIPANTS' COMFORT
- ❑ Lighting adequacy
- ❑ Refreshments
- ❑ Restroom locations
- ❑ Coat/luggage provisions
- ❑ Glasses/water
- ❑ Pens/pencils/paper
- ❑ Comfortable seating, ventilation

ADMINISTRATIVE ARRANGEMENTS
- ❑ Greeter
- ❑ Whiteboard
- ❑ Timing of breaks
- ❑ Name tents
- ❑ Voice amplification test
- ❑ Timekeeper
- ❑ Facility maintenance contact
- ❑ Participant list
- ❑ Name badges
- ❑ Agenda
- ❑ Seating arrangements

Review Materials

Content Exercises

1. List five points of knowledge that would help newcomers.
2. List five points of knowledge that employees expect of a supervisor.
3. What primary subject matter should, and should not, be addressed in a handbook or other written materials?
4. Describe how specific job tasks might be learned.

Practical Applications

1. Inquire about newcomer assimilation practices at your workplace.
2. Acquire an employee handbook or written materials for newcomers and determine if it applies to a) the executives, b) part-time employees and c) temporary employees.
3. Based on your experience, what practices do supervisors use to train subordinates?
4. Inquire about the subject and manner of managing/controlling meetings in your workplace. Is there a common view of the value of certain types of meetings, or of meetings in general? Pick out some specific notable practices.
5. Inquire about personnel appraisal practices in your workplace. Are reviews committed and uniformly carried out? Is there a form to be completed? Are the factors generic or specific? Outcome related?
6. What do employees see as positives and negatives of any appraisal program?
7. What electronic and software applications are used for employee learning in your workplace?

Case-Study Discussions

Case 3.1

New-Employee Communication

A family of entrepreneurs owns a local convenience store, two fast-food stores and two restaurants. The restaurants each have about forty employees and the others have a dozen employees each. The manager of each of these stores enjoys his or her latitude in decision making. Finance and accounting systems are generally standard, but other procedures vary. Each unit is considered a profit-making (or *not* profit-making) enterprise. A corporate CEO who visits on occasion and is the final authority on all matters of policy and procedure provides oversight for all of the locations.

The CEO learned of a successful lawsuit by an employee against another company, in which a faulty employee handbook played a role. She hired a personnel service firm to survey the new-hire materials used in the businesses and suggest a strategy for their application to avoid legal risks in her group of enterprises. She expects that the firm will have to have a common handbook for all of its enterprises.

Would that be your recommendation? What crucial messages should be in the new materials? How would you advise the CEO?

UNIT II
PROVIDE FOR PERFORMANCE

To arrange circumstances, conditions and systems to accomplish the purpose of the organizational unit, which necessarily requires integrating and accommodating necessary financial, human and other resources.

CHAPTER 4: WORKPLACE ORGANIZATIONS

CHAPTER 5: ENABLE WORKER PERFORMANCE

CHAPTER 4
WORKPLACE ORGANIZATIONS

Chapter Objectives

- Differences in economic sectors
- The framework of a workplace
- The role of a worker in a production process
- The worker in a hierarchy
- Methods of management direction
- Components and principles of organizations
- Rights of employees and management
- Roles of human resource management

A View of Different Economic Sectors

When we report to a new workplace it's common to feel overwhelmed and uncertain amid the activity. Sooner or later it becomes clear that there is more order than was first apparent and the activity is arranged and synchronized to facilitate the desired outcomes. Whether the work is coding, completing tax forms or constructing a building, *resources* and *systems* are engaged to achieve the purpose of the unit.

An *organization* is the arrangement of resources and application of methods with which to achieve an orderly, efficient and effective workplace condition. This is common to organizations but there are classifications of their general purpose (i.e., public service or profit-making, and more definitely by industry, such as retail, communications, etc.).

This chapter focuses on the interaction of management, workstations and conditions throughout the U.S. and addresses characteristics of international personnel management as well. Such a broad spectrum provides a wider view of our subject than the characteristics of only a single piece of the economic pie. However, the breadth of scope does require some definition of the major segments within the total picture.

Our domestic economic activity is divided into organizational groups with very different intentions: the *public* (government), *nonprofit* (tax advantaged), and *private* (for-profit) sectors. Each of these sectors is influenced by internal and external forces.

Generally, the public sector is devoted to public service and is characterized by political influences; the private and nonprofit sectors enjoy, or suffer, the will of economic fluctuations. Primary and common elements among the sectors are the *resources*, *production processes*, *organization* and *management structure* through which financial and human resources are applied to accomplish the desired purpose of an undertaking.

Public Sector

The public sector's general purpose is to protect and provide for citizens. Its momentum develops from shifting social and economic conditions, legislative initiatives, special and political interests, and the innate energy to perpetuate its functional existence. Public sector management is elected and politically appointed (e.g., the Secretary of Education) and overlays career managers in the different units of government. It is a large, complex and diverse sector distinctive in services at federal, state and local levels. Civilian government jobs (excluding military) comprise almost 10 percent of those in the nation, equating to roughly 15 million employees. Public services are financed by taxpaying entities.

Another characteristic of public sector employment is the prominence of written regulations and legally prescribed standard procedures. That condition limits the latitude of positions and personnel. In employment, standard forms, processes and patterned interviews are detailed and the norm. For example, verbiage from *The Handbook on Alternative Work Schedules*, produced by the U.S. Office of Personnel Management, evidences the culture: "Under 5 U.S.C. 6121(5), a compressed work schedule means that an employee's basic work requirement for each pay period is scheduled (by the agency) for less than 10 workdays. See the definition and requirements for regularly scheduled work in 5 CFR 610.102 and 5 CFR 610.111(d)."

Federal Government

Within the public sector, the federal government employs about 3 million people in approximately 100 different departments and agencies. Personnel are dispersed across the world. Federal activity includes national defense, justice, law enforcement and welfare. The style of management in many units might be called collective governance, and accountability is elusive. Management is remote from the citizenry they are to serve and suffer the additional disadvantage of being close to politicians and their particular interests.

Several characteristics of the human resource staff in federal government apply less to state and local units. For example, federal public service attracts many with interest to "contribute to the advancement of the quality of life in society."[91]

Incumbents in many positions in the federal workforce enjoy exceptional *job protection* based on civil-service principles so employees can "be protected from improper political influence and from reprisal for the lawful disclosure of information in whistle-blower situations."[92] The Office of Personnel Management (OPM) is responsible for preventing political favoritism in federal employment.

---

[91] Richard J. Stillman II, *Public Administration: Concept and Cases,* 9th ed. (New York: Houghton Mifflin, 2000), 343–4.
[92] Alan Clardy, Ph.D., "Policies for Managing the Training and Development Function: Lessons from the Federal Government," *Public Personnel Management* 37, no. 1 (Spring 2008).

The use of objective testing to help ensure *fair or merit-based selection practices* requires monitoring around the globe and is a weighty challenge. It's been remarked that "human resource staff are used to [measure] processes rather than outcomes."[93]

> **As a result of mutual self-interest among employees, an organization manifests a fundamental drive to perpetuate itself.**

The required practices of due process and just cause in *terminations* are established through civil-service rules, policy or handbook statements. These requirements, widespread union membership, and the fact that federal work activity is insulated from all but severe economic swings provide an uncommon level of *employment security*. This advantage is reflected in a study that indicated public employees have a lower tolerance for risk than those attracted to the private sector.[94] Such job security doesn't exist to the same degree in local government as it does in federal government positions.[95]

Managing thousands of federal units requires definitive governance. Laws are promulgated to help assure that most public programs and procedures are free of influence from politicians or their staff.

State Government

About 5 million workers are in the employ of the fifty state governments. Public service in the states is devoted to natural resources, education, local governments, and law enforcement and suffers some political management. Federal government patterns have influenced control mechanisms and "merit" employment in the formation of state government. However, "each state's civil-servant system is unique, featuring varying levels of . . . sophistication and continuing levels of patronage."[96] Two states, Georgia and Florida, have adopted private sector practices to the degree that they are atypical and cannot be included in general comments about the public sector and civil-service provisions.

Local Government

A number of government jurisdictions considered local are chartered by the state. Among them are counties and 13,000 special districts such as townships, school districts and watershed districts. Elected county commissioners are often engaged with roads, parks and corrections facilities. Some counties are larger than the states of Connecticut and Rhode Island.

---

[93] Stephen E. Condrey, ed., *Handbook of Human Resource Management in Government*, 2nd ed. (San Francisco: Jossey-Bass, 2005), 25.
[94] Michael Roszkowski and John Grable, "Evidence of Lower Risk Tolerance Among Public Sector Employees in Their Personal Financial Matters," *Journal of Occupational and Organizational Psychology* 82, no. 82 (June 2009): 453–463.
[95] Matt Sherman and Nathan Lane, "Layoffs of Public Employees in the Current Recession," Center for Economic and Policy Research, September 2009.
[96] W. David Patton et al., *Human Resource Management: The Public Service Perspective* (New York: Houghton Mifflin, 2002), 54.

Protected job and merit conditions common in federal and state governments are not so prominent among county and city governments. Sometimes a city manager may only appoint a person from a certified list of names provided by a civil-service commission.[97] In contrast, there is a common view that some county governments, not subject to public scrutiny, have a minimum of regulations that allow for political patronage and related corruption.

In many municipalities, officials relate closely with community businesses and apply at-will employment[98] that is very common in municipal service.[99] About 30,000 municipalities, with approximately 12 million personnel, apply a council-manager government, with some combination of an elected mayor or councils. Primary local concerns are public safety and sanitation.

Nonprofit Sector

Nonprofit organizations are the smallest of the sectors, with about 9 million U.S. employees, 5 million full-time volunteer positions and millions more part-time volunteers. Hospitals, charitable groups, cultural organizations, professional associations and fraternal organizations all use volunteers and depend on grants, fees or donations.

Cooperative enterprises (often agriculture based), such as Land O'Lakes, American Crystal Sugar Company, and the Associated Press, are economically self-sufficient. The commonality of these institutions exists in their advantageous tax status. They have no owners and are governed by an oversight board that is accountable for compliance with regulatory bylaws under state and IRS codes. Sometimes there is a self-serving executive compensation motive, but they normally fulfill a single and legitimate social need.[100]

Many groups within this sector are energized by addressing the needs of those they serve. Charitable organizations are normally labor intensive, depending heavily on volunteers, and are typically financially vulnerable. Considerable effort is expended toward fundraising through telemarketing, mailings and grant proposals. A descriptive theme of this sector might be "service to humanity is the best work of life."[101] Many of these organizations are torn between altruistic values and economic reality, with the result that work-life perks are common and personnel decisions (such as unnecessarily granting protective job rights) sometimes reflect costly benevolence that would be considered irresponsible in the private sector.

Private Sector

The engine of the U.S. economy is publicly or privately owned commercial activity, which accounts for almost 90 percent of our employment and produces 100 percent of our wealth. Walmart is the largest single employer, with about 1.5 million employees. Service firms, including restaurants,

---
[97] *Anderson v. City of Minneapolis,* 363 N.W.2d 886 (Minn. Ct. App. 1985).
[98] At-will dismissal (without cause) offset by the right to quit without explanation.
[99] Fox Larsen and Assoc. LLC, Total Compensation Benchmarking Survey, 2007, IPMA.
[100] The Center for Cooperatives at the University of Wisconsin estimates that this group includes 2 million jobs and $75 billion in wages and benefits. (Released 2012.)
[101] From the Jaycee Creed.

hotels, health care firms and financial service companies, comprise over 50 percent of activity following a decline in manufacturing and agricultural employment during the last century.

There are more than 100 million workers in this sector. Within that vast number, most are employed by small employers, defined by the U.S. Small Business Administration as those with less than $7 million in sales and fewer than 500 employees. Most businesses have fewer than 100 employees and compete among themselves for customers and economic survival. (Sixty percent of all business initiatives cease to exist after ten years.) Accountability is normally centered in one or two positions. Profit-making opportunities exist in the fields of finance, health, agriculture, personal services, manufacturing, energy, recreation and hospitality, all subject to financial risk and the chance of failure.

This is a dynamic and competitive environment often characterized by free-thinking entrepreneurs who bask in the risk, challenge and independence of their work. The nature of each firm is unique, and the latitude afforded to personnel varies with the style of management.

Differences and Similarities

One basic difference among the major domestic economic sectors is that of financing. Private and nonprofit firms are *financially self-sufficient*. State and local government have *taxing authority* and are obliged to function within a budget. The federal government has taxing authority but is casual about budgeting and financial accountability.

A second and obvious difference among sectors is the presence or absence of regimen. Public sector organizations have mandated responsibility for affirmative action, due process in separations, subjects of supervisor training, performance reviews and employee unions. The nonprofit sector will frequently opt to adopt similar practices through policy. Those in the for-profit sector have the latitude of accepting or rejecting such practices and most often choose to take their own path.

There are differences in the employment stability between public and private entities as well. Public sector employees are frequently engaged in long-term administrative undertakings. They have far greater assurance of being employed and paid next month than do workers in private firms subject to economic swings.

The *control* exercised in public personnel management matters, particularly in state and federal levels of government, includes scores of standard procedures, approvals of those hired, and finite procedures for how people are dismissed. Extensive and standard training of employees and supervisors on cultural matters, practices, procedures and conduct are the norm. Scores of statutes[102] mandate federal training and associated recordkeeping on the subjects of equal opportunity, customer service, ethics and individual appraisals. In training situations, employees are to be informed how trainees are selected, and told in advance of what subjects and methods are to be experienced. Such absolute and definitive influence is rare in the private sector.

In the for-profit sector, law has provided enumerable parameters and rules in personnel matters, but government influence isn't always paramount in the workplace. In daily decisions,

---

[102] Alan Clardy, "Policies for Managing the Training and Development Function: Lessons from the Federal Government," *Public Personnel Management* 37, no. 1 (Spring 2008).

many owners and managers are likely to prefer urgency and lower cost rather than respond to "regulatory interference." The owner of a firm may well make a preferential summer work hire, often the son or daughter of a customer, or overlook an employee's occasional unpaid overtime work. Such transgressions stir more frequent law enforcement issues in the private sector than in the public sector.

Union membership exists in the public sector to a much greater degree than in the private, though there are some limits to the subjects open for bargaining and prohibitions on the right to strike. Union influence and power exists substantially through the advocacy of politicians and political action. Desirable federal and state employment conditions are duly reflected in political support for those who have advocated in their interests.[103] The workers in many public institutions commonly enjoy the consideration of seniority for promotions, longevity and automatic step-pay increases as well as termination protections. These troublesome conditions were also pursued by private-sector unions in early industrial labor contracts but are not common in contracts today.

International Circumstances

Personnel management overseas is distinctive in many respects, primarily because of severe differences in culture and government. Our political and commercial position in the world results in international involvement within each of our economic sectors. We find ourselves in diplomatic, military, humanitarian and business relationships worldwide. The scope of social and economic challenges around the world is incomprehensible, beginning with tragic environmental and human rights conditions and issues.

Beyond a core of industrialized Western nations, there is a different world in terms of morality, ethics, politics and social norms. Specific workplace issues include bribery, extortion, safety and sanitation. Particular challenges in the management of workers include the absence of collective bargaining rights, the common existence of child and forced labor, and flagrant social prejudice.[104]

Our federal defense and state departments have centuries of experience with unique overseas living conditions and protocols of management. Commercial and human service organizations typically enter new overseas situations through modest investments in the host country, seeking representation and creating a presence, contracting and gradually increasing commitments and risk. Today, commercial, nonprofit and federal organizations conduct activities in more than 100 foreign nations. "The bigger the firm, the more likely it is to be a global player";[105] after all, the fact that 95 percent of the world's consumers live outside the U.S.[106] won't be overlooked by entrepreneurs.[107]

---

[103] However, political activity by public-sector employees can be limited. See Joan E. Pynes, *Human Resources Management for Public and Nonprofit Organizations*, 3rd ed. (San Francisco: Jossey-Bass, 2004).
[104] *The Labour Principles of the United Nations Global Compact: A Guide for Business*, International Labour Organization (2008).
[105] Chris Rowley and Malcolm Warner, "Introduction: Globalizing International Human Resource Management," *International Journal of Human Resource Management* 18, no. 4 (May 2006): 704.
[106] U.S. Chamber of Commerce.
[107] Chris Rowley and Malcolm Warner, "Introduction: Globalizing International Human Resource Management," *International Journal of Human Resource Management* 18, no. 4 (May 2006): 704.

Toys and clothing are manufactured in Asia, and many technical call centers are in India or the Philippines. Multinational firms like General Electric and Deere & Company have large subsidiary manufacturing installations overseas and hundreds of small import and export firms exist worldwide. Subway and Avon franchises are well known in developed countries. Nearly 90,000 employees of American firms live "outside"; two-thirds of them are expatriates.

The unique nature of overseas activity is evidenced by the extent of training and education activity at our Foreign Service Institute, which offers civilian government employees 700 courses and enrolls 100,000 students each year. Others with overseas interests meet education needs through consulting firms, educational institutions and on-the-job training.

The challenges of overseas workplace practices, culture and language for U.S. managers and professionals are significant. Staffing and education needs are ongoing because the tenure of most Americans working overseas is short. Cultures vary immensely; what is desirable and legal in one culture may not be the case in another. In the Mideast, criminal penalties can be severe; in China, Russia and Japan, lifetime employment is normal, social injustices can be common and the use of child labor may be the norm.

A Framework

Beginning with a concept of what product or service is desired, whether in public, private or nonprofit sectors, a *framework* is formed as a basis for action. This template includes functional units of work, reporting relationships and the application of resources. That *organization* supports and enables a *work process* and a means (or hierarchy) through which management directs, coordinates and controls activity. The components and systems will be brought to life by executive motivation[108] (personal and financial) and subsequent energy that cascades through the human assets.

> **The form of an organization is the arena in which workers are to perform.**

The effectiveness of the organization's framework and processes enables or encumbers the effectiveness of its human assets. For example, directions from management can arrive completely and in a timely manner leading to efficient workflow, or be incomplete or confusing and result in process disruption. If there's trouble early in a process, every workstation downstream is likely to be impacted.

The Work Process

The design and application of organization components are crucial in determining *performance* of a worker or unit; the conditions affect the output. To provide order, a manner of getting things done must be arranged through which the human, physical and financial resources are applied

---

[108] There are different views of important elements in organizations. Meier supports consideration of political influence, among others, as a common value. Kenneth J. Meier, "Governance, Structure, and Democracy," *Public Administration Review* 70 (December 2010): 284–291.

and coordinated. (Think assembly-line workstations.) The common point of linkage between units represents not only a communications connection, but also a point of unit supervision. Workstations and unit supervisors become interactive and interdependent with others, resulting in a web of related activity and relationships. Providing proper timing and supportive sub-systems will produce a *predictable and orderly condition* and support the success of a workstation.

The Command Structure

Management allocates resources, develops communications systems and determines levels of authority through which activity is directed and feedback received. Most often the top executive is an owner or their representative, or, in the public sector, a political appointee. Sometimes hierarchy of command in the private sector is intentionally fluid and imprecise in keeping with a chosen style of management, but points of power will always become evident as situations demand. Rarely is it unclear "who runs things around here."

An organization's *management structure* identifies relative levels of command, exhibits major units of activity and indicates the responsibility and accountability of management and professional positions. There are *vertical paths* of communication existing among levels of management, through which a system of command is exercised. Another, generally *horizontal*, structure follows the *process* of work. Additionally, there are critical but informal messaging between positions to lubricate production of the service or product. Any position has an immediate boss that gives direction and determines pay level, but often, another authoritative position with responsibility for the process directs the flow of activities. A position that is subject to direction by dual points of influence is at a point of *matrix management* (and possible confusion).

In very small organizations, the boss is the central point of management and coordinates all matters. With such latitude, policy and practice often depart from the normal and permit taking advantage of opportunities. The nimbleness of small organizations requires adaptable personnel; though such personnel may be challenged to perform, they frequently enjoy uncommon learning experiences and satisfaction in accomplishment.

Illustrated depictions of job relationships and hierarchy, usually known as *organization charts*, can be a useful tool in education and analysis. Ancillary units that are not within the core production scheme, such as finance, research and human resources, are commonly referred to as staff functions. Proper position titles, or at least functional headings, are used, but names of personnel are omitted because of periodic changes. Omitted, too, are paths of informal communications, points of extraordinary influence, goals, management style, and indications of collaboration, all of which exist in organizations. Small organizations have little need for diagrams because the point of power, relationships and decisions are few and obvious.

> **An orderly, effective and efficient arrangement of work and resources enables output and prevents delays, errors and failures in the wheels of productivity.**

There are valid objections to developing and maintaining structure charts, and some managements do without them; others have them only for use by executive management. Such charts do require upkeep, particularly if names are used. The boxes may also suggest undesirable and unintended constraints or be misleading because a system is far more complex than diagrams depict, and organizations, particularly those of modest size, are more malleable than a diagram suggests. A rudimentary diagram and explanatory remarks follow.

> **Depictions of organization hierarchy are common, but they do not represent the complexities of an organization.**

Functional Hierarchy Diagram
Private (Public)

```
                    Executive
                  (City Manager)
                        |
                        |————————— Administrative
                        |            Assistant
    ┌───────────┬───────┴───────┬───────────────┬─ — — — — ┐
Purchasing    Sales         Finance         Warehouse    Contracted
  Agent      Manager                         Manager       Janitor
(City Clerk) (Public Safety)               (Public Works)  (Legal)
                |                |                |
            Assistant to      Systems          Human
            Sales Manager   Management        Resource
                |                              Manager
    ┌───────────┼───────────┐                    |
Salesperson Salesperson Salesperson          Warehouse Crew
   East        City        West            (Maintenance Crew)
  (Police)    (Fire)   (Code Enforcement)
```

Administrative Assistant: Sometimes a top manager wants an assistant to be paid a salary and be exempt from overtime. This permits additional hours of work without premium pay and, in the view of some, provides the position an elevated stature. The level of authority and importance of the work must justify exemption from wage and hour obligations. If the duties are substantially clerical, without decision-making authority, the incumbent must be paid premium pay for more than forty hours of work, regardless of title and method of pay.

Purchasing Agent: The fact that a position is represented by the box parallel to other management positions does not indicate the position is of the same responsibility or pay level, but simply reports to the same level as the others.

Sales: In any analysis, these three positions would be examined to determine whether the work areas are sufficiently well defined to avoid territorial conflicts.

Assistant to Sales Manager: The "to" is important. If the title were "assistant manager," the box would be directly under that of the sales manager, establishing a direct line of authority over subordinates. As it is, this position indicates no supervisory authority over the salespeople but is devoted to assisting the sales manager in other matters.

Contracted Janitor: In this particular diagram, the dotted line is used to indicate that the work is not performed by an employee but by an outside contractor.

Systems Management: This title reflects a paired (two-member team) business system improvement workstation.

Human Resource Manager: This scheme has a personnel "specialist." The reporting relationship of this position suggests that support services are only provided to the warehouse unit, which may not be the actual case. A simple line diagram does not always accurately reflect the alliances or total duties of a position. In this case, if the employment activity is heavy in warehouse activity, there is reason for this reporting relationship. However, if the job has responsibilities for compensation and compliance in the total organization, the position could logically report to the executive level. A *reporting relationship*, and even the distance of an office location from the executive area, can have a considerable effect on the influence of a function.

Elements of an Organization

Purpose

General purposes of organizations include profit making, human or public service and perpetuation of the organization. A *mission statement* is often used to express a central point of purpose for focus. "To be a premier provider of quality training and development services" or "To respond to emergencies quickly and do all possible to protect and save lives and property" are examples. Regardless of whether a mission statement is available, organizations can, over time, wander from their original and/or desired purpose.

Sometimes an organization uses a *guiding statement* not only to express where it wants to go, but its manner in doing so. A guiding statement might express principles the organization intends to follow, such as "To be an efficient and effective organization of integrity."[109] Other principles, such as those involving the environment or fair employment, might be expressed as a management position or part of a mission statement.

Sometimes a *vision statement* is composed that reflects an ultimate aspiration or pursuit of a higher order, often that of an owner. The Shelter Inc. organization aspires to provide "a home for everyone." A municipal government envisions a "safe community."

Direction

The direction, manner and energy that drive and direct an organization come from leadership and/or management, whether in a political, entrepreneurial, career or social service construct. The mission, expectations, resources of choice, and systems evolve from the manner of management or the adoption of existing format and culture. The controls of activity include standards, reports, supervision and legal compliance provisions. Management personnel are expected to model and foster the direction, values and beliefs set forth by the organization's founders and stakeholders.

Large organizations normally engage principles, policies, positions and programs in forming the manner of management. Smaller organizations reflect the personality, beliefs and manner of one or several executives. Because most non-public firms are small, the style and supervision among a high percentage of employers can best be described as customized, nondescript and ad hoc, within the parameters of society and law.

After a decade or more, a management group changes, new priorities erupt, and enthusiasm for a particular manner of management fades. Nevertheless, valuable aspects of the theories linger among employers who find the ideas compatible with their intentions and thinking.

Periodically, a "new" style of managing becomes popular among gurus. Readers will benefit from some understanding of several very different management methods with focuses on 1) employee performance improvement, 2) the pursuit of goals through collaborative effort and 3) the delivery of quality output through work process control. These different schemes for managing sometimes exist in a substantially pure form, but more often are combined and indefinite. There was an additional management movement before the turn of the century dedicated to employee focus on customer service. There are still pockets of this initiative, but much of its popularity has waned. It can be concluded that, with the exception of the federal government, most management is not a single form or method, but some of this and some of that, which results in what is known as mutt management.

Performance Management

Performance management is a contemporary form of management adopted by much of the public sector. There are enumerable variations and fluid definitions of the program, so the federal

---

[109] The value and role of a mission statement was revealed in the last editorial of a 168-year-old English tabloid that met its demise by hacking telephone conversations of celebrities: "Quite simply, we lost our way."

government model is herein most often referenced. The U.S. Office of Personnel Management depicts the system as an action plan of five components: planning, monitoring the performance of work, employee development, rating performance and rewarding. The focus is on using a worker appraisal to improve employee performance toward goals delineated for the position; in other words, there is clear supervisor direction and control with the assumption that the successful performance of each job is integral to the accomplishment of the management plan.[110]

Performance management as a strategy, like other methods, is not without critics. There are obvious issues with 1) the excessive supervision of those workers who are fully competent in their work or believe themselves to be, 2) the continuous search for meaningful goals after several years and 3) supervisor interviews that are not constructive. "In most organizations, performance management has a poor reputation . . . the reason is simple: managers focus on forms, system and processes. What they need to do is focus on the quality of their conversations."[111]

Management by Objectives (MBO)

This method uses collaborative human effort toward a specific high-order management goal to be achieved within cost limits by a certain point in time.[112] Commonly, these targets are goals to be accomplished within time spans of twelve or eighteen months. For example, an objective might be "To increase sales volume 10 percent in the next calendar year with no increase in expenses" or "Reduce plant waste 4 percent in the month of July with no expense." Fundamental to this program is the determination of meaningful objectives by management, such as to improve quality. Subordinates undertake supportive objectives to help in the achievement of those pursuits. This cascade of related objectives down the hierarchy serves to focus energies.

Objectives are not beyond manipulation, and their achievement can lead to the neglect of other normal performance expectations. Objectives, not methods, are prominent in MBO systems. Since administrators focus on results but not on how goals are met, one employee could derail another and team unity would be threatened. Indeed, the achievement of a goal by one employee, should it prevent associates from reaching theirs, could have adverse consequences. Tying a reward to achievements that should be expected for established pay is wasteful. Whereas an incentive bonus will have an uncertain effect, a clear statement of expectations by a supervisor will stimulate desired results.

Process Management

The process management methodology focuses on creating a faultless process that flows from customer interests and satisfaction back through the work process to alter the point of supplies and materials to achieve objectives. Employee appraisals aren't factors in this scheme, given a process free of disruption created from teams of employees improving the process. This exhibi-

---

[110] Mike Schraeder and Mark Jordan, "Managing Performance," *Journal for Quality and Participation* 34, no. 2 (June 2011): 5.
[111] Octavius Black, Debbie Marshall-Lee, "Dynamic Performance Management: How to Deliver More, with Less, Forever," *Industrial and Commercial Training* 43, no. 5, Abstract (2011).
[112] Peter F. Drucker, *The Practice of Management* (New York: Harper & Row Publishers, 1954).

tion of a positive and trusting view of human resources differs significantly from performance management, which provides backseat driving of employees. The style is different, too, in the use of statistics to analyze production variances to control the process. If it's helpful, workers interact directly with the customer to provide the desired product or service.

Congruency

Occasional events and influences, such as the economy or a misguided executive, can distract or mislead units of an organization, so efforts are necessary to prevent actions beyond desired parameters. Proclamations, policies, objectives and mission statements, as well as uniform and consistent procedures, prescribe the boundaries of management authority to keep the desired course in view. Monitoring activities, policies, reports, budgets and requisitions are instruments that also serve this end.

Policies or positions are promulgated by top management and implemented through the hierarchy. Organizations would be well served to communicate positions and/or policy on fundamental subjects of equal opportunity and employee health and safety, and not leave these core commitments to chance. Expressions of a position on a subject ("only quality products are to be shipped") may or may not be written. It's notable that primary management expectations to report to work as scheduled and perform to standards aren't always clearly communicated and understood.

Policies direct and control via a written pronouncement.[113] They disseminate a uniform and consistent position. When effectively implemented, policies unite organizational elements and serve as authoritative thinking to be applied throughout the defined unit. The laws or regulations driving public sector activity are more comprehensive, rigid and inviolate than positions or policy in the private sector that can be more readily altered.

Developing a policy is a time-consuming and arduous task. Before issuance it must be completely correct and clear. It should be drafted, rewritten, tested over time, authorized and implemented with appropriate distribution. Policies can express, but should not compromise, management prerogatives. Well-written policies should set forth the parameters felt to be necessary but not prevent the application of good sense in the circumstances. Zero-tolerance policies are frequently regretted because the unanticipated will surely occur and the policy dictates a poor decision.

Language must be carefully chosen. To correctly paraphrase a legal statement is difficult and foolhardy for anyone unqualified. There is considerable difference in meaning among "may," "should," "must" and "can." It must be clear where and when the policies apply and to whom. Policies may express a preferred behavior or have an absolute tone.

Most federal edicts take months or years to be drafted and approved, and tend to anticipate every conceivable situation. In federal and state agencies, converting legislative language to an understandable regulation is a high-level skill.

---

[113] Kenneth J. Meier, "Governance, Structure, and Democracy," *Public Administration Review* 70, (December 2010): 287.

POLICY ISSUES

Vacation/Personal Time

- To whom does the policy apply?
- What are the qualifications for earning the paid time off?
- Is time earned following a full period of service or accrued each month?
- Do periods of absence count toward qualifying?
- What is the basis for calculating pay?
- Is the time on vacation considered as time worked for calculating overtime pay?
- At what point is any time earned? Can paid time off be taken immediately?
- In what periods of time can/must personal time be used? One half-day? One week?
- What effect does a holiday have when it occurs during a vacation period?
- Can earned personal time be carried over from one annual period to another?
- Does time accrue indefinitely? Any limit? Optional uses?
- Can unused time be exchanged for money? Calculated at what rate?
- Can time be transferred from one employee to another employee?
- Can all of the time earned be used in one absence?
- What happens to earned time upon voluntary/involuntary termination?

Standard Programs and Procedures

Standard programs and procedures are basic methods to manage desired behaviors and achieve a uniform congruent condition. Common programs address benefit plans, communication with employees and injury prevention activities. Standard procedures constitute a sequence of disciplined activity, such as documenting employee status changes, established by management. In the private sector, established programs and standard procedures are not to be confused with occasional projects or a normal or usual practice. The term "practice" or "norm" can be applied to undocumented or nonstandard patterns or routines; the distinction can be important in controversies between employees and employers.

Culture and Character

The nations around the world have discernable social and economic differences. In the U.S., sections of the country have different characteristics, values and identities. Within communities, particularly large cities, there are communities and neighborhoods of distinct ethnicity. Workplaces, too, often have unique and prominent characteristics, sometimes so distinctive as to form a common point of identity (e.g., "They don't pay much" or "The environment is noisy and dirty"). The public image of workplaces can be misleading, but worker off-site conduct, ethics, business standards, employee attitudes and publicity contribute to a mental picture. Clues about the internal aspects of an organization, such as an urgent or sluggish pace of work, an observed conflict between employees, spotless housekeeping or an empty office area before quitting time, are often observable to a workplace visitor.

The reality of an organization is in the demonstrated values and what is observed, be it positive or negative, rather than what is proclaimed. In a 2011 Supreme Court ruling, Justice Ginsburg alleged that the "company culture" of Walmart was biased against women. A workplace is not defined by referring to workers as "associates" or claiming that "people are our most valuable asset." The talk must be walked.

Organizational Change

Organizations are always subject to changes because of politics, law, economics, technology and other influences. Events such as changes in management are most disruptive to personnel. The

---

COMMON POLICY AND PROCEDURE SUBJECTS

Legal or Mandated Policy
- Sexual harassment
- Family leave (FMLA)
- Safety provisions as required
- Affirmative action[a]
- Military leave of absence[b]
- Performance appraisal (some government units)
- Substance abuse policy (some industries, some states)

Frequent Policy Subjects
- Substance abuse testing
- Complaint or grievance system use
- Equal opportunity (fair employment practices)
- Vacation and holiday eligibility and benefits
- Use of company or agency electronic equipment
- Prohibition of personal communication devices

Policies of Occasional Application
- Conflict of interest prohibition
- Personal leave of absence
- Nepotism prohibition[c]
- Supervisory approval of overtime of hourly workers
- Searches of lockers or baggage
- Conduct regarding visitors and strangers

Policy Subjects to Be Applied with Caution and/or Caveat
- Prohibition of solicitation and distribution
- Adopting a probationary employment period (unless required
- Discipline penalties
- Committed performance appraisal
- Severance pay
- Promotion from within
- Causes for dismissal

---

[a] Required of public employers.
[b] A federal regulation, this also may be required in other legal jurisdictions.
[c] A federal regulation that may also be required by state government.

effect can be sudden or cumulative. For example, in March 2012, an executive of Goldman Sachs published an essay on how in one decade this premier firm characterized by integrity, humility and teamwork degenerated into one that called customers "Muppets," talked openly about how they were "ripping off their clients" and became known as the evil empire of finance.[114] This is a discouraging picture of eroded beliefs and values. To better understand the subtle ways an entity can fail employees and customers, consider JacLynn Herron's memoir *Singing Solo: In Search of a Voice for Mom*, a nursing-home case study.

Anticipated or planned change can be managed. Programs and projects to cope with mergers, downsizing and redirection, or to institute quality standards or MBO,[115] are systemic management initiatives moving a unit in a positive manner. The term most often used for projects undertaking such major improvements is *organization development* (OD). A process begins by conducting a study of key internal conditions, including systems and attitudes, often using employee input to form base information with which to identify the triggers that can result in change. This, plus data from related external sources (customers, suppliers), is used for diagnosis and action planning through which the new condition will be pursued. The presence of unions must be addressed in organizational change, because often "they favor seniority-based systems and resist change."[116]

Action plans to achieve the desired result can include changes in management, systems or policy and normally include massive employee education to establish a new mind-set. The intention is to move an organization from condition A to condition B, and often is undertaken using outside expertise. The orderly change of conditions minimizes upset to systems and people and can repair unsettled conditions.

Principles of Organization

The success of a unit depends on the effectiveness of the elements of organization. There are general notions of desirable organization design. These serve as considerations in the formation of new entities and as points of examination in *organization analysis*.

A good share of factual and useful information about a workplace and its culture is generated from people who engage with it. The questions below are typical of those that might be asked of workers to explore the effectiveness of conditions and to surface issues in regard to the methods and manner of organization management.

1. Are you provided with necessary supplies and materials in a timely manner?
2. Are employee absences, injuries and discipline handled uniformly in different departments?
3. How well are new technologies and practices implemented?

---

[114] Greg Smith, "Why I Am Leaving Goldman Sachs," *New York Times*, March 14, 2012.
[115] See Peter F. Drucker, *The Practice of Management* (New York: Harper & Row Publishers, 1954), and George Odiorne, *Management by Objectives* (New York: Pitman Publishing, 1965).
[116] J. Edward Kellough and Sally Coleman Selden, "The Reinvention of Public Personnel Administration," *Public Administration Review* 63 (March/April 2003): 170.

4. Do supervisors have too many or too few workers to attend to?[117]
5. Is there a reasonable balance of work among positions?
6. Do the production systems flow without interruption?
7. Are the supervisor and department current with technology?
8. Are positions treated in a uniform and consistent manner?
9. Are you aware of any recent work or process failures?
10. What are the performance standards for your workstation?

The Rights and Roles of Workers and Managers

Common to all organizations are the distinctive rights of management and those of non-management workers. Common law has adopted a number of *management rights* and actions that allow employers sufficient authority to maintain the needs of productivity. Contemporary legislative actions and courts protect the civil and human *rights of employees*. It's important to understand general parameters of employer-employee relationships. Issues and disputes between the groups are most commonly about rights, compensation and conduct. If there are questions on issues about rights, inquire of those in upper management with expertise. (See the following chart of Management and Employee Rights.)

> **Organizations are vulnerable to economic and political influences, management failings, self-interests and forces of nature.**

A Variety of HRM Priorities

The Function

In private and nonprofit organizations, there is often uncertainty of the role and differences in the responsibility, authority and duties of HRM as a distinct function. Its influence depends largely on the conditions provided and expectation of executive management. The form of the hierarchical level of those responsible is important: the authority and accountability assigned the function, the executive support and latitude provided, and the ability of those assigned. The function is commonly directed to provide:

- Applicable principles and policies
- Special knowledge
- An influence on conditions

---

[117] This question relates to the appropriate number of workers for which supervisors should be responsible (i.e., their "span of control"). It can differ based on whether the work is routine and homogenous or diversified, difficult and dispersed. Is there ease of communication or close proximity? There is no definitive research. See Kenneth J. Meier, "Governance, Structure, and Democracy," *Public Administration Review* 70 (December 2010): 284–291.

- Legal compliance
- A legal staffing process
- Uniformity, consistency and equity
- Pay guidelines
- Administration of benefit programs
- Two-way communication systems
- An efficient personnel record system
- Coaching and training on legal matters and risks
- Oversight of personnel management situations

Organizations often outsource training, payroll, executive employment, benefit administration and related communication. Designated oversight of these activities is necessary, and because payroll benefits are financial in nature, the accounting unit might be assigned some responsibility.[118] However, who does what isn't important if the work is done well.

In start-up situations, preparation for even the first person to be hired requires preparatory groundwork: providing for forms, work analysis and job specifications, initial pay and benefit positions, and satisfying safety requirements. The training of supervisors, methods of communication and the implementation of sustaining programs, including unemployment and workers' compensation, must also be readied.[119] Individual managers should understand their role in personnel management matters: Is there authority to hire, fire, and change pay? An HR specialist may be contracted to see an organization through the start-up stage until a structured condition with policy and programs is in place.

The Specialist/Practitioner

Personnel management in an organization is instituted from the executive level. People successful in HRM activity often demonstrate a high order of interpersonal skill, functional and organizational knowledge, confidence and grit. This last attribute is necessary because achieving policy, program and legal compliance with a modest level of authority requires a willingness to engage peers, managers and executives.

Designated practitioners normally have special knowledge or skill in some aspects of the vocation, such as payroll or recordkeeping, but less often have the knowledge to monitor legal exposure, or the stature to influence the methods or manner of management. The nature of activity and influence of a practitioner help distinguish HR *managers* moving the organization forward from *administrators* who primarily maintain established policies, programs and procedures.

In the private sector, when the number of employees exceeds 100, there is often a recognized need for a full-time specialist. Survey data indicates that municipalities with populations exceeding

---

[118] Guy Logan, "HR Loses Outsourcing Powers as Finance and CEOs Take Over," *Personnel Today*, March 31, 2009.
[119] Sally Coleman Selden, Ingraham, Jacobson, "Human Resource Practices in State Government," *Public Administration Review* 61, no. 5 (September/October 2001): 599.

MANAGEMENT RIGHTS

- Start, stop and direct organization activity.
- Hire and terminate employees; assign work.
- Determine standards of performance.
- Change the organization's nature, personnel needs and methods.
- Establish reasonable standards of conduct.
- Determine methods and rates of compensation (within parameters).
- Determine the duties, staffing complements and work schedules.
- Adopt operating policy and positions, such as prohibiting conflict-of-interest and residency requirements (public sector).
- Expect compliance with reasonable rules, policies and procedures.
- Expect cooperation, honesty and productivity.
- Expect employees to report as scheduled and attend to tasks.

EMPLOYEE RIGHTS

- Exercise free speech (but not if disruptive or injurious).
- Expect personal privacy to be protected.
- Organize for collective bargaining.
- Serve as jurists in federal courts.
- Expect freedom from illegal discrimination because of race, religion and other protected characteristics.
- Refuse imminently dangerous work.
- Disclose to authorities illegal activity of the employer.
- Receive equal pay for equal work (gender).
- Be protected from bullying and harassment.
- Expect reemployment after approved absences for military duty or family medical leave.
- Receive medical care cost and compensation for job-related injury or illness.
- Be eligible for group medical insurance continuation after separation.
- Expect the satisfaction of commitments made by the employer.
- Receive equal opportunity for jobs, training, promotion and other opportunities.
- Be notified of impending major staff reductions.
- Be instructed on hazards, safe practices and evacuation procedures.
- Be free from retaliation for exercising employee rights.
- Be protected from discharge for reasons deemed illegal by law.
- Have the freedom to file for unemployment and injury benefit compensation.

2,000 add HR specialists or practitioners to staff.[120] Human resource managers in most organizations are often *generalists*, meaning they perform a variety of duties. In large organizations, *functional specialists* are used specifically for matters of employment, training, benefit administration, safety, or union relations.[121]

Generally a specialist's influence and activity with staffing and pay is more frequent at the hourly position levels and gradually diminishes at the point of politically appointed government positions and, in the private sector, at the level of management involved in budget decisions. HRM decisions affecting the top executive group are typically handled by a board of outside directors.

Sometimes HR personnel are expected to provide management with a legal and ethical compass on workplace matters. Management or employees may also have an expectation that the HR function is to be an *advocate* for employees and human rights. Guidelines for business management conduct by Kenneth Goodpaster[122] are noteworthy: avoid and prevent harm to others, do not lie or cheat, respect the rights of others, keep promises, obey the law and be fair.

It should be expected that time dedicated by a specialist will result in higher standards, better decisions and more complete and accurate accomplishment. However, as a general rule, the more integrated the function is with the "doers," the greater the contribution to organization management. Provided the skills, knowledge and time, operational supervisors can and do fulfill personnel management duties. When the activities become adjunctive to a unit and activity is more ancillary than integrated, supervisors can become less familiar and responsive.

HRM practitioners have an advantageous view of the organization. Like finance, HRM is central to units, functions and activities. Practitioners become acquainted with all the work, units and management. A disadvantage of functional specialists in the private sector is that they have no authority over workers and must master other methods of winning the cooperation of managers and supervisors. In state and federal public organizations HR operatives often have authority over process that has been granted through congressional (political) enactments that can result in discord with personnel supervisors.

Tools of the Practitioner

There are skills and areas of knowledge common to those accomplished in personnel management. Given the opportunity, most of these are mastered in the first dozen years of occupational activity.

Knowledge

- Management's purpose, mission and positions
- Occupational principles and desirable practices
- Purpose and objectives of HRM

---

[120] Siegrun Fox Freyss, ed., *Human Resource Management in Local Government,* 3rd ed. (Washington, D.C.: ICMA Press, 2009).
[121] W. Lee Hansen et al., "Needed Skills for Human Resource Professionals," *Labor Law Journal* 48, no. 8 (August 1996): 524–534.
[122] Kenneth Goodpaster, *Ethics in Management*, Harvard Business School, 1984.

- Employment law
- Applicable regulations
- Systems for production and command
- Principles of workplace psychology
- Management training and education resources
- Occupational associates and organizations
- Sources of regulatory and functional information

Skills
- Job ranking
- Job study
- Determining hiring criteria
- Determining performance criteria
- Interviewing
- Meeting management and facilitation
- Writing
- The practice of discretion
- Compensation administration
- Records administration

Summary Remarks

An organization determines its objectives and the methods by which they will be satisfied. The desired outcomes of a workplace are most readily realized with orderly systems and the timely application of resources. Because the organization and the performance of its human resources are integrally involved, the refinement, repair and redesign of an organization and any of its elements is within the purview of personnel management.

    The chapter opened with definitions, commonalities and distinctions of human resource management in three primary economic sectors, each of which has a different fundamental purpose and appeal for workers. In each sector, organizations have frameworks comprised of functions, units, streams of authority, communication and processes through which command and productive action take place. The interaction of an organization and a worker affects the performance of the other. Internal systems are subject to influences from inside and outside, and can affect personnel comfort and compatibility.

    Methods and tools used to manage the structure and system include mission statements, policies, processes and structures. Organizations apply resources, support and communication to make workstations and workers effective.

Some primary measures of the effectiveness of the arena and its support are the operating system efficiency, the functioning of policy and procedures, and the presence or absence of conflicts and dysfunctions.

Applicable Competencies

Interviewing, listening, observation, and intuitive and analytical abilities.[123] Personal integrity is necessary because of work with compensation, personal information, background investigations and management plans.

Applicable Resources

Credibility; knowledge of the structure, policies, law, compensation principles, culture and the expectations of management.

Review Materials

Content Exercises

1. What are four tools through which HRM work is accomplished?
2. List four differences between public and private HRM.
3. List three elements common to all organizations.
4. List three historical strategies used in personnel management.
5. List five distinctive rights of management and five distinctive rights of workers.
6. Be prepared to define the following: *management, mission, position, policy, program, nonprofit, procedure, management rights, HR specialist, hierarchy of command, organization development.*
7. Name four primary pursuits of HRM.
8. What are some conditions or systems that affect employee productivity positively? Negatively?

Practical Applications

1. Acquire any examples of policy statements, MBO plans, mission statements, organization diagrams or written procedures.
2. Make inquiries at your workplace to form a view of prominent HR influences and roles, plus any that seem overlooked.

---

[123] Additional competencies include verbal and written communication skills, computer use, presentation skills and sensitivity to diversity. W. Lee Hansen et al., "Needed Skills for Human Resource Professionals," *Labor Law Journal* 47, no. 8 (August 1996): 524.

3. Can you think of one or two circumstances when your work has suffered an interruption because of a lapse in organization effectiveness?
4. Identify a principal contribution credited to organization expert Peter Drucker.
5. Research news sources to identify several organizations undergoing systemic changes. Speculate on the issues.
6. Name four identifiable conditions or changes in workplace culture that you have experienced.

Discussion Assignments

Research and Discussion Assignment 4.1

Personal Communications Policy

Inquire about the manner of control exercised over the use of personal and electronic communication devices at your workplace. Is this a subject of policy, rule or an unwritten position? Is the expressed concern (if any) about organization liability, productivity or privacy? Is there a distinction made between break-time and work-time use? Are there different positions for handheld devices, computers and networks? If applicable, how are rules enforced? Are they accepted? Effective? Is the policy practical? Is it uniformly and consistently applied? Do you believe this is a suitable policy subject? What means would be best used by management to affect this issue?

Research and Discussion Assignment 4.2

The Role of HRM

Generate a preliminary list of commonly accepted functions of HRM and address the following questions.
1. What HRM differences (if any) between public, private and nonprofit organizations are likely to cause problems or reeducation for a specialist moving from one sector to another?
2. Which (if any) of the items you listed seem heavily influenced by federal law?
3. How are these matters administered in your workplace? Do the functions of compliance, employment or pay have a designated responsible person? Or do responsibilities for some seem unclear or ignored?
4. If there is an HR specialist, to what position does he or she report?
5. If the specialist position is titled HR manager, does the title seem appropriate?
6. So far in your study, have you recognized any misconceptions you may have had about HRM?

Advanced Study for Chapter 5

As preparation for the next chapter, prepare a brief discourse (3–4 minutes) on the research contributions of one of the following subjects: 1) McGregor's Theory X and Theory Y, 2) Herzberg's two-factor theory or 3) Maslow's hierarchy of needs.

CHAPTER 5
ENABLE WORKER PERFORMANCE

Chapter Objectives

- Influences on employment conditions and environment
- Positive and negative employment conditions
- Applicable workplace research
- Methods of worker and management communications
- The composition of a good place to work

On Being a Good Place to Work

There is an endless mix of management styles and cultural conditions in organizations—some more comfortable for an individual worker than others. Myriad physical, mental and emotional conditions are afloat in organizations, many of which influence the workstation and that worker. A number can have notable positive or negative influence on employees, such as working conditions and supervision, as well as opportunity for personal accomplishment and recognition. Work environments and workstations differ and change as do individual differences among us, so a recipe for achieving "a good place to work" depends on the individual and the workplace at a specific point in time.

Employee-Employer Relationships: A Mix of Elements

Different Arenas of Employment

Physical and mental working conditions in economic sectors, industries and particular occupations attract or deter individuals. Workers make choices for vocational pursuits based on their experience and self-understanding.

Recall that the for-profit sector is generally competitive and is attractive to those willing to pursue risk and reward. It includes a number of remarkably different industries with prominent characteristics: agriculture, entertainment and hospitality segments are often seasonal and involve irregular office hours; forestry and mining demand moving material and equipment in variable weather; and manufacturing work normally involves an array of physical tasks and environmental conditions.

Those who feel called to make a societal contribution can find ample opportunity in the broad and diverse public sector. In state and local employment especially, the motivation to perform community service is prominent. Public sector employment, by virtue of its financing and constancy, is characterized by employment security. Such characteristics are initial considerations in a person's preference of occupation and employment.

Differences in Employers

The nature of most organizations is unique, but primarily determined by its product or service, location, and its owner or management. Top executives of for-profit organizations are normally in a position to abruptly shape and alter the internal workings of the entity, such as changing hiring or compensation practices. Public and nonprofit organizations are subject to governing bodies that normally exercise more deliberate direction and are more resistant to change.

The general manner of management, or that which is applied in a particular unit, will influence the nature of the working environment and employee attitude. Practices can enable individual workers to innovate, function freely and be effectively utilized, or leave workers feeling limited and frustrated.

Investments in human resources are of value when, like dollars, the returns are maximized. Pursuing the *full utilization of able and available human personnel* is a cornerstone of personnel management. Managers foster and enable employees by providing challenging work of interest, timely and useful equipment, supplies and support, a favorable atmosphere, high standards and goals, recognition and encouragement, and incentive opportunity. One view of enabling the full potential of an employee is through a management-by-faith strategy instituted at 3M, maker of Scotch™ tape and Post-it® Notes; CEO William McKnight suggested, "Hire good people and leave them alone."

The multitude of employer characteristics mixing with the incomprehensible differences in people constitutes an unstable, unpredictable condition to be managed. Small units within a large organization can have unique practices that differ from a dominant pattern of a larger unit; the style of supervision of one group can be desirable, yet across the room, workers can be subject to abuse. The federal government, a few large private sector organizations, and franchising firms in particular intentionally use control mechanisms and standardization to achieve virtual uniformity of the major aspects of their environment, including those that form their relationships with employees.

Employers Have Parameters

It's commonly believed that entrepreneurs can "do their thing"; however, this is true only within conditions set and enforced by government. Stipulations to being in business vary in their degree of disturbance and cost. Employers must operate within a realm of fair and equitable employment, hazard abatement, and payroll and recordkeeping. Employers involved with natural resources such as oil, gas and timber are subject to controls that affect *what* they can do in their productive process. Other employers are subject to *how* they carry out their activities; for example, those in the health care industry are affected by record privacy and regulations regarding blood-borne pathogens. Government intrusions sometimes frustrate those in free enterprise who prefer options and latitude, but are welcome to those who prefer stability and routine. Federal and state employer operations are circumscribed not only by *what* must be done, but also *how often*, the *manner* and *when* things are done.

A Parade of People

Employees of an organization will eventually leave, which is why a workforce is dynamic. Management must accept and prepare for the complexities and adverse consequences caused by personnel changes. Routine employment activity, efficient training procedures and, in many organizations, generous benefit plans are in place to slow the parade of people passing through most jobs.

Most people seek stable employment circumstances, but in our open economy, where two incomes are common, some wage earners prefer temporary or part-time work. Seasonal industries offer temporary work; the fast-food industry is largely staffed with jobs that are routine with modest pay. Those employers are comfortable (and profitable) with a continuous flow of generally young personnel beginning their vocational pursuits.

Occasionally the number of employee terminations among employers in an industry is used as an indicator of employee attitudes and satisfaction. It's a common belief that lack of employee turnover indicates a desirable condition; this may be true in some circumstances and false in others. The long tenure of an employee may mean the worker is simply repeating their first year of mediocre work at greater and greater cost to the employer. Short-term employees may be leaving because their situation and income needs change. The departure of a long-term employee may represent an opportunity to increase productivity.

Turnover rates normally include all employees, good or mediocre. They also include those who leave for uncontrollable personal reasons that are unrelated to the employer. Management should particularly focus on its relationships with *key employees*.[124] If measures of employee losses are used in administration, know the story behind the numbers.

It's been suggested that most employees work in a groove, maintaining a static employment condition of comfort. About a quarter are considering leaving for one reason or another and a similar percentage feel contentment as part of the team. Accepting the premise that a good number of staff is thinking of leaving encourages an ongoing effort to *court*, and not *neglect*, valued employees.

Corresponding Needs and Wants

The employee-employer relationship is an exchange of work for compensation within a larger realm of associated conditions and obligations of the parties. It begins when the parties exchange information (advertisements and resulting application forms) about what each has to offer the other. Just as an employer seeks certain attributes in job applicants, characteristics of employers are examined for compatibility and suitability by applicants. The employer wants reliability, use of the worker's abilities and hopefully some allegiance; the employee seeks suitable compensation,

---
[124] David Satava, "The A to Z of Keeping Staff," *Journal of Accountancy* 195, no. 4 (April 2003): 67–70.

interesting work and employment stability. Employers must understand the attributes of both parties and judge the probabilities of a successful marriage.

As understandings between the parties form, so do expectations of one by the other. A concept of a mutual and unwritten understanding ("a psychological contract") is attributed to theorists Chris Argyris and Donald Schön. Additionally, an organization or its representative might foolishly suggest the probability of future career advancement, job enhancement, or enhanced compensation or environmental conditions.[125] If such matters are unfulfilled, such "contractual violations" result in dissatisfaction, a severe wound to these relationships.

Differences in People

Any workplace can be unpleasant for one person but a great place for the person working beside them. Any work situation results in different mental and emotional responses from the people working there. Human differences are not only complex and unique, but even stimuli varies; a specific program or condition will cause a different response by the same person in different circumstances, and employers try to provide *a mix of appeals* for a variety of applicants and employees. The study of workplace behavior is one of the paths open for continued study of HRM.[126]

> **Creating an expectation in the mind of an employee that is unfulfilled can result in disappointment, the loss of management credibility, and legal exposure.**

Some institutions and firms have the resources to address almost every personal interest, such as having the benefit of a concierge available to help employees get personal chores done or offering medical insurance for pets. Nevertheless, organizations with the most comprehensive benefit packages[127] may not be able to provide the occupational role or opportunity for challenge sought by a particular worker. Individuals can find a niche of satisfaction and opportunity, as well as downsides, throughout the world of work.

The Influence of Unions

Federal and state legislation declares that most profit-making employers and many public agencies must permit the formation of unions and engage in bargaining with unions of employees. A small percentage of employees in the nation's workforce choose to enroll with unions. Among the reasons are to improve employment conditions and job security, to collectively address perceived injustices, to express dissatisfaction with management, or because of peer pressure.

---

[125] Relationships are based on unwritten expectations as well as standard written commitments.
[126] A scholarly article addressing workplace behavior theories is Sunil Ramlall's "A Review of Employee Motivation Theories," *Journal of American Academy of Business* 5, no. 1/2 (September 2004): 52–63.
[127] Some uncommon employee relations programs include eldercare benefits, matching gifts, and paid personal absence days.

The pursuit of changes in the working environment by unions has been notable in our nation's history, and union members remain a factor today by virtue of political influence as well as collective bargaining power. A union focuses on the well-being of its members, providing help with their complaints and grievances, and improving their condition by way of labor contract negotiation. Unions in general have been successful in improving employment conditions and contributing to personal and job security of members. Pressures from employee collectives commonly force management to grant more influence and costs than they would like. In rare occasions the success of unions has contributed to financial stress in industries such as steel and automobiles. Keep in mind, however, that management in the for-profit sector can always say no to union demands and take the risk of a business shutdown.

As a result of greater national affluence, a decline in massive industrial (versus service) employers, legislative advantages to workers, such as safety and benefit regulations, and greater wisdom on the part of management, union membership has declined. Today about 11 percent of the workforce is organized into unions.[128] Thirty-six percent of members are in the public sector,[129] while less than 7 percent of private sector employees are union members.

Nationwide organizing efforts are continuously underway. Unions normally seek to influence members of the workforce in their homes with publications expressing union views. Rumors and secretive behavior among workers may signal an attempt to organize. Private sector management will normally resist unions because they dislike the imposition, preferences for seniority rather than merit, conflicts, and threat to the enterprise that labor power can represent. Employees who are union members and also appreciate their employment sometimes struggle with occasional conflicts within their dual commitments and allegiances.

While unions and management share an interest in perpetuating the employer's organization, they have different secondary purposes, positions and priorities that can result in conflict between the parties. Nevertheless, employers adopt different views of collective bargaining. Federal agencies and some states take a political posture of passivity toward union membership. The federal government has been an advocate for unions since the National Labor Relations Act of 1935. Unions of teachers and state and local employees are among the largest in the country. There are groups excluded from the mandated bargaining rules of the NLRA, including supervisors and managers, agricultural workers and, of course, public employees subject to other legislation.

Matters in the arena of labor-management relations are crucial in the maintenance of positive employee relations: resolving employee grievances, training supervisors on workplace practices, and administering contracted provisions, such as seniority and pay schedule applications. If a union wins representation rights, then negotiating a contract and maintaining management prerogatives become challenges.

Relationships with labor unions are challenging and require professionalism. There are finite *legal parameters* and legal vulnerability of employers in union-organizing campaigns. Management,

---

[128] Large unions include the American Federation of State, County & Municipal Employees; with over 1.3 million members, AFSCME represents considerable political power.
[129] John Schmitt and Kris Warner, "The Changing Face of Labor, 1983-2008," Center for Economic and Policy Research, November 2009.

and especially supervisors, must tread carefully in what is said, lest they commit an "unfair labor practice," which is a routine allegation of management malpractice by unions in organizing strategy.[130] Management cannot interfere (or appear to interfere) with union activity, threaten or discriminate against employees because of union activity, or refuse to bargain with a government-certified bargaining representative of employees.[131] It's recommended that expert counsel be used in organizing situations.

Contracts with a union are renegotiated every few years. The two principal parties select negotiating committees with an identified spokesperson and establish a protocol for their interactions over the course of their meetings, typically beginning with an exchange of issues or demands of the parties. The parties are "to meet at reasonable times and confer in good faith with respect to . . . conditions of employment in good faith."[132] The work of an organization might be interrupted as the result of a *strike* by union employees or a *lockout* of the employees by management. The lockout at the American Crystal Sugar Company ended after almost two years. Four hundred of the original union members reported for work in June 2013.

Unions and management have a mutual interest in the survival of an employer, so over the time of discussions, demands are normally ameliorated without reaching the point of a shutdown. It's general practice that management will insist on and win a "management rights" clause intended to protect their prerogatives. Unions will demand union security clauses that 1) require all personnel in the organized unit to be union members[133] and 2) stipulate that the union's dues be automatically deducted from the payroll checks prepared by the employer. If union membership and monthly dues payments are guaranteed, a union establishes permanency, becoming an ongoing stakeholder and an element of workplace culture. Most for-profit employers strongly resist agreeing to union security provisions, but these are crucial to the union.

There are distinct differences between public- and private-sector union negotiations. Private sector employers have the obligation to negotiate over wages, hours and working conditions under the NLRA and the Railroad Labor Act.[134] The Civil Service Reform Act of 1978 provides for organizing and bargaining in federal agencies. Most federal employees can organize but cannot always strike or negotiate wages. Thirty-eight states[135] have labor laws applying to public employees, and some have legislation specifically addressing teacher unions. Teachers can bargain in Tennessee but other public employees cannot.[136] Therefore, public-employee bargaining situations must be examined state by state.

As a study of this issue points out, "The majority of states with public-sector bargaining laws prohibit strikes and stipulate that a bargaining impasse must be resolved by arbitration (e.g.,

---

[130] In 2008, there were 20,000 charges of unfair labor practice and 40 percent had merit. Fay Hansen, "Talking Unions," *Workforce Management* 88, no. 12 (November 16, 2009): 16–18.
[131] W. David Patton et al., *Human Resource Management: The Public Service Perspective* (New York: Houghton Mifflin, 2002), 107–108.
[132] 29 U.S.C. § 158: US Code – Section 158:(d).
[133] Some states have enacted a "Right to Work" law that states that employees have the right to work without being required to join a union.
[134] The RLA applies to the railroad and airline industries.
[135] States prohibiting public bargaining include Arizona, Colorado, Louisiana, Utah, Virginia, Arkansas and New Mexico.
[136] Siegrun Fox Freyss, ed., *Human Resource Management in Local Government*, 3rd ed. (Washington, D.C.: ICMA Press, 2009), 106.

see statutes in Iowa and Wisconsin and the law providing for collective bargaining for New York City employees). In some other states, strikes by certain groups of employees whose services to the public are defined as nonessential to the public interest are allowed, whereas bargaining impasses involving critical employee groups must be resolved through arbitration."[137]

An employee's support of a union is usually associated with the likelihood of improved personal well-being via higher compensation, representation in the case of a misstep and support for protecting job security. Some workers, required to become members or pay the fees by virtue of contract provisions, resent it. Others have little loyalty because they joined as the result of peer pressure. Still others may be attuned to "belonging" to an organization, are perpetual protesters or are devoted to social change. Few unions are a totally positive or negative factor in the workplace, and their voice is heard at the time of individual grievance situations and during negotiations.

> **Research provides some understanding of workplace behavior patterns and tendencies, but the behavior of individuals is distinct.**

Influential Researchers

There are principles of worker psychology that are accepted as base knowledge in understanding the relationships between employers and employees in the United States. The studies of only several researchers[138] are mentioned herein, and additional study of the subject of *employee motivation* is recommended.

Abraham Maslow[139] postulated a *hierarchy of needs* that has gained wide acceptance. His studies indicated that while people first and foremost work for food, shelter and personal needs, those who have satisfied those survival needs work to satisfy interests of a higher order. His theory sheds light on the relative priority of employment and income in social structure. Beginning with the most basic needs and climbing toward the more personally satisfying activities, the postulated increments of human pursuit are generally as follows:

1. Biological and physiological needs (food, sleep, air)
2. Protection and safety (shelter)
3. To be cared about and loved; a sense of belonging
4. To have self-esteem and the esteem of others
5. To learn and satisfy a need for greater knowledge
6. Time for the appreciation of beauty
7. Personal achievement and satisfaction

---
[137] John Remington et al., *Human Resources Law*, 5th ed. (Upper Saddle River: Prentice Hall, 2011): 234.
[138] The thinking of Maslow and Herzberg is generally accepted. Readers may also benefit from the work of Rensis Likert and David McClelland.
[139] Maslow's original work was published in his book *Motivation and Personality* and identified a hierarchy of five needs. Research by others refined that work.

The personal-needs hierarchy is a general progression and, of course, can't account for uncommon events and those troublesome individual differences.

A second researcher who helped define characteristics of workers was Frederick Herzberg.[140] His studies suggested that many negative aspects of employment can be attributed to the environment, such as unpleasant relationships with others, inadequate or unfair compensation and offensive supervision. Over the years, Herzberg also emphasized the *negative effects of perceived inequity* or unfairness felt among workers.

> **"People work for themselves, not the company."**
>
> —From Mary Walton, *The Deming Management Method* (New York: Putnam Publishing Group, 1988), 91.

Herzberg also helped establish the importance of a job as a potential source of employee satisfaction and motivation, thus highlighting the advantage of enhancing jobs to challenge and interest an employee. Major positive aspects of employment tend to emanate from the work itself, such as challenge, responsibility, interest and achievement. The commonly used terms *satisfiers* and *dissatisfiers* in employment grew from his work.

The work of these two individuals has been both enhanced and challenged but remains foundational to the pursuit of positive employer-employee relationships. *Work-and-life balance*,[141] another theory that is being widely discussed in this century, was yet to reach a mature status equal to these early studies.

The Conditions of Influence

Different workplace conditions can result in periods of *employee dissatisfaction*, can *enable* and *retain* employees, or be of negligible impact. It is the nature and understanding of management and its direction and control that sets the course. Employee interests are most commonly job satisfaction, the priorities and ability of management, personal opportunities within that scheme, the personalities that will be engaged and compensation. Applicants and employees generally gravitate toward employers that seem to evidence a favorable measure of those matters and try to avoid or escape employers believed to have undesirable circumstances. Research continues to increase the body of knowledge that can clarify the complexities and dynamics of the workplace, including:

> **Historically, workers had to fit their lives around their workplace. In this century, employers permit some jobs to be performed in concert with the life activity of employees.**

---

[140] Herzberg's work was originally published in *The Motivation to Work* (1959). In the last fifty years, some further considerations have evolved.

[141] A 2008 study verifies workplace flexibility as a factor that enables "a more facilitative relationship between employees' work and family life." Jenet I. Jacob, Bond, Galinsky, "Six Critical Ingredients in Creating an Effective Workplace," *Psychologist-Manager Journal* 2, no. 1 (2008): 141–161.

- A study of IT personnel in thirty-eight states revealed that women preferred *family-friendly benefits*, while men wanted *increased responsibilities* and greater *clarity of job expectations*.[142]
- Retail clerks indicated that the *image of the employer* for whom they worked was significant in their desire to stay in their job.
- Temporary and part-time personnel react to the *safety risks* and job threats more than full-time workers.[143]

The availability of monies with which to provide desirable programs or efforts is always a consideration. Some employers have more dollars than others, and some have higher priorities at any point in time. Even if a key element of satisfaction/dissatisfaction is recognized, the *costs* might be too great for even a sizable employer to provide.

Employment and Job Security

Some employees live with anxiety about job and income loss. Threats exist because of personal health concerns, failure of the employer, obsolescence of the occupation, elimination of the position, economic conditions or inadequate performance.

Employers can temper fear and uncertainty about the prospects of economic setbacks and job loss by sending positive but realistic and factual messages about the future. Reassuring feedback about job performance is welcomed by anyone. The importance of giving people a thoughtful heads-up to anticipated staff reductions is sufficiently important that federal legislation has been enacted to require warning people of impending job loss. (See discussion of the Worker Adjustment and Retraining Notification Act (WARN) in chapter 9).

An employer's history of *employment stability* is a most valuable consideration in achieving the status of "a good place to work." Employers with such an advantage should publicize it, though with due caution since everything seems to cycle. In the face of technology, our global economy, and personal vulnerabilities, some uncertainty will always exist.

It's common to think of the stability of work in terms of a specific job with a specific employer. There can be opportunity, however, for employers to motivate, engage and impress workers by providing vocational training and education for *occupational opportunities* in an industry or profession beyond those available with the present employment condition. Workers have benefited from learning how to operate or program a robot that replaced them at their workstation. *Job security* and *employment security* are not synonymous. In our economic and technological system, vocational enhancement and redirection becomes increasingly necessary.

---

[142] Soonhee Kim, "IT Employee Job Satisfaction in the Public Sector," *International Journal of Public Administration* 32, no. 12 (2009): 107–109.
[143] Yueg-Hsiang Huang, Peter Chen, "The Job Satisfaction of Part-Time Workers Hired without a Safety Threat," *Work* 21, no. 3 (2003): 251–256.

Compensation

Direct Pay

Generally, workers allocate a consistent degree of their life energy to their job irrespective of pay level. However, pay must be perceived as *adequate and equitable* or it will become a source of dissatisfaction. A pay increase felt to be inadequate or perceived as inequitable relative to the increase of others will most assuredly be problematic. Because internal pay comparisons are more evident and personal, they have "a greater effect on most work attitudes than external comparisons."[144]

Exceptional pay will serve to keep people, but can't be expected to prompt greater effort. Only lucrative, well-designed and closely administered incentive programs can increase productivity, and then only among workers willing and motivated to react to the opportunity. Chapter 6 is devoted to pay programs.

Benefits

Benefits are a principal element in forming the image of an organization, encouraging applicants, and fostering the high retention of employees, both good and mediocre. An employer contribution to medical care insurance (a basic need of high cost) is a powerful attraction in the eyes of most workers. Mid-life employees will maintain employment because they appreciate employer contributions to their retirement, but they are not likely to work harder.

Paid Time Off

Holiday, vacation, and personal time programs and work hour flexibility can contribute to a positive work-and-life balance, but can't be expected to result in greater output of work. A normal and reasonable expectation of nine paid holidays and the potential of three weeks' vacation in the for-profit sector are viewed as satisfactory by most. Paid time off beyond that level contributes to a feeling of good fortune but isn't likely to motivate or provide a positive return on the investment.

Working Conditions

Basic elements of the physical and often emotional working conditions are most often fixed by the workplace. Workers generally accept the working conditions in a chosen occupation as a matter of fact and with little emotion. However, employment insecurity, disrespectful supervision, and disturbing and/or unpleasant associates can cause discomfort and dissatisfaction.

Scores of matters can cause positive or negative reactions by workers, even in an office setting. The office may be too noisy, hot or cold, or the workstation too public or too removed from desirable social opportunity. A wondrous facility—and there are many—can engender pride ("You should see

---

[144] Ted H. Shore and Judy Strauss, "Effects of Pay and Productivity Comparisons in the Workplace on Employee Attitudes: An Experimental Investigation," *International Journal of Management* 29, no. 2 (June 2012): 677–681.

our cafeteria!"). Fortunately, humankind includes a breadth of workers who can tolerate working under the ocean, on the moon, in freezing temperatures or in underground mines prone to explosions.

> **It's not always about the money.**

Accommodating Personal Needs

Employee satisfaction or dissatisfaction with the employment relationship can swing on an employer's ability or willingness to accommodate a worker's life situations. There is increasing expectation on the part of workers that management will willingly alter normal workplace procedure so employees can undertake *personal chores* or *family obligations* during normal work time. A decision affecting a request for absence because of a stressful family matter or an opportunity for an educational experience can result in long-lasting employee appreciation, or, if denied, resentment.

Offering job sharing, telecommuting, choices in benefit offerings and counseling through employee assistance programs contributes to comfort and retention, though the cost-to-benefit ratio for an employer is normally uncertain. The adoption of programs should be economically justified, but is most often rationalized. While management may often like to enhance the benefit package, it needs to sacrifice investment in a different resource and consider the precedent and long-term implications.

The Job and Placement

The consideration of *proper job placement* exists throughout the study of organization and personnel success. The match of worker abilities, interests and aptitudes with the physical and psychological demands of a position directly affects the satisfaction of an employee as well as the productivity and costs for the employer.[145]

Changing the *design of a job* might improve the match between the worker and the assignment. Increasing the responsibility through job enlargement and/or adding related activities that can increase the employee's contribution are possibilities. Efficiency often creates more available time at a workstation and a supervisor should be observant of those opportunities for productivity improvement, especially with some "workers at the lower levels . . . of the echelon."[146] However, a supervisor should consider "the differences in employees' technical and psychological readiness before any specific job design is implemented."[147] For the worker, the advantages of such changes can result in less boredom, increased use of abilities and more self-sufficiency, leading to a greater contribution to the company.

The nature of the work itself can provide learning, creativity and prideful influence on outcomes of a unit[148] and can serve to *motivate* as well as *retain* personnel. Meaningful work, by one

---

[145] National Career Development Association (NCDA), "The Professional Practice of Career Counseling and Consultation: A Resource Document," 2nd ed., files.eric.ed.gov/fulltext/ED387742.pdf.
[146] Kae H. Chung and Monica F. Ross, "Differences in Motivational Properties between Job Enlargement and Job Enrichment," *The Academy of Management Review* 2, no. 1 (1977).
[147] Ibid.
[148] Jenet I. Jacob, Bond, Galinsky, "Six Critical Ingredients in Creating an Effective Workplace," *Psychologist-Manager Journal* 2, no. 1 (2008): 143.

definition, is work that satisfies both the need to make a living and the need to make a difference. When an employer can offer both, they are providing employees with "a more complete work experience."[149]

Sir Ken Robinson of the U.K. believes that employees can settle into their element when their *talent converges with their passion*. Doug Claffey, CEO of WorkplaceDynamics, believes "You cannot pay more money to someone to remain engaged in a bad workplace . . . they get excited about doing something meaningful with people they believe in and enjoy working with."[150] Successful job placement has financial advantages for both parties, plus a psychological benefit for the employee.

Unfortunately, a significant percentage of adults are unsure of the vocation and conditions to which they are best suited. Trying to find an occupation that provides personal preferences under the pressures of a job search for a source of employment income can be distressing. Workers often enroll for jobs that are of little interest and have little likelihood of any long-lasting positive outcomes. Despite interests voiced by an eager applicant, an employer must explore an applicant's vocational indicators and try to ensure *suitable job placement*.

Social Relationships

Personal relationships that exist, or are absent, on the job have a positive or negative influence on the desirability of a workplace. Some people might extend their tenure with an employer primarily because they don't want to lose their friends at work. Recall the earlier findings of Maslow for *needs to belong* and to enjoy the *affection of others* and think about the popularity of interpersonal contacts on Facebook. This is not to suggest that group picnics and parties to stimulate connections will automatically have a positive result on employee retention. A 2011 survey of several thousand employees by Harris Interactive revealed that a holiday party was far down the list of employee choices for a holiday perk.[151] Money, paid time off, a grocery gift card and a number of other benefits were preferred. Of course, antisocial or "scary" associates represent a negative social condition.

A prevalence or absence of positive social connections can result from the layout of a workstation or unit. It's difficult to cultivate social ambiance, but sometimes it is a matter of fostering what has freely developed. Social relationships can contribute to employee tenure and thus benefits both parties without substantial cost.

Another aspect of the social climate in a workplace is the existence of positive and negative biases in regard to politics, race, religion and gender. Managers crossing the threshold of the workplace must subdue any thinking that might lead to prejudicial behavior on their part and be alert to unpleasant remarks in the work area. People can't readily change years of attitude conditioning, but can behave with civility during the hours of work, and *must* respect social and legal limits.

> **We like to spend time "where everybody knows your name."**

---

[149] Teresa Daly of Navigate Forward, supplement, *Minneapolis Star Tribune*, June 17, 2012.
[150] "Top Workplaces," supplement, *Minneapolis Star Tribune*, June 17, 2012.
[151] Glassdoor workplace-information website, survey by Harris Interactive, November 2011.

Personal Recognition

The desire to be noticed and appreciated is innate to us all. Daily greetings and pats on the back, particularly in public, stir each of us to some degree. Supervisors should understand the value of personal identity and the use of employee names, as well as acknowledgment and recognition of positive contributions of a worker.

Giving credit to a worker should be sincere and specific in terms of that which is notable, and should occur soon after the occurrence. The public awarding of certificates or certifications for attendance, production or other achievements is common. Records can be used to methodically recognize workers for annual birthdays and five-year intervals of lengths of service.

Singling out workers, however, can have undesirable consequences. An "employee of the month" selection makes *someone* feel special, but can also be viewed as favoritism by a score of others. Award behavior must be worthy, distinctive and clear to others in order to prevent adverse consequences.

Fairness

Justice and fairness are primary values in the American social structure. Nevertheless, offensive discrimination on the basis of race, religion and gender was common in our workplaces until equal-opportunity political action in the twentieth century. As a result of that redirection, most managements place a high value on fairness in their personnel choices, employee treatment, and assignments, resulting in more favorable employment conditions as well as increasing diversity.

> **"If you strip it away, my take on great places to work is they've established community... there's a sense of belonging."**
>
> —From J. Forrest, "Employee Strategies," supplement, *Minneapolis Star Tribune*, June 17, 2012.

The initial and continuing base for fair employment standards are legal mandates for valid criteria and the tools used in making choices among workers. Fair treatment in employment is an expectation of the general population, and management missteps, or the perception of unfairness, generates disfavor.

Engagement and Affiliation

A key element of engagement is creating a sense of community and camaraderie that includes transparency, trust, communication, participation and a focus on individuals. Both productivity and tenure can be increased when employees feel like a valued contributor in the organization, and "organizations that provide employees with opportunity to participate in the decision-making process are less likely to be the targets of unionization."[152]

---

[152] Joan E. Pynes, *Human Resources Management for Public and Nonprofit Organizations*, 3rd ed. (San Francisco: Jossey-Bass, 2004), 369.

Profit-sharing and stock purchase plans for the workforce are financial techniques to bind a person's well-being with that of the organization. However, simple participation in department projects and programs as provided by the supervisor, interactions with management on meaningful subjects, and knowledge of activities, successes and failures of the unit also bond. Study groups are not uncommon in large firms, but Google management encourages special-interest groups to increase the mooring of their people, supporting groups of skiers, dog owners, singers and those interested in "topics from wine to hiking to quilting to Dungeons & Dragons" that total thousands of employees.[153]

Opportunity and Growth

Potential for motivation and retention of an employee can swing on the opportunities afforded by an employer. People routinely seek increased income, but there are also folks motivated to improve their personal competencies. Such personal ambitions aren't always on display, so supervisors must be attentive to any clues and, at some point, have a discussion with subordinates on the subject. The files of many personnel should have notes of their occupational interests.

> "It ain't brain surgery. Every person in an organization has value and wants that value to be recognized. Everyone needs appreciation and reinforcement. Taking care of employees is perhaps the best form of kindness."
>
> —Colin Powell

The culture of an organization and management leadership can foster the availability of work or learning possibilities. The *broadcasting of job opportunities* and *periodic inquiries about an employee's career interests* are two practices to accommodate interest in advancement. It's common that technology- and communications-oriented units readily fund training for technical devices used on the job. Opportunities to promote from within should be fully explored. Opportunities for internal learning assignments or advanced education are powerful motivators for the perpetual learners among us.

The Manner of Management

The effectiveness, efficiency and manner of management conduct are principal determinants of how workers view an employment situation. A system can create feelings of pride and the comfort of predictability or be dysfunctional and disappointing.

Different styles of management, as discussed in chapter 4, provide different degrees of employee autonomy. Employees react favorably or unfavorably along the continuum of latitude provided by the systems.

---

[153] Mike Swift, "At Google, Groups Are Key to the Company's Culture," *San Jose Mercury News*, June 2011.

Social Responsibility

There is worldwide interest and questions surrounding the responsibilities that employers have to society and our planet. S*ustainability* is about maintaining the earthly matters necessary to our survival.[154] To many people, active *social responsibility programs* (such as sustainability and affirmative action) adopted by an employer reflect a management of high character and an organization with which they are proud to be associated. On the other hand, actions that express a disregard of environmental concerns, such as inappropriate disposal of toxic waste, can cause employee distaste.

A broader scope of social responsibility includes *management ethics, human rights and responsibilities to workers, the environment* and *society* in general. Efforts to influence employers toward social consciousness and action normally come from the general public, government actions, stakeholders of an organization, enlightened citizens or the personal values of owners and executives.

Global concerns include child and forced labor, social discrimination, employee safety and health, business and political ethics, termination injustice and the absence of workforce diversity and collective bargaining. The federal government has addressed these conditions primarily through statutory requirements (equal opportunity, collective bargaining, safety) and our resulting norms are generally viewed positively among many nations. However, there is evidence that our workplaces still suffer injustices such as favoritism, the disrespect of others, dishonest appraisals and undeserved disciplinary actions.[155]

International concern with these matters adds credence to our nation's societal choices and the resulting form and direction of our human resource management. It may also evidence economic justification for our investments in equal opportunity and justice in workplaces. We play a leading role in the growing global pursuit that employers "do no harm" and be "good corporate citizens."

The most prominent of societal concerns faced in the U.S. is sustaining the physical environment. Matters of concern in this arena include global warming, air and water pollution, and energy and water consumption, which are clearly broad societal concerns, but don't relate to the people management function as closely as do concerns of the *human condition in workplaces*.

Many applicants and employees react favorably to organizations with broad corporate social responsibility commitments,[156] but only 6 percent of HRM professionals believe that HR has a primary role in environmental matters. Employee training and communications programs, however, are often supportive of social value activity that management endorses.[157] Managements will increasingly adopt and define their position in social responsibility matters.

While there are many pursuits of corporate social responsibility in this country, the environmental matters in the private sector are problematic. Private sector enterprises are driven by motives of profitability, perpetuation and personal interests. All of these can conflict with financial investments

---

[154] Michael Czinkota, Ilkka A. Ronkainen, Michael H. Moffett, *Fundamentals of International Business* (Indianapolis: Wessex Press, 2008).
[155] Amanda Rose, *Ethics in Human Resources*, highered.mcgraw-hill.com/sites/dl/free/0077111028/.../EHR_C02.pdf.
[156] C. B. Bhattacharya, "Using Corporate Social Responsibility to Win the War for Talent," *MIT Sloan Management Review* 49 (2008): 483–494.
[157] Elaine Cohen, Sully Taylor, Michael Muller-Camen, "HR's Role in Corporate Social Responsibility and Sustainability," SHRM Foundation, 2012.

in long-term environmental matters. Interest in more worldly matters may best be a personal matter (i.e., off the job)[158] and require compromise in an employment situation.

Ethics

The perception of management's *ethics* can be a factor in employee relationships. The lapse of ethical conduct on Wall Street and the failure of accountability by Congress regarding the 2008 housing crisis that grew into a general economic downturn give reason to question the degree of ethical standards in the highest echelons of commerce and government. There were no consequences for those responsible, though many financial organizations were discredited and millions of citizens suffered severe economic damage and job loss. Month after month, pharmaceutical, government, financial, food and manufacturing institutions continue to become publicly embarrassed because priorities to perpetuate the organization and serve self-interests trump established social values.

Effective Systems

Uniformity and Consistency

Predictable decisions are the norm in public employment but not always in the private sector. Economic changes, occasional turmoil and a general aversion to time-consuming regulations and documentation can make a profit-making environment vulnerable to inconsistency, preferential treatment or inequity. Uniform and consistent practices are the norm, but perceived injustice or favoritism does occur. One of the underlying contributions of a designated HR management presence is ensuring common practices and preventing inconsistencies among units.

Order, Predictability and Discipline

Any organization expects employees to follow patterns of acceptable attendance and productivity whether rules or the established culture are well communicated or not. Some management fosters an environment of mutual trust and believes that expressing negative rules of conduct that are rarely violated is unwise. Workers who tend to associate with management or consider themselves professional might see a prominent list of admonitions as an affront. Nevertheless, just exhibiting the proper example may not fulfill management's obligation. Employees deserve to have been informed about expected effort, attendance, off-site conduct and ethics. Suitable opportunities can be found to send periodic messages on those subjects without applying an unnecessary "bully pulpit."

One of the distinguishing differences between the public and private sectors is the tolerance afforded public employees for misconduct and marginal performance versus the private sector's weapon of dismissal under the employment-at-will doctrine. A specific frustration is the inability to

---

[158] Gerard Zwetsloot, "From Management Systems to Corporate Social Responsibility," *Journal of Business Ethics* 44, no. 2/3 (May 2003): 201–207.

exercise effective control over the use of paid sick-time benefits and other unnecessary absence.[159] Rationalizations like "needing a mental health day," "just taking a day off" or simply "they owe me" abuse implied contracts with trusting management. Similarly, trust can result in personnel who abuse the system by leaving early to make up for arriving late. Misuse of time, along with theft of supplies and products, are major costs for employers.

Discipline for deviation from norms should be definitive and consistent. Applying a penalty for violating a standard of conduct or performance should be limited to the specific offender rather than taking an action that penalizes an entire department of people. Performance deficiency demands recognition of the difference between inability and lack of effort; one can be corrected through retraining, but the other must result in some form of discipline.

An employer's objective should be to accomplish a redirection of errant conduct in a manner perceived to be fair in the eyes of the entire workforce.[160] The common and initial course of action in dealing with unacceptable behavior is to talk about it, making sure the desired conduct is clear in terms of what and why, and to point the offender in the preferred direction. The level of any disciplinary action should correspond to past practice and the severity of the transgression. Offenses that are injurious to the employer or another person normally result in far greater penalty than when the issue is attendance or errors of minor cost. If the first coaching effort isn't sufficient, progressive measures are applied to correct unacceptable variances.

Disciplinary action must desirably specify the offense and provide an opportunity to listen to a defense, apply due process and create documentation. In union situations, be cognizant of the Weingarten Rule, which grants employees who are represented by a union the right to a supportive representative in disciplinary meetings.[161]

Supervisors

The role of supervisors and their support of employee performance in maintaining positive employee-employer relationships can't be overvalued. The position influences the success or failure of multiple people. The task tends to become more difficult as the level, skills and ability of subordinates increases. Professional personnel have special knowledge, have typically enjoyed functional latitude and often have a constituency; as such, they respond better to leadership rather than the use of management authority.

These first-level management positions and the people that occupy them are crucial in how a workplace is viewed as a place to work. An organization will do well to fill supervisory positions with those who possess leadership traits, such as the desire and patience to be supportive of workers. Those who supervise must also be prepared with training, technical and organizational knowledge and know how to express directives.

---

[159] The normal sick-day use is three to four days per year. Typically, only a third of those days are actually used because of illness. Commerce Clearing House, Unscheduled Absence Survey, 2007.
[160] One common effort to be corrective rather than punitive is the practice, sometimes legislated, of providing an employee abusing illegal substances the option of a treatment program rather than dismissal.
[161] *NLRB v. J. Weingarten, Inc.*, 420 U.S. 251 (1975).

Any negligent or undesirable conduct by a supervisor is more readily identified in small organizations because of transparency. In large organizations with less visible conditions, favoritism, bullying and abuse by supervisors can occur more readily. In organizations of every size and reputation there are people in supervisory roles that should not be. Some were appointed supervisors because of exceptional technical or production skill. Many are well intentioned and motivated but aren't provided a mentor, are untrained or simply don't have the ability to lead or manage.

In the continual discourse about the appraisal of personnel, the focus is normally on the supervisor as a rater of others. However, perhaps the first and most important positions that should have conduct and performance evaluated are these representatives of management, who are in daily communication with, and impact the performance of, the mass of employees. Recall that about a third of supervisors are considered poor by subordinates. Some factors of satisfactory performance include the following:

- Each workstation functions effectively and efficiently.
- Timely and quality output of the unit is consistently accomplished.
- Physical and human resources are suitably maintained.
- Communication channels with employees are active.
- Relationships with other units are effective.
- Notable issues are addressed with the department head.
- Mutual respect exists among subordinates and discord is minimal.

The Role of Employee Communications

Management Messages

A web of communication linkages among units of workers is a principal means through which processes are accomplished. Large organizations, by virtue of their size, require considerably more management attention to accomplish unadulterated, timely and full dissemination of directions and other messages. Feedback to the top carries reports of results and issues. Small units can call the gang together and "talk it over."

Management messages to employees are most often intended to:

- Provide directions
- Fulfill government message mandates
- Inform personnel of news and changes
- Enlist employee support for special matters
- Promote the attributes of the employer

Principal Subject Matter

The primary communications for production purposes are generally routine. The greater challenge is the information that flows up and down the hierarchy about other matters of benefit to workers and managers.

Employers have a heavy obligation and legal exposure because of obligatory messages they are required to convey and/or post under state or federal law.[162] Many posters are notification of *employee rights* and others of *employer obligations and prohibitions*.[163]

> **Effective messages are those that reach the total of the intended audience in a timely manner and in a clear, concise, complete and correct form.**

Required Posters

- Equal opportunity
- Fair labor standards (minimum wages, overtime and child labor)
- Retirement rights
- Polygraph testing limitations
- Family and medical leave eligibility
- Medical insurance continuation rights (COBRA)
- Benefit plan description and funding status (ERISA)
- Affirmative action status (if a government contractor)
- Harassment policy and prohibition
- Workers' compensation rights
- Unemployment compensation rights
- Notification of safety hazards and protective measures
- Federal contractor worker pay rates
- Safety and health rights
- Plant closing notification
- Drug-testing requirement for commercial vehicle operators
- Safety record postings
- Emergency evacuation diagram and training[164]

---

[162] Some small employers may be excluded.
[163] There may be additional subjects required by state law.
[164] Individual states also have poster requirements to be accommodated, such as New York (AIDS), New Hampshire (vacation shutdown) and Vermont (meal breaks).

Other than these matters, there is rarely any selected subject matter or planned delivery for exchange with workers. Communication is often centered on the newcomer handbook, posters and occasional bulletin board announcements about unexpected events. There is a strong need to know what's happening in our work life. It's common for employees to remark, "No one tells us anything." Satisfying the "need to know" contributes to positive employee relationships and fosters a positive relationship with management.

Carrying out general employee communication requires management commitment and the dedicated effort of a skilled and curious writer. Responsibility must be assigned and support provided in the form of access to executives and other sources of information, such as customers, the industry and the community. The designated communicator should explore industry and community matters, news about vendor, customers and political interests, and matters about the facility, equipment, interesting employees and events, management decisions, products, success, errors and more. A variety of media should be used for full and effective understanding of messages.

Common Methods

Established Channels

Because of the mass, complexity and importance of management messages, a number of routine and systematic channels, such as the chain of command, mailings (e.g., benefit change announcements), websites, group meetings and production-related forms are commonly used. *Bulletin board postings* require administration and normally have fixed messages of mandated policy, position statements on topics such as the holiday schedule, complaint process, and periodic education, or social event notices. *Published materials* include policy and procedure manuals, employee handbooks and product or service information manuals. Each of these tools is part of a larger effort that can benefit from oversight and accountability for accuracy, proper dissemination and maximum results. Information that is posted electronically includes benefit information and file access, job opportunities, training materials, and policies and procedures.

Supervisors

Supervisors typically act as the voice of management in the transmission of messages and can provide responses to any questions or concerns from workers. Adept supervisors sift through daily prattle and learn of irritations and changes in an employee's life that could impact scheduling. Unity of thought among employees about an event or issue should be transmitted from supervisors up the chain of command. The smaller the organization, the more likely top management will receive important feedback.

A *personal meeting* with an employee is usually for notification of pay or assignment changes, disciplining, coaching, seeking systems improvements or giving credit for good work. *Small-group meetings* conducted by supervisors are often used to transmit messages from higher management about changes and matters impacting the objectives of the total unit. When complex matters need transmission, a subject specialist is often used. Meetings of supervisors that don't result in some feedback of value to management are rare. Principles and techniques for meeting management are discussed in chapter 3.

There are sound reasons why people like a personal visit with their supervisor. They want to hear how they are doing, voice a complaint or concern and get deserved kudos. In terms of short interactions, a coaching hint or a quick acknowledgment are positive experiences. A talk with the boss can result in more positive feelings about job security and less uncertainty. Interviews about career paths and opportune assignments serve as recognition and can contribute to retention. It doesn't take much prompting to have a positive outcome when the meeting is about the employee; virtually all workers try to do a good job[165] and have joint interest in employment circumstances. Performance shortcomings, personal pay matters or discomforting subjects like discipline are best dealt with in a personal meeting devoted to that single purpose.

Remote Connections

Contemporary management includes many organizations with centralized executive management but geographically remote personnel, in which case teleconferencing is commonly used. Exceptional efforts are often made to overcome the distances and facilitate bonding among workers and with management. Many firms connect with those working elsewhere through websites. An eldercare firm with dispersed workers schedules personal visits of employees to a central location, has annual employee picnics, dinner theater events and periodic health training sessions to foster relationships among personnel. Another firm arranges gatherings for bowling and ball games and uses monthly staff meetings, newsletters and a number of routine communication methods to ensure employees feel connected to one another.

> "Eliminate slogans, exhortations and targets for the workforce—they never helped anybody do a good job."
>
> —W. Edwards Deming, from Mary Walton, *The Deming Management Method* (New York: Putman, 1988). See also W. Edwards Deming, *Out of the Crises* (Cambridge: MIT Press, 1986), 35.

Exit Interviews

Exit interviews can generate revelations or issues of workers, but those leaving can be hard to corral, have no advantage to talking and can incur some risk; many prefer to avoid an interview. Certainly someone other than the supervisor should be assigned as the interviewer. The interviews of disgruntled employees can be particularly beneficial in the event they are harboring the thought of legal action. In such circumstances, reacting promptly and positively to correct the matter on behalf of the employee is a desirable tactic.

---

[165] Seymour Martin Lipset, "The Work Ethic, Then and Now," *Journal of Labor Research* 13, no. 1 (Winter 1992).

Walk-Around Visits

Some owners and managers are very successful in exchanges with people during a *walk-around* of work areas. A manner demonstrating interest and trust can result in the collection of considerable workplace intelligence and can assist in building relationships.

Focus Groups

Distinctive in that they involve group thinking rather than the views of an individual, and generate expressions rather than data, focus groups can "produce highly useful information about practices and services that surveys miss."[166] "Focus groups are a method of group interviews in which the interaction between group members serves to elicit information and insights in response to carefully designed questions."[167] Expert moderators who use carefully formed questions typically lead them. Groups of eight to twelve randomly selected participants meet at least twice for a one- or two-hour period.

Attitude Surveys

Managers of large groups sometimes use voluntary written or electronic interrogative devices to collect general employee views about pay or issues and lift them to a level that can affect change. Such surveys should be fully supported by decision-making management, carefully prepared, provide actionable feedback, be statistically valid and result in demonstrated changes.[168] One firm provided feedback with a report stating "You said this . . ." followed by "We did this . . ."

Management's willingness to react is necessary before questioning employees about their honest views. The privacy and confidentiality of employees' input is a significant concern to employees. If confidentiality cannot be satisfied or a portion of the workforce is not sufficiently literate, other feedback methods should be used. If surveys are not professionally conducted and don't result in obvious changes, the result is a negative mark for management.

> **Feedback from workers can identify faults and failures that need repair.**

---

[166] Nancy Grudens-Schuck, Beverlyn Lundy Allen, Kathlene Larson, "Focus Group Fundamentals," Iowa State University Methodology Brief (May 2004).
[167] New York State Teacher Centers, August 14, 2012. Website tutorial.
[168] If management is unwilling to change a condition, omit the inquiry. A 5 percent return of solicitations is too few; announce that the project has been abandoned.

Transmissions from Employees

Informal Paths

The navigation of messages from employees up the management hierarchy is more difficult than the slide downward. A channel must permit employee concerns and complaints to reach an appropriate level of management. Individual comments as well as patterns of employee remarks can be flags and indicators about employee interests and thinking but can sometimes get minimized or lost in transmission. Higher management should demonstrate interest in messages sent upward. Without an outlet for frustrations and complaints, such as hotlines, surveys, free-flowing complaint processes or perhaps a complaint resolution system, employee frustration can reach serious levels and might contribute to feelings of despair or the organization of a union.

The initial and primary navigation method used by workers is interaction with their supervisor. A supervisor serves as management's listening post as well as mouthpiece. Because some employee concerns are about their supervisor, it's necessary to have alternative methods so messages can bypass these managers and be heard.

Large firms sometimes use commercial telephone call centers so employees can anonymously report matters such as theft, discrimination, wage and hour violations and fear of violence. Some organizations provide an interactive Internet exchange. Suggestion and complaint boxes and formal complaint procedures collect expressions of dissatisfaction but requires demonstrated administration.

Management sometimes claims "open doors" for employees but these are often ineffective. Workers are deterred from entering the open door because of discomfort with an office setting, fear of retaliation by their supervisor for going "over his/her head" or finding that a manager is unwilling to contradict their supervisor.

In small firms, the owner is normally close to most activity and deals with issues. Some small-business owners have a sit-down with each employee every year. Whatever the size of the unit, concerns and complaints not addressed will adversely affect relationships between the parties and may mask legal issues with high cost potential.

If issues of workers are unheard, discounted or no action results, management may find itself listening to a third-party (union or government) representative that the law insists *will* be heard. The procedures for dealing with employee messages should be a subject of basic management training and oversight.

Structured Paths

A formal program to foster messages and positive attitudes is often used as part of the upward communication strategy. Very similar to grievance procedures that are negotiated with unions, complaint and suggestion programs provide a channel through which an employee can seek resolution of perceived injustice. Formal systems are characterized by a clear written procedure, ease in voicing the concern, defense against reprisal, a pursuit for confidentiality, and *intent for resolution*. Principles and procedures typically applied are:

- Several optional points of initiating contact
- Fact-finding
- Prompt feedback
- A central position for coalescing issues
- A documented step-by-step process
- Permission for a support person in meetings with management
- A central, neutral party to investigate, mediate or judge

Union Messages

A collective body of employees magnifies voices and influence in regard to workplace issues. An exchange of points of view on distilled, targeted subjects is inherent in across-the-table bargaining between management and union representatives. Employees not associated with a union can also gather and approach management for changes in working conditions. This, too, is collective employee action that is protected from reprisal under law.

A *grievance procedure* is a top priority of unions in collective bargaining and is routine in labor agreements; in the public sector, these procedures are usually required by regulations. Such procedures are used to surface and resolve specific employee issues or complaints other than normal bargaining subjects.[169] Grievances progress through increasingly higher levels of the hierarchy of the two organizations until the matter is resolved, arbitrated or dropped because the costs of continued action by one or both of the parties is greater than the possibility of the positive result or benefit to be derived.

Action Programming

Approaches to improving contributions of, and relationships with, employees can be simple or difficult but always require some strategic thinking. Some matters might only require buying a new piece of equipment, coaching a supervisor or issuing a one-minute directive. Improvements can be accomplished in individual units with initiatives to change the manner of supervision, communication, training or the level of worker participation.

On the other hand, a desire to shift the thinking of the entire workforce can involve massive education and many months of time. Executive management is the source of energy, authority and any significant changes to an organization. They have the insights, information, power and finances with which to "get things done" and must provide the expectations to do so.

---

[169] Certified unions must also provide "fair representation" to members of the bargaining unit, though they might not be members of the union.

Fundamental Policies and Positions

As a result of actions by the federal government, some basic management principles are standards of our society and conditions expected in a workplace. However, it's up to management in the private sector to create its chosen principles by addressing its values and beliefs and the degree to which it wants to be a "good place to work." Core thinking may or may not be in writing but can constitute a basis for management decisions and directions that can enhance favorable employment circumstances. Examples include:

- Management conduct is ethical, honest and legal.
- Human resources are supported, respected and valued.
- Standards of conduct and performance are maintained at a high level.
- Investments are made in the human resources.
- Decisions accommodate long-term needs.
- The satisfaction of customers is a fundamental pursuit.
- Responsiveness to stakeholder interests is a fundamental pursuit.
- Management adheres to the established mission.

Conditions and Standards for Adoption

Organizations commonly adopt an array of practices and programs devoted to fostering positive employee relationships. Over time, the addition of remote units and new managers, overall growth, and financial fortune changes tend to dissipate original management beliefs and intentions. Maintaining valued principles and beliefs requires sustained effort. Below is a list of performance standards management might monitor:

- Executives are evaluated against base values.
- Organizational systems result in a timely and quality product or service.
- Effective communications systems are operable.
- Standards of conduct and performance are understood.
- The environment is without fear.
- Due process is applied in the pursuit of justice.
- Extraordinary behavior is recognized and rewarded.
- Those who supervise others are carefully chosen and provided sufficient training.
- Impediments to the performance of personnel are minimized.

Summary Remarks

Qualifying an organization as a good place to work is based on an individual's judgment; what is desirable for one worker may not be viewed similarly by another. Each workplace has unique qualities and management. This chapter identifies management's challenge to deal with the conditions and environment of the workplace.

Workplace psychology provides a number of primary principles upon which management can forge desirable employment conditions. The provisions that can be satisfying and enabling to employees include: the nature of the work assigned, freedom from encumbrances, adequate compensation and supervision, supportive physical working conditions, employment security and recognition. Creating and maintaining a workplace environment that is inviting and has a minimum of discouraging elements enables productivity and fosters the retention of valued personnel. Two principal research contributors referenced herein are Abraham Maslow and Frederick Herzberg. Readers are urged to study these and other contributors to effective personnel management.

One primary subject of the chapter is the sense of involvement generated through employer-employee communication. Frequently an afterthought, such communication is a primary means through which positive employee relationships can be formed. Established methods to carry management messages down the hierarchy, and employee messages up, are helpful to achieving collaboration and avoiding issues and frustration.

A format for developing and/or maintaining positive relationships between management and staff is offered that includes management standards and values to embrace.

> **Employers will benefit from providing opportunity for adequate earnings, advancement, fair treatment, free expression and meaningful involvement.**

Applicable Competencies

Initiative, analytical and communication skills; the ability to organize and carry out projects; knowledge of basic workplace psychology, the industry or business sector, community benefits, compensation levels and practices.

Applicable Resources

Management's collaboration and allocation of resources and programming to achieve positive employee relationships.

Review Materials

Content Exercises

1. What are five of the major positive or negative employee relations elements listed in the book to which you can relate?
2. Why are unions formed?
3. Why is there less union membership now than historically?
4. What is a difference between unions in the public and private sectors?
5. If you were trying to improve a workplace, what would be some initial steps?
6. What points of action are available to management that might affect relationships with employees?
7. What are some subjects of joint interest to management and employees?

Practical Applications

1. List employee relations tactics and programs that your employer applies well.
2. If you have worked for both large and small organizations, create a chart showing distinctive differences you have seen between each type of organization concerning employee and management relationships.
3. If your workplace has a complaint and/or grievance system, obtain a copy of the process and compare it with those of other organizations, which can be found either online or shared by others.
4. If you have worked in a union workplace, what routine issues or conflicts other than pay seemed to exist?
5. How might a message be formed and transmitted expressing that your employer has a favorable history of job security and/or competitive compensation levels?
6. Conduct research to find out details about the law in your state (if any) regarding a public employee's rights to bargain.
7. List the prominent methods used for messages to go up and down the hierarchy at your workplace.
8. Consider whether there is any personal acknowledgment at your workplace of doing your job well or achieving an employment anniversary or birthday date. What is your reaction to this policy or practice?

Case-Study Discussion

Case 5.1
Providing Communication Paths

Over the course of several weeks, the manager of a software development firm employing several hundred people learned of three disturbing incidents and was unsure what to do about them. First, he was told that on a day when he'd been absent, two employees had come to his office, found it locked and were overheard saying, "So much for open doors!" Second, an employee hired last year recently had stopped the manager in the hall and told him that she understood at the time of her hire that she would be granted three weeks' vacation rather than the normal two, but her supervisor didn't have the same recollection. She was upset and sought resolution of her complaint. Third, the manager had just received a report from the state labor department about an investigation they had conducted on-site that was an unpleasant and total surprise.

The manager couldn't help but wonder if policy deviations and a seemingly casual reaction to a government investigation by the support staff suggested some laxity or lack of understanding on their part. He was perplexed, too, because he didn't believe he had ever claimed an open-door policy! However, he was surrounded with a staff of thinkers, and asked several members to visit with him about his concerns.

What seems to be missing in management? What are the system concerns? What options and results would you expect from this meeting? What changes would you foresee?

Case 5.2
Discussion Preparation: Working Environments

1. Based on your personal experience and observations, how would you characterize the manner of management generally practiced in the public, private, nonprofit and international sectors?
2. What might be seen as the positive and enabling characteristics of each of the sectors?

UNIT III
SUSTAIN A QUALIFIED WORKFORCE

To provide working conditions and compensation that serve to maintain a desirable workforce.

CHAPTER 6: DELIVER PAY

CHAPTER 7: BENEFITS FOR RECRUITING AND RETENTION

CHAPTER 8: SAFEGUARD THE HUMAN RESOURCE

CHAPTER 6
DELIVER PAY

Chapter Objectives

- The value of earnings opportunity in the workforce
- Methods of paying wages and salaries
- The construction of a pay program
- The development of pay guidelines
- Considerations in pay decisions
- Common pay administration issues
- Integrity in pay matters

Providing Employment Income

For most people, continuous income is the greatest of personal needs. Pay from work provides the wherewithal for personal security and satisfying wants. Governments spend vast sums to sustain minimum personal income levels of those with limited employment opportunity. Employment compensation is obviously a primary necessity to retain and nurture a workforce, but important, too, are employee perceptions about compensation. This chapter addresses the manner and circumstances of how employers deliver pay.

> **Management balances the investment in compensation dollars with other financial needs.**

Planning for Pay

Wages and salaries are paid to workers in exchange for their contribution to the organization's effort. Both employers and job applicants normally have a general expectation of the value of a job's contribution. Regardless of the nature of the work or the size of the organization, how others pay for similar work is one of several considerations in compensation decision making.

- What am I presently paying for this work?
- What is being paid for jobs with greater, and less, difficulty and responsibility?
- What do competitors pay for similar work?
- What is a rate the candidate will accept as fair?
- What can be afforded?

These common employer pay questions relate to underlying principles, expressed as follows, for managing wages and salaries. *Costs, adequacy* and *equity* among workers are the basis for structured and orderly wage-and-salary programming.

- Payroll is a cost and investment to be judiciously expended.
- The pay of any associates doing similar work is considered in pay decisions.
- Pay levels must satisfy recruiting and retention needs.

Pay management embraces a host of variables that leave it far from exacting. An expression that a pay figure "is the correct pay rate" for a position is rare compared to the assessment that "that seems about right." Despite the use of mathematics and wage-and-salary schedules that specify rates of a specific position, the numbers used *are* imprecise. Wage-and-salary management is neither science nor art, but it is logical and methodical and prevents employee uncertainty and dissatisfaction.

It's generally true that pay levels are based on the *difficulty, contribution and conditions of the workplace, competitive rates, fairness* among employees and any *legal parameters*, such as minimum wage. A small employer often thinks of previous pay experience and practices in making pay decisions. In large organizations with a multitude of different jobs and levels of performance, programs are more complex; competitive pay information is collected, positions ranked against others in the interest of fairness, and standard practices are applied among units to achieve consistent and uniform practices.

As with other HR functions, start-up situations require study and tentative positioning so that a semblance of pay orderliness for jobs can be instituted early in the organization's formation. Preparations include:

- Identification of the nature of the work
- Formation of an initial structure of position levels (higher to lower)
- Competitive pay data collected and considered
- Determination of management intentions about pay (competitive, minimum, high)
- Determination of pay criteria (time spent, incentives)
- Determination of variable pay (e.g., bonuses)
- Allocation of the responsibility for oversight of the function and pay decisions
- Calculation of the degree that benefit offerings will influence wages and salaries in the total compensation

In the first days of organizing, positions are not usually well defined; there may be too few for definitive ranking, and ancillary compensation programs aren't yet determined. In those circumstances, the primary source for initial pay decisions becomes *competitive marketplace data*. Very often, new private sector enterprises offer a minimum of benefits because the ability to pay for them is uncertain. Even so, the attraction of a "ground-floor opportunity" in a new undertaking can excite many candidates.

Common Methods of Pay

Pay levels and methods should be established that provide satisfactory income to maintain a workforce. Some methods are instituted to drive greater efforts. Changes to pay programs are periodically necessary to maintain competitive levels. Normally this is accomplished through a *cost-of-living percentage of increase* added to the pay structure. These accommodating marketplace increases are usually passed on to employees on a common date or included with another increase for reasons such as merit. *Merit increases* are awarded to workers who are improving their skills and knowledge. *Performance bonuses* are granted for uncommon accomplishment. Readers will find that the terms used for pay grants are not uniform and can even be inaccurate and misleading (e.g., merit increase is expressed for a marketplace advancement).

> **A primary determinant of pay level is the value of the work in the competitive marketplace.**

Fixed Rate

The predominant method of earning pay is based on the *amount of time* an individual contributes their skills and efforts for the benefit of an employer. It's common practice that workers such as machinists record *hours worked*, including overtime, and are paid, often weekly, based on these hours. The salary of those not required to receive overtime pay is often paid on a monthly basis. Such workers are often expected to complete responsibilities or processes that periodically require more than eight hours of work a day or forty hours a week.

The productivity of most personnel over the course of a day is commonly viewed to be below 80 percent of a full effort. The nature of many workers is to function at one speed and to maximize break time. It's not uncommon that some employees will "spread the work out" or "take their time" when tasks demand less time than is scheduled. To track the attention-to-task of remote personnel, management may use electronic recording to register worker progress against a schedule.

Two variations of fixed pay are *skill-based pay*, which allows individuals who

> **Pay systems are based primarily on the jobs in an organization, not on the parade of individuals passing through.**

apply multiple skills to earn an elevated rate, and *team-based pay*, which is an application to stimulate *unity of effort* and accomplish results with a group of associates.

Pay for Output

Trying to make the most of payroll dollars in the private sector has resulted in plans to pay for *results* rather than *time*. An amount of output, such as miles driven per day, patients consulted or units machined, is converted to a dollar value of pay. Arriving at a reasonable output performance standard can be administratively costly and a point of disagreement between the parties. Industrial engineers are often used to conduct time-and-motion studies of the work and methods in the formation of these standards. Management does not always understand the potential *unit cost reduction* achievable through incentives and is not always willing to accept the administrative costs and extraordinary paychecks for the output that can result.

Incentive plans are best applied in an efficient, predictable production system and with a competitive, energetic environment. Prompt payouts of rewards reinforce good effort. Realistic rewards should be 12 percent of the base salary and higher to stimulate the extra effort. The potential productivity improvement in situations suitable for incentive stimulation is notable. Matching the proper kind of workers to the pay system is a challenge of personnel selection and placement.

Sales Incentives

Sales positions in our economic system occupy key roles in profit-making organizations. Whether market creators or order takers, they are at that transaction point that converts output into *revenue*. Inside sales workers, such as those in telecommunications, or outside sales workers, who travel and are exempt from overtime pay, are normally salaried. They frequently enjoy some variable pay opportunity (e.g., salary plus bonus) or can be compensated totally on results via commission.

Sales incentive plans typically have unique features based on industry or organization peculiarities and are often managed (and/or manipulated) by sales management. A simple plan might provide a relatively low base salary or alternatively a draw against commission earnings. Route salespeople, who deliver merchandise like food and beverages, are often provided an incentive to increase market share by pushing their product. Some pest-control service people receive 20 percent of total billing in order to keep them on the move. Hair stylists and barbers are typically paid on a production basis (50+ percent). Sales incentives that pay a percentage of the sales dollars generated above a quota of sales volume are common in communications, software and other industries. Some product sales commission plans reward 2–5 percent of the gross, net or invoiced dollars. New accounts are often paid at a higher percentage than established accounts. Established accounts may generate less reward because of extraordinary service requirements by technical support staff.

It's difficult to arrive at a realistic sales projection or quota as a base point for incentives in the face of unknown economic and business conditions in the future. Management will frequently add an annual quota increase to the sales of a worker for the next business year regardless of circumstances. This assumes increased market opportunity and controls compensation expense.

It's rationalized as an incentive "carrot," but erodes the integrity of sales management. The practice is so common that experienced salespeople accept it as a matter of course.

In most circumstances, a salesperson's degree of success is the result of major economic swings, customer business decisions and other circumstances rather than actual sales skill. Success can be a matter of being in the right place at the right time. A customer can eliminate a product or change suppliers because of pricing, over which the salesperson has little input and no control. Rewards for a successful sale could be lost if the product was of poor quality and consequently returned, or delivered late through no fault of the salesperson. On the other hand, an unexpected windfall sale might result because the salesperson stumbled across a cousin in a purchasing department, or because of misfortune to a customer's normal supplier. Such situations create difficult issues of fairness and equity in plan design and administration, and their common occurrence helps explain why sales management wants control over pay decisions in the sales unit.

Variable Pay

Variable pay in the form of profit-sharing cash awards, bonuses and gainsharing are often paid relative to an output standard accomplished over a twelve-month period. Variable pay applications have the advantage of responding to a particular accomplishment while not adding to the base compensation level, which would automatically perpetuate and compound the dollars in future years. A variable reward is a common and valuable technique, but must be properly controlled and explained as a *one-time award*. Recipients must understand that a different standard and decision may be made in future performance periods.

> **The purpose of variable pay must be well defined, communicated and monitored. If participation grows, standards could be compromised, thereby eroding the value of the plan.**

The rewarding nature of variable pay is a very strong factor in positive employee relations, but "There has been little or no information on how variable pay plans have actually impacted business results."[170] Initial variable pay programs should be positioned as pilot efforts because of the possibility of miscues in plan design.

In about one-third of private sector firms, *bonuses* of cash or gifts, usually of about 10 percent of base salary, are awarded when business is profitable, but most often only to management personnel. By definition, bonuses are "in addition" to the agreed-upon wage or salary. Eligibility often requires employment at the *time of distribution* if pay programs are intended to promote retention. Previously negotiated bonuses are actually deferred compensation because they are *not* "in addition."

Bonuses are paid for a variety of reasons, such as the sharing of financial success, because other companies do it, or even from guilt because of suppressed base pay. At times of business strife,

---
[170] Lance A. Berger and Dorothy R. Berger, eds., *The Compensation Handbook*, 5th ed. (New York: McGraw-Hill, 2008), 236.

retention bonuses are sometimes granted to key personnel to discourage their loss. Well-founded bonuses are generated by a profit-sharing formula or serve as individual performance awards for identifiable, defensible and notable contributions. Performance rewards should be significant (8–10 percent minimum) to be sufficiently valued, and are most effective when granted near the point of performance rather than delayed until year-end.

Many experts believe that proper bonus actions make meaningful contributions to motivation and retention. They also represent a cost and, if poorly handled, may be viewed as unfair to others.

Employer *profit-sharing* plans typically provide varying amounts of cash and/or deferred cash based on the level of financial results of the organization.

Gainsharing plans provide a group cash reward based on collective improvements in costs and productivity. Results are determined by comparing cost improvement over the previous year. The degree of any improvement results in formula-based payouts. Such plans foster collaboration, cost awareness and participatory effort.

Executive Pay

The pay practices for the top echelon of officials and executives in all the economic sectors are normally excluded from general pay policies and programs. These personnel can put the organization at risk or lead it to success, and so have extraordinary authority, responsibility and risk of job loss; as such, employment contracts at this level are the norm and establish performance standards such as increasing market share, executing a merger, establishing a specified return on investment (ROI) or accomplishing an acquisition objective. Because a top executive faces daunting challenges and the risk of short tenure, generous severance payments are often contracted in return for confidentiality and non-compete obligations. To encourage management stability, agreements also provide significant deferred compensation, often in the form of stock options. An equity interest is more likely to be granted in large, publicly owned firms than in smaller firms where ownership is closely held. A compensation package may include supplements to the normal employee insurance and time-off and retirement benefits as well as perquisites such as club memberships, a vehicle and extraordinary expense allowances. Privately held organizations often establish a compensation committee from among the board of directors to negotiate the accord. Chief financial or legal officers often administer these agreements.

Organizing Pay Practices

Framework

Organizations create and apply methods of compensation based mostly on the nature of the work in the unit. Jobs that involve mostly physical labor are typically paid with an hourly rate that is simple, understandable and minimizes controversy. Incentives for production or sales units are desirable when the worker is the predominant determinant of output. Group pay methods are used to stimulate collaboration of productive effort. Profit-sharing techniques are applied to foster a participative culture. Organizations use any or all of these approaches to achieve the most effective use of dollars.

Programs

Fixed and documented guidelines foster consistent, uniform and sound decisions and are a basis for educating supervisors and employees about desired practices. The preamble to such guidelines should include to whom the program applies; sales, union and executive personnel are commonly excluded from a general program. The increasing percentage of other-than-full-time employees in organizations is resulting in the documentation of guidelines for employees in a variety of employment statuses.

Protocols and Practices

Despite the unique nature of millions of organizations, the formation of direct pay schemes, as herein addressed, follow a clear pattern in private, public and nonprofit workplaces regardless of size. Protocols and *functional principles* exist because rational, methodical decision making is commonly understood and applied. Even the smallest of firms pursues equity, consistency and understanding about practices among workers.

Small-business managers learn about pay and competitive levels through acquaintances or business associations. A few neglect to *verify actual job content* relative to a position title, to

---

PAY PROGRAM CONTENT

PURPOSE OR INTENT: This section typically references the need to recruit and retain personnel, along with the pursuit of equity and legal compliance.

SCOPE: Identifies the employee groups to whom the program applies.

COMPONENTS OF THE PAY PLAN: Includes reference to ranking, surveys, steps or open ranges.

RESPONSIBILITIES: Defines who will do what (e.g., write job descriptions, provide oversight). In the public sector, a governing body such as the school board or city council often oversees activity.

TIMING: Avoids any commitment to pay-review frequency, and instead declares flexibility.

AUTHORIZATIONS: Provides some identification of the executive level necessary to approve hiring pay, titles and pay changes, and establishes the practice that an employee should be notified of a pay change only after approvals.

consider related compensation, such as benefits, or to inquire about the frequency of overtime. Titles are often fallacious—one executive noted that "It's easier to give someone a more grandiose title than more money"—and are not to be relied upon. A pay rate judged against comparable pay rates in the marketplace may be low because it is that of a *new employee* or because it's the foundation rate for additional incentive earnings. Likewise, a job rate can be high because it's temporary and/or doesn't provide benefits. Proper research is a necessary ingredient of market pricing and compensation data in general.

Developing Pay Levels

The amount of money that people are paid emanates principally from the difficulty and responsibility of the work they perform; pilots, for example, earn more than flight attendants. Methods of determining pay differentials among jobs can begin with a simple best-guess ranking of their perceived value. A small business is well aware of who can lay bricks and who can only be the helper. Ladders of increasing job difficulty can usually be agreed upon with a minimum of disagreement. However, it's the determination of the *degree of difference* between the jobs—should the pay spread between the levels be small or great?—that requires complete and accurate analysis.

There is disconnection between the professional determination of pay grades and what people may actually be paid. Without dwelling on the possibility of some disorder in management, there are workers paid on the basis of extraordinary skill, misinformation, poor judgment, or a political, business or family connection. When a strong program exists, these difficulties can be minimized.

Job Knowledge

Time should be devoted to achieving an understanding of essential job content for each job with different tasks or responsibilities within a group. When current and complete job descriptions are available, they provide the basis for study that can then be used to develop pay levels. The supervisor of the position can answer most questions about the job, but the person doing the job knows it better than anyone else. See chapter 1 for more information about the study of work and positions.

Job Ranking

The method of ranking to be used corresponds to the complexity and nature of the jobs to be addressed. Ranking approaches include *educated guessing*, *market pricing*, *grouping of similar jobs* and *comparison of inherent factors* of one job to another. One elementary technique is to construct an initial hierarchy based on present employee pay practices and "slot in" new positions. Executive ranking is normally based within the industry, often using IRS financial scope data as the basis. Salespeople who are compensated primarily through an incentive system are normally unranked.

Almost 100 years ago, industrial engineers identified four primary factors common to all jobs that differentiated the difficulty between them: *skill*, *effort*, *responsibility* and *working conditions*.

Since the original research, those elements have been further refined into about a dozen more definitive factors. Rather than best-guess ranking, job evaluation instruments provide a form for analysis and comparison of the inherent factors in jobs.

In 1923, federal personnel management adopted a merit system of employment and pay rather than previous patronage practices. The Classification Act was enacted to initiate "standardizing the classification and grading of civil-service positions according to duties in ascending order of responsibilities."[171] In 1930, premier firms General Electric and Westinghouse Electric adopted a job evaluation plan developed by the National Metal Trades Association. Since then, this rational, methodical manner of job ranking has cascaded down to, and through, state and local government units and sizable organizations in the private sector.

Job evaluation, not to be confused with *personnel evaluation*, requires results to be viewed as credible by the worker as well as by management. To that end, management must understand and support the effort and assign able administration. If self-interest or disinterest in the system exists to a significant degree, an outside service can be contracted to add a professional face to the program, change a method, ensure fairness or resolve issues.

A central program can transcend units, even those that are remote, to achieve a system that ensures validity and equity throughout the organization. The adoption and maintenance of a job evaluation system is costly, and many small private and nonprofit firms elect not to incur the cost and rely on marketplace compensation intelligence. Following are the factors commonly used in job study evaluation.

> **Understanding job content and its contribution to the system is fundamental to proper job ranking.**

---

[171] W. David Patton et al., *Human Resource Management: The Public Service Perspective* (New York: Houghton Mifflin, 2002), 39.

Common Job Content Factors

EDUCATION AND TRAINING: The level of knowledge and schooling necessary to perform the designated duties (software use, vocational training, certifications, scholarship).

EXPERIENCE: The necessary practice time before knowledge and skills reach competency (one week, one month, two years, five years).

JUDGMENT: The importance of normal decision making and the consequences to the organization. (Do decisions follow established procedures or create risks to assets or the enterprise?)

ANALYSIS: The complexity of options and unknowns inherent in the work (routine situations only, known possibilities to consider, unpredictable circumstances).

COMMUNICATION: The complexity, risks and frequency of communications of consequence (interaction with supervisor, executives, or customers; necessary technical expressiveness; level of desirable tact or diplomacy).

ACCURACY: The necessary degree of correctness, and consequences of a likely error (inaccuracy with product specifications, production schedules, customer orders or delivery data).

SUPERVISION: The accountability for the direction and control of other people directly or indirectly (the number of subordinates and complexity of their activities).

ORIGINALITY: The necessity for creative thinking; the expectations for new methods, strategies or products (repetitive work, adjustments sometimes necessary, creates new programs or products).

RESPONSIBILITY: The relative importance of accountability (impact on costs, revenues, profitability or public safety or image).

AUTONOMY: The latitude for independent action (work is checked daily, policies are available, decisions are rarely reviewed).

CONFIDENTIAL MATTERS: The degree and frequency of normal exposure to confidential matters and the likelihood of unfortunate disclosures (pay matters, medical or personal histories, trade secrets, business strategies).

MENTAL AND VISUAL EXERTION: The predominant level of concentration, stress and attentiveness required (casual attention, constant concentration, the burden of success or failure).

PHYSICAL DEMANDS: The level and constancy of difficult physical exertion (lifting, awkward positions, excessive hours).

WORKING CONDITIONS: The severity and constancy of exposure to undesirable conditions (normal office, heat or cold, confined space, hazards, travel).

The most common plans used in larger organizations are based on factors like these to guide judgments. Following is a sample single factor applicable to all jobs. In this example, the determined level of required education is compared to the level of education required in other positions. This example uses a numerical value for each of the established factors, and the points assigned for each factor, such as supervision required or responsibility, can be added to arrive at a total job value expressed in points.

A FACTOR DESCRIPTION

Education

POINTS	MOST SUITABLE DESCRIPTOR
0	a) Activity involves no reading or writing
3	b) Elementary skills applied: simple reading, writing, adding, subtracting
6	c) Routinely applies simple formulas, calculates numbers, reads instructions and completes forms
9	d) A more advanced level of knowledge than (c) but not as advanced as (e). (This is a flexible category for calculating pay grades.)
15	e) Applies technical knowledge as learned from study during apprenticeships, years of experience or technical-school study
24	f) Applies principles and formulas in the development of products or processes

---

Any plan adopted by an organization should be expected to be used for years, and should be fully tested prior to final adoption. The method of evaluation must provide a consistent result; to "adjust" an established plan tampers with its validity. Tests of a plan's accuracy include second evaluations with a different committee, use of a different technique and the application of face validity; that is, considering the fit of the job in the hierarchy over time.

Organizations can create their own plan, purchase one, or use a consulting service. Public organizations often use instruments adopted and provided by an association. At the federal level, classifications are determined by plans of the Office of Personnel Management.

A committee of three to five management or staff personnel who are familiar with the job(s) to be studied is normally convened by an administrator/facilitator for the evaluation of one or several positions. The facilitator sets ground rules, including admonitions to pursue objectivity and to disregard the job incumbent and job title. Any evaluation by a single person will be based on limited job knowledge, subject to bias and without the consensus that is necessary for credibility of the result. Committee membership should always include a supervisor representing the job, and a parade of other management personnel who "pass through" committee duty. Their participation is an exercise in management education and spreads credibility for the program. Any project session might include three or four positions to rank and last about two and a half hours. Orientation and the first job study normally require one hour; after struggles with the first position, the process moves more quickly.

Learning the Pay Market

The primary determinant of a pay level is that which is generally paid for comparable work in the same industry or geographical area. The important undertaking of collecting and considering pay data useful in constructing an organization's pay pattern can be difficult because of the *challenge of locating and accessing comparable data*. Whatever the pay level that management wants guidelines to reflect, whether market level or higher or lower, an adequate and accurate reality of the market must be known for the basis of any decision.

Employees expect their pay to be fair relative to that of associates.

Large firms, nonprofits, counties and cities use *pay surveys*, sponsored by an industry or association among similar organizations, from which to draw pay-and-benefit data for comparison. Some surveys are produced as a participative effort and others can be purchased. Occupational surveys are conducted by accounting and engineering associations but normally aren't validated, are self-serving and are largely ignored by compensation practitioners. Small employers learn about community pay practices informally from advertisements, applicants and associates.

Sound pay management depends on sufficient and accurate knowledge of the competitive pay in the labor market.

The jobs contained in a survey are selected *benchmark jobs*, and survey participants, or those using the survey, may only be able to legitimately match with 25 percent of the positions. The duties described for the benchmark job must match the internal position, including the role of the job in the organization. A controller position in a small firm is not comparable in scope to the controller of a large multinational firm. Titles are not used beyond the initial locator search for similarity. Supplementary compensation, such as benefits, cost-of-living adjustments, automatic increases, or bonuses, must be considered; *medians* of pay cannot be compared to *means*. There must be close comparisons for data to be useful.

The best survey practices include periodic sit-downs of representatives of the survey and participating administrators to examine each position's content, organizational role and ancillary compensation to ensure an adequate match. Common levelers are the use of 2,080 work hours in a year and 173.3 hours in a week.

There are competitive commercial and association surveys in most communities but *participation* in a select survey involves years of building credibility and relationships. The exchange of pay information among competitors involves an unwritten *understanding of non-disclosure*. Shared data is to be used for study and calculation, not illicit recruiting, curiosity or competitive advantage. Working with compensation data requires a level of discretion that not everyone possesses. Fortunately, observing so many numbers results in disinterest and an inability to recall any of them. An administrator who is curious or judgmental about personal pay situations represents a risk. Disclosure of pay information can be harmful to individuals and the organization. On the other hand, *employees have a legal right to disclose their own pay*, so pay comparisons among employees cannot be prohibited.

Constructing Pay Guidelines

Given the *ranking* of positions and some benchmark *pay comparisons*, a *pay line* for a unit can be constructed by *interrelating the two factors*. By posting points of pay data and job rank on a vertical and horizontal axis, a *scattergram* is formed. Given sufficient and accurate data, a trend line of best fit through the points of data can be calculated and/or drawn. The data fixes anchor points of the relationship of job rankings and points of market pay that represent a job value. Scattergrams are used for the calculation of ranges or to establish fixed rates. The points of intersection can represent a single position or group.

A pay line can be developed in either a linear or a curvilinear form.[172] *Pay lines of exempt positions* are usually curvilinear to reflect the reality that positions nearing the top of the hierarchy have an increasing pay differential.

Pay Grades

Pay grades, or *classifications*, are spans of similarly ranked positions to which the same rate, or range, of pay applies. They are determined with a consistent arithmetic spread among the "clumps" of ranked jobs along the horizontal axis of a scattergram display. Vertical lines of demarcation, with a consistent spread along the horizontal axis, form the width

Competitive Pay Scattergram

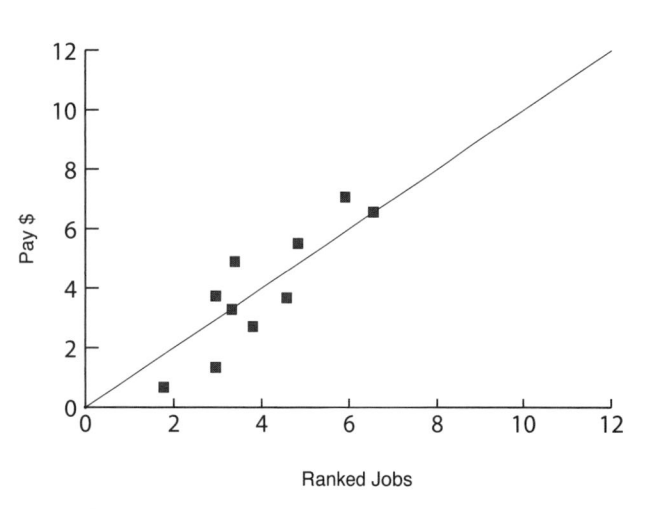

Each point represents the pay for a position with another employer against the horizontal scale of relative job value determined by the employer's ranking.

---

[172] Lance A. Berger and Dorothy R. Berger, eds., *The Compensation Handbook*, 5th ed. (New York: McGraw-Hill, 2008), 56.

(span) of the classification. Similarly determined spans of dollars on the vertical dimension will form the top and bottom of a *range* exhibited graphically as a vertical rectangular box. Manual trial and error of different lines of demarcation on the vertical of the axis is useful in order to minimize grade splits where there is little job weight distinction. Such tweaking of the arithmetic classification spreads during the original construction of a point plan can prevent a position with a score of 109 being in a higher grade than another position with a total of 108 points, an insignificant difference between two estimated points. Such diligence contributes to equity but must always be a rational standard formulation; the size of groupings must always be consistent.

The number of pay grades in the pay plan relates to the degree of pay discernment desired among positions in the hierarchy. In private-sector pay grade systems, there are often eight to twelve grades or pay ranges for nonexempt positions, or about $1,500 per increment. Exempt positions to be paid from $24,000 to $150,000 may use twelve to twenty grades, each with $7,000–$9,000 between classification midpoints.

Some federal government agencies and states have several thousand grades, with the result that differences in job difficulty and pay are minimal among grades. Some of this results from individual agencies having different, customized structures because units believe their work to be unique and incomparable to that of others. There has been strong effort to reduce the number of grades and simplify administration in the federal agencies and state governments. At the other extreme, too few grades spread pay parameters enabling lavish spending within the wide parameters and compromising cost control.

Pay Range Midpoints

Pay structure midpoints are the points of *convergence* of a job rank or *grade center point* and the survey *pay center points* for jobs in a classification. Range midpoints in much of the private sector are guidelines and not targets for specific pay points; accelerating the progress of pay can be wasteful, and, after all, a midpoint is an approximation, as is a judgment about performance. In many public sector units with pay program transparency, little cost control, and political oversight, midpoint pay is considered the norm.

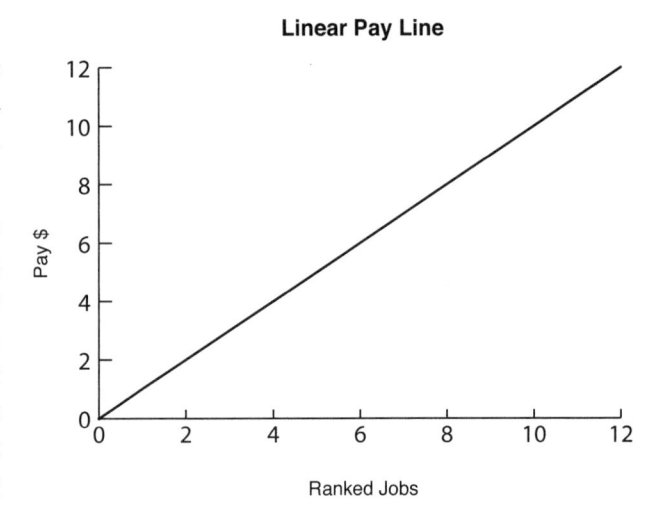

Linear Pay Line

Pay Ranges

A *grade* is along the horizontal axis and has parameters for jobs of similar difficulty. *Ranges* are the top and bottom parameters of money available for jobs in that group (grade). Pay increments on the vertical line of a diagrammed structure provide management guidance for the top and bottom of

Pay Range Structure

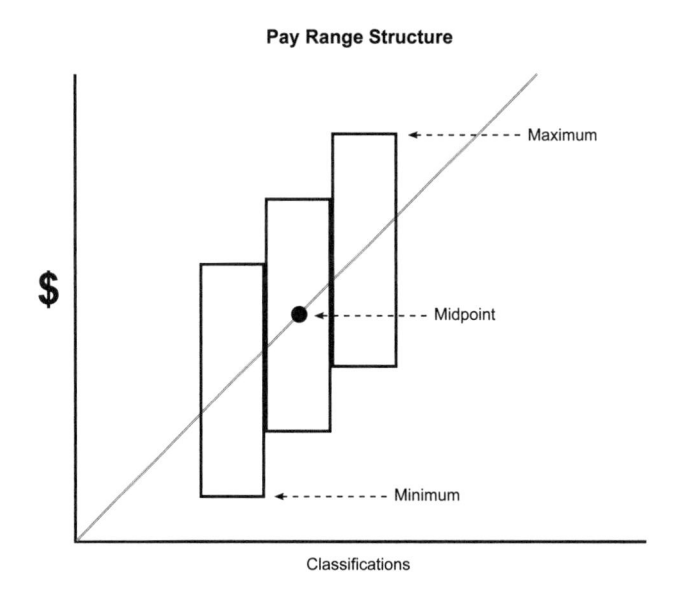

a position's pay. In the case of a single job rate scheme (a list where there are no ranges), there is a single point of normal pay.

Parameters of pay ranges serve to provide dollars for performance above the norm, allowances for lower pay for the inexperienced, and some latitude to achieve equity. Protocol is to calculate the range limits from the dollar midpoint of the classification. Normally the range of pay is about + and – 20 percent for nonexempt positions and + and – 35 percent for exempt positions. Ranges are sometimes divided into pay zones of thirds or quartiles. These segments are helpful in pay practice studies and in communication with employees; for example, "You are paid in the middle area of the range." For administrative purposes, the illustrated range-of-pay format is normally displayed in a form similar to the single-rate structure, illustrated below.

Pay Schedule

Where employees number more than a dozen, a pay schedule or pay template of range parameters in some form is constructed for reference by management and may be published as it is negotiated in union contracts. A pay schedule displays management's current wage and salary position and orderliness of the pay program. Its existence can also counter special-interest occupational survey data that employees may pull from the Internet. A typical production unit pay schedule of job rates is displayed below.

Pay Schedule
Effective January 2013

Grade	Title	Rate Range Minimum	Midpoint	Maximum
8		$13.00	$14.00	$15.00
7	Assembly Crew Leader	$12.00	$13.00	$14.00
6	Inspector / Repair Person	$11.00	$12.00	$13.00
5		$10.00	$11.00	$12.00
4	Customer Service Office Administrator	$9.00	$10.00	$11.00
3	Assembler	$8.00	$9.00	$10.00
2	Materials Handler	$7.00	$8.00	$9.00
1		$6.00	$7.00	$8.00

Vacant spots in a pay schedule indicate that there are no current positions or ranked positions at that level.

Pay Decisions

Compensation

The financial aspects of compensation costs are crucial to nonprofit and private enterprise organizations. Pay adequacy depends on the allocation and availability of dollars. In the public sector, self-serving political interests, whether overt or covert, are normally involved and can corrupt sound financial judgment. Mortimer Zuckerman, owner of the *U.S. News & World Report*, wrote that "lavish, unaffordable over-promises have been made to public service employees . . . . public unions often elect . . . politicians, who upon election, repay their benefactors by approving salaries and benefits."[173] More responsible decisions are often made at the municipal level, where there is more taxpayer influence.

Using the Pay Range

Minimum $	Midpoint	Maximum $
Zone 1	Zone 2	Zone 3
Learning Status	Satisfactory Performance	Top Performance

Pay decisions involve considerations of costs, equity and adequacy. Careless short-term pay decisions by management can have horrendous long-term cost consequences. Some practices swell costs over the years without a return on the investment. Automatic pay increase provisions for longevity (most often up to a cap[174]) obscure increasing expenses. A public sector survey found automatic increase techniques actually reflect "open-range scenarios."[175]

Supervisor Decisions

Recall that the primary pay level of an individual is based on the *marketplace value of the position*. Annual and performance pay adjustments as made by supervisors are only a relative tweaking of the substantive basic figure. Pay increases will normally occur only when a marketplace increase is implemented in the total structure. In light of that limited financial opportunity, an employee may seek an opportunity elsewhere and leave the firm. In that case, a promotional opportunity becomes available.

Influences on Pay Decisions

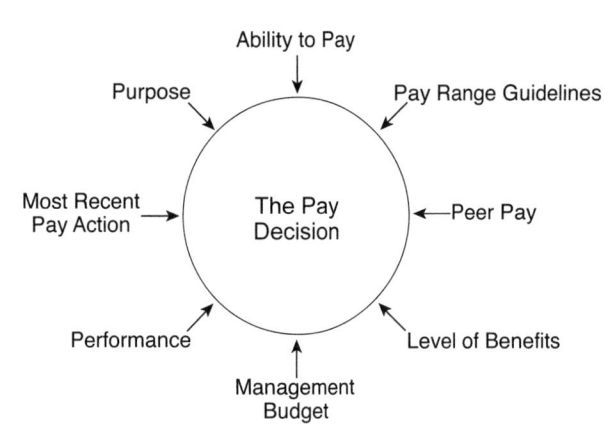

The Pay Decision is influenced by: Purpose, Ability to Pay, Pay Range Guidelines, Peer Pay, Level of Benefits, Management Budget, Performance, Most Recent Pay Action.

Most employees think of their performance as the primary consideration in pay changes; it is a matter over which they have some control. Of course, a worker's normal perception is that he or she is a good

---
[173] Mortimer B. Zuckerman, "Why We Need a New Approach to Public Unions," *U.S. News & World Report*, June 18, 2012.
[174] See Personnel Ordinance No. 30A of Carroll County, Maryland, and practices in Dorchester County, South Carolina.
[175] "2007 Total Compensation Benchmarking Survey," IPMA, http://ipma-hr.org/sites/default/files/pdf/BestPractices/Benchmarking.pdf.

performer. This personal bias among employees makes discussions about pay difficult for supervisors, particularly with employees at low-income levels.

Negotiating Wages and Salaries

Pay determination is not always within the sole purview of management; initial thinking can be affected by negotiation with an individual or a union. As with any negotiation, negotiating compensation is an effort through which two or more parties seek to maximize their personal interests or at least arrive at a satisfactory agreement.

Negotiations normally begin with an expression of a position or "wish list." Usually these positions are expressed in terms like dollar amounts or days of paid time off. However, as an exchange proceeds, there are subtle references or messages for optional possibilities. The nature of labor management discussions is presenting and justifying one's position regarding the issue and pointing out the downside of the other party's position. Over time, whether minutes or months, negotiators stress their priority points and soften their position on less critical matters in search of compromise and agreement. A position of certitude escalates the risk of negotiation failure and agreement loss. In negotiating with a union, the risks are that employees will strike or that the employer will close the doors or seek replacement workers.

Labor union contract negotiations often continue for months and, in rare cases, years. Under legal parameters, collective bargaining is to be honestly conducted in good faith to achieve an agreement about wages and benefits, hours of work and working conditions. Labor contract meetings are conducted in privacy by two teams of people "across the table," with one spokesman per team. If an agreement is not reached, it's normal for a government official, such as a mediator, to enter the scene to help the parties come to terms.

Administration

Duties and Responsibilities

Wage-and-salary administration is devoted to carrying out management's directions. The responsibilities can be assigned to unit managers, or, in larger firms, delegated to a central administrator. Decisions regarding individual pay levels generally remain with department management. The administrative duties include the defining of jobs; ranking, surveying and monitoring pay activity; and maintaining the pay guidelines. In keeping with their responsibilities, administrators will find themselves defending a job classification and applying pay range controls that interfere with a manager's desired course of action.

Structure Adjustments

Pay guidelines are normally adjusted each year or two based on increases in competitive pay levels. Normal practice is to periodically increase the pay line (midpoints) along its length by a percentage. Management might choose for pay guidelines to be higher or lower than those of the determined marketplace. Guidelines can also be set to anticipate the market or to lag behind. In the latter case, the established line is fixed at a point in time and the pay schedule becomes increasingly delinquent by a small degree until an adjustment is made.

The cost-of-living index is often mentioned relative to annual pay adjustments. Many labor contracts of an earlier era negotiated its use as a basis for automatic annual increases in pay. The cost-of-living increases as reported, however, have only a loose relationship to the annual increase in pay levels. It's not unusual to see a differential of 3 percent between the measured increase in cost of living and pay increase level. Nevertheless, while actual annual increases in pay are what compensation managers study, employees and the public equate the need for an annual increase with the cost-of-living index. Union negotiators, of course, seek to justify wage demands using consumer price index (CPI) numbers when it is advantageous to do so.

Most multi-location organizations consider pay levels for management and professional jobs recruited nationally to be sufficiently similar across the nation that one pay guideline is useable. A broad range of pay (top to bottom) in higher ranked positions permits ample latitude for employment conditions.

Pay scales for nonexempt personnel differ in locales. Pay level can differ between suburban and urban pay areas because of commuting and parking fees. Pay also differs by geography and size of community. Hourly and clerical pay is notably different among Chicago, Tulsa, Cody and Keokuk.

Special ranges are sometimes necessary to account for peculiar market or job value conditions. At different times, the market demand has been elevated for computer technicians, nurses, family doctors and commercial truck drivers, necessitating special temporary pay levels. Such situations invariably interfere with the pursuit of long-term pay equity but tend to eventually revert to a normal social structure level. Whatever supervisory or outside influences make administration temporarily troublesome, such as a temporary shortage of nurses or computer system managers, adjustments to the primary pay line should be resisted.

> **Protect the integrity of a classification list, pay line and pay system from political and temporary influences. The only basis for permanently increasing or decreasing the established rank of a position is a significant change in job content.**
>
> (Federal government rules permit changes of classifications, but when an incumbent leaves the position it "reverts to the original.")

Pay Program Anomalies

There are a number of uncommon circumstances in pay administration. Pay levels of some employees might linger at the bottom of the range because of performance or supplementary tips or consideration. A grandfathered-in employee may be red circled (above range parameters) in deference to long service. A special high salary may also exist because of someone qualified as "super skilled." A pay rate at the top of a range can be frozen until the range is increased. All of these exceptional situations intrude on cost control and equity with other jobs and genders and should be eliminated when possible.

Pay compression typically occurs when the pay of one or more employees, probably through earning incentive or overtime premium, meets or exceeds the pay of the worker's supervisor who is working a similar number of hours. A minimum spread between an employee and the supervisor is desirably 12–15 percent. It's common to relieve such compression situations by reducing or increasing the hours and/or increasing pay of one or the other. Compression can also occur when the rates of new hires, driven by market conditions, overcome the pay of those previously hired.

> **Effective pay management requires judicious pay decisions and close oversight.**

Communications about Pay

Communication of general information and principles applied to the wage-and-salary program satisfies curiosity, answers questions and demonstrates transparency. Compensation in the public sector tends to be as open as public inquiry requires. Fixed-rate scales and sales incentive plan formulas in the private sector are normally fully disclosed; however, a person's pay is considered a personal matter and is generally understood not to be disclosed to any other worker by any manager or supervisor.

Legal Compliance

Management must know and comply with state and federal wage-and-salary law. Common violations are neglect in *paying for overtime* and *gender pay inequity*. Employers must have "an acceptable business reason" for unequal pay between males and females at the same location. Inequities are under the spotlight of both the courts and lawmakers.[176] Performing work during breaks and lunchtime can also be problematic. A 2012 court decision in California established that if employees continue work under their own volition, the employer is not required to "police meal breaks and ensure no work is being performed."[177]

Summary Remarks

The pay provided for work is central to the employee-employer relationship. It must be deemed sufficient and fair by the worker and cost-effective by the employer. If not, the relationship is at risk, though there can be other compensations to aid retention.

There are large amounts of dollars involved in payrolls. The effective management of those expenditures impacts the staffing, productivity and retention of employees; legal compliance; and, in the private and nonprofit worlds, organizational survival.

---

[176] Ruben Bolivar Pagán, "Defending the 'Acceptable Business Reason' Requirement of the Equal Pay Act," *Journal of Corporation Law* 33, no. 4 (Summer 2008).
[177] California Supreme Court Case No. 8166350, April 2012.

EMPLOYEE RIGHTS
FOR WORKERS WITH DISABILITIES PAID AT SPECIAL MINIMUM WAGES
THE UNITED STATES DEPARTMENT OF LABOR WAGE AND HOUR DIVISION

This establishment has a certificate authorizing the payment of special minimum wages to workers who are disabled for the work they are performing. Authority to pay special minimum wages to workers with disabilities applies to work covered by the **Fair Labor Standards Act (FLSA), McNamara-O'Hara Service Contract Act (SCA), and/or Walsh-Healey Public Contracts Act (PCA)**. Such special minimum wages are referred to as "**commensurate wage rates**" and are less than the basic hourly rates stated in an SCA wage determination and less than the FLSA minimum wage of **$7.25 per hour beginning July 24, 2009**. A "commensurate wage rate" is based on the worker's individual productivity, no matter how limited, in proportion to the wage and productivity of experienced workers who do not have disabilities that impact their productivity when performing essentially the same type, quality, and quantity of work in the geographic area from which the labor force of the community is drawn.

WORKERS WITH DISABILITIES

For purposes of payment of commensurate wage rates under a certificate, a worker with a disability is defined as:
- An individual whose earnings or productive capacity is impaired by a physical or mental disability, including those related to age or injury, for the work to be performed.
- Disabilities which may affect productive capacity include blindness, mental illness, mental retardation, cerebral palsy, alcoholism, and drug addiction. The following do not ordinarily affect productive capacity for purposes of paying commensurate wage rates: educational disabilities; chronic unemployment; receipt of welfare benefits; nonattendance at school; juvenile delinquency; and correctional parole or probation.

KEY ELEMENTS OF COMMENSURATE WAGE RATES

- **Nondisabled worker standard**—The objective gauge (usually a time study of the production of workers who do not have disabilities that impair their productivity for the job) against which the productivity of a worker with a disability is measured.
- **Prevailing wage rate**—The wage paid to experienced workers who do not have disabilities that impair their productivity for the same or similar work and who are performing such work in the area. Most SCA contracts include a wage determination specifying the prevailing wage rates to be paid for SCA-covered work.
- **Evaluation of the productivity of the worker with a disability**—Documented measurement of the production of the worker with a disability (in terms of quantity and quality).

The wages of all workers paid commensurate wages must be reviewed, and adjusted if appropriate, at periodic intervals. At a minimum, the productivity of hourly-paid workers must be reevaluated at least every six months and a new prevailing wage survey must be conducted at least once every twelve months. In addition, prevailing wages must be reviewed, and adjusted as appropriate, whenever the applicable state or federal minimum wage is increased.

OVERTIME

Generally, if you are performing work subject to the FLSA, SCA, and/or PCA, you must be paid at least 1½ times your regular rate of pay for all hours worked over 40 in a workweek.

CHILD LABOR

Minors younger than **18 years of age** must be employed in accordance with the child labor provisions of FLSA. No persons under 16 may be employed in manufacturing or on a PCA contract.

FRINGE BENEFITS

Neither the FLSA nor the PCA have provisions requiring vacation, holiday, or sick pay nor other fringe benefits such as health insurance or pension plans. SCA wage determinations may require such fringe benefit payments (or a cash equivalent). **Workers paid under a certificate authorizing commensurate wage rates must receive the full fringe benefits listed on the wage determination.**

WORKER NOTIFICATION

Each worker with a disability and, where appropriate, the parent or guardian of such worker, shall be informed orally and in writing by the employer of the terms of the certificate under which such worker is employed.

PETITION PROCESS

Workers with disabilities paid at special minimum wages may petition the Administrator of the Wage and Hour Division of the Department of Labor for a review of their wage rates by an Administrative Law Judge. No particular form of petition is required, except that it must be signed by the worker with a disability or his or her parent or guardian and should contain the name and address of the employer. Petitions should be mailed to: Administrator, Wage and Hour Division, U.S. Department of Labor, Room S-3502, 200 Constitution Avenue, N.W., Washington, D.C. 20210.

Employers shall display this poster where employees and the parents and guardians of workers with disabilities can readily see it.

For additional information:
1-866-4-USWAGE
(1-866-487-9243)   TTY: 1-877-889-5627
WWW.WAGEHOUR.DOL.GOV

U.S. Department of Labor | Wage and Hour Division

WH 1284
Revised July 2009

Retrieved from http://www.dol.gov/whd/regs/compliance/posters/disab.htm.

Pay practices in all the economic sectors are based on several guiding principles: sufficiency of allocated finances, the primary role of competitive pay and external equity, the need for job ranking and internal equity, and the value of an established program to enable timely, uniform and consistent pay administration.

Whenever feasible, supervisors should be trained to participate in job ranking and in communicating the application of applied principles to employees in order to avoid uncertainty and to establish pay administration as a positive aspect in employment. There may not be full-time wage-and-salary specialists in small organizations, but job knowledge, internal fairness, collection of competitive pay data and compensation controls should be applied.

The success or failure of a pay system is measured by success in recruiting and retaining valued employees. However, if no one ever leaves for greater pay or opportunity, it may suggest unnecessary largesse and waste. The availability of effective job ranking and survey data, and an absence of complaints and legal issues, evidence program effectiveness.

Applicable Competencies

Discretion, ethical standards, and knowledge of jobs and laws. Skills of value include those of job analysis, ranking, survey participation and management of processes and meetings.

Applicable Resources

A compilation of wage-and-salary practices, appropriate survey data, a job ranking method, pay change forms and job descriptions. Knowledge of state payroll regulations, equal pay and any labor contract stipulations. Management support and favorable community and industry relationships.

Review Materials

Content Exercises

1. Describe the distinct advantages of incentives, profit sharing and bonuses.
2. Describe the concepts of a *benchmark job*, *ranking* and *broadbanding*.
3. List six factors common among jobs that can be compared.
4. List four job evaluation factors that are prominent in your job and two that are of little import.
5. Be able to define two of these three terms: *compensatory time*, *commission*, *variable pay*.
6. What are several negative aspects of broadbanding? A positive?
7. From among the following positions, identify two that you would think most likely to be priced on the basis of the national or local market and two probably unlikely to serve as survey benchmarks: electronic component assembler, chief financial officer, systems analyst, regional sales manager, tower crane operator, salesperson.

8. Define the term *cost of living* and explain how it is related to pay adjustments.
9. What is a term for a pay line that purposely deviates from a market pay line?
10. What are two reasons a worker's pay might linger at the bottom of the pay range?
11. Name several principal determinants of a worker's pay and several of less import.

Practical Applications

1. Determine if your employer has a written pay program, maintains job descriptions or has a method of job evaluation.
2. Inquire about the sources of outside pay data used by your employer.
3. In recent years there has been a view that some executive compensation in the private sector is excessive. Conduct research on this opinion and investigate current political winds on these situations in preparation for discussion.[178]
4. In anticipation of the next chapter, prepare a synopsis of the state workers' compensation program, or the obligations of a large employer under ERISA or COBRA.

Case-Study Discussion
Collaborative Study 6.1
Group Job Ranking Exercise

One way of ranking jobs is for a committee of unbiased participants to agree upon a ranking or number of points for a position. This short exercise exposes participants to the difficulties of job knowledge uncertainty, disagreements in consensus development, biases in the pursuit of consensus and factors used in job evaluation.

Directions

A small group of four or five participants should be gathered for the job evaluation exercise. A participant/facilitator should be determined to guide the discussions and control the time. A note taker will be necessary to record the judgments of raters. With clear direction and cooperation the exercise might be completed within an hour. Rating the first two job functions may take twenty minutes, but those remaining will require less time. The post-exercise discussion should require a second hour. Participants should be instructed by the facilitator that it's the job, and not a person, being evaluated, and that disagreements that occur can only be briefly addressed. Bias should be subdued. One of the two common jobs below should be selected. The rating template that follows should be used for rating both jobs.

---

[178] A good example of a recent article can be found at http://www.theglobeandmail.com/report-on-business/careers/excessive-executive-pay-bad-for-business/article12029730/.

Facilitator Instructions

1. Once the committee is gathered, select one of the two jobs summarized below.
2. Spend five minutes to discuss and understand the basics of the job.
3. Each participant is to independently and without discussion decide on the (numerical) degree of the five numbers across the page believed to be the most applicable.
4. After one minute, the decision of each rater should be expressed (in points) and, without comment, recorded in turn. Differences in understanding and judgment will become apparent, but there is not sufficient time to address them all.
5. After all participants' ratings are recorded, briefly explore the possibility of total agreement (but don't spend more than three minutes doing so). Proceed to the next factor. The work must move forward one factor at a time. For this exercise, the administrator must avoid solving controversies but with experience will develop skills in overcoming logjams.
6. After discussion of the ratings for each factor, a narrowing of differences should be explored. Compromise will occur, but a participant might be adamant, requiring revisiting the issue later.
7. Arrive at the total points of the six factors by individual raters and compare for the degree of variation. Individual ratings will differ but the sum of points for individuals may be similar.
8. Expect the sum of the points to be in a range of 22–28. To have all ratings within that range would be substantial accord. Exploring any ratings outside those parameters may not be time well spent.

Grocery Store Cashier

A workstation has a cash register and typical conveyor belt over which groceries and sundry items pass to be priced, registered and paid for by customers one after another; customers may use several methods of payment. Incumbent jobholders stand and drag customer purchases past a bar-code reader. Accuracy and a level of courtesy are expected. The position requires that price sheets be used on occasion, and receipts must always be provided to the customers. Incumbents are expected to respond to customers in a helpful manner about items they couldn't find or that were unavailable. Supervision and assistance is nearby.

Dental Hygienist

The workstation consists of a dental chair where dental treatment is performed. The position assists a dentist and also performs routine treatment without the dentist at the site. Incumbents stand in close proximity to patients and, by following established procedures, perform scaling, polishing, x-raying and charting of a patient's teeth. The position requires technical knowledge, and the satisfaction of federal and state regulations and licensing regarding radiation, blood-borne pathogens and waste treatment.

POINT EVALUATION TEMPLATE

POINTS TO BE AWARDED	Minimal/ Incidental 1	2	Most Jobs 3	4	Difficult/ Demanding 5
Factors					
Necessary weeks of occupational training	1	2	4	6	8
Months of work to achieve competency	1	2	4	6	8
Difficulty and frequency of judgments	0	2	4	8	10
Necessary communication skill	0	2	4	6	8
Workstation conditions	0	2	4	6	8
Physical demands	0	2	4	8	10

Concluding Discussion

Conduct a group discussion of the job rating process and experience regarding 1) misunderstandings or assumptions about position duties, 2) differences because of a participant's additional knowledge of the job, 3) the interpretation of descriptive phrases, 4) the tendency toward consensus, 5) the level of credibility and accuracy resulting from wide and knowledgeable participation and 6) the difficulty of individual rater certitude.

CHAPTER 7
BENEFITS FOR RECRUITING AND RETENTION

Chapter Objectives

- The purpose and role of benefits
- The scope of benefit programs
- Principal programs
- The value of benefits to individuals
- The importance of promoting benefit value
- Mandated programs
- The role of regulations

Considerations in Planning

Benefits represent high costs to large employers but require much less attention by small firms with minimal offerings. Employers who provide a broad scope of benefits do so to *compete in recruiting and retaining valuable employees*.[179] Four paramount group benefits play a role in U.S. employment relationships: some amount of *paid time off, retirement and savings compensation, medical care cost support* and *income replacement programs*, such as unemployment and workers' compensation, which are mandated by government.

Public-sector medical care and retirement programs are politically mandated and are generally viewed as generous, particularly at the federal level. The U.S. Bureau of Economic Analysis reports that since the turn of the century, benefits have increased about 4 percent for government workers and 2 percent for private sector employees.

There are stark differences between the "fringe" benefit packages of small and large employers. Data from the U.S. Census Bureau reveals that the public sector and large firms in the private sector (17,000 with more than 500 employees that employ a total of 60 million workers) typically offer paid time off, health insurance and retirement plans. At the time of writing, about

---

[179] A few large employers provide benefits that will be only minimally effective in this regard and might be considered a matter of paternal largesse or of not being outdone by others. Examples might include day-care services or help with transportation costs.

85 percent of organizations with more than 100 employees, and all public sector employers, enroll applicants in some form of employer-sponsored medical and retirement plans.

Small firms may only be able to grant some paid holidays and limited paid vacation. There are 4.5 million firms with fewer than ten employees that employ 20 million workers. Firms of less than fifty employees will typically not provide employer-paid medical insurance or retirement benefit programs.[180] Many of those employed in very small firms are among the 47 million (16 percent) of the population without health care insurance.[181] It's worth noting that many small growth firms in the electronic and communications industry with good profits can compete for talent on the basis of compensation packages with organizations of any size.

The national period of transition in the delivery of medical care services to our population as a result of the Affordable Care Act will probably continue for some years. Of the 85 percent of the present population with medical insurance, 60 percent are covered through programs sponsored by employers, with government programs and personal insurance plans as the primary sources for the remainder.[182]

Benefit programs were first developed during World War II. Wages were frozen and staffing difficult, so employee group insurance was offered as a recruiting tool. With the addition of other fringes over time, benefit program management and financing have become major industries. The complexity of benefit programs and the related administrative liability of employers have grown to the extent that outside specialty firms are commonly contracted as plan administrators.

Providing benefits hasn't proven to increase productivity but does improve recruiting results and the retention of employees. In that regard, those employers who have the means to make substantial contributions to benefits have some staffing advantage over those who do not. Organizations typically invest in benefit comparability with other organizations whether it is proven to be cost-effective or not. Investment decisions based on the actions of others or because of pressures from stakeholders might better be based on a *cost-to-benefit analysis*. It's possible that an attribute of an employer, such as location, prestige, or social contacts, has a particular appeal to an individual and a benefit package may not always be viewed as a paramount consideration by applicants.

Private sector employers are likely to plan some features in accord with their nature, such as profit sharing or discounts on company services. Project-based or seasonal enterprises that employ particular talent for short-term employment situations may ignore retirement or health care programs entirely in favor of providing extraordinary take-home earnings.

In most start-up situations, insurance firms of various types and purveyors of fund management, if deferred plans such as retirement are contemplated, are selected to make competitive proposals early in the formation of the business. New firms can be at a disadvantage because the costs of benefit provisions can only be estimated at the time of installation.

Government Influence

The federal government plays a large role in regulating and increasing employee group benefits in all the economic sectors. Federal and state governments have legislated a number of *social*

---

[180] "National Compensation Service: Employee Benefits in the U.S." March 2009, Bulletin 2731, Department of Labor.
[181] "Civilian Health Care Coverage." U.S. Census Bureau Press Release, September 3, 2009.
[182] National Council of State Legislatures, NCSL Overview 2011, September 2011.

welfare programs that are obligatory for employers. Unique paid holidays, such as Patriots' Day in Massachusetts and Pioneer Day in Utah, are granted for public employees.

Since employers first became obligated to collect income taxes for the federal government, government initiatives on behalf of public and private sector employees became obligations of the employer. The private sector finds it necessary to maintain a presence in the political arena in order to temper legislated costs and errant political actions.

Common Private Sector Employment Benefits

Employee Interests	Government Programs	Employer Offerings (Optional)
Income protection	Unemployment compensation / Injury compensation	Severance pay
Permanent personal injury	Social Security disability pay	Temporary disability pay until Social Security disability commences
Job rights protection	Military absence / Family leave absence / Federal jury duty	Personal leave of absence / Some jury absence time/pay
Medical care	Required personal option	Medical care insurance contribution
Paid time off	For federal and other public employees	Holidays / Vacations
Security/aging provisions	Social Security / Medicare	Profit sharing / Pension plans / Savings plans
Survivors insurance	Minor stipend upon death	Paid life insurance
Ancillary (limited)		Education assistance / Transportation assistance / Child care assistance

The Character of the Workforce

The nature and demographics of the workplace influence the composition of a group benefit system. Besides group insurance, paid time off and deferred retirement programs, which typically apply to employees in general, some plans appeal to specific groups. Day care is useful in recruiting among women, and savings plans might have a financial appeal to the older segment of the employee population.

Employees also relate to different concerns and interests at different times in their lives. An employer's contribution to retirement or a health club might be of minimal interest to a young unmarried worker, while additional paid time off or an educational experience opportunity might be attractive to these younger employees.

The complexity of addressing the needs and preferences of the workforce is partially dealt with through an annual open enrollment period required by the IRS. During a several-week period in autumn, employees have the opportunity to change benefit options because of changes in their personal circumstance. An opportunity of choice, even on relatively small matters, provides an element of tailoring benefits to fit personal needs.

Costs

Defining factors in recruiting and retention success are the *availability of dollars* for employment enhancements and the *employer's choice of investment*. In a few private firms, the benefit costs are a small percentage of total costs; in another industry, the investment may be large or unnecessary, and the planned turnover of personnel may be more cost-effective.

The cost-effectiveness of certain benefits with specific individuals at any point in time could be nil. How the costs of retirement and medical care programs are split between the employee and employer is also a consideration in plan design. Small firms more often require more contributions by employees.

The cost of benefits in large organizations is reportedly an additional 40 percent of the direct payroll costs. The U.S. Bureau of Labor Statistics reports the average benefit levels in small private-sector employers at 30 percent, which indicates less compensation for those employed in smaller firms.[183] It's uncertain whether such figures include millions of very small employers and those who are self-employed. Keep in mind that benefit costs include expenditures for those just "passing through" or making a modest contribution to an employer. Management should craft benefit offerings for maximum cost-effectiveness and be wary of using misleading information and statistics as benchmarks.

> **Benefit program offerings should be carefully studied for long-term cost consequences.**

Competitive Patterns

Most large for-profit firms exceed or follow the pattern of their industry or organizations of like size to ensure competitiveness. Public sector management seeks to be competitive with larger firms of the private sector, and charitable nonprofits usually lack the financial resources to compete with other sectors in the fringe benefit arena.

To learn the competitive landscape, industries often share general benefit information within related groups. Health insurance and retirement plans embody masses of detail and can be difficult to decipher. Sometimes consultants are employed by large firms to conduct surveys among targeted comparable firms. Small employers can often find benefit information through the Chamber of Commerce, an association of employers, or personal contacts and applicants. At the

---

[183] Retrieved from www.bls.gov/news.release/pdf/ebs2.pdf.

federal level, the Office of Personnel Management provides management survey services. Other public sector units enjoy access to similar government units, and many readily find data from county or city associations.

Flexible and Free Time

The most common of all benefit options offered in the private sector is approved personal absences, including sick days, holidays and vacation time, which provide time free from work obligations. Public sector holidays and vacations are mandated through legislative actions, and even the smallest of private employers are likely to pay for popular national holidays that fall within the normal workweek. Sometimes it's necessary to accommodate national holidays with alternative time off; retail and entertainment businesses often conduct work on holidays, and many manufacturing processes operate continuously, twenty-four hours a day, seven days a week.

Adaptable Work Schedules

One of the most appreciated benefits developing predominantly in the twenty-first century is for employers to grant flexibility with work days and hours of work. The historical pattern of manufacturing shift work and 9:00 a.m. to 5:00 p.m. office hours is still most prevalent, but there is increasing flexibility of the *location* and *time of day* that work obligations are fulfilled to accommodate the personal needs of employees. Present practices include telecommuting and flexible-hour arrangements, optional paid time-off days and compressed workweeks. Such accommodations normally provide many workers increased job satisfaction.[184] The hours on-site are normally stipulated to remain within parameters of customer needs or efficiency.

Even in a trusting employment culture, adopting programs that permit employee flexibility requires management and clear guidelines for some measure of control. *Telecommuting* requires trust and can be quantified. While the hours of work remain subject to overtime laws, OSHA does not inspect homes for compliance. Issues can surface with other employees who would like such an arrangement but whose jobs in a process may not be suitable for such adaptation. These employees should be provided with an explanation of which positions can be remote and which cannot.

Pay for Time Off

As a matter of social obligation, the federal government requires agencies to grant time off in a number of circumstances regardless of the consequences. In most cases, pay for the time off is not required, although state governments may require pay for employee time spent voting or for jury duty. Most European nations mandate that employers grant two to six weeks of paid vacation.

Virtually all U.S. employers grant some paid time off to regular full-time employees as a normal employment benefit. Patterns of paid holidays and vacations are readily found in the community or within a particular industry. Program and administrative issues in time-off matters

---

[184] *The 2009 Guide to Bold New Ideas for Making Work "Work,"* Families and Work Institute, 2009.

center on the *qualifications for eligibility*, the method of *calculating pay*, record keeping, and regulatory requirements for state and public employers. The size of the employer tends to be a factor in the number of days granted, with greater frugality among small employers.

Sick Days

Many employers provide *paid sick days*, sometimes as they are requested and sometimes within the scope of the company's personal time program. There are often three to five paid days a year available with larger employers when an employee suffers injury or illness not related to work. Sixty percent of large employers grant five days each year[185] and some states mandate a defined short-term-illness benefit for all employees.[186] Such benefits often require a qualifying time period beginning with one day after three months of employment. Skagit County (Washington) makes one paid day available each month for medical purposes, which includes the care of immediate family. It caps accrual at 120 days, but these days are not subject to cash out.

Sick leave "is intended as a form of income protection and is not to be considered as paid time off that is owed to an employee."[187] Other managements simply administer a practice of "no work, no pay." The U.S. Bureau of Labor Statistics reports that almost 40 percent of all private sector firms allow no sick pay.

Paid time-off programs (PTOs) combine the paid days an employee normally uses for illness and vacation and provides flexibility for free time. These arrangements overcome issues about the legitimacy of absences but can result in unnecessary costs through time off for non-existing illness. The number of days granted are often generous (twenty to thirty days each year) and can be used for any purpose. Policy may provide for the cashing out of unused days upon separation, which could be considered additional pay for days worked. Few such programs exist among smaller employers, where personnel costs are crucial to business success, but are common with large employers.

Long-Term Disability

LTD income plans are established for extended medical conditions and have finite qualifications similar to those of the Social Security Administration. Benefits might continue until a person becomes eligible for Social Security benefits. The plans are often funded through insurance contracts with a benefit of two-thirds of the previous base income level. In many programs, this partial pay replacement is an elective and normally requires an employee contribution.

---

[185] Kerstin Aumann, Ellen Galinsky, and James T. Bond, National Study of the Changing Workforce, "Times Are Changing: Gender and Generation at Work and at Home," (Families and Work Institute, 2008), 21.
[186] California, Hawaii, New Jersey, New York and Rhode Island mandate a defined short-term benefit.
[187] Personnel Policy and Procedure Manual (1996).

Holidays

Holiday choices are heavily influenced by national holidays,[188] the industry pattern, customer needs and the day of the week on which the holiday occurs. Employers often customize some of the dates of their paid holidays because the dates vary with days of the week and might fall on weekends. The general practice is to observe Sunday holidays on Monday, and Saturday holidays on Friday. Many organizations post the holiday schedule at the beginning of the year.

There are six "basic" holidays in the United States, but another half dozen are also popular, with a normal of about ten. Sometimes a list of holidays provides an employee option in the form of a floating holiday. States may declare pay for holidays for Jefferson Davis's birthday or Confederate Memorial Day.[189] Open and honest efforts should be made to accommodate *employee religious holidays*. If a holiday falls during a vacation period, it must be determined if the vacation is to be extended, if the day off is sacrificed or if pay is to be granted in lieu of the day.

Vacations

There is typically written vacation policy that expresses the qualifications and time-off parameters. A conservative schedule might establish eligibility of five consecutive days after completing twelve full months of active employment, and ten days after thirty-six months. One study reports that the annual average vacation used by U.S. employees is sixteen days.[190] In small private firms, it would take considerable tenure to reach that amount of paid vacation.

Administrative guidelines should explain how and when employees are to request time off and any period when vacations are prohibited. It is important to declare whether vacation accrues as service time increases each month, or if vacation is earned only after the completion of periods of time based on the employment date.

Unemployment Benefits

Employees who lose their job through no fault of their own (typically because of economic cycling) are provided employer-funded sustaining income for a limited period under state law. Each state taxes employers and has different standards for employee qualifications and compensation, though most have a waiting period of a week before benefits are paid. There are normally serious sums of employer dollars involved, and each claim needs prompt study for legitimacy. Claims may be denied if the claimant has income beyond the termination date, if sufficient hours had not been worked to qualify for the benefit, if the employee is unavailable for work or if the employee was dismissed for gross misconduct. Incompetence or some absences may not be sufficient reasons to deny a claim. Administrative expediency is a factor because the time permitted to challenge claims

---

[188] Congress dictates holidays for federal employees.
[189] Richard A. Leiter, ed., *National Survey of State Laws*, 3rd ed. (Farmington Hills: The Gale Group), 1999.
[190] Kerstin Aumann, Ellen Galinsky, and James T. Bond, National Study of the Changing Workforce, "Times Are Changing: Gender and Generation at Work and at Home," (Families and Work Institute, 2008).

is limited by regulation. A few claim-handling service firms exist, but local in-house administration can normally be accomplished in concert with other absence control efforts.

Workers' Compensation

State law also provides for a measure of income replacement when employees suffer death or personal injury by accident arising from employment. "Employment" commonly includes business travel time or off-site work completed for the employer. Insurance firms or state agencies administer the programs in accord with state regulations. Weekly payments are often about two-thirds of average wages, and employers can transfer a measure of liability to third parties (e.g., insurance carriers). These third-party administrators (TPAs) obviously have self-interests greater than they have for the employer, so at least any large-dollar settlement decisions should be studied for reasonableness. The dollars of employer cost for funding this benefit is roughly split with one-third each for medical care cost, weekly cash payments to those off work and the insurance provider.

> **Income replacement programs established by regulation and administered by third parties must be closely monitored for payment of only justified claims and the proper (cost-effective) funding or tax rate contribution.**

Injury absences are part of a total absentee control effort, and it's desirable that the worker's recovery is monitored to achieve an early return to productivity. The prompt reporting of injuries to the claim processor is necessary and can be done via Internet, mail, fax or telephone. Considering medical liability, a thorough investigation of each alleged injury or illness should be carried out with dated documentation of details and witnesses. Normally, essential administrative detail is documented on forms headed "First Report of Injury." Because there are occasionally fraudulent claims, a reliable occupational health care provider's expertise can be an asset.

In most states, employers have a contracted insurance or legal obligation to return injured workers to productive employment as soon as possible. Return-to-work assignments with limited duties are temporary and must be within medical parameters. They are often for an undetermined period without the option of termination for *temporary* medical conditions. Suitable work for which the employee is qualified is to be offered at a reasonable pay rate and duration. Personnel returning to work following an injury, and their supervisor, should have a full understanding of the essential duties of the work and of the physical restrictions and capabilities that have been determined by medical professionals.

The actual and potential costs of health care service, disrupted production, mishandled work as a result of employee absence, unwarranted financial settlements and fraud all suggest attentive management of workers' compensation situations.[191] Even more preferable is preventing injuries to human assets (see chapter 8).

---

[191] John Remington et al, *Human Resources Law,* 5th ed. (Upper Saddle River: Prentice Hall, 2011), 157.

Unpaid Personal Absence (Not Medical)

Occasionally, employees request unpaid time off with the opportunity to return, for educational, bereavement, travel or other personal situations. Large organizations with some workforce flexibility often establish permissive policies for such circumstances. Smaller firms with fewer staffing options prefer to avoid policy commitments and deal with each request individually.

Jury Duty

When employees are summoned for jury duty, most employers make every effort to provide the time off, but some resist granting time off for state court service. A summons can be appealed, and depending on the nature of the reasoning can be retracted. One estimate of the U.S. Bureau of Labor Statistics reports that almost 90 percent of employers permit non-prejudicial absences for such civic duty. Employers of exempt personnel continue their pay if the duty occurs during a week in which they work. No federal law requires pay to nonexempt personnel, except federal employees, who receive regular pay when serving on juries. Many employers provide a supplement to nonexempt personnel for jury pay in order to protect employee earnings. In New York, employers with more than ten employees are to pay nonexempt employees for the first three days of jury service.

Military Duty Absence

It's public policy to encourage voluntary or involuntary service in any of the Armed Forces, including National Guard units. Discrimination against those who accept military obligations is prohibited. Except in emergencies, an employee is obligated to give his or her employer as much advance notice of a required absence as possible. The employer must consider the employee to be on an approved absence during military duty, but pay is not required. An employer cannot refuse to allow an employee time off to attend obligatory drills or training. The employee is entitled to elect to continue health coverage during military leave for up to eighteen months and is to accrue vacation pay during military leave.

Upon termination of military leave, which can continue for up to five years, the employee is generally entitled to reemployment in the position he or she would have attained had there not been absence for duty. If service is longer than 180 days, the employee's application for reinstatement must be filed within ninety days of completion of duty. The Uniformed Services Employment and Reemployment Rights Act (USERRA) governs employers' responsibilities to such employees and should be the source of information for administrative purposes. Veterans Affairs public-service volunteers have been known to place advocacy before technical accuracy, so the written (legal) word should be used rather than electronic inquiries. The law applies to all employers.

Family and Medical Leave

Most employees of large and midsize organizations are entitled by law to unpaid leaves of absence for serious personal and family medical reasons. The time off is intended to help employees balance their work and family obligations. Employees are permitted to use the time in an intermittent manner, such as being absent during certain hours of the day. The benefit is largely unused because the time off is normally unpaid, and people will often use any paid time-off options, such as personal or vacation days, before opting for unpaid time.[192] Employers can require that accrued days of absence be used first. Those on approved leave continue to accrue service seniority and benefits.

Providing a job guarantee for an uncertain and/or extended time normally creates a staffing problem for the employer, but this is of no consequence under the law. The probability that an employee will not be returning is also immaterial; the job or its equivalent must be available upon the employee's return. Be warned that an employer cannot threaten job loss of employees for exercising their leave rights.[193] Any retaliation is also specifically prohibited.

The Family and Medical Leave Act (FMLA) guarantees employees twelve weeks of leave with employment reinstatement during any twelve-month period, to be used for birth or adoption of a child; to care for a spouse, child or parent who has a serious health condition; or for treatment of a serious condition disabling the employee for at least three days. The families of employees who are serving in an active military capacity are covered by amendment HR 498, which extends benefits for needs of military families "to care for" a service member.

A legitimate absence is one that requires inpatient care at a hospital or continuing care by a licensed health care provider for such matters as heart conditions, appendicitis, pneumonia and pregnancy. Illnesses such as the flu, earaches, headaches, upset stomachs and cosmetic surgery do *not* qualify for FMLA. An employer's rejection of a chiropractor for not being a qualified health care provider in California was overturned.[194]

About 40 percent of the nation's workforce and 300,000 institutions are subject to this mandated benefit. A covered employer under the FMLA is one that has employed more than fifty employees for twenty or more calendar workweeks in the current or preceding calendar year. Some states have lowered this threshold; for example, Minnesota has a statute that covers employers with twenty-one employees or more. Employees are eligible if they have been employed by the employer for at least twelve consecutive months and have worked at least 1,250 hours in the twelve-month period immediately preceding the request for leave.

Employers covered by FMLA are required to broadcast FMLA rights to employees in three ways: (1) by posting a notice, (2) by providing FMLA information in a written handbook or a similar document and (3) by giving the employee notice of his or her obligations once a medical absence begins, or be subject to the damages suffered by the employee.[195]

The administration of the FMLA can involve Americans with Disabilities Act considerations. The leave can run concurrently with workers' compensation and may also involve collective bargaining provisions, all of which necessitate simultaneous compliance. Make note that if an absence control plan exists, an employee on both workers' compensation and FMLA can be required to come to the worksite to report their condition. Covered employers are wise to use available resources to ensure knowledgeable administration.

---

[192] California mandates six weeks of pay and New Jersey requires two-thirds of pay for six weeks.
[193] *James Daugherty v. Sajar Plastics, Inc.*, U.S. Court of Appeals No. 06-4608 (6th Cir. October 16, 2008.
[194] *Faust v. California Portland Cement* (Ca. Ct. App. May 10, 2007).
[195] *Ragsdale v. Wolverine World Wide, Inc.*, 535 U.S. 181 (122 S. Ct. 1155 March 19, 2002).

U.S. Department of Labor
Wage and Hour Division

(Revised 2012)

Fact Sheet #28: The Family and Medical Leave Act

The Family and Medical Leave Act (FMLA) entitles eligible employees of covered employers to take unpaid, job-protected leave for specified family and medical reasons. This fact sheet provides general information about which employers are covered by the FMLA, when employees are eligible and entitled to take FMLA leave, and what rules apply when employees take FMLA leave.

COVERED EMPLOYERS

The FMLA only applies to employers that meet certain criteria. A **covered employer** is a:
- Private-sector employer, with 50 or more employees in 20 or more workweeks in the current or preceding calendar year, including a joint employer or successor in interest to a covered employer;
- Public agency, including a local, state, or Federal government agency, regardless of the number of employees it employs; or
- Public or private elementary or secondary school, regardless of the number of employees it employs.

ELIGIBLE EMPLOYEES

Only eligible employees are entitled to take FMLA leave. An **eligible employee** is one who:

- Works for a *covered employer*;
- Has worked for the employer for at least *12 months*;
- Has at least *1,250 hours* of service for the employer during the 12 month period immediately preceding the leave*; and
- Works at a location where the employer has at least *50 employees within 75 miles*.

* Special hours of service eligibility requirements apply to airline flight crew employees. *See* Fact Sheet 28J: Special Rules for Airline Flight Crew Employees under the Family and Medical Leave Act.

The 12 months of employment do not have to be consecutive. That means any time previously worked for the same employer (including seasonal work) could, in most cases, be used to meet the 12-month requirement. If the employee has a break in service that lasted seven years or more, the time worked prior to the break will not count *unless* the break is due to service covered by the Uniformed Services Employment and Reemployment Rights Act (USERRA), or there is a written agreement, including a collective bargaining agreement, outlining the employer's intention to rehire the employee after the break in service. *See* "FMLA Special Rules for Returning Reservists".

LEAVE ENTITLEMENT

Eligible employees may take up to **12 workweeks** of leave in a 12-month period.

Source: U.S. Department of Labor

Health Care

The Scope

Health care is a major concern, increasingly so as families grow and people age. Employer group insurance plans provide a range of medical care, including doctor visits, medicine, hospitalization and surgery to an estimated 150 million workers. The contribution of employers to employee and family health care costs is valued highly and is a strong appeal in recruitment and retention. It's probable that with increased health care benefits under the Affordable Care Act, its significance as a recruiting advantage will diminish among employers with modest plans.

Plans vary in construct, but all provide similar medical care to different degrees and costs. (Dental and vision coverage are often limited.) Employees normally can choose one level of benefit or another. Some insurance plans, such as Blue Cross, are offered on the basis of a *fee for service*, and other providers collaborate in *preferred provider* consortiums, which service about 60 percent of covered employees. Health maintenance organizations (HMOs) provide a range of services from specific care providers for a *fixed fee*, servicing 20 percent of covered employees. A few large employers presently self-fund their benefits without an insurer but normally do insure for catastrophic cost claims.

Current Status

The scheme of health care in the U.S. is undergoing extensive revision as the result of the Patient Protection and Affordable Care Act (PPACA, PL 111-148) enacted in 2010. A national health care system will form in the years and decades ahead as a result of that legislation. In its present form it provides that employees and employers can maintain the traditional employer-sponsored insurance or either party can withdraw from that arrangement. Employees will have individual insurance opportunities from which to choose, or must pay a tax. The objective is to maximize insurance protection for the nation's citizenry. Whatever choices are made by employers and employees, the employer investment in the combined medical benefit and direct pay can be expected to remain substantially the same; in other words, previous levels of direct pay increases may be tempered if there are greater contributions to health care benefits.

Costs

Costs are a paramount factor in all benefit offerings but particularly for medical care plans. A notable amount of that cost results from government mandates for eligibility and required care. The approximate annual insurance cost for a single employee is about $5,500 and $15,000 for a family.[196] Private sector firms with health plans reportedly paid an average of $10,730 in 2011, according to benefit consultants Towers Watson.

Cost control starts at initial plan design. At that point, certain coverage options can be excluded or the expenses for a treatment limited.

---

[196] Kaiser Family Foundation Report 2011.

Personalizing Coverage

Large employers frequently install plan features with which employees can save money by channeling dollars to specific expense areas. This is a popular benefit-personalization tactic valuable to an employee and cost-effective for the employer. A *flexible spending account* (FSA) permits the direction of improved coverage for dependent care or additional survivors insurance rather than for dental care. A *health savings plan* can have pre-tax money deducted for application to future out-of-pocket expenses. Both the employee and employer gain a small tax advantage under present IRS rules. These programs obviously apply where a breadth of benefit possibilities exist. They are often foreign to employees of small firms where there is no health care benefit.

    Many large employers also provide in-house health care programs as an option for employees. Toyota, Disney, Pepsi and some public employers provide clinics to carry out preventive programs like education and inoculations, and doctors and nurses are available to minimize the time employees may spend seeking medical attention. More firms provide only supplemental educational programs at no expense to employees, or opportunities for programmed physical exercise through low-cost fitness center memberships. Sometimes financial incentives are offered to promote employee fitness and reduce potential insurance costs. Typically there is a small but appreciative group of people who take advantage of these opportunities.

Health Insurance Continuation

Employees who enjoy medical insurance normally have the opportunity to continue their insurance for themselves and dependents for a period of eighteen months at their own expense upon termination. Termination for misconduct is a disqualifying event for COBRA.

Health Privacy

The need to protect the *privacy of employee medical information* is not only a matter of ethics but law. Many state laws address the subject of access to personal records. Controlling medical and other personal information requires established recordkeeping procedures and attentive oversight.

> **Employers that have access to personal health information are subject to strict regulations regarding information privacy.**

    Required procedures for ensuring the privacy and security of health information are found in HIPAA[197] and HITECH[198] legislation. These regulations establish guidelines for securing patient confidentiality and standardizing an electronic interchange of data. All health care providers, health organizations and government health plans that use, store, maintain or transmit patient health care information are required to comply with the privacy regulations of HIPAA.

---

[197] The Administrative Simplification provisions under Title II of the Health Insurance Portability and Accountability Act.
[198] The Health Information Technology for Economic and Clinical Health Act.

Information indiscretion is particularly challenging in medical care facilities. In recent years, a group of California hospitals was fined $800,000 for breaches of file security, two hospitals in Minnesota fired thirty-two employees and in Everett, Washington, thirteen employees were dismissed for mishandling personal medical information.

Survivors Insurance

A common benefit is insurance on the life of an employee during his or her period of employment. The amount is often linked to the level of pay or is a common amount for all in a group. The insurance is usually a modest amount, which is paid to a beneficiary designated by the employee. Sometimes employees have the option of purchasing an additional amount of coverage at their own expense. Almost all such insurance is term insurance that exists only during employment and has no cash value except upon death during employment. A lesser amount of insurance for dependents is sometimes offered at the expense of the employee.

An accidental death and dismemberment (AD&D) benefit may also be offered. This benefit provides additional cash if the employee's death is accidental or if there is loss of a limb. These term insurance benefits are considerably less costly than most benefits. Some states provide an elevated survivors benefit to public safety personnel killed in the line of duty.

Retirement and Deferred Income Plans

Employee retirement is normally financed over the years through Social Security, accumulated personal funds, and employer pension or savings plan participation. Social Security and pension benefits are determined by the years of work and earnings level. Other voluntary plans, such as profit sharing and private-sector savings plans, are subject to benefit variability given their dependence on the employer's financial results. Beginning in the latter years of the previous century, the number of employer-sponsored savings plans increased markedly, while pension plans have declined.

Retirement benefit plans are promulgated through legal and trust documents and involve finance institutions, IRS determinations, beneficiary designation records, account records and reports to the government. The complex requirements and continual changes in regulations require considerable expertise, mostly provided by service firms that manage and administer benefit plans for employers as a third-party business.

If pension, profit sharing, savings, individual retirement account and stock bonus plans meet stringent regulations, they are permitted to be *qualified plans* and enjoy significant tax advantages to the employer and participants. One regulation is that plans can't discriminate in favor of highly compensated employees.

Plans must specify an approved schedule of qualifying for benefits. Vesting is a feature whereby employees become entitled to an increasing percentage of their benefits over time with an employer. Historically, pension plans were designed to develop benefits at a rate that would help retain workers over many years. Today, as the result of political action, the least liberal vesting schedule allowed by law is 20 percent per year. Employees receive the vested portion of their accounts at termination, disability, death or retirement. Distributions from funds may be made in a lump sum or in installments over a period of years. If employees become disabled or die, beneficiaries can receive the vested portion immediately.

The federal government provides its employees the opportunity to participate in three primary retirement plans: a basic pension plan, Social Security and a Thrift Savings Plan.

Pension Plan Construct

A pension plan is established and maintained by an employer to provide for the payment of a known *retirement benefit* to employees for a time period of the employee's choice after a fixed number of years of service. A formula determines the specific dollar benefit based on contributions by the employer. A monthly benefit might be calculated using a dollar figure ($30) times the years of service (20) to equal the total ($600) monthly stipend.

Pension plans, popular in the twentieth century, are totally funded by the employer in good times and bad. Many millions of union workers are pension plan participants; in the private sector, only 16 percent of workers are enrolled in such plans. Employers prefer savings plans without a fixed financial commitment. A single plan, common to a single industry or union, can involve a number of employers.

Pension plans among state and local government units take several forms, but are funded through legislative action. The system used in Minnesota, where a single public-employee fund applies to all city, county and state employees other than teachers, who have a separate retirement plan fund, is typical. Similarly, fire protection and police often have segregated funds. New York State has eight plans for different public employee groups.[199]

Savings Plan Construct—401(k) and 403(b)

Today, the most popular plans for long-term savings are 401(k) or 403(b) savings plans, which can provide for both employer and employee contributions of pre-tax dollars. The common 403(b) or 401(k) designations relate to sections of the enabling legislation. Under these plans, participants select a limited percentage of their compensation to contribute to savings and makes a choice of how the monies are invested. Funds can be invested in several different types of financial instruments with different degrees of financial risk, including an annuity that will guarantee a fixed level of income.

These plans provide methodical personal savings and significant tax savings for the employees' benefit. Depending on the plan design, neither the employee nor employer may have an obligation to contribute. Often, an employer will match at least a portion of the employee's contributions to achieve a blended and larger end result. For example, an employer could contribute a 50 percent match of the employee's contributed dollars to a maximum of 4 percent of the participant's compensation each year. Private and nonprofit employers can automatically enroll new employees (who have the option of declining), which serves to increase plan participation.

---

[199] E. J. McMahon, "Defusing New York's Pension Bomb," Empire Center for NY State Policy Research Bulletin, June 7, 2006.

The nation's largest retirement plan is the federal Thrift Savings Plan (TSP), with 86 percent participation by 4 million employees, including postal and military personnel, and $200 billion in funds.[200] It is free of ERISA regulations but is secured by the resources of the federal government. Participation by public employees in 403(b) plans has always been high. State and local plans include 20 million participants who are funded with $7 million.[201] The Department of Labor reports that 401(k) plans in the private sector have 72 million participants with accrued financial assets of $3 trillion.

Deferred savings can also be financed through profit-sharing contributions of private sector employers. Further information about these plans is found later in this chapter.

Individual Retirement Account (IRA) Construct

These arrangements exist primarily to provide self-employed individuals with a tax-advantaged method of saving. There are limits to how much individuals can contribute to their account on an annual basis, and the dollars and investment returns may be taxed as income upon withdrawal.

Federal Social Security

The Old-Age, Survivors, Disability, and Health Insurance (OASDHI) program was established to provide aging and disabled Americans with sustaining income, and is now commonly known as Social Security. Benefits are financed by employee and employer contributions and are distributed to *retirees* (69 percent), *disabled workers* (17 percent) and *survivors* of a deceased worker (14 percent). For many older Americans, Social Security is their only source of income (20 percent). The Social Security Administration and the Internal Revenue Service are jointly responsible for administration.

Ancillary Benefits

While health care, retirement and time-off benefits are the most common and heavily used, other benefit offerings, such as those described below, are common among the nation's employers.

Employee Assistance Programs (EAPs)

It is increasingly understood that people suffer mental and emotional health issues as well as those physical in nature. Employee assistance programs (EAPs) are popular employer-sponsored counseling programs designed to provide assessments of individuals and make referrals to professional services for employees and their families. The larger the organization, the more likely such a benefit plan will exist. These programs are not unlike urgent care in our normal medical system—a diagnostic initiative. They can provide treatments for a specific concern (e.g., for an issue such as substance abuse) or for a broad range of issues.

---

[200] Doug Halonen et al., "Federal Thrift Becomes Top Dog," *Pensions and Investments* 37, no. 3 (February 9, 2009): 1–28.
[201] GAO, "State and Local Government Retiree Benefits: Current Funded Status of Pension and Health Benefits," GAO-08-223 (January 29, 2008).

Under a typical EAP, the employer contracts with a third party to provide services or refer employees for problems related to substance abuse, parenting, grief, stress, adoptions, marriage, litigation or finances. Institutions that provide EAPs as an employee benefit believe that the expense is justified by reduced health care and absenteeism costs and increased productivity.

Educational Support Programs

Educational support programs normally provide assistance to full-time employees through in-house seminars or offer reimbursements for books, tuition and fees to attend outside educational programs. Programs often require classes to be work- or degree-related and participants to have one year or more of employment to qualify.

Employee Stock Ownership Plans (ESOP)

An employee stock ownership plan is a benefit provided by private firms that awards employer stock to accounts of individual employees. The amount of stock each individual receives is typically based on compensation level, years of service or both. The perceived value and consequence of such plans are usually minor in large firms, but can be meaningful to long-service employees in small, stable companies. The intention of such plans is to establish a financial partnering affiliation with employees and to become, in part, "an employee-owned company" more than to provide significant retirement savings.

Profit Sharing

A profit-sharing plan is established by an employer to share financial success with employees in order to win their allegiance, generate motivation or as a reflection of personal values. The employer makes an annual discretionary contribution of profits to an account of each employee, usually based on the compensation level of each participant. A trust invests the monies, the results of which hopefully bring advantageous financial gains for the employees. The sharing of financial returns with employees in the form of ESOP and profit sharing is most meaningful when such programs are an element in *a partnering culture*.

Others

Financial accounting is unreasonable or administratively impractical in cases of certain events and incidental gratuities, which can be granted as *de minimis* fringe benefits. Examples include holiday events and gifts (if not cash), occasional tickets to sporting or other events, coffee and doughnuts, lunch or occasional use of office equipment. There are specific taxation standards for gift certificates and eating facilities.

Organizations often provide meeting space for events with outside interest groups, such as civic activities or charitable causes. Be cautious in accommodating groups with political, religious or racial overtones because of the precedent set and/or an appearance of favoritism.

Non-financial Benefits

Employees frequently benefit in the form of psychological or non-financial satisfaction as a result of performing their work. People can develop strong bonds and satisfactions through their work, relationships with supervisors or the organization's value system. Such individual feelings and the degree to which they exist or affect behavior and productivity can be difficult to discern. (See chapter 5 for information on enabling employee performance.)

Non-financial benefits can often be more fully realized with small employers because of the likelihood of close personal relationships, a variety of duties or, by necessity, a role of responsibility. A view of the workplace is an individual matter, and a single positive aspect will often trump more pay or time off. The majority of research about workers overlooks the largest number of employees who are employed in our small commercial enterprises, so reported studies are misleading.

Communicating Benefit Value

The value of benefits is in the eyes of the beneficiary. Individuals react to what appeals to them and what they understand. An investment return on benefits can be increased by management efforts to communicate the advantage and value of ancillary compensation to the employee and their family members. A MetLife survey in 2010 indicated that benefit communication efforts *do* result in positive employee satisfaction.

Large employers may communicate through interactive computer programs, individual benefit (or "total reward") statements or review meetings. Obscure benefits, such as free downtown parking, survivors insurance, and excessive weeks of vacation that benefit very few, have little impact.

Public and large company personnel take generous benefits for granted. Employees who spend their work life in large organizations often assume that other workers enjoy similar vacation periods, health care, day care and paid sick days. The disparity in workplace benefits can be used to advantage by those with generous benefit packages.

Employees should understand the scope and value of even secondary compensation programs. The value of workers' and unemployment compensation as income security are worthy subjects of communication efforts. A structured pattern of publishing educational materials and announcements of improvements at group meetings can be helpful.

Most programs and their provisions involve detail. Educational efforts must consider the impatience of some and limited ability of others in absorbing material. Many employers rely on *third-party administrators* to answer questions, but alternative tactics should also be employed to cultivate education and appreciation and connect the benefits availability with the management. The Employee Retirement Income Security Act (ERISA) requires plan administrators to communicate regularly with participants and beneficiaries about the benefits to which they are entitled. These communications are also filed with the federal government.

A *summary plan description* provides adequate information to medical plan participants and beneficiaries to ensure that they understand important provisions. The document must include information on benefits, trustees and eligibility, instructions on filing claims and a description of the participant's rights. A retirement plan annual report to participants, Form 5500, is filed with the government.

Benefit explanations and messages must be absolutely correct. Indeed, overstating a benefit could result in a legal decision to provide the misstated excess. Disclaimers should be used to limit liability of expressions whether in conversations or in writing.

Administration

Benefit administration matters begin at the time of hire with the initial plan enrollment and continue throughout the period of employment and commonly thereafter. Benefit education, enrollment, recordkeeping, employee notifications, claims processing and other details all require *forms*, *procedures* and *practices*. A plan administrator must have copies of the plan description, the latest annual report, and copies of documents available at all times for examination by participants and beneficiaries.

> **Each group benefit plan has a basic legal plan document that provides the legal basis for administration and decisions.**

Many employee benefit plans of employers with more than 100 employees fall under protective provisions of ERISA, a federal law administered through the Department of Labor and IRS that governs pension and welfare benefit plans sponsored by private and nonprofit sector employers. ERISA does not mandate any employee benefits but it controls and specifies regulations for those plans implemented. ERISA prohibits certain financial transactions by trustees with funds in their care and requires identification of those individuals and entities with fiduciary responsibilities to participants of the plan. There have been some profit-sector employers that have failed to meet their pension-funding obligations, resulting in ERISA establishing the Pension Benefit Guaranty Corporation (PBGC) to ensure pension plan commitments. This legislation also establishes extension requirements of employers to communicate the financial status of plans to participants.

The complexity of employee benefit plan management, with its myriad details and provisos, can only be fully understood through legal examination of the formal plan documents. These include trust documents, insurance contracts, summary plan descriptions, handbooks and other required mailings to employees, IRS qualification determination letters, forms (enrollment, beneficiary designation claims), notices (COBRA), government report forms, investment and third-party administrator agreements, employee status records and more.

Most employers have shed the administration of medical and retirement plans to third-party administrator firms. An employer's decision to outsource specific duties is usually because of the extent of the distraction from primary organizational pursuits and the absence of the necessary time. A third-party administrator can help with selecting insurance carriers and investment firms, employee communications, disbursements, legal compliance and the filing of reports. Third-party claim processing relieves the employer of administrative violations and unpleasant disputes. As with other contracts for outside services, a business agreement should fix the accountability for fulfilling the employer's legal obligations and any financial obligations.

Summary Remarks

Principal employee benefits are paid time off, contributions to health care insurance, retirement or savings programs and those mandated by governments. The most prized by the vast majority of workers is health-care cost assistance. The disparity of employee benefits based on economic sectors, financial conditions and size of employers is extreme; there are "haves" and "have-nots." The public sector and large private sector firms satisfy obligations and then offer more benefits involving substantial costs. Small private and nonprofit organizations might offer only several days of time off with pay during the year.

The primary purpose of employee benefits is to be competitive in recruiting and retention, but there are extreme programs that go beyond those objectives. Any benefit program should be based on a study of cost relative to value in the particular workforce. The appeal of a benefit is related to individual differences and circumstances.

Some organizations constantly promote the value of the programs they offer; many others, after initial orientation and enrollment, do not. Small firms can win positive and close partnering relationships with employees through non-financial benefits like participation in decisions, the granting of influence and responsibility, and the assignment of desirable work.

Benefits management, with its extensive detail and legal aspects, is a challenging specialization, beginning with original plan design and cost projections and then dealing with plan, legal or tax changes. Health-care insurance contracts, pension and savings plan regulations, and, considering the Family and Medical Leave Act, even time-off administration are complex and create legal exposure for employers.

One measure of benefits management effectiveness is the degree of success in recruiting and retention. Positive input from employees and timely services suggest effectiveness, as does an absence of administrative errors or any regulatory violations.

Applicable Competencies

Effective administrative skills, understanding benefit options and applicability, cost consciousness, and the communication skills to promote the value of the plans.

Applicable Resources

Access to investment, administration, fiduciary, plan design and legal expertise. Familiarity with applicable ERISA provisions and requirements. Knowledge of competitive circumstances, benefit plan documents, and descriptive terms and implications.

Review Materials

Content Exercises

1. Define the following: *COBRA*, *FSA*, *TPA*, *ESOP* and *PBGC*.
2. A time-off policy may use the expressions *pay in lieu of* and *accrued*. Be prepared to explain these terms.
3. Name three methods through which an employer should notify employees of their FMLA rights.
4. What is the greatest average number of employees an employer can have without being subject to the FMLA?
5. Why might a bulletin board posting be more effective for announcing holidays than listing them in a handbook?
6. Be prepared to explain the differences among pension, 401(k), 403(b), profit sharing, retirement and savings plans.

Practical Applications

1. How does your employer track, record and/or report the days of time off for nonexempt and exempt personnel?
2. Does your state have laws requiring paid or unpaid time off for jury duty or voting? Explain.
3. Share information about one long-term disability benefit, employee assistance plan, or the existence of health reimbursement or flexible benefit opportunity with your employer.
4. Examine your benefit plans and define your eligibility for two of the following benefits: vacation, paid holiday, medical care, 401(k), 403(b) or pension.
5. Explain your employer's sick-day pay and any control practices.
6. Outline the purpose or general subject matter of a medical summary plan description, FMLA policy or COBRA notice letter.
7. Report on the primary eligibility requirements, disqualifying factors and pay provided by workers' compensation or unemployment insurance in your state.
8. What are the cost factors that determine the premiums or taxes for workers' and unemployment compensation in your state?
9. At your workplace, how is vacation time determined and what is the basis of pay? Does it accrue? Is it paid at termination, including dismissal? Is there a state statute about vacation pay at termination?
10. What is the practice of your employer regarding light duty after a work injury, if such situations arise? What does statute or the insurance contract say about an employer's obligation and employees' rights in regard to workers' compensation light-duty work opportunities?

11. What major changes have transpired in the health care benefits of employers nationally since passage of the federal health care law in 2010? What shifts have occurred in coverage, costs and benefits? What state and national political issues remain?

Case-Study Discussion

Discussion Exercise 7.1

Workplace Health Care Changes

This case is designed to consider and evaluate the current conditions of employee medical care benefits against the conditions that existed prior to 2010. For decades, generous group health care plans for employees had been established in large institutions and firms, commonly providing insured doctor, hospital, and prescription care, and sometimes vision and dental care, for employees who made modest contributions to the costs. Mid-sized private sector firms, with somewhat more cost sharing by employees, typically used insurance firms for financing basic health care plans, which frequently did not include vision and dental care. Very small firms commonly did not offer any health care benefits.

Research and prepare for discussion, necessarily in general terms, a comparison of the present patterns of workforce health care benefits in both large and small employers with the conditions that existed in 2010. Make a note of your information sources.

Examine different sizes of employers: those with more than 500 employees, employers with about fifty workers and those with fewer than five employees. Consider changes in:

- Patterns in coverage of employee benefits
- Employer and employee costs
- Claim filing and processing
- The percentage or character of the uninsured population

CHAPTER 8
SAFEGUARD THE HUMAN RESOURCE

Chapter Objectives

- The obligations of employers
- Advantages of an injury-free workplace
- The scope of regulations and standards
- The format of a safety program
- Methods of preventing accidents

Workplace Health Threats

Introduction and Scope

Our daily existence is subject to health hazards, including accidents and various viruses. We create some of our own hazards too, such as mismanaged cruise ships and automobiles that go too fast. We reduce the risks we may encounter with protections like storm shelters and home security systems; the government takes a role through such actions as mandating automobile seat belts and life jackets in boats.

There is a need for precautions in workplaces, too. Each year more than 4,500 workers are killed on the job, with a ratio of about ten private sector employees to one civilian public sector employee.[202] Almost 4 million reportable (professionally treated) injuries occur each year, a third of which are in manufacturing and construction industries with the remainder in the service sector, with notable percentages in retail and health care.[203] Clearly, while every employer has responsibilities for employee safety, the industrial venues face far greater challenges in preventing injuries than do office environments.

Particularly dangerous occupations are in commercial fishing, forestry, and iron and steel construction. Transportation workers, including drivers and pilots, have a high rate of fatalities, and pharmacies are increasingly subject to robbery and violence. Injuries are most prevalent in meat processing (knives and saws), foundries (molten metal) and health care work (physical exertion). Injuries are often strains and sprains, falls, lacerations and punctures. Backs and hands are frequent points of bodily injury. Drugs and alcohol play a role in about a third of the incidents. The Bureau of Labor Statistics provides such data.

---

[202] U.S. Department of Labor, Bureau of Labor Statistics, October 25, 2012.
[203] Ibid.

The federal government's record with preventing injuries in workplaces is relatively enviable in comparison with that of the rest of the world. Sadly, "over one million work-related deaths occur annually and hundreds of millions of workers suffer from workplace accidents. . . . 12 million children are injured in workplaces each year, around 12,000 of them fatally"[204] around the world. Moreover, "occupational health and safety laws cover only about 10 percent of the people in developing countries, omitting many hazardous industries and occupations."[205]

There is progress, led not by the United Nations or a nation's leadership, but by importers and buyers of products. The European Union, as well as the United States, has fixed standards for safety, sanitation and the use of child labor in purchasing agreements. To enter the international marketplace, at least most manufacturers in developing countries must adopt safety and quality standards in their production that is acceptable to Western (and Japanese) standards. When the economic condition of a country is at a lower level and considered to be "undeveloped," the presence of effective workplace safety is rare.[206]

In the U.S., employers have *statutory responsibilities* for the health and safety of their workers. History demonstrates that until the federal government legislated illness and injury prevention standards, acceptable safety precautions in workplaces would generally have a low priority. Contemporary employers are expected to anticipate threats and disasters and provide prevention steps and provisions for evacuation and medical care. In some segments of the economy, safe practices are integral to activity, as with the routine use of construction hard hats, maritime life preservers and vehicle backup alarms. Safety precautions and regulations are totally ignored in many offices.

Safety planning and activity begins before a business is launched or an office opened. Present or potential hazards should be listed and alleviated. The facility should meet local fire protection and sanitation ordinances. The purchase and installation of equipment requires attention to innate hazards; purchased chemicals must be evaluated for toxicology and protective equipment for suitability. Exit signage and clear pathways must be provided. Employees new in a workplace must be informed of hazards and instructed on how to avoid injury.

Management's motivation for safeguarding employees is not only to send people home in a healthy condition, but also to *protect a valuable asset* and *prevent impediments to the organization's pursuit of its purpose*. Maintaining systems that keep the organization active and free of disruption contributes to its continuing existence. The full utility of a worker is obviously compromised when an injury or illness occurs. Then, too, there are the *costs* of accidents.

Every employer must prepare for the emergency care and treatment of personnel.[207] Security, facility maintenance or personnel units are commonly assigned safety responsibilities. Regardless

---

[204] Remarks by Jukka Takala, Chief of the International Labour Organization's Health and Safety Programme, *New Internationalist*, no. 317 (October 1999): 6.
[205] Joseph LaDou, "International Occupational Health," *International Journal of Hygiene and Environmental Health* 206, no. 4/5 (June 2003): 303–313.
[206] An observation by John Bottger, who as VP of Land O'Lakes developed businesses in four continents.
[207] In 2010, people were not warned for hours after a triple murder at the Huntsville, Alabama, campus of the University of Alabama "because the people involved in the activation of the system were involved in responding to the shooting."

> **The General Duty Clause of the Occupational Safety and Health Act**
>
> "Each employer . . . shall furnish to each of his employees employment and a place of employment which are free from recognized hazards that are causing or likely to cause death or serious physical harm to his employees."
>
> —29 CFR 1910 (Public Law 91-596)

of the point of accountability, there must be a specific designation of program responsibility.

Historically, industrial work was considered the most hazardous. Today, the administrative and professional personnel who comprise the largest segment of our workforce are also vulnerable to an increasing variety of threats. Offices are subject to noise, ventilation and chemical hazards, as well as to violent acts by people. On average, two U.S. employees are homicide victims in their workplace every day.[208] Superstorm Sandy and Hurricane Katrina were indiscriminately deadly, and retail clerks have been trampled to death when opening the doors of retail stores.[209] In 2010, without warning, a disgruntled taxpayer flew his airplane into IRS offices in Austin, Texas, leaving two people dead.

Even with these newer threats, there are fewer injuries and fatalities in the nation's workplaces than in earlier years. The development and implementation of thousands of regulations have resulted in major improvements, but so too has the growing percentage of workers in much safer employment occupations.

The threat of toxic workplace air continues to be a challenge in workplace safety. J. Paul Leigh at the University of California, Davis, says data reveals that each year 200,000 people die prematurely from previous exposure to contaminated air in the workplace.

> "Employees have both the need and right to know the hazards . . . and what protective measures are available."
>
> —Fact Sheet No. OSHA 93-26

Injury Prevention Tactics

Essential elements of occupational injury and illness prevention include 1) *making prevention a management priority*, whether motivated by caretaking, financial loss or law, 2) *identifying and overcoming hazardous conditions or practices*, 3) *training employees* to use safe practices and insisting they be applied and 4) *understanding legal requirements*. Risks of injury are more likely to occur when management discounts the threat of injury, rejects the investments that might mitigate them or is ignorant of the regulations designed to prevent them.

Normally fire safety provisions are built into a facility's infrastructure, maintained by building management and monitored by an insurance firm. Small offices may conduct a study of hazards

---

[208] Roberto Ceniceros, "Stricter Company Policies Help Lower Number of Homicides in Workplace," *Business Insurance* 43, no. 24 (June 6, 2008).
[209] DOL News Release of Walmart employee death, May 26, 2009.

and find few issues for concern; nevertheless, contingency planning for emergencies from power failures, storms, sabotage, violence or explosion is an obligation of the employer. Organizations in several states that are oriented toward physical labor or the processing of metal or chemicals are required to have a documented safety program with specific content. In Minnesota, industrial employers with more than twenty-five employees are to maintain a workplace accident and injury reduction (AWAIR) program.[210]

The existence of international terrorists has focused new attention on public health and safety in the nation. Government recognizes the need to protect our imports and food, water, and chemical and nuclear facilities. Employers have improved new-employee background investigations, established identification systems, moved to control deliveries, installed access controls and added surveillance equipment and guard staff.[211] Many establishments, and necessarily government facilities with more than fifty employees, have written security programs. It's reasonable to expect that employers, and especially federal government units, will promulgate additional security measures as new techniques for violence—and thwarting it—develop.

Federal agencies have long been burdened with safety and security measures because of the government's enormous size, files of personal information and national security responsibilities. The scope of federal activity is revealed in the following excerpts from an Occupational Safety and Health Act (OSHA) fact sheet.

"During FY [fiscal year] 2004, approximately 165,000 occupational injuries and illnesses involved civilian federal employees. In addition to the human dimension of this issue, workers' compensation billings for all federal employees in 2004 totaled more than $2.3 billion."

Federal management therefore has the following requirements:

- Conduct occupational health and safety training for top management, supervisors, safety and health personnel, employees and employee representatives.

- Conspicuously display a poster informing employees of the provisions of OSHA, Executive Order 12196, and the agency safety and health program under 29 CFR Part 1960.

- Designate an official with sufficient authority to manage the agency occupational safety and health program.

---

[210] An amendment to the MN OSHA, Jan 1, 1991, MN Statutes, Sect. 182.653.
[211] G. Seivold, ed., *2008 Security Regulations, Compliance and Liability Prevention Manual,* (New York: Institute of Management Administration, 2007).

Safety Program Structure

A written program represents management direction and can outline the scope and desired steps to be carried out.

Injury Prevention Program Content

Policy Statement

A directional statement can express the priority, responsibility and purpose of an effort. Any statement should reflect the reality of management's position and be *customized*. The OSHA general duty clause can serve as the basis for a statement because it represents the employer's obligation. However, its use of the term "furnishes" suggests a condition that exists, so using an expression that indicates the *pursuit* of hazard-free conditions is preferable. An example of such phrasing is: "Will seek to provide a healthy workplace for employees." Foolhardy slogans in the safety arena, including the popular "Safety is our goal," appear when the organization's true and obvious objective is not personal or public safety, but profit.

Goals

A realistic, measurable objective adds substance to a program. A foggy platitude ("to reduce injuries to the minimum") lacks a thoughtful commitment and omits any means of determining success or failure. A goal "to complete each successive calendar month without worker injury or illness requiring a doctor's care" is an understandable and measurable target.

Organization

The implementation of a program requires directed activity and communication. Top management should provide visible support to a program. There should be demonstrations of executive interest through inspections, injury site visits and meeting attendance. Involving management by notifying it of periodic results, key incidents and any health concerns should be routine. Organization possibilities include:

- Designation of a *coordinator* that maintains records, researches technical matters and interacts with top management.
- *Supervisors* responsible for the working conditions and safe conduct of their employees. Their job description should declare this accountability and appraisals should assess it.
- Knowledgeable input and support from building and equipment *maintenance supervisors and security sources*.
- A *collective effort* involving all those with a stake in preventing health and safety issues.

Participation

A *safety committee* of employees has an irreplaceable base of knowledge and can make immense contributions to hazard abatement and injury avoidance. The "doers" of the work know where hazards and unsafe practices exist and will win more cooperation and support among associates than will appeals by management. Membership often rotates and committees regularly carry out walk-around inspections. *Records* of committee initiatives and activity should be maintained.[212]

Hazard Identification

Hazards should be identified and documented; they serve to fix targets for injury prevention efforts. Office situations are often examined casually, but blocked exits, unsafe wiring, unstable files and the presence of toxic chemicals (often used in copy machines) commonly exist. Potential hazards outside the building (steps, ice) can also be serious. A list of all inherent and potential hazards should be maintained.

Accident Reports

Accidents, or incidents without injury, are an opportunity to take preventive action and should be addressed. The First Report of Injury (FROI) form of the insurance provider helps in determining the cause of an accident. These forms are to be completed and submitted soon after any injury. The diligence expended to identify *causes* rather than just the rote completion of a form evidences the degree of commitment to injury prevention efforts.

Facilities

Many workplaces have hazards innate to the facility, such as stairs, wiring or slippery floors, and these should not be overlooked. An incident such as a terrified 1200-pound steer careening loose on a slippery floor among hundreds of employees in a meat-slaughtering plant may be rare, but contingency plans do exist in those facilities to minimize the possibility of injury.

Training

Educating employees about hazards, evacuations, the use of protective equipment and safe practices is an essential element in protecting personnel. The conditions of the particular workplace necessitate *customized education*. Recording the training exposure and the distribution of written material to employees is legally required in certain conditions, but represents good administration in any case. Examples of an accident report and safety rules follow.

---

[212] CFR 1910.132: Inspections can focus on hazards, points of previous accidents, new-employee procedures and other changes in the workplace.

Accident Investigation Report

Name of Injured Person: _____

Telephone Number: _____

(Circle one):   Male   Female

What part of the body was injured? Describe in detail: _____
_____

What was the nature of the injury? Describe in detail: _____
_____
_____

Describe fully how the accident happened. What was employee doing prior to the event? What equipment or tools were being used? _____
_____
_____

Names of all witnesses:

_____   _____

_____   _____

Date of Event: _____   Time of Event: _____

Exact location of event: _____

What caused the event? _____
_____
_____

Were safety regulations in place and used? _____
_____

Employee went to: Doctor's Name: _____
                   Hospital Name: _____

Recommended action to prevent reoccurrence:
_____
_____
_____

_____   _____
Supervisor Signature   Date

> # DRIVER CONDUCT TRAINING INFORMATION SHEET
>
> The following rules apply for employees driving vehicles requiring a commercial driver's license (CDL).
>
> 1. Drivers and passengers of any company vehicle will wear seat belts at all times.
> 2. Drivers will ensure that cargo is properly loaded and secured.
> 3. Vehicles will be maintained as specified.
> 4. Drivers are to complete daily vehicle inspection reports and take any necessary action.
> 5. Drivers are to cooperate in our substance abuse prevention programs.
> 6. Employees violating federal, state or local laws while driving are subject to dismissal.
> 7. Radar detectors are prohibited.
> 8. Drivers are to comply with on-site traffic signage.
> 9. Hitchhikers are prohibited.
> 10. Text messaging while driving is prohibited.

In some work environments, behavior such as running, horseplay and fighting might occur and is often specifically prohibited. Any established safety rules should be applied to everyone, including visitors and executives. A list might prohibit having weapons on the property, wearing rings and bracelets near machinery, using protective equipment improperly and walking to the parking area at night unescorted.

Workplace Inspections

Routine inspections by committee members or management personnel are used to identify unsafe practices and conditions. Programs often specify these as part of the program. Depending on the workplace, points of inspection can include environmental factors (air, noise), structural conditions, walking surfaces, storage structures, sanitation facilities, material-handling equipment, fire protection and first-aid readiness, electrical connections, material handling, trip and fall hazards, methods used to perform work and the adequacy of tools and equipment.

Medical Care

The locations of medical care and supplies should be specified in the program, and supplies updated as necessary. Public safety employees (first responders), by virtue of the frequency and severity of exposure, are often granted extraordinary medical examinations and services beginning with pre-employment examinations.

General Safety Code of Conduct Newcomer Checklist

Check the item below when you understand its meaning. When completed, sign the bottom of the form.

I understand that I am responsible for the following:

___ Following safe work practices

___ Reporting any unsafe practice or condition

___ Promptly reporting any accidents or injuries

___ Maintaining my work area and any other areas assigned

___ Knowing the location of first-aid supplies and how to get assistance

___ Reporting any threats of violence, intense anger, strange behavior or remarks about weapons or explosives

___ Avoiding the use, sale, possession, or influence of alcohol or other controlled substances while at work

___ Recognizing the emergency alarm, location of exits, procedures for evacuation and the point of congregation

I understand and agree to each of the above expectations.

_____   _____
Signature   Date

The above items are representative. Violation of any of them can result in discipline.

Employee Health

The level of employee health impacts attendance and group insurance costs. Larger organizations sometimes provide health education, counseling, in-house nursing and a provision for exercise; if these exist, such efforts should be documented. The number of employees using the program obviously impacts the cost-to-benefit ratio.

Tests for Illegal Substance

Employers who choose to test employees for unacceptable substance use, or who are required to by federal law, may have state law with which to conform. Federal employees enjoy particular freedoms from such testing on the basis of privacy rights. The management position and procedure should be documented.

Applicable Standards

Any state regulations on drug or safety matters deserve mention in a program so they remain on the administrative agenda and are not overlooked. Current OSHA and local safety standards that apply should be in addendum to the program document for reference.

Measuring Results

The program should set forth an accepted basis for determining the success of safety efforts. The number of injuries over a span of time, expressed targets or industry patterns tracked over the years can be used. Accidents not resulting in injury are rarely recorded but are helpful.

Annual Audit and Report

A periodic review of program activity and conformance should be routinely conducted for management information. Principal considerations should be the number and seriousness of accidents and injuries, documentation accuracy, the depth of study of causes, program administration, the state of safeguards and conditions, and the conduct and attitude of (random) employees. A respected stakeholder who is not directly involved in the routine of the program and is free of self-interests should conduct the audit.

Other Resources

Insurance carriers who cover workers' compensation risks and fire insurance firms often provide inspections and advice on safety matters. Small employers with limited resources should insist on such services. In addition, trade associations and employer groups may provide help to members, and within a particular industry there may be an association of safety specialists who collaborate. OSHA offers assistance that will be addressed later.

Regulations

Workplace safety regulations are promulgated by a number of federal agencies, including the Environmental Protection Agency, the Nuclear Regulatory Commission, the Federal Aviation Administration, the Mining Oversight and Accountability Commission, and the U.S. Coast Guard. These agencies address matters related to their particular pursuits. The Occupational Safety and

Health Act (OSHA) is the most widely applicable. It establishes standards for ship fitting, demolition, manufacturing and underground work, and has tremendous impact in medical care procedures. The material in this chapter is based primarily on the general industry standards of OSHA.

Child Labor Safety

The Fair Labor Standards Act addresses child labor safety matters as well as wage and hour standards. More than 3 million teenagers under age eighteen are employed during the summer months; nearly 2,000 suffer injuries each year, and scores die as a result of their employment. This occurs despite law that prohibits their employment in hazardous jobs. Those less than age eighteen are prohibited from operating cutting and shearing machines or from driving delivery vehicles. In 2005, Walmart paid a fine of $135,000 because in several states their teenage workers operated chainsaws, paper balers and forklift trucks.

Transportation Drug and Alcohol Testing

The Department of Transportation (DOT) is a notable partner in occupational safety and health by virtue of legislation that was primarily enacted for public safety in the form of the Federal Motor Carrier Safety regulations, which require various forms of *drug and alcohol testing*. Such testing impacts hundreds of thousands of employers in the trucking, rail, aviation and mass transit industries, as well as in construction, delivery, disposal and recycling organizations. Drivers, pilots and other safety-sensitive positions, such as those involved with loading and unloading, inspecting, servicing or repairing a commercial vehicle, are subject to testing. Employer programs must apply written procedures and practices in order to comply with regulations.

> **Operators of commercial vehicles are subject to drug and alcohol testing.**

The largest occupational group covered by the regulations is the 6.6 million commercial truck drivers. The trucking rules generally apply to anyone required to hold a commercial driver's license (CDL), even if they do not drive across state lines. Commercial motor vehicles mean those used in commerce to transport passengers or property with a gross vehicle weight rating of 26,001 or more pounds.

Tests analyze hair or urine samples of drivers for marijuana, cocaine, opiates, amphetamines and phencyclidine. The program includes pre-employment, periodic, reasonable cause, post-accident and random testing. A screening test and a confirming test to verify any positive initial test are required. Employees who test positive on both tests are unqualified to operate a commercial motor vehicle or assist in other duties related to the operation of the vehicle, such as loading.

Applicants who test positive should not be hired, though it is possible that future laws may provide windows for medical marijuana users. Applicants who fail tests should not be labeled substance abusers or addicts, but they cannot perform any safety-sensitive functions. The federal regulations do not require employers to provide employees with an opportunity for rehabilitation

> **Medical Testing Agreement**
>
> The City of _____ has adopted a drug and alcohol testing policy. An applicant for any City position may be subject to testing under the policy and may be asked to provide a urine specimen after receiving a conditional offer of employment. You may legally refuse to undergo a drug or alcohol test. If you refuse, the City's conditional offer of employment may be withdrawn. If you undergo an initial screening test with a positive test result, a confirmatory test will be performed. The full Drug and Alcohol Testing Policy is available in the Human Resources Department at the City Center, during regular business hours.
>
> If requested, I agree to submit to a physical examination to determine my physical fitness for employment or continued employment in the event I am employed.
>
>   Signature of Applicant:_____
>
>   Date:_____

and treatment unless they are returning to a safety-sensitive function and such treatment has been recommended by a substance treatment professional.

Federal contractors who do substantial business with the government are designated as drug-free workplaces. The employers are mandated to notify job candidates of the policy and, because of the interdependency of the federal government, are to provide employees with education and rehabilitation opportunities.[213]

Smoke-Free Regulations

There is no federal law prohibiting smoking in the private sector, but Executive Order 13058 (1997) requires federal facilities to be smoke free. Most states and many cities have laws limiting smoking, resulting in a patchwork of circumstances. Illinois enacted a statute in 2008 that bans smoking in virtually all enclosed workplaces statewide, including bars and restaurants. However, an Allen County, Indiana, law bans smoking except in bars. Localities are permitted to enact more restrictive regulations.

Smoke-free employers have contributed to employee health across the nation. Many employers have initiated cessation programs in the interest of employee health.

---

[213] The federal Drug-Free Workplace Act is administered by the Department of Labor.

Campus Alarms

Another public safety statute[214] involving employers applies specifically to higher education institutions, both public and private. As the result of murders at a number of college campuses, those institutions that benefit from federal dollars are required to establish a program safeguarding the school population from violence. Primary provisions of the regulations are to maintain a multiple-channel warning system of any crimes or threats. A program of recordkeeping, emergency action, and education is to be included in student recruiting and orientation materials.

Workplace Violence

Incidents of violence in the workplace are an increasing threat. Incidents include physical assault, threatening behavior and bodily harm. Media reports of serious behaviors in both the public and private sectors are common. According to the U.S. Department of Justice, nearly a million violent crimes occur each year at job sites. The U.S. Bureau of Labor Statistics reported there were more than 500 workplace killings in 2009, most by gunfire. These acts are committed not only by employees, but also by acquaintances of employees and total strangers. The perpetrators sometimes feel they were treated unfairly or suffer some other state of despair.[215]

Three notorious incidents occurred in post office facilities between 1986 and 1991, during which a total of seventeen people were killed. In the first two weeks of 2010, a Las Vegas courthouse was the scene of a murder; three men were killed and five wounded by a gunman in a plant in St. Louis; two more were killed and three wounded in an Atlanta courthouse. No workplace is immune from the possibility of violence or murder, hence the consideration of contingency preparations and the need for management concern.

Employers should be diligent about who is hired and who continues to be employed. Employers can be held liable for acts committed by their employees when reasonable care in the selection or winnowing processes has not been exercised. Employers are well advised to seek the help of employees in identifying possible points of threat.

In addition to *employee awareness education*, other precautions should be considered:

- Limit access to the workplace, train receptionists, and have an alarm.
- Make hazardous and valuable materials inaccessible.
- Provide mail-handling protection, such as initial isolation.
- Use lighting effectively.
- Avoid isolating workers.
- Provide a parking lot escort at night.
- Connect with public safety agencies; uniformed law officers should be welcome visitors.
- Carefully terminate the employment of those perceived to represent a threat.

---

[214] The Clery Act, 20 U.S.C. § 1092 Sec 1092, as amended July 1, 2010.
[215] Workplace murders, mostly shootings, average 550 each year. See USDL-13-1699, U.S. Bureau of Labor Statistics.

- Prepare for unpredictable disasters and intruders.
- Be alert to possible retribution in dismissal actions.

Ergonomics

Most worksites have conditions with covertly hazardous activity that may cause illness or injury. The study of the interaction of workers, tools and their environment is termed *ergonomics*.

Typical points of injury involve muscles, joints and bones because of repeated vibration, twisting, bending, lifting and awkward posture. Corrective action can be taken by redesigning a job or the method of doing it, and changing platform elevations, tools or the arrangement of components. It's estimated there are about 500,000 injuries of this nature each year. An employer's accountability for ergonomic safety exists by virtue of OSHA's general duty clause, which sets forth general employer responsibility and serves to empower the agency when specific standards do not exist.

Standards of OSHA

There are a multitude of conditions required of public and private employers, expressed in the Occupational Safety and Health Act of 1970. The act's provisions apply to 8 million workplaces and almost 100 million workers. There are sections for general industry, maritime, construction and agricultural application. Public sector employees in Connecticut, New Jersey and several other states have other regulations, but state or federal OSHA regulations dominate the national employment scene and constitute a pillar of workplace safety.[216] Employers are expected to know and apply the standards to which they are subject and must have copies of the standards on-site. Employees are granted the right to request inspections, to join in an inspection and to refuse to perform dangerous acts.[217]

For introductory purposes, a synopsis of the most commonly applicable general standards follows:

Medical Care Provisions (29 CFR 1910.151)

Workplaces are to be provisioned with first-aid supplies and, if medical care is more than four or five minutes away, a qualified first-aid provider.

Sanitation (29 CFR 1910.141 (a))

There are general standards requiring dry working platforms, vermin control, drinking-water access and cups, and a specified number of toilets and hand-washing facilities.

---

[216] *All About OSHA,* OSHA 2056.
[217] *Employee Workplace Rights,* OSHA 3021.

Fire Prevention Provisions (29 CFR 1910.155)

Fire prevention and control are often the responsibility of maintenance and facility management. These include an operable automatic fire suppression system, ready and accessible fire extinguishers and the proper storage of flammable materials.

Emergency Evacuation Plans (29 CFR 1910.38)

The act requires *an action plan* for the evacuation of the workplace. Employers of ten or more workers are to have this plan in writing. A plan is to include a method of alarm, security and shutdown assignments and procedures, escape route assignments, a list of telephone numbers for emergency contacts and employee training of duties.

Emergency Action Plan Content

1. Identify and publicize a point of command that is to receive and widely broadcast an alarm.
2. Acquaint workers with the alarm and its method of delivery (horn blasts, public address system, siren) that signals evacuation.
3. Acquaint workers with evacuation routes, which should be free of obstructions, and exits, which should include lighted signs. A diagram of exit paths should be posted in each department.
4. Assign special actions, such as locking the safe, or assistance duties, such as evacuating the handicapped.
5. Instruct that upon the signal, occupants are to exit the facility and congregate at locations indicated on the exit route diagrams.
6. A primary and secondary position responsible for instituting an alarm should be designated.
7. Conduct a practice drill each year.

Hazardous Chemical Training (29 CFR 1910.1200)

Many chemicals, such as cleansers, are hazardous. Workplaces may have materials that are corrosive, radioactive or contain lead, and older buildings often have asbestos. (See 29 CFR 1910.119.) It's estimated that some 25 million employees work in the proximity of such hazards, and all have the

Material Safety Data Sheet Excerpt

Section IV - Fire and Explosion Hazard Data

Flash Point (Method Used)	Flammable Limits	LEL	UEL
Extinguishing Media			
Special Fire Fighting Procedures			
Unusual Fire and Explosion Hazards			
			OSHA 174, Sept. 1985

Section V - Reactivity Data

Stability	Unstable		Conditions to Avoid
	Stable		
Incompatibility *(Materials to Avoid)*			
Hazardous Decomposition or Byproducts			
Hazardous Polymerization	May Occur		Conditions to Avoid
	Will Not Occur		

Section VI - Health Hazard Data

Route(s) of Entry:	Inhalation?	Skin?	Ingestion?
Health Hazards *(Acute and Chronic)*			
Carcinogenicity:	NTP?	IARC Monographs?	OSHA Regulated?
Signs and Symptoms of Exposure			
Medical Conditions Generally Aggravated by Exposure			
Emergency and First Aid Procedures			

need and right to know about the hazard and the protective measures available. A written program is required, and should list the materials, labeled hazardous containers, location and application of material safety data sheets provided by manufacturers, and records of employee training. Some states, including Maine, New Hampshire and West Virginia, have their own regulations. An abstract of material safety data sheet content is presented in this section for referral.

Blood-Borne Pathogen Hazards (29 CFR 1910.1030)

OSHA estimates that more than 5 million workers in health care and public safety occupations are exposed through bodily fluids to diseases including AIDS, tuberculosis and syphilis. Physicians, dentists, paramedics, laundry workers and nurses work with the possibility of infectious exposure on a daily basis, particularly from blood. Vulnerable, too, are law enforcement officers who not only encounter open wounds but are occasionally spat upon in confrontations.

A dental office visit includes the presence of gowns, gloves and facemasks, metal containers for sharp instruments, sterilization equipment, covered handles and chair coverings. What is not apparent is the *cleaning and sterilization protocols* required, nor the rigid procedure to be followed when blood or saliva is transmitted. When a worker is exposed through a needle stick or blood splash in the eye, a *medical evaluation* by a licensed health care professional is required. Employers are to pay for medical care after exposure as well as time lost.[218]

A stringent detailed standard covers all employees who could "reasonably anticipate" to contact infectious material in the course of their work. A written exposure control plan is to include:

- Procedures and disinfectants used for sanitation
- Procedures for the disposal of contaminated wastes and sharp instruments
- Compliance instructions (hand washing, use and care of protective equipment)
- Codes and labels used with hazardous materials
- A copy of the standard
- Employee education about HBV, HIV and other hazards

Chemical Process Safety Programs (29 CFR 1910-119)

Piping and mixing chemicals are common in many industrial processes. This standard is intended to prevent accidental releases of hazardous chemicals and human exposure. It requires extensive and detailed *documentation* of the system components, along with documented potential equipment and human failures. The standard also demands engineering and maintenance *training* and the upkeep of technical changes.

---

[218] *Secretary of Labor v. Beverly Healthcare-Hillview,* 541 F.193 (3rd Cir. 2008).

Personal Protective Equipment (29 CFR 1910.132)

One million work establishments with about 12 million employees find hazards that necessitate the use of personal protective equipment (PPE). Any employer involved with material handling, toxic materials and other-than-sedentary activity should research PPE on the OSHA website. The conditions might require technical studies of noise exposure and air contamination levels. The assessment is to be in writing, signed and dated. Employers must provide and pay for welding gloves, goggles, hard hats, respirators, face shields, specialty foot protection and other standard protective equipment. The employer must provide training on when and how to use any equipment, and keep records of such training. Some common conditions requiring PPE are listed below.

- The possibility of falling objects requires head protection in the form of helmets to absorb the shock of a blow to the head.
- Liquid chemicals, acids or caustic liquids can be abated by eye or face protection.
- Excessive noise can be tempered with ear protection and earplug pieces.
- Foot injuries due to either falling objects or sharp objects piercing the sole can be reduced with safety shoes.
- Harmful dusts or sprays can be controlled with respirators if effective engineering cannot abate the threat.
- Harmful substances and risks of lacerations or punctures suggest the use of gloves.

OSHA Administration

Information and Records

Employers are responsible for keeping employees informed about safety regulations via a job safety and health protection workplace poster (OSHA 2203 or state equivalent). Employers must maintain a list of hazards, with the notation of the recorder and date. Many industrial employers must maintain a log of injuries and illnesses of the last year and post annual summaries (OSHA 300A). White-collar industries with very low injury rates, and employers with fewer than eleven employees, are exempt from these requirements. Work-related reportable injuries include those that result in limited work activity, loss of consciousness, job transfer, termination of employment or professional medical treatment.

> **Failure to resolve employee complaints about unsafe conditions may result in a visit by government officials.**

CHAPTER 8: SAFEGUARD THE HUMAN RESOURCE

OSHA's Form 300 (Rev. 01/2004)

Log of Work-Related Injuries and Illnesses

Year 2009
U.S. Department of Labor
Occupational Safety and Health Administration

Form approved OMB no. 1218-0176

Attention: This form contains information relating to employee health and must be used in a manner that protects the confidentiality of employees to the extent possible while the information is being used for occupational safety and health purposes.

You must record information about every work-related death and about every work-related injury or illness that involves loss of consciousness, restricted work activity or job transfer, days away from work, or medical treatment beyond first aid. You must also record significant work-related injuries and illnesses that are diagnosed by a physician or licensed health care professional. You must also record work-related injuries and illnesses that meet any of the specific recording criteria listed in 29 CFR Part 1904.8 through 1904.12. Feel free to use two lines for a single case if you need to. You must complete an Injury and Illness Incident Report (OSHA Form 301) or equivalent form for each injury or illness recorded on this form. If you're not sure whether a case is recordable, call your local OSHA office for help.

Establishment name **ABC Co.**
City **Anywhere** State **USA**

Case no. (A)	Employee's name (B)	Job title (C)	Date of injury or onset of illness (D)	Where the event occurred (E)	Describe injury or illness, parts of body affected, and object/substance that directly injured or made person ill (F)	Death (G)	Days away from work (H)	Job transfer or restriction (I)	Other recordable cases (J)	Away from work (K) days	On job transfer or restriction (L) days	Injury (M1)	Skin disorder (M2)	Respiratory condition (M3)	Poisoning (M4)	Hearing loss (M5)	All other illnesses (M6)
1	Tammy Newcomer	Chemist	2/5	Lab	Breathing difficulty—inhaled chlorine gas		X			13				X			
2	Pat James	Electrician	3/4	Maintenance Dept.	Gunshot wound, left shoulder, from ex-wife		X			25	28	X					
3	Jose Ortega	CNA	6/30	3rd Fl. South wing	Hernia, lower right abdomen, from lifting				X		5	X					
4	Georgina Gonzella	Welder	6/29	Welding Area	Welder flash, both eyes from TIG welder		X					X					
5	William Handwerk	Temp Help	8/7	Shipping Dept.	Broke wrist from fall to dock floor				X	5	15	X					
6	Privacy Case	Janitor	10/4	Rm 6, 2nd Fl.	Needlestick from used springs, right hand				X								
7	Ellen Bass	Press Opr	12/5	Sheet Metal Dept.	Hearing loss, right ear				X							X	
					Page totals ►	0	3	1	3	43	48	4	0	1	0	1	0

Be sure to transfer these totals to the Summary page (Form 300A) before you post it.

Public reporting burden for this collection of information is estimated to average 14 minutes per response, including time to review the instructions, search and gather the data needed, and complete and review the collection of information. Persons are not required to respond to the collection of information unless it displays a currently valid OMB control number. If you have any comments about these estimates or any other aspects of this data collection, contact: US Department of Labor, OSHA Office of Statistical Analysis, Room N-3644, 200 Constitution Avenue, NW, Washington, DC 20210. Do not send the completed forms to this office.

Page ___ of ___

Source: www.osha.gov

For safety-sensitive personnel, the following matters require records of the company's educational efforts.
- Emergency evacuation plan
- Blood-borne pathogen program
- Hazardous chemicals program
- Drug plan procedures for drivers
- Drug misuse standards
- Suspicious behavior training
- PPE use
- Chemical process systems
- Industrial truck-driving training
- Radiation exposure prevention training

Inspections

OSHA officials are authorized to enter any workplace or environment where work is performed, but most often appear at industrial sites with high injury potential. Many inspections result from employee complaints to the agency. It's preferable to permit an inspector immediate access; otherwise, a court order can be secured and the inspection will take place. An official compliance officer should display credentials and will want an employee representative to participate in an inspection.

A program administrator can take steps to be ready for regulatory inspections, the first step being not to be surprised or unprepared. Preparation includes complete and accurate reports of injuries, the list of hazards, compliance with standards, an evacuation program and the required postings.

The compliance officer will observe safety and health conditions and practices, consult with employees privately, and may take photos and instrument readings, examine records, collect air samples and evaluate medical care provisions. At the conclusion of an inspection, the compliance officer conducts a closing conference with the employer and the employee representative. During the closing conference, the employer may wish to produce records to show good-faith compliance efforts and to provide information that can help OSHA determine how much time may be needed to abate any alleged violation. Making any commitments at this point is unnecessary and may be unwise. Employers are well advised to be cooperative and businesslike. Arrogance, or attempts to be social, can be counterproductive.

Common causes of employer noncompliance with OSHA standards include:
- Neglecting the identification and labeling of hazards
- Neglecting to notify employees of hazards (including toxic chemicals)
- Lack of a required written program
- Faulty electrical wiring

- Neglected lockout procedures for a machine under repair
- Unused machine guards
- No poster of employee rights
- Inadequate training and injury records
- Faulty care and use of scaffolding and ladders
- Failure to use respirators in foul conditions

Safety Assistance

OSHA consultation assistance is available to employers who want help in establishing and maintaining a safe and healthful workplace. The service is provided at no cost to the employer. No penalties are proposed or citations issued for hazards originally identified by the consultant if they are duly corrected. OSHA provides a wealth of information that can be helpful. OSHA publications are available from the U.S. Government Printing Office or via the OSHA website.[219]

Summary Remarks

U.S. employers are responsible for preventing worker injuries in the workplace. Besides the prevention of human suffering, it's advantageous for employers to protect their human assets and to avoid interrupted production and adverse costs.

An array of regulations has been promulgated under a number of statutes applicable to different industries with specific conditions and practices to be implemented. They are based on hazards (noise, radiation), age (prohibition of dangerous work by individuals under the age of eighteen), occupation (safeguards to avoid bodily fluids), industry (transportation drug testing), and governmental jurisdiction (local fire suppression ordinances). The Occupational Safety and Health Act expresses that "the employer is responsible" for hazard abatement. That responsibility, and its array of conditions, evidences the need for HRM standards and ongoing oversight.

Injury avoidance begins with demonstrated management interest followed by orderly oversight; points of hazard should be identified, and first-aid supplies and emergency evacuation training should be provided. Dedicated inspections to audit the proper use of protective equipment, availability of readied fire extinguishers and an absence of unsafe conditions or practices should be a management routine. Any applicable safety standards should be satisfied.

Effectiveness in protecting human resources is generally measured by tracking the number of lost-time injuries or the number of incidents that required professional medical care during a time period. In the total private sector in 2011, non-fatal but reportable injuries to workers occurred at a rate of 3.5 per year per 100 employees.[220]

---

[219] See http://www.osha.gov. Recommended are the *Small Business Handbook* (OSHA 2209), *Recordkeeping Forms* (OSHA 300), *All About OSHA* (OSHA 3302), and *Fire Safety* (OSHA 3256).
[220] U.S. Department of Labor, Bureau of Labor Statistics, October 25, 2012.

Applicable Competencies

Knowledge of applicable safety and health regulations and reports, injury prevention techniques, and meeting and management skills.

Applicable Resources

OSHA regulations on-site, management commitment, designated responsibility, a written program, workforce participation, egress diagrams, medical supplies, available medical care, lists of hazards to be abated, effective supervisors, adequate maintenance of facility and equipment, and trained, disciplined and cooperative workers.

Review Materials

Content Exercises

1. List five industries or occupations that carry notable risk for occupational injury.
2. List three risks that can exist in office environments.
3. List three major federal laws that encompass employee safety in public and private organizations.
4. Identify two reasons each why management might or might not assign a high priority to injury prevention.
5. What is the one principal standard used to protect employees at work?
6. Be prepared to define *HAZCOM*, *MSDS*, *PPE*, *OSHA*, and *NIOSH*.
7. What is the distinction of a safety-sensitive position?
8. Explain the potential hazard of a repetitive motion activity and which OSHA standard would apply.
9. Name four common compliance violations.
10. Name three sources of safety management information available to most employers.

Practical Applications

1. Visit with a supervisor who is knowledgeable about safety matters and learn of at least two hazards in your place of employment and how they are addressed.
2. Identify and research an OSHA standard applicable to your workplace, such as the first-aid provisions or hazardous chemical standard. Compare the regulation to the practice.
3. Acquire a copy of one of the following for use in group study or personal reference: a list of safety rules, egress diagram, drug-testing policy, or a safety-related policy or program.

4. Determine the position (if any) responsible for primary safety administration in your organization. Learn about this position's place in the hierarchy, scope of activity and the defining statement regarding safety used in the job description.

5. If your state has a law regarding drug and alcohol testing (other than for transportation occupations), what are some legal requirements of the employer?

6. If your employment is subject to safety laws other than OSHA, such as those related to mining, aviation or maritime, prepare a short explanation of the key provisions and priorities.

7. Is your workplace covered by federal or state OSHA regulations?

Case-Study Discussions
Case 8.1
The Blood-Borne Pathogen Standard (29 CFR 1910.1030)

This standard is primary in the health care sector, schools, assisted-living environments and all first-response circumstances. It applies to millions of employers and can affect millions of employees.

This exercise involves research and study by a large study group that will result in a unique and mutual understanding of this common OSHA standard. There are six different sections of the standard to be assigned, each to a specific small group of students. Groups might be aided by picturing the circumstances of a dental office or first responder. Each student independently pursues the assigned study between classes. Students should read the standard and consider any applicable personal experience or visual aid that would provide a learning supplement for the class.

On the assigned report day, each study group should meet together for fifteen minutes to agree on key points, to review any learning aids for the group and to form a brief presentation. A designated group should select one or two students to summarize and present the key points of the subject (e.g., the purpose of that particular section of the standard) to the total body of students. Six or seven minutes should be spent for their preparation of a six- or seven-minute "show and tell" report. The total of reports will provide a broad summary of this OSHA standard.

Individual group subject assignments:
1. The purpose, scope and hazards targeted by the standard
2. The designated points of exposure and the exposure control plan
3. The requirements for the training and education of employees
4. The scope and methods applied for cleaning and disinfection
5. Exposure incidents, reactions and follow-up provisions
6. Coding, labeling and disposing of contaminated waste

Case 8.2: Blood-borne pathogens

Suzie is applying for a new position as HR director in a dental clinic, her first position in the medical field. In the preliminary interview, something was said about how this new position would make it possible to add some previously neglected new-employee training on the subject of the blood-borne pathogen exposure plan. Suzie doesn't know anything about blood-borne pathogen exposure and thought she should learn about pathogen training plans in case the subject came up in her next interview.

Suzie's research revealed that pathogen training plans were a critical legal and personnel health obligation in the industry. She found a few uncommon and unfamiliar terms used in reference to the training and speculated that while some of the subject matter might be suitably handled by a staff person, other material should be left to experienced department experts.

How should Suzie prepare for this potential interview subject? What should she know at a minimum? Of a dozen or more required training points, list any that you expect Suzie will believe can be addressed in new-employee orientation, and which should be left to department experts. What three or four terms applied in this regulation do you think she should be familiar with? Form several ideas on how the necessary education of new employees on such a comprehensive and complex subject might be accomplished.

Case 8.3: The Catch-all Clause

Harvey had a machining job at a new workstation. This machine was somewhat more complicated than the one he worked on previously and so the job paid a little more. It was similar to his last job in that it involved picking up a casting from a pallet, performing milling operations, and putting it aside to a pallet for finished product. In this job, the incoming pallet was stacked higher because the pieces were only about twenty-five pounds. Orville, the previous worker on the job, had developed a sore back doing the work, which is why Harvey was provided the opportunity. Harvey was healthy and didn't have any trouble for about a week.

After two weeks on the new job, Harvey found that lifting the castings to and from the machine when the pallet was full (in other words, stacking the top layer) was difficult and strained his back. He also found that picking up pieces and putting them aside when the pallets were about empty made his lower back ache. He asked the supervisor if the loads of castings could be positioned better, but the supervisor didn't see how and nothing was done. Harvey learned that Orville had complained, too. Harvey asked his union steward if anything could be done. The union steward talked to the safety coordinator, who replied that the supervisor didn't think anything could be done. Besides, the coordinator was confident that every OSHA regulation was satisfied, and there was no standard for such a situation. Harvey's back got worse.

One day an OSHA officer appeared before the receptionist and wanted to tour the plant. The safety coordinator was very confident of compliance, but was shocked in the closing conference when the inspector made reference to a citation for a violation. What steps might have been considered by the company? What OSHA standards were overlooked?

Case 8.4

Lyle Zabel, an experienced office manager, was sent by a temporary agency to assist an entrepreneur named Al who was just starting a business. Al had started three field crews of six people each in the last ten days, working on irrigation projects in rural areas. In town he had a warehouse area with racks, a loading dock and a small office with some furniture. He needed payroll and purchasing procedures, and help with administrative matters in general. He had ordered several computers and an industrial lift truck for handling the warehousing of irrigation pipe on storage racks, which were to be delivered next week. This would be Al's physical location, and there was an office.

In a brief meeting between the two, Lyle assured Al that with another part-time office person, phones and a corporate credit card, he could establish the administrative necessities, collect employee information, find forms, get the crews paid and relieve Al of most of the paperwork he so disliked. Lyle set about establishing his relationships with the bank and vendors, and checked proper licensing with the state attorney general. Lyle also thought to call an OSHA office with his personal cell phone to inquire about any safety regulations, a subject that Al hadn't mentioned. In the five-minute conversation that ensued, Lyle learned there could be a dozen safety issues that should be addressed (he finally quit taking notes), as well as required training to be conducted. He realized that he needed a copy of OSHA's general industry safety standards for the details.

What items did he find in the safety standards that must be acted upon? What training would be required? What provisions adopted? Where might he find some help on safety matters?

UNIT IV
MANAGE LEGAL MATTERS

To satisfy legal requirements related to the workforce and carry out procedures and practices that reduce adverse legal exposure.

CHAPTER 9: ENDING THE RELATIONSHIP

CHAPTER 10: RECORDS, PRIVACY AND REPORTS

CHAPTER 11: LEGAL COMPLIANCE AND RISKS

CHAPTER 9
ENDING THE RELATIONSHIP

Chapter Objectives

- Types of employee separations
- Legal exposure for employers
- Steps to mitigate liability and avoid litigation
- Valuable procedures
- Differences between public- and private-sector dismissal practices

An Overview of Separations

The relationship of an employee and employer will come to an end. At some point, one or the other of the parties initiates action to dissolve the relationship; very rarely is it a truly joint decision. One or both parties will probably suffer emotional pain and/or financial setback, and because of the potential for legal issues, management must use caution when a termination threatens.

Different forms of separations can be confusing because of the terms and language applied. Separations are permanent, and either voluntary or involuntary, not to be confused with temporary layoffs or leaves of absence. People removed from the payroll can be *fired, dismissed* or *terminated*, all terms that suggest misbehavior. Other common expressions are *downsized* or *released*, which normally indicate that the separation is without prejudice, often occurring due to reduced activity or reorganization. The terms *separation* or *termination* are often used interchangeably and indicate removal from the payroll and a break in service with the organization. *Furloughed* is vacation time in military parlance, but when used to camouflage involuntary separation in the civilian sector can be viewed as deceptive; whether the departure is permanent or temporary is unclear. The preferred expressions for an absence that both parties expect to be temporary are a voluntary *leave of absence* or an involuntary *layoff*.

Voluntary Separations

Employees are generally hesitant to leave a position that provides their income. Workers often endure significant job dissatisfaction, inconvenience and even abuse when they don't have a suitable alternative source of earnings. There are many reasons why people choose to leave an employment situation. They may be dissatisfied, because of unfulfilled expectations, uncomfortable with their peers or supervisor, unable to arrange transportation or child care, relocating or accepting a more favorable job. As a matter of courtesy, most employees give notice when they know they will be quitting the relationship.

When it's known that an employee is leaving, management faces the option of immediately severing the relationship or permitting the employee to continue work, which could help operations but carries some risk of subversion, theft or sabotage. In lieu of continued work, an immediate separation in the private sector might be with or without pay for the period of notice, normally two weeks. It's desirable to acquire a written statement when the employee initiates the separation, and even better if the statement reveals the reason, which may eliminate later questions about the cause of the separation.

It's common when sizable staff reductions are planned to offer an inducement for workers to leave with *voluntary "early retirement" agreements*. Such agreements are commonly based on qualifying periods of service and age. In 2006, Ford was offering hourly workers $100,000 to leave, no matter how few their years of service. In the same year, GM offered employees with ten years of service $140,000; those with less service received $70,000. It should be noted that these were especially tough times in the auto industry.

If employees believe they were *forced to quit*, the situation may be construed to be a "constructive discharge" by a court, which alters the situation to a management act and opens the liability for jobless pay, penalties and other employer costs.[221]

An employee who voluntarily leaves can occasionally provide useful feedback in building positive employee relations. To encourage open and honest *exit interviews*, a meeting is normally assigned to an interviewer other than the immediate supervisor. Normal subjects of inquiry include wages and benefits, and views of the company, job and supervisor. Very often it's difficult to arrange a meeting, and most employees are hesitant to offer anything negative. There is no personal advantage for them to disclose their views, and there could be fear of adverse consequences for doing so. Revelations of abuse or unfulfilled commitments require prompt follow-up and reaction. Management should work with the departing employee to correct an undesirable condition or possibly mitigate any mistreatment.

Administrative (Without Fault) Separations

Employees who are considered inactive due to temporary illness, an extended period of layoff or being in an on-call status normally remain listed on the payroll. Removing such employees from payroll should be in accord with a consistently applied policy and protocol. Separation from the payroll for administrative reasons may result from no work activity for one year or for a period of elapsed time that equals the employee's period of time on the payroll.

---

[221] See *Humana, Inc. v. Fairchild*, 603 S.W.2d 918 (Ky. App. 1980).

CHECKLIST FOR SEPARATION

Employee name:_____ Date:_____

Termination date:_____ Unit:_____

ITEMS TO OBTAIN

- ❏ Keys
- ❏ Corporate credit cards
- ❏ Security cards
- ❏ Uniform
- ❏ Work materials
- ❏ Manuals
- ❏ Telephone and computers
- ❏ Transportation items
- ❏ Any confidential materials
- ❏ Resignation letter
- ❏ Passwords
- ❏ Method of future contact

NOTIFICATIONS

- ❏ Insurance continuation opportunities (COBRA)
- ❏ Non-compete obligations
- ❏ Confidential information obligations
- ❏ Transition assistance (copy machine access, etc.)
- ❏ Benefit option information in writing by expert

ACTIONS

- ❏ Provide any monies due
- ❏ Collect information on work-in-progress
- ❏ Mail COBRA notice
- ❏ Collect personal records from supervisor/medical units
- ❏ Initiate notification to payroll and benefits
- ❏ Seek and document a reason for separation

Involuntary Terminations

Staff Reductions

The number of personnel in a company can vary because of market needs, technological developments, economic variations and voluntary separations. County road workers and city parks and recreation staffing will change with seasonal *reductions in force (RIF)* when less work is available. The same kind of fluctuation occurs in agricultural and entertainment venues (canneries, Disney World).

Staff reductions are normally intended to reduce unnecessary costs. Any cost-to-benefit calculations should account for costs of severance pay, outplacement services, unemployment costs, potential lawsuits and loss of competencies.

When there is less work to be done, management can recover previously outsourced work, grant unpaid time off (with or without benefits), reduce hours, share work assignments, not hire replacements and release part-time and temporary personnel. A few firms with strong commitments to their human assets go to great lengths to avoid sending people home. Reductions in the workforce are unpleasant but can also be viewed as an opportunity for an overall study of staffing in search of improvements in the way work is done and the business conducted.

About half the states have legislated shared-work programs. These spread the work hours at a workplace among employees, benefiting management by avoiding terminations of valuable people and reducing the need for unemployment benefits. Measuring work time in units of less than a full day is commonly expressed in terms of FTE, or full-time equivalency. Reducing hours of a position is common in the public sector; for example, teachers might be employed at half time (.5 FTE).

The reason for staffing reductions should be clearly defined and communicated to employees. Not doing so can result in erroneous perceptions, unnecessary issues and magnified upset by employees. The method used to reduce the staff should be formed with the management that will suffer the losses as well as those who must carry out production. The plan should address work needs, schedules, job changes, training and communication needs.

Applying a Process

Separations and layoffs should be handled through a process and not treated as an event. Union contracts spell out layoff procedures, including bumping, which favors length of employment rather than competency. A few states have legislated performance as a factor for teacher reductions in force.[222] To avoid bias, reduction programs should begin by identifying the work that must be maintained and then staffing excess by occupation. It becomes more complex when exploring the possible combinations of jobs and talents of personnel to arrive at the most effective and efficient workforce. The assessment of workers one to another may be influenced by unique or broader skills of some. In general, deviations from retention by length of employee service can be expected to result in challenges to the process. Documentation of the rationale and decisions in anticipation of legal challenge is sound practice.

---

[222] These states are Colorado, Tennessee, Delaware and Oklahoma.

An Emotional Event

Leaving a place of employment results in sadness, depression, anger and even violence. Hundreds of dismissed employees react violently each year, and workplaces suffer scores of murders. Criminologist James Fox postulates that uncertain reactions may be more probable when employees believe "work is everything." The release of a large group of people can adversely affect the economy and social stability of entire communities.[223] To minimize the unpleasant consequences of abrupt staff reductions, Congress legislated that employers notify groups of employees facing job loss. (See WARN, discussed below.)

Job Loss Notification (WARN)

The private and nonprofit sectors are subject to the Worker Adjustment and Retraining Notification Act (WARN), which requires most employers of 100 people or more to provide sixty days of advance notice (which can often be difficult) regarding large-scale worker separation anticipated to affect at least fifty members or one-third of the workforce. Notification is to be made to all affected employees, the local mayor, union officials and state employment services. A number of states, including California and Tennessee, require smaller employers to make announcements as well.

Dismissals

A worker's usefulness relates to his or her contribution; incompetence or disruption is unacceptable. Those who cannot perform an essential function of their job or whose conduct compromises the organization's effectiveness are candidates for dismissal. Good, reliable employees with low output are candidates to receive corrective training or to transfer to more suitable work. Organizations with a culture of employee caretaking often apply that human sensitivity to dismissals and find another place for failing personnel. If that doesn't work out, the choice is between termination and inefficiency.

Dismissal situations aren't common, and most managers don't have a refined pattern of action and expressions with which they are comfortable. "It just hasn't worked out" is one expression used, as is "We are letting you go," both of which leave some ambiguity regarding specific status. "You are fired" is clear but suggests a degree of rancor and sounds unnecessarily harsh. "The decision has been made to remove you from our payroll" has the advantage of clear intent and a minimum of emotional implications.

Managing Dismissals

The need for dismissals and the resulting possibility of adverse legal actions and litigation can be minimized by establishing procedures, training supervisors and providing process oversight. Because employee discharges create legal exposure, preventing them is important. Defensive measures are embodied in routine management activities, many of which have been mentioned earlier in this book.

---

[223] Richard S. Deems, Ph.D., *How to Fire Your Friends* (Lincoln, NE: Media Publishing, 1989), 21.

- Careful selection and background examinations of personnel will minimize subsequent issues.
- Placing personnel that "fit" their assigned work increases favorable assimilation.
- An extended trial period for newcomers is a lengthy test of acceptability. In the public sector, a probationary period of six months to a year is the norm for public safety personnel, and a period of several years is typical for educators, who then become tenured.
- Ensure that newcomers clearly understand expectations and standards in regard to output and conduct.
- Provide a positive, helpful work climate; be a good place to work.
- Broadcast an at-will relationship clearly and routinely so that employees understand their status. Its expression in offer letters and other new-employee materials are initial steps, but ongoing documented messages are important.
- Apply disclaimers in documents to the effect that no employment contract exists unless there is an agreement in writing approved by an official.

Alternative Dispute Resolution (ADR)

Dealing with employee issues can ease emotional upset. ADR applies mediation or arbitration by third parties to resolve employee-employer disputes, and serves to conclude issues between the parties in the same manner as union contract grievance procedures. The ADR systems are less time-consuming, costly and public, are applied more quickly than litigation and result in less rancor.[224] ADR is adjunctive to actual legal proceedings and protocols and is considered quasi-legal. Third-party involvement may be a late step in a due process system or be applied within a process of litigation to reach a settlement. The systems should be established with the guidance of an attorney and agreed to by the parties in advance. The agreement to involve ADR as needed is part of the documentation signed at the time of hire.

Mediating labor contracts and arbitrating grievance matters have long histories in labor relations and remain common today. Public sector disputes may be referred to a private sector provider or submitted to a state agency. All federal agencies are to have policies on the voluntary use of ADR to resolve issues.[225] Both the Americans with Disabilities Act and the Civil Rights Act of 1991 encourage the use of ADR procedures, including media-

> **SAMPLE ADR AGREEMENT**
>
> **The employee and employer agree that any and all complaints, disputes and claims against each other not settled by previous resolution steps will be resolved by binding arbitration by the National Arbitration Forum.**

---

[224] Todd B. Carver, "ADR: A Competitive Imperative for Business," *Dispute Resolution Journal* 59, no. 3 (August/October 2004), 67–68.
[225] Robert E. Woods et al., *A Guide to Dispute Resolution for Business* (Minneapolis: Briggs & Morgan, 1995).

tion, to resolve employment disputes. An analysis of more than 2,000 public and private arbitration cases revealed that public-sector management decisions were upheld 56 percent of the time compared to 49 percent in the private sector. Perhaps because of due process practices, public sector discharges for performance failures were upheld at a rate of 62 percent.[226]

Public Sector Practices

The normal procedures for dismissals in the civilian public sector (excluding political appointees) are distinctly structured and definitive as compared to those applied in most of the private sector. Public sector dismissals tend to require more evidence, are generally applied for more serious offenses and follow documented action steps.[227] Proceedings can carry on for many months, in contrast to a norm of just hours or days in the for-profit sector.

Job Rights

Most government employees, by virtue of law, have a degree of *proprietary job rights* that can only be overcome through an extensive dismissal protocol. This job protection exists mostly at the federal level and, to a diminishing degree, at lower levels of government. There are media reports of frustration by taxpayers because of the lack of public sector dismissals (frequently regarding schoolteachers), most often in regard to severe and costly employee incompetence and negligence.

A bit of American history explains this favored status. In the nineteenth century, government employees were hired because of their political affiliation via a patron. Whenever the political winds changed, there were massive job losses (no-fault separations) as the new regime created job vacancies for their own people. History reports that it took the murder of President Garfield by a disgruntled job seeker to bring order to the staffing of federal jobs via legislative action. The Pendleton Act created the Civil Service Commission in 1883, and instituted the hiring of federal government people on the basis of merit, permitting their dismissal only on the basis of just cause following the application of due process.[228] These principles and civil-service organizations cascaded down through the government hierarchy to state and local levels. These "merit" concepts are fixed through statute, labor agreements or policy statements. The doctrine is also applied among human service organizations in the nonprofit sector, but much less so in commercial entities that require efficiency in order to endure.

The basis for proprietary job rights emanates from the Constitution, which provides that "no person ... shall be deprived of their ... property without due process of law."[229] An HRM resource states, "Public sector employees are viewed as having a bona fide *property* right in their jobs once

---

[226] This study covered a period of twenty-four years of arbitrations in the state of Minnesota. It was conducted by Prof. Stephen Befort of the University of Minnesota Law School and Prof. Mario Bognanno of the Carlson School of Management. Laura J. Cooper of the University of Minnesota Law School reported this excerpt of results in the *Star Tribune* on September 17, 2010.
[227] "Misconduct must be substantiated and sufficient for justifying just cause." Siegrun Fox Freyss, ed., *Human Resource Management in Local Government*, 3rd ed. (Washington, D.C.: ICMA Press, 2009), 231.
[228] Stephen E. Condrey, ed., *Handbook of Human Resource Management in Government*, 2nd ed. (San Francisco: Jossey-Bass, 2005), 20.
[229] Kenneth L. Sovereign, *Personnel Law,* 4th ed. (Upper Saddle River: Prentice Hall, 1999), 59.

they have passed their period of probation."[230] Again, those completing the probationary period will qualify for "permanent appointment."[231] Those job rights are manifested in requirements for "indisputable just cause" with findings arrived at through due process in the face of discharge.[232] The demands of the process result in better-grounded actions than in the private sector.

Job protection isn't true in all government entities. Many local government units have been influenced by private sector practices and have obviated job rights. One county procedure manual makes it clear: "Employees are not granted proprietary interest in their job and a department head may dismiss any employee for any reason."[233]

Inadequate employees, particularly at the federal level, are sometimes tolerated due to the fact that dismissal is an unpleasant, lengthy and difficult task; replacements can be slow in coming, management may not support dismissal actions and there is a reluctance to be involved in any resulting legal actions.

> **When management is without freedom to dismiss at will, standards of conduct and performance must be well understood, quantified and documented to support discharge actions.**

Key Terms

Thousands of organizations, primarily public, that commit to due process in discipline and just cause procedures use different definitions of these phrases.

Due process for an offender can mean that he or she is informed of the offense in writing; is granted time to examine the evidence, correct the problem or prepare a defense; or is given the opportunity for response, representation help or appeal.[234] Very often an organization, whether subject to a union contract or not, embraces progressive discipline, which involves an exact predetermined sequence of greater penalties, as an element of due process.[235] A critical component of due process "is that [termination action] be preceded by notice and an opportunity for hearing."[236]

Legitimate business necessity is normally accepted as *just cause* in downsizing situations impacting an entire organization, but in the case of individuals can mean an individual's failure to perform an important element of the job or a finding that the worker is detrimental to the organiza-

---

[230] W. David Patton et al., *Human Resource Management: The Public Service Perspective* (New York: Houghton Mifflin, 2002), 360.
[231] Sally Coleman Selden, Ingraham, Jacobson, "Human Resource Practices in State Government," *Public Administration Review* 61, no. 5 (September/October 2001), 599.
[232] Merit System Principles, 5 U.S.C. § 2301 (2006).
[233] See the process in the Lake County Personnel Manual, Lake County, IL, February 9, 1999.
[234] W. David Patton et al., *Human Resource Management: The Public Service Perspective* (New York: Houghton Mifflin, 2002), 82.
[235] "And with the reason in writing." Dorchester County, South Carolina, Procedures Manual, July 7, 1997.
[236] Mohave County, Arizona, Merit System Rules, Article 7: Corrective Actions, Rule 701, Discipline A (1), (May 2, 1994), 1: "Generally, disciplinary measures begin with a less severe action and become increasingly severe if new offenses occur. In some cases, however, even in the absence of prior disciplinary action, a particular offense may be so serious in nature as to warrant immediate dismissal or suspension."

tion. It has also been ruled that "cause" must be of a substantial nature, such as sexual harassment, fighting, résumé fraud, assault, insubordination or drunkenness. Just cause can also refer to violation of reasonable rules, expectations or clearly understood warnings, as well as valid evidence of inadequacy or a fair judgment by an important decision maker.

> **Follow declared discipline protocol. Deviating from an expressed discipline or discharge process is likely to result in aborted justice and undeserving people remaining on the payroll.**

Dismissal Without a Reason (At-Will)

Most states have adopted the judicially created at-will doctrine that permits the termination of employees outside the public umbrella "for any reason or no reason at all." This century-old concept simply means that employers and employees can enter or leave the employment relationship freely.[237]

> **A termination is a process, not an event.**

The application of this doctrine is prevalent in the private and not-for-profit sectors, but there are some alternative tactics. In public sector organizations that operate under this concept, political changes make personnel vulnerable to cronyism by the new management. As a result, new decision makers commonly grant city and county managers employee contracts with severance provisions, lest politics or whimsy result in errant dismissal.[238]

The at-will concept displays a distinct but diminishing disparity between arbitrary judgment and the societal preference for justice and job security as represented in government institutions. There is no federal statute for government employee discharge protections except at the federal employer level.

Wrongful Discharge

The at-will doctrine is not totally unfettered; state and federal statutes prohibit dismissals for certain reasons, thus creating the possibility of a *wrongful discharge* of employees who don't enjoy job rights. Those managing dismissals should know the specific restraints in their state as well as those that exist generally at the federal level. The following list of state statutory provisions represents a developing social view.

---

[237] EEOC, Civil Action No. 4:08-CV-2816 (AR), April 17, 2009.
[238] W. David Patton et al., *Human Resource Management: The Public Service Perspective* (New York: Houghton Mifflin, 2002), 222.

- The at-will principle cannot be applied when its existence has not been clearly communicated to the employee (California).
- The principle is set aside if assurances of future job security have been expressed (Connecticut, Massachusetts).
- Civil service or union contract provisions have precedence (a common proviso).
- In some states, when explicit reasons for dismissal have been expressed by the employer, the doctrine has been compromised.
- Expressing an annual wage to be paid can suggest a contract for that period of time (South Dakota).
- If an expressed process is not properly followed, a dismissal could be revoked.
- So long as a test of *good faith* and *fair dealing* is practiced, the doctrine is permitted to prevail in some jurisdictions. In contrast, other jurisdictions reject any obligation of an employer on the basis that due process and just cause must be honored.
- Some states require that at-will dismissals for off-duty conduct must be supported by evidence that there was damage to the employer.[239] Under the policy of some federal agencies, terminations are prohibited for conduct "which does not adversely affect the performance of the . . . service."
- Some states prohibit dismissals through legislation for the use of legal products (e.g., cigarettes), for not participating in a charity drive, for off-duty conduct that is not illegal (e.g., drinking) or on the basis of criminal history or substance abuse.

Federal law also compromises the at-will doctrine, which cannot be applied to dismissals in the following circumstances:

- A civil-service employee protected by just cause (CRA)
- For legitimate union activity (NLRA)
- For refusing to perform unsafe work (OSHA)
- To prevent qualifying for a benefit (ERISA)
- An employee served with a wage garnishment (CRA)
- For serving on a federal jury (Jury Act)
- For refusing to perform an illegal act (state laws)
- A returning veteran for a one-year period (USERRA)
- In retaliation for reporting illegal actions of an employer ("whistle-blowing")
- For exercising personal constitutional rights (U.S. Constitution)

---

[239] See *Conway, Inc. v. Ross*, 627 P.2d 1029 (Alaska Supreme Court, 1981).

OSHA® FactSheet

Whistleblower Protection for Railroad Workers

Individuals working for railroad carriers are protected from retaliation for reporting potential safety or security violations to their employers or to the government.

On August 3, 2007, the *Federal Railroad Safety Act* (FRSA), 49 U.S.C. §20109, was amended by *The Implementing Recommendations of the 9/11 Commission Act* (Public Law 110-53) to transfer authority for railroad carrier worker whistleblower protections to OSHA and to include new rights, remedies and procedures. On October 16, 2008, the *Rail Safety Improvement Act* (Public Law 110-432) again amended FRSA, to specifically prohibit discipline of employees for requesting medical treatment or for following medical treatment orders.

Covered Employees

Under FRSA, an employee of a railroad carrier or a contractor or subcontractor is protected from retaliation for reporting certain safety and security violations.

Protected Activity

If your employer is covered under FRSA, it may not discharge you or in any other manner retaliate against you because you provided information to, caused information to be provided to, or assisted in an investigation by a federal regulatory or law enforcement agency, a member or committee of Congress, or your company about an alleged violation of federal laws and regulations related to railroad safety and security, or about gross fraud, waste or abuse of funds intended for railroad safety or security. Your employer may not discharge or in any other manner retaliate against you because you filed, caused to be filed, participated in, or assisted in a proceeding under one of these laws or regulations. In addition, you are protected from retaliation for reporting hazardous safety or security conditions, reporting a work-related injury or illness, refusing to work under certain conditions, or refusing to authorize the use of any safety- or security-related equipment, track or structures. You may also be covered if you were perceived as having engaged in the activities described above.

In addition, you are also protected from retaliation (including being brought up on charges in a disciplinary proceeding) or threatened retaliation for requesting medical or first-aid treatment, or for following orders or a treatment plan of a treating physician.

Adverse Actions

Your employer may be found to have violated FRSA if your protected activity was a contributing factor in its decision to take adverse action against you. Such actions may include:

- Firing or laying off
- Blacklisting
- Demoting
- Denying overtime or promotion
- Disciplining
- Denying benefits
- Failing to hire or rehire
- Intimidation
- Making threats
- Reassignment affecting promotion prospects
- Reducing pay or hours
- Disciplining an employee for requesting medical or first-aid treatment
- Disciplining an employee for following orders or a treatment plan of a treating physician
- Forcing an employee to work against medical advice

Deadline for Filing a Complaint

Complaints must be filed within 180 days after the alleged adverse action occurred.

How to File a Complaint

A worker, or his or her representative, who believes that he or she has been retaliated against in violation of this statute may file a complaint with OSHA. The complaint should be filed with the OSHA office responsible for enforcement activities in the geographic area where the worker lives or was employed, but may be filed with any OSHA officer or employee. For more information, call your nearest OSHA Regional Office:

Source: www.osha.gov

Training and Tactics

Dismissals should be anticipated and contingency plans prepared for that probability. There are conditions and desirable procedures for personnel selection; so too should there be guidelines for dismissal processes. The following points of learning apply to management training and could be used as part of a management reference handout.

- Provide employees with training, fair opportunity and the time necessary to achieve standards.
- Consider salvage efforts of established or responsible workers through retraining or alternative work.
- Acquire signed acknowledgments of warnings.
- Prohibit abrupt dismissals; establish the practice of sending disruptive people home pending a decision of the discipline to be administered.
- Do not embarrass the employee in the process.[240]
- Fulfill union and policy procedures and commitments.
- If the reason for dismissal is for unacceptable conduct, be sure it can be demonstrated that the behavior was detrimental to the organization;[241] otherwise use a lesser sanction.
- Be sure the expressed reason for action is true and is not masking revenge or bias.
- If performance is the issue, be sure the standards are well known and evidence clear.
- Collect and retain sufficient evidence in a timely manner. Identify witnesses and document their statements.
- Confirm that the pay level and personnel records are consistent with the impending action.[242]
- Consider the consequences or fallout of the timing of the action. Can work processes adjust? What message will others receive from the action?
- Seek the critical analysis of an associate or expert to examine the justification, fairness and absence of retaliation or other inappropriate motives in the pending action.[243]
- Notify appropriate management of an issue.
- Be able to articulate why the employee is more of a liability than an asset.
- Employees and the public expect a sound, explainable reason and civility in manner.

---

[240] See *Darst v. Interstate Brands Corp*, U.S. App. (7th Cir. 2008).
[241] John Remington et al., *Human Resources Law*, 5th ed. (Upper Saddle River: Prentice Hall, 2010).
[242] The Administrative Dispute Resolution Act of 1990, 5 U.S.C.
[243] Conduct must have an adverse effect. See *Conway, Inc. v. Ross* 627 P.2d 1029 (Alaska Supreme Court, 1981).

Monitoring Discharges

Employers, particularly in the private sector, are vulnerable to legal challenges of discharge actions by enforcement agencies and individual civil actions. Primary threats are allegations of illegal discrimination and retaliation. For example, vengeful action against a troublesome employee, such as one that always complains or initiates numerous grievances, might be masked under a claim that the employee is a poor performer. Allegations of *defamation of character* can be generated by careless discussions of an employee's shortcomings in or out of the workplace. As noted above, at-will discharges even have limits to their application in different legal jurisdictions. All dismissal actions need a review procedure to confirm true and just cause, along with any necessary due process and legality; the risks inherent in discharges must be minimized.

It seems appropriate in dealing with this subject to reiterate that there is no guarantee of legally accurate content herein for any particular situation. Employee terminations are replete with legal parameters that differ among government units, states and the passage of time; refer to current circumstances in your state. Some situations may require the following:

- Ensure that law does not prohibit discharge for the reason being considered, including exceptions to at-will termination. Employees on approved leaves of absence (FMLA, military leave) are afforded job protections.

- Manage supervisor language lapses that can create liability. Casual remarks about "putting an oldster out to pasture" or expressing belief that a pregnant worker "shouldn't do heavy work" can be ruled as evidence of illegal discrimination.

- In some situations, securing an agreement to waive the rights of an employee to any personal damages in exchange for some consideration by the employer, such as severance pay, is an option to consider. Law declares that an employee cannot waive their legal rights. If peculiar circumstances suggest an agreement, it's recommended that legal assistance be employed.

- Confirm that dismissal action is in keeping with past practices in similar situations.

- If the employee is a member of a protected class of employees, thus elevating the risk of litigation, reexamine each step to ensure there are no flaws or uncertainties about management's actions.

- Use legal counsel when appropriate, particularly if some form of quid pro quo is contemplated.

- Prevention of legal actions is fostered when work environments are respectful of employees, bullying isn't tolerated and employees are free to vent concerns.[244]

---

[244] James Fox, Criminologist, Northeastern University (Massachusetts), quoted in the *Minneapolis Star Tribune*, September 30, 2012.

Managing the Meeting

A properly choreographed process includes a formal notification of termination, usually during a personal meeting. A suitable time and location[245] should be arranged, necessary materials should be on hand, a clear expression of the action and reason should be in readiness, and preparations made for emotional reaction (security, tissues). Dismissals are commonly viewed as the most unpleasant duties of supervisors. If personal contact is impossible, written communication of dismissal should be sent by certified mail. A recent example of an emotional, impersonal and disparaging dismissal event occurred when the chief executive of a large media firm dismissed an employee during a conference call to more than one thousand employees.[246]

Important, too, is management of the meeting aftermath. A suitable explanation of the employee's absence must be crafted for associates, preferably one agreeable with the employee, to minimize speculation and gossip. A standard sterile expression, such as "Dorothy Dix has left us for other opportunities," should be used. Any disreputable remarks about the employee can result in alleged defamation.

Preserve the individual's dignity.

---

[245] Richard S. Deems, Ph.D., *How to Fire Your Friends* (Media Publishing, 1989), 39.
[246] Nicholas Carlson, "Listen to AOL CEO Tim Armstrong Fire a Patch Employee in Front of 1,000 Coworkers," August 12, 2013, http://finance.yahoo.com/news/listen-to-aol-ceo-tim-armstrong-fire-a-patch-employee-in-front-of-1-000-coworkers-140600015.html.

TERMINATION MEETING PLAN

- Prepare an agenda of the subject matter.
- Know the full story, evidence and previous steps.
- Arrange a private place for the conversation that will be free of interruptions.
- Gather appropriate payroll and benefit material.
- Arrange for an associate to attend as a witness.
- Identify property of the organization to be retrieved.
- Be aware of the protocol and past practices of appeals.
- Prepare an unobtrusive exit for the employee.
- Plan for security readiness (consider the possibility of violence).[247]

CONDUCT

- Be decisive, clear, honest and final.
- Review the process steps to date.
- Accept the responsibility of representing management; don't "pass the buck."
- Avoid arguments.
- Don't agree to write any letters of recommendation; they are often misinterpreted and writing them sets a precedent.

POST-MEETING

- Document the meeting events, particularly any threatening behaviors.
- Have the witness document critical points.
- Don't talk to others about the meeting.

---

[247] Following his dismissal in Minneapolis in September 2012, an employee returned and killed five people, including the owner of the small enterprise and a transit UPS driver. Provide vigilance, especially in the case of any employees exhibiting troubled behavior, and a method of alarm.

Helping Employees Recover

Payments

Severance payments are sometimes granted at the time of involuntary termination. It may be considered recompense when the employee is released immediately in lieu of earnings they would have had during the period of notice. The value of any greater gift is subject to question; sometimes rationalized as an investment in goodwill, it might also reflect charity or guilt. In any case, it is difficult to discern any positive return on investment. One survey of 147 organizations indicates about half of employers grant severance pay, and a third of those are granted only in select situations. Years of service or the level of the job in the hierarchy usually determines the amount. Public employers seemed most often to use both of those factors.[248] At the executive level in the private sector there can be "golden parachute" severance agreements that provide a soft landing if a change in ownership results in job loss.

Buy-out agreements sometimes provide payments in exchange for a release or waiver signed by the employee to relieve the employer of potential legal actions. Drafting such agreements requires expertise and will not erase an employee's civil rights. Payments due, whether for work or accrued, including payable vacation, should be delivered in accord with state law, which may mean at the moment of dismissal.

> "There are occasions when it is wise to have the benefit of an associate's thinking."
>
> —M. P. MacDougall, Senior VP, Human Resources, Hoerner Waldorf Corporation

Transition Assistance

Those who are involuntarily terminated can benefit from some understanding, help and hope. Normal personal upset can be tempered by an offer to help the transition from this job to whatever the future may hold. The help may be as simple as being prepared with answers to questions about unemployment compensation and insurance and handling the situation in a courteous and professional manner. The degree of transition assistance granted will vary based on the nature of the separation, level of the position and the individual.

A primary value of job search assistance is the immediacy of hope and action to help the employee move forward rather than to succumb to despair. In no-fault situations, an employer may provide office use or call acquaintances on behalf of the terminated employee. Professional outplacement firms are often contracted by larger organizations to help individuals or masses of personnel, usually those who are "white collar" or technical. Such firms provide help with search techniques, the preparation of materials and the development of interview skills.

---

[248] "How Employers Are Handling Severance," *HR Focus* 86, no. 11 (November 2009): 7–13, 40.

Summary Remarks

Workers come and go through organizations, and their exiting requires management just as well as their entry. Most separations are without fault, with the action resulting from the personal circumstances of the employee, business conditions, new technology or organizational changes. Substantially all personnel are productive and worthy, so most separations are hurtful and costly to some degree.

"Letting people go," whether temporarily or permanently, is an unpleasant personnel transaction and fraught with potential legal consequences for employers. Sizable staff reductions require the advance notice of employers by virtue of statutes. Dismissal actions should be based on ample evidence of disruptive activity or incompetence of the employee. Seemingly innocent words and actions during involuntary separations can result in allegations of wrongful discharge or defamation.

Public sector units have a historical pattern of conducting termination based on just cause and due process. Practices in private sector firms range from some that are similar to the government practices toward those consisting of abrupt and arbitrary dismissals resulting in legal complications. There is a growing societal standard demanding due process and respectful treatment of all employees at a time of separation.

Management can take measures to avoid terminations altogether and to minimize adverse legal actions. Some of these preventive actions include careful selection, attentive supervisor practices and training. Management actions should be within a framework of understanding about the worker's employment status, applicable regulations, and wrongful discharge parameters, but allegations of illegal discrimination, defamation and contract violation can always occur. Defensive measures may not seem to be required in states permitting dismissals at will, but it's good practice to be prepared for adverse consequences.

Effective staff reduction is accomplished when allegations of legal wrongdoing are avoided and remaining activity is efficient and effective. Properly conducted separations and outplacement programs help minimize costs and pain, and ease negative and vengeful thinking toward employers.

Employee losses are often measured as a rate of turnover. Such a general index is of limited value because of the varying value of personnel; the loss of a single chef or researcher is of far greater consequence than that of a dozen café bussers or lab technicians.

Applicable Competencies

Sensitivity; knowledge of state laws regarding termination, final pay and vacation compensation; recognition of illegal reasons for discharge.

Applicable Resources

Administrative, dismissal and meeting checklists, an expert for counsel, an ADR process, transition assistance resources, trained supervisors.

Review Materials

Content Exercises

1. Define *downsizing, layoff, termination, due process, just cause* and *at will*.
2. How might an employer stir allegations of 1) defamation of character or 2) constructive discharge?
3. Explain an advantage of taking prompt dismissal action on marginal new workers.
4. Explain general differences between dismissals by government agencies and the norm in the private sector.
5. Explain how language in an employee handbook might impact a discharge.
6. What are applications and exclusions of WARN?
7. How might an employee react to dismissal?
8. What actions should or should not be part of a dismissal notification?
9. What actions might reduce the number of discharges?
10. What steps might reduce an employee's desire to take legal action upon dismissal?

Practical Applications

1. Examine and report on conduct that qualifies and disqualifies a dismissed worker from unemployment benefits in your state.
2. Be prepared to relate a personal experience of layoff, discharge and/or outplacement assistance.
3. Find a salaried employee severance pay policy or an instance of seniority being applied in a layoff situation under a union contract.
4. Report on the discharge procedures used in your hometown municipal government unit. If possible, acquire a copy of the procedures.
5. Report on the discharge practices used in your place of employment. Do these include due process? Necessary authorization? Assigned oversight? Are these practices uniformly and consistently applied?

Case-Study Discussions

Case 9.1

Dismissal Practices

Two years ago, an employee irritated a city council member. After some words, the employee retorted, "I can't be fired!" The HR manager told the flustered council member that that was not technically correct, though such termination could be very difficult to carry out. Now there is a new mayor and new council members. The new mayor (guess who) announces that there is a "new sheriff in town." The HR manager is told that the old civil-service rules are "out" and "we're going to run this place like a business." The first item in the transition will be to change this "job rights thing" and adopt the at-will conditions used in commercial enterprises.

What are the differences between these two conditions of employment? What are the pros and cons? What are changes the city administration must anticipate? Are there employee relation issues? What implementation steps might be planned?

CHAPTER 10
RECORDS, PRIVACY AND REPORTS

Chapter Objectives

- Required records and reports
- Systematic information collection
- Multiple depositories of records
- Data privacy and security provisions
- Retention and disposal guidelines
- Information in defense and for precaution

Contents of Records

This chapter is about information used in managing personnel and satisfying government regulations, a subject that doesn't stir much excitement or attention. However, the normal bank of workforce information is a substantial asset for management. Personnel data can be used for controlling absenteeism, fulfilling government report requirements, research, workforce studies and defense in litigation. However, if personnel information is inaccurate, misused or without safeguards, the files, whether paper or electronic, represent a threat.

Despite a variety of electronic and software options, paper remains the core of personnel records. It depicts signatures and authorizations, and cannot be lost or misplaced in electronic space; when handled properly, paper cannot be stolen. The Office of Personnel Management (OPM) uses the content of the employee's hard-copy Official Personnel Folder as its base information. Nevertheless, in all but the smallest of organizations, select information, such as an individual's assignment and status, is accessible electronically in addition to hard-copy documents.

Filed personal information is the property of the employer, but its collection, use, access, disclosure and privacy is regulated by various government agencies, thereby necessitating responsible caretaking. Information about state and federal personnel can be more easily accessed than information about employees in the private sector—though requests can be subject to judicial review[249]—because of public interests in the affairs of government. For all sectors, however, the

---

[249] The Minnesota Government Data Practices Act, Chapter 13 (2005).

U.S. Department of Labor
Wage and Hour Division

U.S. Wage and Hour Division
(Revised July 2008)

Fact Sheet #21: Recordkeeping Requirements under the Fair Labor Standards Act (FLSA)

This fact sheet provides a summary of the FLSA's recordkeeping regulations, 29 CFR Part 516.

Records To Be Kept By Employers

Highlights: The FLSA sets minimum wage, overtime pay, recordkeeping, and youth employment standards for employment subject to its provisions. Unless exempt, covered employees must be paid at least the minimum wage and not less than one and one-half times their regular rates of pay for overtime hours worked.

Posting: Employers must display an official poster outlining the provisions of the Act, available at no cost from local offices of the Wage and Hour Division and toll-free, by calling 1-866-4USWage (1-866-487-9243). This poster is also available electronically for downloading and printing at http://www.dol.gov/osbp/sbrefa/poster/main.htm.

What Records Are Required: Every covered employer must keep certain records for each non-exempt worker. The Act requires no particular form for the records, but does require that the records include certain identifying information about the employee and data about the hours worked and the wages earned. The law requires this information to be accurate. The following is a listing of the basic records that an employer must maintain:

1. Employee's full name and social security number.
2. Address, including zip code.
3. Birth date, if younger than 19.
4. Sex and occupation.
5. Time and day of week when employee's workweek begins.
6. Hours worked each day.
7. Total hours worked each workweek.
8. Basis on which employee's wages are paid (e.g., "$9 per hour", "$440 a week", "piecework").
9. Regular hourly pay rate.
10. Total daily or weekly straight-time earnings.
11. Total overtime earnings for the workweek.
12. All additions to or deductions from the employee's wages.
13. Total wages paid each pay period.
14. Date of payment and the pay period covered by the payment.

How Long Should Records Be Retained: Each employer shall preserve for at least three years payroll records, collective bargaining agreements, sales and purchase records. Records on which wage computations are based should be retained for two years, i.e., time cards and piece work tickets, wage rate tables, work and time schedules, and records of additions to or deductions from wages. These records must be open for inspection by the Division's representatives, who may ask the employer to make extensions, computations, or transcriptions. The records may be kept at the place of employment or in a central records office.

FS 21

Source: U.S. Department of Labor

development and maintenance of elementary personnel information is a requirement, not an option.

Initial information about an employee is collected from an application form and a hiring and payroll authorization document. This information frequently is used to create an electronic database. A subsequent personnel change process updates the records.

Employee files are composed of employment-related information that references or describes a person and actions involving the person. An individual's file content normally documents a profile of an employee's full employment history, but a few employers maintain only the most recent ten to fifteen years of data. Organizations must maintain W-2 tax and I-9 documents, along with personnel change forms that record pay and job assignments during the full period of an individual's employment.

Other job-related information that is typically retained includes ways to contact the employee, hire date, time periods of any extended absences, benefit plan participation, notable incidents and formal training experiences. The file should include necessary records of required notifications and training, waiver authorizations, any individual agreements and a handbook receipt. Records of personnel information might also supply career preferences and performance records. Files should be void of indications of any matters not job related, including family relationships, age, heritage or religious preference. If the retention of such information is necessary for some reason, it is to be kept in a separate high-security file.

In addition to satisfying regulations, the content of records can be compiled to use in benefit plan design, administration, research and decisions. Large institutions tend to bank more detailed personnel information, including professional interests and competencies. Nonprofits develop databases of information about volunteer skills and contacts. The Federal Emergency Management Agency (FEMA) can activate contact with thousands of on-call people through their Automated Deployment Database, which lists individuals by skills, knowledge, experience, performance, location and availability for staffing in emergencies.

Most employers' file cabinets dedicated to HRM activity have sections devoted to the following subjects.

Protecting Privacy

Employees expect personal information in the hands of their employer to be held in confidence. State laws not only grant employees file access but limit access by others. Regardless of regulations, policy and procedure must protect employee rights and privacy. Among the most sensitive personal facts are *medical and financial circumstances* and a person's *Social Security number* (in the interest of identity theft). Connecticut has legislated privacy protection policies, particularly related to Social Security numbers, and Michigan, Texas, California, North Carolina and New Mexico also have protections for Social Security numbers. In May 2011, a health care firm in Minnesota dismissed thirty-two employees for unnecessarily accessing medical records of people associated with a drug overdose incident.[250] Access protection in the form of passwords, codes, entry logs and a gatekeeper is the responsibility of the employer.

---

[250] Allina Hospital, David Kanihan, spokesman, retrieved from *Minneapolis Star Tribune*, www.startribune.com/lifestyle/health/121402894.html.

> **Employee Information Section**
>
> - I-9 forms (work eligibility)
> - Payroll enrollment forms (tax and pay actions)
> - Applications (pending)
> - Individual personnel folders with personal training record
> - Sensitive personal file section (isolated) and/or personal medical file

> **General File Section**
>
> - Policies and past practices
> - Laws and regulations
> - Forms
> - Safety activity/hazard lists/standards
> - Training activity by unit or subject
> - Benefit programs/documents
> - Requisitions/recruiting activity
> - Diversity reports/activity
> - Employee feedback
> - Employee relations programs/activity
> - Pay programs
> - Service/seniority list
> - Position descriptions

Firms engaged in processing medical information, such as health insurance and TPA firms, are required by HIPAA to have a designated "Privacy Officer" to oversee specific security measures. Such precautions include the encryption of data in, and transmitted to and from, electronic databases. Most other employers protect sensitive information, whether electronic or hard copy, by 1) avoiding having sensitive information in the first place or 2) keeping what is filed from exposure.

Access to Personal Records

Though payroll and personnel records are the property of the organization, employees in many legal jurisdictions have the right to view their files. Supervisors occasionally have an interest in information from the file of a subordinate. Many times the record gatekeeper can simply provide that item of information from the file without exposing other materials unnecessarily. Employees in some larger organizations have access to electronic files so they can change an address or benefit beneficiary.

> **Those in any position with access to Social Security numbers, dates of birth and any medical or financial data should be carefully screened for integrity and monitored to reduce risks of identity theft.**

Although some employees expect their file to contain unflattering materials that they don't know about, most documents in a personnel file have been viewed or signed by the employee.

There is little reason to deny access except for notes that may reflect on other people, such as those who provide references or are witnesses to incidents. Those notes should be put in a high-security file when first received.

Don't collect or record unnecessary information.

(Under the Ohio Privacy Act it is a violation of privacy for counties to collect more information than necessary.)

An employer may choose to grant an employee file access only under conditions that have been set by courts and statutes. State law sometimes limits the frequency of viewings, prohibits the removal of material, and provides access only during office hours or in the presence of a management representative. A civil action was initiated when a number of law enforcement officers reviewed a female officer's driver's license photograph in violation of the Driver's Privacy Protection Act. It was revealed in the course of litigation that the officer's information was called up 400 times by 140 other police officers in sixteen different law enforcement jurisdictions, for curiosity as opposed to job-related purposes. The cities involved agreed to pay more than $1 million in damages.

Inaccurate records and their faulty disclosure represent legal landmines.

In the private sector, employers should understand any state law provisions and have a standard procedure and conditions under which an employee is to have access to their file. Only a few states have legislated employee rights to access, including Washington, Oregon, Wisconsin, Alaska and Nevada. Files can be sanitized of references to other people before granting access.

Considerable information about the government is open to the public under the Freedom of Information Act (FOIA), but personnel files are not.[251] The federal Privacy Act of 1974 grants federal employees the right to view and copy their file and insert amendments, and employees can request justification before providing the employer a Social Security number. States legislate on both public- and private-sector privacy matters.

Typical Reasons for an Employee's Request for Access

- Curiosity
- An opportunity to disagree with content
- An opportunity to add material to the file
- The right to copy documents

---

[251] 5 U.S.C. § 552 (FOIA).

Disclosures to the Outside

Occasionally inquiries about previous employees will arise. These normally come via telephone, but may also arrive in writing. To protect the person's privacy, and despite management's desire to cooperate with a request, the normal advice of legal counsel is to *acknowledge only indisputable and documented facts*, such as "Yes, this person was employed during these dates, performing this kind of work at this rate of pay." To say more opens the vault to subjective and controversial information upon which lawsuits can be built. Clever inquirers will doggedly persist with seemingly simple and harmless follow-up questions.[252] Indeed, a caller can easily misrepresent him/herself and be the previous employee inquiring about themselves. In December 2012, two radio announcers impersonated Queen Elizabeth II and Prince Charles as a prank and were given personal medical information about a hospital patient, the Duchess of Cambridge (Kate Middleton). Such mistakes result in strong reluctance to disclose information.

The disclosure of inappropriate information about a previous employee can result in allegations of defamation, blacklisting, privacy intrusions, retaliation and identity theft. In those rare cases where a previous employee proved to be a danger to others, courts in some states have acted to magnify that exposure. Upon inquiry by a potential employer, the previous employer must disclose pertinent facts about the individual as a caution.

Privacy Practices for Previous Employment Verification

1. Supervisors should be prohibited from replying to any personnel information requests.
2. All inquiries are to be channeled only through adequately trained representatives who are to verify the caller, deal only with specified facts and document the exchange.
3. Established practices are to be applied consistently. Trying to help out a favored person can result in an illegal discrimination charge by someone who is denied like consideration.
4. It's preferable to deal with such inquiries only in writing.

Administration

The administration of personnel information includes satisfying regulatory needs including record content, the protection of record information and retention. Management is concerned with disposal, low cost, and current, accurate and available data.

The personnel recordkeeping system grows as the number of employees in the organization increases. Small firms begin with a payroll administrator dropping documents in a file folder; larger

---

[252] Paradoxically, the very inquiries recommended in background investigations are to be avoided by previous employers.

firms establish standard procedures to achieve uniformity. Medium and large employers form policies and programs and invest in electronic Human Resource Information Systems (HRIS) software.

Information about personnel that is processed through an organization must be properly channeled and items occasionally erased. An effectively administered program requires management of the identified information selected for processing; methods of transmittal, filing, retrieval and disposal procedures; and administrative attention to the detail of the forms, content and authorizations. All of these elements are dependent on a routine, expedient transmission system that begins with the submission of a timely, accurate and complete change notification document by the supervisor.

Once a system and protocols are implemented and established, an administrator can maintain the procedures. Frequently the task of coding or encrypting data and input to electronic files is done in conjunction with payroll activities. A position description outlining common administrative duties is provided at the end of this chapter.

As with other HRM activities, there is necessary preparation for recordkeeping before any employment and production activity. Government tax and internal authorization forms, change documents and secure file cabinets should be available. Initial management education should include the rules on personnel file access and instructions on completing and using personnel change notification forms.

Record System Schematic

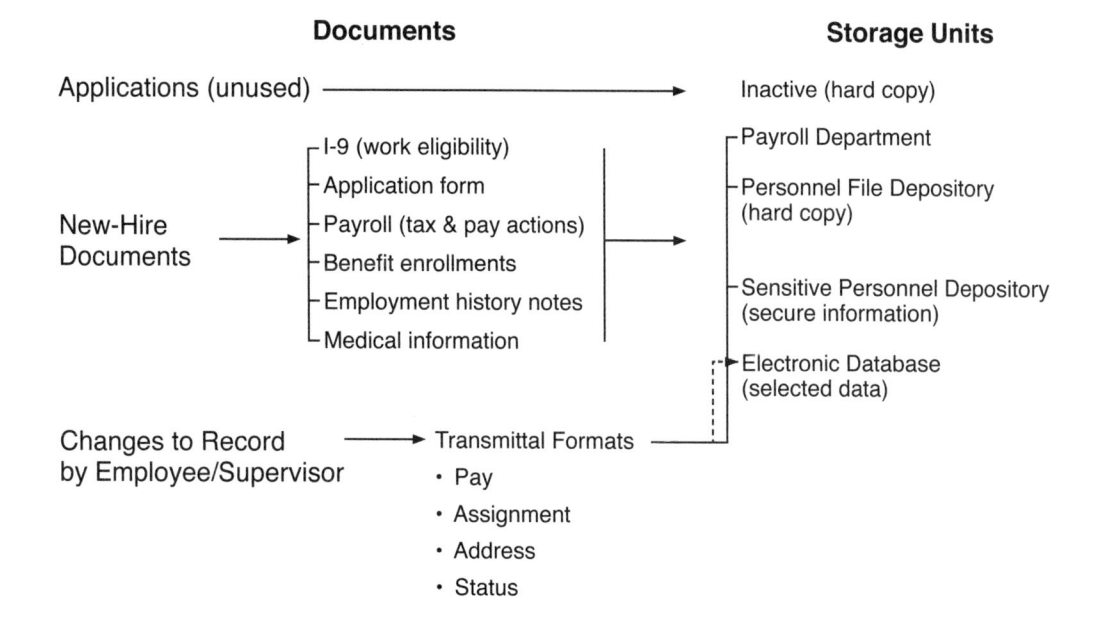

Documents   **Storage Units**

Applications (unused) ⟶ Inactive (hard copy)

New-Hire Documents ⟶
- I-9 (work eligibility)
- Application form
- Payroll (tax & pay actions)
- Benefit enrollments
- Employment history notes
- Medical information

Storage Units:
- Payroll Department
- Personnel File Depository (hard copy)
- Sensitive Personnel Depository (secure information)
- Electronic Database (selected data)

Changes to Record by Employee/Supervisor ⟶ Transmittal Formats
- Pay
- Assignment
- Address
- Status

Forms

Forms for collecting and transmitting information, such as the *application* and *personnel change notification form* must be readily understandable, easy to complete, free of unnecessary inquiries and organized for electronic input; clear instructions for forwarding should be included. There should be provisions for the initiator and designated authority to sign and date. A sample is provided below. Such a document can usually fulfill multiple changes, such as adding someone to the payroll, initiating pay, changing an employee address and termination.

PERSONNEL CHANGE NOTIFICATION

Employee Name: _____ Date: _____

PERSONAL CHANGE

Employee (Existing Information): _____

_____

New Information: _____

_____

STATUS CHANGE

(Temporary Leave of Absence, Layoff, Recall, Quit, Other)

From: _____ To: _____

Reason: _____ Effective Date: _____

If termination, eligible for rehire?   Yes: ____   No: ____   Conditional: ____

PAYROLL CHANGE

Circle one: New   Pay Change   Termination   Title   Other:_____

From: _____ To: _____ Effective Date: _____

Remarks/Reason:

_____

_____

Initiator: _____   Authorization:_____

Date: _____   Date:_____

File Administrator: _____

Cc: Payroll: _____

Multiple Depositories

Regulations require that there be *multiple files* in order to isolate some information. The Americans with Disabilities Act requires that medical information be isolated from the normal personnel file, and the Department of Transportation wants drug-testing data likewise separated from general matters. A *high-security file*, separate from the general personnel file folders, is used for information that reveals age, religious preferences and racial declarations that are collected for affirmative action reports or other purposes. This file can be used for additional sensitive information such as personal contracts, background investigation notes, test scores, financial information and any references to political activity, none of which are relevant to daily employment activity. This information should be in a locked-safe depository in a remote or inaccessible location. Preferably it will not be entered into a computer database.

The use of electronic data tends to increase with the size of the organization and the extent to which the workforce is geographically dispersed. Most organizations maintain enough information in a database to at least generate lists of employee service (or seniority) and addresses or contacts. Training and testing applicants on computers is common, and the records of these activities may be stored electronically. At the other extreme, employees in many organizations are not computer literate. Dual messaging methods are used in most workplaces to account for audience differences and to increase the likelihood that messages are received.

Authorizations and Facilitation

Personnel change documents must be monitored for suitable authorization before filing. Typically new hires, pay changes and terminations require an executive signature. It's usually more efficient if a trusted administrator can see to the recording of routine transactions and just forward issues and matters requiring closer control to an executive. A designated administrator and authorization protocol should be documented in sizable firms, lest management directions dissipate over time. In the author's hometown, the city's human resource director processed an unchallenged form that increased her pay and advanced her rank.

Personnel transaction forms are to move from point to point expeditiously. It's desirable that an employee's recorded job status and pay are current on a next-day basis. Documentation of injuries, absences and all matters should be prompt so that any information retrieved from files is accurate and current. Frustration is commonly caused when a necessary authorizer is traveling and a payroll change deadline or job offer is delayed.

Mandated Information

Considerable required data stipulated by regulations from the Wage and Hour Division and the IRS is kept in the payroll department rather than in an individual's personnel folder.

   a. Demographic data, such as Social Security number, date of birth and a copy of the formal hire document are commonly filed with the payroll records.

   b. Personnel transactions, such as job changes, layoffs and leaves of absence, are documented via a personnel change notification document and filed in the personnel folder.

c. Hiring activity documentation (date and pay) is necessary for EEO regulations and must be retained generally for one year from the date of application lest there be questions of discrimination. Retain the associated application form, tests, advertisements, hiring orders and results of any medical examinations.

d. Benefit plan documents and records of employee benefit materials must be kept indefinitely.

e. Safety programs, hazard lists, medical reports, training records and written records of injuries by employers with eleven employees or more are necessitated by OSHA.

f. Commercial driver qualifications, records, license copy, driving history, violations and test results are required by the DOL and should be placed in the high-security file.

g. A file of I-9 documentation should be maintained for all employees, even employed family members. Copies of the materials used to complete the right-to-work declaration, such as a birth certificate, should not be copied and retained lest they are later determined to be fraudulent. The fines for neglecting work eligibility confirmation can accumulate to large sums. Employers should have the *Handbook for Employers*, produced by U.S. Citizenship and Immigration Services.[253]

Precautions

Not only could exposed personal information damage an employee, but filed material could be costly to management in litigation. Files can be sanitized of material that is irrelevant (disciplinary actions of five years ago), condemning (résumés with undesirable information), erroneous (faulty appraisals) and disadvantageous (notes of departures from policy); questionable note or code marks on application forms should also be removed.[254]

In disputed matters, such as defending a dismissal, documents are normally viewed as more credible than hearsay, and documentation can be helpful in legal defense. Nurses learn early in their training that "If it isn't recorded, it didn't happen." Documentation can be the point upon which a legal decision may swing and large sums of money turn. Such records include:

- Performance appraisal reports
- Disciplinary warnings (preferably signed by the employee)
- Documentation of notifications for insurance options
- Agreements with employees
- Conditions of an employee leave of absence
- Memos of uncommon incidents
- Receipts of handbook rules and stipulations

---

[253] M-274 (Rev. April 30, 2013) N, found at http://www.uscis.gov/sites/default/files/files/form/m-274.pdf.
[254] In *Ramsey v. American Filter Co.*, 772 F.2d 1303 (7th Cir. 1985), a note on an application form cost an employer $92,500.

- Authorizations to investigate background
- Evidence that mandated safety training has been conducted
- Evidence that efforts have been made to accommodate those with disabilities

As previously noted, individual files should be devoid of references to age, race, religion, Social Security number and gender as well as of information regarding personal financial and family matters.

Absent or mishandled bits of information can have serious legal and/or costly consequences. Many federal government regulators are engaged in the examination of individual personnel records of employers, examining age certifications, I-9 forms and time records for overtime violations. Safety compliance officers are interested in injury reports, training records and injury prevention activities. Keeping records in a state of readiness is due diligence.

Personal information should not leave the premises. In 2006, the national media reported that a laptop computer was left in a public place, and copies of the personal data of about 28.6 million veterans disappeared. In March 2010, 3.3 million students with federal loans had personal information stolen from the files of a private firm. The need for control of personnel information is obvious. If the information is truly required by outsiders, such as for legal actions, it can be subpoenaed.

Accounting

Assets and resources are subject to management accounting. At any point in time, financial management knows the status of its dollars, and transportation firms know the location and availability of its equipment. In order to maximize the utility of assets, the present status of human assets (both active and inactive), too, must be known. If these assets are not on the job and contributing, where are they, and when are they available? Individual department heads normally track the status of their people, but when large numbers of people are involved, a worker can be forgotten for several days or even completely fall through the cracks.

Payroll procedures enable tracking of attendance of hourly paid workers but not explanations of absence. A central administrative position charged with daily payroll and attendance reports can maintain a registry of any worker status that deviates from the norm.

Absent personnel who are accruing benefits and receiving regular pay are costly assets that are worthy of oversight. Monitoring the expected dates of return for ill employees, expediting the return to work of those absent because of injuries, and tracking the use of scheduled vacation or floating holidays require complete and accurate staff work. Program-approved absences most often require only recording. The tracking of open-ended, uncertain periods of absence, such as illness or jury duty, requires more administrative attention.

Retention and Disposal

Records of personnel that are working and being paid are considered *active* records. Those of workers who are on the payroll but not presently working are considered *inactive*. The files of those who have left the payroll are placed in a *terminated* file section that is normally kept handy for several years before being removed from the filing system.

It's necessary to dispose of obsolete and unnecessary records because of space costs and latent legal concerns. The responsibility of managing the disposal of all records may rest with a top legal or financial officer because of his or her understanding of file retention legalities.

Explicit regulations about the retention of most personnel information are scattered among a score of different statutes, including FLSA, CRA and ADA, and are often unclear.[255] There are differences among agencies, different rules that apply to government contractors, and differences depending on states and the number of employees of the employer. Website references may be helpful in identifying those differences.[256] Organization *guidelines for record retention and disposal* that have been suitably approved should be documented as policy or standard procedure for application.

Following is a general pattern of file retention practices, but state laws can vary and these guidelines may not apply in a particular situation. Don't be in a hurry to dispose of the files, even for employees who separated several years ago.

- Unused applications and résumés: 1 year after application date (résumés can constitute a legal landmine if they contain undesirable information)
- Payroll and tax records: 4 years after employee termination
- Hiring job orders, notices and advertisements: 1 year after beginning search date
- Application and activity files: 6 years after termination
- I-9 employment authorization: 1 year after termination
- Credit or consumer report information unrelated to the job must be destroyed (burned, pulverized, smashed or shredded)[257]
- Safety training records: 3 years after termination
- Employment contracts: 3 years after termination
- Medical information: 6 years after termination
- Injury/illness reports, drug and alcohol test reports: 5 years after termination
- Diversity reports (EEO, affirmative action): 2 years after report date
- Benefit plans, annual reports and notices: 6 years after termination
- Litigation-related records: Until the matter is resolved

The laws of each state in which the employer has employees must be applied. For example, while the above list provides general guidelines, Rhode Island has a General Records Retention Schedule with different and additional stipulations. Among them in Section GRS9 are:

---

[255] Jonathan A. Segal, "Is It Shredding Time Yet?" *HR Magazine* 2, no. 2 (February 2003): 109.
[256] Wallace Bonapart and Cornelia Gamlem, "Federal Record Retention Requirements for Employers," Society for Human Resource Management, December 2002.
[257] The Federal Fair and Accurate Credit Transactions Act of 2003 requires destruction of credit report information.

- Unused applications: 3 years after termination
- Sexual harassment allegations: 7 years after termination
- Background investigation reports: 3 years after termination
- Military and injury records: 30 years after termination

Hard-copy files to be retained are normally relegated to an inactive file status and put in a paper storage location, computer data file, or are microfilmed or microfiched. Don't overlook that a certain degree of collection activity is necessary to compile a complete inactive folder. Usually supervisors and department heads have records that should be included when an employee's file is made inactive; otherwise these documents can end up in trashcans, dumpsters, landfills and ultimately court because of the management neglect. Telephone records, voice mail and computer files must be erased or retrieved from discarded electronic equipment in order to avoid identity theft and the violation of personal privacy.

Public organizations use a definitive and formal record structure. Federal agencies have extraordinary record security provisions dealing with national security. The West Virginia Division of Personnel has recordkeeping requirements applicable to state and local units, a synopsis of which serves well as a summary of this section:[258]

> Records should never be destroyed without verifying . . . . retention requirements. . . . Agencies [who] may develop . . . more stringent [procedures] . . . may wish to create a master list of personnel-related records . . . establish a [retention] schedule . . . [and] retain documents that are relevant to anticipated, current or future litigation. Consult with legal counsel prior to removing and disposing . . . maintain the confidentiality of records . . . remember to back up files . . . keep in locked cabinets in a secure area . . . destroy records carefully.

Reports

File information is commonly used for periodic and "on request" reports that contribute to management in general and to specific decisions under consideration. Routine reports to management might address diversity, attendance and employee benefits participation data.

Reports to government bodies include annual EEO and affirmative action reports; the Personal Responsibility and Work Opportunity Reconciliation Act (PRWORA) requires employers to report those who complete W-4s for employment to a state agency within twenty days in order to facilitate the enforcement of child support payments across the nation. Injury reports were discussed

---
[258] West Virginia Division of Personnel, "Guide to Selected Human Resource/Payroll Record-Keeping Requirements," February 2007.

in chapter 8. Benefit communication and the availability of official documents of programs for regulators were mentioned in that chapter as well.

Summary Remarks

Recordkeeping of personnel and related activities, which begins on the first day of employee work and continues through termination, is a fundamental program of HRM. Documenting and/or recording employee activity satisfies *government regulations*, serves to *protect the organization* and provides *basis for decisions*. However, having possession of personal information about people creates liability and vulnerability for an employer. This information must be managed, secured and properly used.

Effective and efficient recording begins with simple forms, has an established and routine system with which every supervisor is knowledgeable, and includes authorization protocols and secure depositories. The following conditions are representative of desirable records management:

- Required information is efficiently collected and maintained.
- Required notifications of employees are evidenced.
- Documentation of incidents is available.
- There is order to necessary and desirable information files.
- There is designated responsibility and accountability.
- Suitable technology and computer software, and other physical resources for efficient collection and secure storage, are applied.
- Information is filed in such a manner that data can be acquired and/or compiled in a timely manner.
- Records and depositories have controlled access and security provisions.
- Protocols for internal and external file access are established and enforced.
- Information is current and readily available for the use of management and government regulators.
- Guidelines for compliance with retention requirements are established and applied.

Applicable Competencies

Organization, accuracy, administrative skills, computer literacy and a discreet nature. Knowledge of recordkeeping and disposal regulations.

Applicable Resources

Access to IT expertise, well-designed instruments for data collection, protocols and management support.

SAMPLE JOB DESCRIPTION

POSITION TITLE: Personnel Records Administrator   DATE: Jan 2, 20__
DEPARTMENT: Human Resources   REVISED:_____
APPROVALS SUPERVISOR:_____
REPORTS TO: HR Manager

SUMMARY STATEMENT: Administers those policies, programs and procedures related to personnel records, regulations and transactions, including those related to confidentiality and personal privacy. Remains cognizant of the status and absence of all accounting employees. Provides reports and records for regulators and management in an efficient, discreet and cost-effective manner. Endeavors to minimize benefit costs of workers' compensation and unemployment.

SCOPE: A technical organization of about 500 employees. This position serves as the focal point of attendance control, documentation of all personnel actions (hires, separations), current and accurate records and personnel databases (electronic and paper).

MAJOR ACCOUNTABILITIES:

10%	1. Initiates individual employee records from new-employee enrollment materials (application, I-9), maintains activity records of employees during employment tenure and applies proper record retention practices.
10%	2. Maintains forms, databases (paper and electronic), and personnel information transmission systems (routing, authorizations) to meet regulatory and management needs.
5%	3. Monitors approved leaves of absence (FMLA, military, jury duty) in accord with policy and regulations.
10%	4. Receives notices of unemployment benefit claims and evaluates them for legitimacy; may represent the company at hearings as directed.
5%	5. Submits injury reports to insurance providers and tracks employee medical status and availability.
10%	6. Promotes employee attendance and the return of employees to limited work assignments.
15%	7. Maintains record access and security.
10%	8. Trains and coaches supervisors on absence policy and control and on the proper completion and use of change notices and other forms.
5%	9. Generates reports for government agencies (EEO, injury) as required and for management (attendance, census lists) as requested.
10%	10. Remains informed of regulations regarding leaves of absence, workers' compensation, privacy and other related legalities.
5%	11. Monitors and records evidence of insurance benefit notifications.
5%	12. Collects all record information upon employee termination and stores materials in accord with file retention policies.
	13. Performs other duties as required in accord with policies, rules and expectations.

ENVIRONMENT CONDITIONS: Normal office conditions with occasional meetings in the community.

EQUIPMENT USED: Normal office equipment with use of computer and other electronic devices (HRIS software), file folders and file cabinets.

MENTAL REQUIREMENTS: Exceptional clerical aptitude and detail accuracy, dexterity, tolerance of routine. Capacity to apply multitudes of regulations and procedures to a system. Appreciation for protecting employee privacy.

PHYSICAL REQUIREMENTS (AS PRESENTLY PERFORMED): Ability to see, hear and communicate in person and electronically. Very light lifting and normal office activity. Low and high reaching into file cabinets.

SELECTION CRITERIA: Must have demonstrated responsible attention to duties with detail and little supervision. Ability to communicate and coordinate activity with employees, payroll associates and supervisors. Must know or have the facility to learn computer software application, workers' and unemployment compensation regulations, standard procedures. Will preferably have demonstrated facility for cost control, work simplification, innovation, and skillful interaction with people.

PERFORMANCE STANDARDS:

Employee

- Reliable in attendance and promptness
- Attends to tasks

Position

- Knows and satisfies applicable regulations and procedures
- Knows the status of each employee every day
- Information transmission to and from supervisors is clear, accurate and prompt
- All claims for unemployment benefits are legitimate or challenged
- Injured personnel return to full work status as soon as possible
- Access to personnel files is in accord with desired procedures
- Required and requested reports are submitted promptly
- Desirable and required training records and waiver evidence are recorded
- Group insurance and FMLA notice requirements are fulfilled

Review Materials

Content Exercises

1. Name two primary reasons for maintaining personnel files.
2. Who do personnel records belong to?
3. Name three physical components of a normal personnel record system.
4. Name three policy or procedure needs of a system.
5. How long should an unused application form be kept?
6. What is the minimum period of time that the file of a terminated employee is retained?
7. What information about a previous employee can be safely disclosed to outsiders?
8. Name two potential adverse allegations if personnel information is misused.

Practical Applications

1. Inquire about personnel record administration in your organization. Number of folders per employee? Security and access provisions? Retention guidelines?
2. Acquire a personal action form, new-hire form or a previous affirmative action report.
3. Inquire about the filing, access and types of information available electronically. If your firm processes medical information, report on the duties of the privacy officer.
4. Does your state require that employees have file access? Are there any conditions of that access?
5. Ask to see your personnel file. How is the access process handled? Does it contain a handbook receipt? Signed application? Inappropriate matter?
6. If you possess information about several commercial HRIS software programs, prepare some remarks about their differences.
7. What electronic and/or hard-copy reports are routinely generated from personnel files at your place of employment?
8. How is the gatekeeping of personnel and medical files handled in your organization? Is a specific position delegated? Who facilitates when the normal incumbent is absent?

Case-Study Discussions

Collaborative Study 10.1

Components of HRIS

This assignment is designed so it could be used as a collaborative exercise for up to five separate small teams of a larger study unit. It would be an extensive but worthwhile task for an individual reader. At its conclusion, the exercise should have addressed most of the considerations and options associated with personnel record systems. Each small team has a discussion/recommendation assignment, the summary of which is to be shared with others.

A leader would form the groups, make the subject assignments and see that primary factors of each of the input reports are displayed for communal benefit. Each group must identify a principal spokesperson.

The situation: A new HR specialist is assigned the task of recommending a personnel record system. The company, a growing manufacturing firm, currently has 100 employees but is a federal contractor and is expecting a number of military clothing contracts requiring several hundred more personnel. Management's interest is to establish a personnel record system that anticipates the greater number of employees and prepares for government affirmative action and other compliance demands.

The specialist decides to call on present employees, vendors and other acquaintances (including IT people) who might contribute to developing a plan for recommendation to management. The specialist knows that recording names and addresses for employees is necessary—at least every employer collects that data.

The five groups should arrange to meet separately in order to compile recommendations and procedures for one aspect of the total system. It's reasonable to expect that some overlapping views will take place among the inputs, requiring accommodation and refinement of individual group suggestions. Some issues may remain unresolved. The five group assignments, or units for an individual reader, are as follows:

CONTENT AND CAPABILITY: What capabilities, banks and data outputs are necessary or desired and can be anticipated from management? What types of information and report needs can be foreseen for a database? Any employee interface? This team should be scheduled and launched early because its output affects others.

HARDWARE AND SOFTWARE SYSTEMS: What equipment, software and workstations make sense? Consult with the group above. Should some data remain only hard copy? What input and access equipment is necessary? What are several optional data-handling installations, considering the needs and cost-effectiveness?

SECURITY: There will be security demands and audits by federal personnel. What security provisions should be planned? Should any sensitive data be excluded from the databases, or can the total system be secured? How might access be controlled from remote points of the system? What safeguards should be designed in software or administratively applied?

POLICIES AND ORGANIZATION: What work groups will be primary in input and output? How should information be collected and transmitted? What staffing is necessary? Which departments will use it? How are decisions made? Where does this fit with other units? Where does the position report in the hierarchy?

ADMINISTRATION: What is necessary in terms of maintenance, security and administration? What input procedures, rules, or controls, and which data retention practices, should be anticipated? What protocols should be established for transmission and access? What are primary duties of a caretaker? Craft a practical and descriptive position title, and consider three primary qualifications.

CHAPTER 11
LEGAL COMPLIANCE AND RISKS

Chapter Objectives

- The prevalence of law in personnel management activities
- Employer requirements under federal law
- The nature of state laws
- Management education
- Common issues and employer missteps
- Auditing and oversight of legal vulnerability
- Minimizing adverse legal actions and costs

The Role of Laws and Regulations

Earlier chapters have made frequent reference to legal applications to personnel management. Laws are core aspects in employment, safety, benefits and employee separations. Employers in the U.S. and generally in the Western Hemisphere are more obligated by social standards than those in most other countries to provide regulated conditions; compliance with law is fundamental. For the most part our employment laws address justice, fairness, welfare and protection in the interest of the American worker.

Employers must navigate through a maze of laws to identify those that apply to them. Statutes have been enacted that apply to a variety of employers and employees through different societal or economic segments, such as industry (maritime regulations), subject matter (honesty testing), individual circumstances (veterans), the general public (ethnicity) or employer size. The Family and Medical Leave Act is applicable to all employers with fifty or more employees in the private sector and some public sector units. The comparable Rehabilitation Act of 1973 applies to the remaining public organizations. Employers are to comply with societal standards of equality, child and worker safety, and parameters for termination and compensation, and provide employees with training and information about their protections and rights. They are to provide special consideration to the disabled and veterans, deliver personal privacy and control abuse to which workers may be subjected. This wide scope of finite standards for employers results in the need for substantial understanding of employment law as an element of HRM.

Some federal laws don't apply to smaller employers (see FMLA above), but states may lower the threshold of the law's application. Regulations for employee safety vary by industry, and about half the states have a safety law other than federal OSHA. Employer practices with overtime eligibility, pay at the time of separation and fair employment should be in conformity with state regulations.

Specific laws apply to federal government entities and government contractors. Over the years, federal government employees have been ascribed significant protection under constitutional law, and state and federal statutes have granted public employment special rights for a century.[259] There are specific protections in government regarding freedom of speech, association and personal privacy because of relevancy to constitutional provisions.[260] However, beyond a few fundamental constitutional protections, employers in all the economic sectors are subject to the same or similar regulations in workforce matters.

Law is the cornerstone of the employer-employee relationship.

Hundreds of laws and thousands of regulations have been promulgated in the interest of both public and for-profit workers. However, when short-term political interests overcome long-term consequences, there can be negative consequences for employees. The legislated employee vesting rules contributed to the demise of defined benefit plans, state overtime laws frustrate the granting of flexible hours, and the penalties for benefit administration errors discourage benefit offerings. The OSHA regulations exceeded legislative intent and required reversal by act of Congress, and in 2012, a frustrated U.S. district judge accused the EEOC of a strategy to sue employers first and "ask questions later," dismissing a class-action lawsuit. Political and regulatory action does not always benefit the general welfare. As a result, HRM professionals find it occasionally advantageous or necessary to undertake political activity.

During the last fifty years, the increase of government regulation has substantially altered the manner of managing personnel. Focusing the choice of personnel on the basis of a position's job-related considerations and essential functions establishes *credibility* in personnel selection. The use of due process procedures formulated through the Civil Service Reform Act and amendments evidences the *pursuit of justice*. *Integrity* is served through transparency of benefit plan details and fixed financial accountability for retirement plan funding. *Standards* have been established requiring valid employment tests, just cause in dismissals and specified safety conditions. A *balance* of labor and management power exists through collective bargaining and the increased application of arbitration in conflict resolution. This increase in functional definition has resulted in human resource management becoming a more respected function; its contributions readily earn it a more prominent role and greater relevancy to management.

---

[259] "Local governments . . . cannot deny a person of rights, privileges, and immunities secured by the Constitution." Civil Rights Act 1811 (U.S.C. 1983).
[260] For a more definitive discussion of the differences between the applicable employment law between municipalities and the private sector, see P. Edward French, "Employment Laws and the Public Sector Employer," *The Public Administrator Review* 69, no. 1 (January/February 2009): 92–103.

The demands of the function include the understanding and monitoring of compliance and defensive measures, policies and positions that reflect developing social and legal expectations, programs to satisfy regulatory demands, standardization of practices, responsiveness to a wiser workforce, and more knowledgeable administrators and supervisors. Defensive measures include announcing disclaimers, providing accurate and timely messages, and responding to discontent and issues. By any measure, such demands and challenges elevate the role of human resource management.

This book is not intended to give legal advice in any particular situation, time or place, but to caution readers that regulations underlay our activity, whether evident or not. Students of the function should know points of risk and defenses. A number of sources of information about regulations, some with a minimum of legalese,[261] and, of course, professional legal counsel are available.

Sources of Regulations

Laws and regulations emanate from a number of different legal jurisdictions. Our legislatures create *statutory law* and our court system generates *common law*. Readers must keep in mind that all laws are enacted with "the consent of the governed" as per the Declaration of Independence. Regardless of our reactions, our laws emanate from those we elect to act on our behalf.

Statutes, the primary source of HRM law, are formed in Congress and promulgated and enforced by *federal agencies*. Legislation usually addresses issues about employee protection and safety, worker welfare and compensation, and reemployment rights such as are covered under the Family and Medical Leave Act. Fair treatment in the workplace was the primary subject in the Civil Rights Act and Civil Service Reform Act.

Regulations are derived from statutes. Agencies such as OSHA dictate the detailed requirements for compliance that are published in the Federal Register. Trade and professional associations and local business groups disseminate the information to members. *Court decisions* develop patterns of law based on preceding and related court judgments. The concept of at-will employment initially formed from a court decision and subsequently has been enacted as a statute in most states. Regardless of how certain the outcome appears, caution should be exercised before seeking a court decision in an employment controversy; high costs are certain, but judgments, whether by judge or jury, are unpredictable.

Executive orders are pronouncements by the president that have the effect of law within the federal government. In 1940, Executive Order 8587 first mandated that federal employees could not be denied opportunity because of race, creed or color.

The complex pattern of mandates and the multiple sources of regulation present a challenge for employers. Readers must focus on the subjects affecting their industry and occupations and develop dependable information sources that will meet their informational needs.

---

[261] An HRM law text for non-lawyers is Remington et al, *Human Resources Law*, 5th ed. (Upper Saddle River: Prentice Hall, 2011)

Basic Standards

Those with responsibilities in personnel management should be conversant of at least the following core of prominent and fundamental federal standards for workplaces. Whether or not an employer's small size excuses a legal obligation, applicants, employees and the public regard these expectations as norm in employment, so employers would do well to adopt compatible positions and conduct.

- Supporting equal opportunity and diversity (CRA, 1964)
- Adhering to child labor prohibitions (FLSA, 1938)
- Verification of employability[262] (IRCA, 1986)
- Personal pay records (FLSA, 1938)
- Prohibiting abuse (CRA, 1964)
- Maintaining safety standards and mandated training (OSHA, 1970)
- Acknowledging collective bargaining rights (NLRA, 1934)
- Employing due process in public sector dismissals (CSRA, 1978)
- Accommodating protected groups (CRA, 1964)
- Implementing employee privacy protections (various)

Federal fines for noncompliance with law can be sizable and are most often imposed on smaller firms who may be uninformed, apathetic or neglectful. Eighty percent of fines are assessed against employers with fewer than 100 employees and 55 percent against employers with fewer than fifty employees. A financial penalty for falsifying a safety or payroll record could be $10,000 and up to six months in jail. In courts, the settlements from about 50,000 sexual harassment allegations each year average about $250,000.

Illegal Discrimination

The principles of fair employment and equal opportunity are a dominant and common workplace standard. A diverse workforce often contributes to positive employee relationships. An objective in the Civil Service Reform Act is a desire "to achieve a workforce from all segments of society."[263] This expression of the pursuit of diversity affects the federal government and those in the private sector with government contracts. Some states and communities have fair employment statutes that are applicable to public and private employers.

Fundamental to a condition of fair employment is the mind-set of management. Managing with a minimum of bias in thought and deed becomes more common as the generational spiral of learning overcomes centuries of misdirected human conditioning. Management that pursues diversity in overt and proactive messaging is in support of the nation's preferred social theme and minimizes legal exposure.

---

[262] In a November 2008 *HR Magazine* article, Bill Leonard reported that following an ICE raid, two HR managers faced federal charges for 9,000 violations of the child labor law.
[263] PL29-454 sec. 2301.

The primary application of equal opportunity is the mandate that choices for assignments are to be made on the basis of *job-related demands* and not on peripheral or irrelevant matters such as color, age or gender.[264] This practice applies not just to hiring decisions but to the wide spectrum of personnel choices, including selection for promotion, overtime, layoff and recall. The Fairness Doctrine applies to equal treatment regarding facilities, approved absences, pay, discipline and standards of conduct.[265]

There are situations where preferential hiring is legal. Recall that employers are obligated to discriminate against those without documented authorization to work. (See also provisions for BFOQ and veteran preference in Chapter 2.)

Applying Fair Employment

An employer's statement about equal opportunity can provide direction and a favorable image but can also be shallow compared to the elevated challenges of affirmative action. Below are sample guidelines for a fair employment program to which an employer and supervisors might commit. The program reflects legal obligations and defensive tactics, and can be used in educating management, forming culture and demonstrating the intent of compliance. Establishing a diverse culture can require much more than exhibiting intentions, including explicit coaching or personnel changes to ensure the desired outcome.[266]

FAIR EMPLOYMENT STANDARDS POLICY

It is our policy to comply with federal, state and local fair employment and equal opportunity statutes and regulations.

PRACTICES:

- Job vacancies will be advertised in a manner intended to reach a diverse audience.
- Choices among people for opportunities in employment are to focus on job-related considerations.
- The steps (tests) used in employment procedures will be valid and applied in a manner consistent with equal opportunity.
- When employees cross the threshold of the organization's property, they are expected to set aside any prejudicial behaviors that are illegal in the workplace.
- Our workplace is expected to be free of disrespectful treatment of people.
- Our supervisors receive instruction on our fair employment practices.
- We endeavor to comply with federal equal pay regulations.
- Disadvantaged applicants and employees are to be accommodated in accord with laws.
- We recognize the personal privacy rights of our employees.
- We intend that any dismissal decisions be made on the basis of business necessity or failure to meet standards for performance or conduct.[267]

By:_____ Title:_____ Date:_____

---

[264] See the methods for identifying and documenting job-related matters in Chapter I.
[265] Title VII of the Civil Rights Act of 1964 covers all private employers, state and local governments, and educational institutions.
[266] Joan E. Pynes, *Human Resources Management for Public and Nonprofit Organizations,* 3rd ed. (San Francisco: Jossey-Bass, 2004), 106.
[267] Not applicable to executive political positions in some public sector organizations.

The most frequent allegations of discrimination are on the basis of *race*, *gender*, *age* and *disability*. Remedies for victims can include issuing back pay, attorney fees and compensatory damages. In the case of harassment, employers may also suffer a requirement of extensive *remedial training* of all employees by discrimination experts.

Harassment and Abuse

Common illegal discrimination includes actions that disparage women, including harassment. There are several forms, however, and not all victims are female. Three male police officers alleged discrimination on the basis of a "hostile work environment" created by their chief who "favored lesbian females."[268]

Federal civil rights statutes do not have a specific provision prohibiting harassment, but the courts[269] and the EEOC have so interpreted law. Harassment can exist when a favor is granted in return for sexual considerations, or when an environment is hostile because of ongoing jokes, sexual innuendos or propositions. Human nature being what it is, harassment will be a perpetual problem and represents significant exposure for employers. The distinction between romance and harassment can swing on whether the flirting is *welcome or unwanted*. Employees subject to the attention of others should be instructed to clearly object to the unwanted attentions or to make a formal declaration of tolerance that management should record. A victim should report the harassment to a representative of management.

Personal relationships between supervisors and subordinates are particularly difficult, because when they go sour, the power role of the supervisor can be used by a (previously willing) subordinate as the reason for participation in the relationship. In-house romances are legal landmines.

Regulators expect employers to have a clearly expressed posture and applied discipline on the prohibition of sexual harassment. Sample policy provided by regulators is very specific and includes proscribed procedures as part of the statement. EEOC model policy or legal counsel should be used as a basis for alterations. As mentioned earlier in the text, it's not recommended that amateurs revise legal and government language. A declared position should address bullying, disrespect and harassment of anyone for any reason in the course of employment. Often, the prohibition of disrespecting a religion is included in the policy statement. The prescribed policy statement of the EEOC includes:

- A complaint process to use
- Assurance of no retaliation for complaining
- A definition of harassment (teasing, propositions)
- A management commitment to prohibit illegal disrespect
- An employee education procedure
- A commitment to investigate allegations
- Documentation of incidents

---

[268] Charges filed in Hennepin County District Court, MN, on February 10, 2010.
[269] The first judicial recognition of harassment occurred in *Williams v. Saxbe*, 413 F. Supp. 654 (D.C. 1976).

- Resolution of the complaint
- Disciplinary action as appropriate
- Periodic reminders of management's concern

Enforcement

Equal opportunity law may be enforced through local, state, or federal EEOC or Fair Employment Practices agency offices, which enforce the CRA, EPA, ADEA, and the ADA, among other statutes.[270] Any employee, or someone on their behalf, can allege a violation of rights under the statutes. A discrimination allegation must be filed (free of cost) within 180 days of the incident and must precede the filing of any lawsuit, this in deference to clogging the court system with cases. Many groundless allegations are dismissed early in the process.

An allegation is evaluated for *reasonable cause*, and officials will seek to conciliate the matter (sometimes with a cash settlement) for a speedy resolution. If conciliation is unsuccessful, an investigation will ensue. An employer's transgression needn't be intentional, but if it resulted in *disparate treatment* or unequal representation, even inadvertently, it can be found to be *with cause*, resulting in further action.

Completion of the I-9 form at the time of employment is a priority. In 2010, there were 2,200 government audits of employer I-9 document files. Enforcement officials may appear unannounced and present a Notice of Inspection. I-9 forms should be in an available file maintained by a designated administrator. Submitting new-hire data for validation to a database of the federal government through the voluntary *E-Verify program* is troublesome

> **Employers are required to investigate all complaints of sexual harassment, but wisdom suggests that all incidents of bullying and disrespect should also be addressed.**

but evidences good-faith effort in compliance. Federal agencies and contractors must use it.[271] If the federal file data is fraudulent, of course, the effort will fail.[272] Practices that will mitigate enforcement issues are following standard practice, completing accurate staff work and investigating missteps to resolution.

Notifications to Employees

There are a number of specific notifications that employers are obliged to provide to employees, the most recognized being the numerous posters of employee rights displayed near gathering places or employee entrances in a workplace. A list of mandated messages is provided in chapter 5. This obligation is a necessary part of fulfilling compliance responsibility.

---

[270] Disability discrimination in federal government is the subject of the Rehabilitation Act of 1973, administered by the EEOC.
[271] *Payroll Manager Newsletter* 25, no. 9 (May 7, 2010): 4–5.
[272] Bill Leonard, "Researchers: Stolen Identities Often Slip Through E-Verify," *HR Magazine* 55, no. 4 (April 2010).

Unions and Collective Action

The rights and possibilities of employees forming a union surface a number of legal risks for private sector employers. Union membership and collective action by employees for purposes of negotiating wages, hours and working conditions are protected activity under the National Labor Relations Act of 1935, also known as the Wagner Act.[273] The protection also applies to small groups of employees who ask to meet with management about the above subjects in units where there is no union. The protection includes a prohibition against any retaliation by management for union activity.

In order to sustain a for-profit organization, management needs to control processes, maintain employee performance and conduct, and manage the costs of its human assets. Unions have different and somewhat contrary priorities: staffing needs, the limitations of management's need or right to outsource work, and, of course, how much money the employer should devote to union labor.

If private sector management resists formal employee organization and collective bargaining, an expressed position should be announced. Employees should know the position and views of management. Readers should refer to chapter 5, which deals with positive employee relation (and union avoidance) tactics. Interacting with labor organizers and negotiators is a unique and rare experience for most managers, and it's common and recommended to consult with knowledgeable experts if union activity develops.

Long-existing law proclaims that employees are free to organize without interference. In that regard, over the years, scores of legal decisions about what constitutes "interference" has resulted in rules of conduct with which the parties must comply. For example, union promotional materials cannot be distributed during work time in work areas, and management cannot prevent discussions about unions during non-work time. In the private sector, the National Labor Relations Board rules on whether a union has satisfied the criteria to be a legitimate bargaining agent for a specific unit of employees; most often the ruling is based on the results of a vote among employees.

Once unions are officially declared as the representative of an employee unit, they will seek to prove their value by *improving working conditions* and *protecting the jobs of members*. Like other organizations, they have a high priority to sustain their existence. To that end, there is an emphasis to secure membership fees by way of dues collection through management's payroll system and to require all potential members to join or at least pay for union representation regardless of whether they choose to join. Unions are bound to represent all the employees in the sanctioned bargaining unit whether the workers are members of the union or not.

Blacklisting, or refusing to hire people for employment because of legitimate union activity, is specifically prohibited under law. Such discriminatory acts are called *unfair labor practices*[274] and can easily occur when management with limited experience in such matters makes knee-jerk reactions or unwise comments to card-signing solicitation or the appearance of union buttons.

Our federal government looks with favor upon unions and takes an accepting or passive role toward membership by their employees as opposed to being contrary or combative as might exist in other economic sectors. However, some units of federal and state employees are not permitted

---
[273] 29 U.S.C.A. § 151.
[274] 29 U.S.C.A. § 158.

to bargain on economic issues. Federal employees in national security and others performing essential public services, such as air traffic controllers and first responders, are prohibited from striking, which is the strongest weapon of a union.

Compensation Matters

Pay for Time Worked

The enrollment of personnel at the time of hire is the point at which payroll activity and *employment status* is initiated. Finance and accounting units normally deal with costs, the delivery of pay and taxes, and the maintenance of financial records, and will sometimes administer the pay program. However, it's common among larger employers that the human resource function sets pay parameters, as they have a greater stake in differences among jobs, job ranking and the role of money in performance.

When pay is based on hours of work, *the recorded time must be accurate*; only several minutes of "slippage" are permitted by regulations. An overtime-eligible employee who does not record time worked during lunch or a break creates liability. In the state of Minnesota, Walmart reportedly settled a lawsuit for $54 million dollars because it "cut corners on meal and rest breaks" of its store employees.[275] Sometimes an employee works a second job for the same employer, performing additional duties unrelated to their core position responsibilities. Regulations require that the total of hours be combined for pay purposes. In the private sector, time off in lieu of pay is only permitted within the same workweek. A few states permit the use of compensatory time for public employees or sometimes for employees in occupations with uncommon scheduling needs.

A number of work-related activities that are sometimes viewed as inconsequential by an employer are in fact compensable, such as picking up the mail on the way to work, or an overtime-eligible employee making coffee before time is recorded. Some examples of matters that have been determined in a court to be *compensable* include*:*

- Putting on or taking off required work gear[276]
- Completing required sales reports
- Attending a required meeting after hours
- Mealtime when it must be at the workstation
- Time spent to conduct work-related travel during the normal workday

Wage and Hour Investigations

Inspections by DOL Wage and Hour Division officials are common in the private sector. They usually result from an employee complaint alleging unpaid overtime dollars in one of the situations above.

---

[275] *Braun v. Walmart, Inc.*, Court File No. 19-CO-01-9790 (Minn. 1st Dist. November 3, 2003).
[276] The time limousine drivers are donning and doffing uniforms has been ruled not compensable, but driving from one job to another is considered work time. Time waiting for a customer has been ruled compensable time. See *Powell v. Carey International,* Inc., No. 05-21395 CIV, 2007 WL 49442 (S.D. Fla. February 1, 2007).

Recall that earlier the suggestion was made that employees be encouraged to voice their complaints to management about perceived injustices before they seek regulatory relief. Listen to employee complaints and head off litigation.

Investigators will probably appear unannounced for a "routine" inspection; all are routine, but most are in response to a complaint. Find time for their visit and exercise due respect. They will conduct themselves professionally and ultimately have their way. Should you refuse them access when they appear, expect them to return with a subpoena and a less positive mood. They will seek evidence of violations through worker interviews and files. They will confirm I-9s and age verifications, and search for overtime pay infractions, including the use of electronic devices by overtime-eligible employees after hours for work in the employer's interest.

Group Benefits

Federal and state benefits for public employees are legislated and enjoy public funding. In the private sector, most benefit offerings are a matter of the employer's choice and ability to pay, and are subject to funding specifications and administrative demands of federal legislation. The financial administration of retirement and health care benefits involves a maze of regulations promulgated through welfare legislation and tax laws.

ERISA requires employers with more than 100 participants to file reports and audits for not only retirement and health care plans but also for some insured disability and prepaid legal and severance plans. Certain plans are exempt because they are paid out of the employer's general assets, such as sick leave, short-term disability plans, and vacation and holiday pay.

Accommodations

Requiring employers to fulfill an obligatory administrative role between employees and the government (with associated liability) began long ago when employers first became the income tax collectors. Statutes impose a number of required employer accommodations on behalf of employees, including veterans, those with disabilities and those whose religious practices conflict with normal workplace practices. Continued job rights after a military or medical absence, and special accommodations for breast-feeding moms, are mandated. Employers must be able to prove they have fulfilled their responsibilities to inform employees on specific benefit matters.

Disabled applicants are to receive affirmative help (for example, interpreters) and preferably an interview to explore job opportunities as part of affirmative action. Search for available work is expected and demonstrates good faith. Very often, interviewers see only the limitations of a person and not the abilities, or in the case of a limited worker, overlook the possibility of a changed workstation. It's important when considering a candidate to explore whether the employee is able to accomplish the *essential functions* of a job and not to disqualify anyone on the basis of incidental duties that can be otherwise satisfied. Accommodations needn't involve sizable sums of money or be a burden on other employees. If employers judge an applicant who is limited to be unqualified, they should be prepared to demonstrate the legitimacy of that decision to officials.

Veterans enjoy favorable treatment in the form of preferential hiring and dismissal protection in public employment, but the same is not true with all private employers. Some view preferential consideration as reverse discrimination, and so some states enact laws in an effort to protect employers from liability for their affirmative action.

Annual affirmative action plans and reports that demonstrate employer outreach toward minority groups are required in the public sector as a means of increasing representation of protected or disadvantaged people. A number of for-profit firms voluntarily undertake affirmative action. Others don't pursue government contracts because of the substantial demands of the program. Directed affirmative recruiting requires a different mind-set than simply being fair and equal in evaluating all the applicants.

ANNUAL AFFIRMATIVE ACTION PLANS

Affirmative action plans to increase representation of protected classes are a requirement of federal and state government and their contractors; others voluntarily adopt them.[277]

An affirmative action plan is a formal written document that includes:[278]

- An equal-opportunity policy statement
- Public and employee communication provisions
- Assigned responsibilities
- A workforce analysis by category of a minority group
- Action plans to improve minority representation

Subjects of State Law

States commonly promulgate laws that extend the application of federal regulations to smaller employers in their state. It's common to require higher minimum wages as a floor for intrastate employee earnings.[279] Other common enactments apply to permissible paycheck deductions and the promptness of pay upon discharge. Utah requires weekend work to be at premium pay. In Michigan, compensatory time off may be used, and in Wyoming it can be applied for state and county employees. Some states permit lower minimum wages for employees who are routinely tipped or who are in training. These matters normally become a matter of course for payroll practitioners in

---

[277] Remington et al., *Human Resources Law*, 5th ed. (Upper Saddle River: Prentice Hall, 2011), 61.
[278] Ibid.
[279] A jury awarded 116 California Walmart employees $172 million for being denied lunch breaks required by California law.

a state, but payrolls prepared by out-of-state payroll administrators can overlook such stipulations and become problematic. Employers must make note of applicable accommodations in their circumstances and be prepared to satisfy them. Readers are urged to research the regulations and agencies for human resource laws in their state.

Legal Landmines

In addition to the well-known legal standards about discrimination and safety generated by statute, numerous rare situations can be problematic, a number of which have been previously mentioned. The potential for claims of fault against management is always lurking. Employees are well informed about their legal protections in general, and allegations of legal transgression might surface months after an incident.

> **Supervisors and managers must learn of legal obligations and risks, ways to deal with them, and the potential consequences of not doing so.**

Careless, uninformed or innocent remarks can create legal exposure not only for an employer but for individual supervisory representatives of management as well. Exaggeration during recruiting may not surface until years later as an allegation of *misrepresentations* of job advancement or income opportunity. A *breach of implied contract* can be based on a careless statement in a handbook or offer letter.

Untrue statements, such as referring to someone as dishonest or a thief before conviction, can result in a charge of *defamation*, not only against the organization but against the person who spoke.[280] Indeed, innocent remarks about the existence of a probationary period can compromise the legitimacy of an at-will employment condition. The use of words like "black" or "Muslim" in referencing minorities can cause startling interruptions in conversation with some people. The use of certain legitimate words are misconstrued and assumed to be disparaging by advocates for political correctness. Adjustments to diversity continue to improve, but be aware that some words can be viewed negatively and use them with caution.

Electronic communication devices come with risks. Employer-owned devices should be subject to policy, include security measures, and be returned when an employee is separated. If an employee uses a personal device for business purposes, accessing the messages can be difficult and costly. The parameters of use that management desires should be repeated often so new personnel are informed and the rules are fully understood.

Negligent hiring can result if someone who is employed without a thorough background investigation proves to be criminal. Employers can be charged with *negligent retention* if an employee's threatening or violent behavior is unaddressed by management and leads to someone getting subsequently injured.

---

[280] *Weissman v. Sri Lanka Curry House, Inc.*, 469 N.W.2d 471 (Minn. Ct. App. 1991).

Employees can have cause for court action if an employer is believed to have *retaliated* against an employee who did something management felt to be to their detriment (e.g., filing an injury claim) but was, after all, legal.[281] If there is vengeful action suffered for reporting an employer's violation of law, either written or oral, the charging employee has protection.[282]

Records are subject to subpoena in court actions, and false appraisals or the total absence of documentation can be problematic. Inaccurate reports and careless recordkeeping can even result in evidence that incriminates the employer. If any legal action is pending, related records should not be altered or destroyed.

The employment of *underage workers* for incidental chores is problematic and a common point of investigation by regulators. Typical violations of law are not having age verification documents, working youngsters beyond the hours stipulated by state law, assigning hazardous work or placing young employees where alcohol is served.

Personal privacy is a constitutional right that constrains the conduct of *searches*, particularly in public employment. Law enforcement and health care employers must be particularly diligent in how they handle information to which they have access. Privacy can also be an issue if background inquiries of a candidate are made without authorization to do so, as could happen if the necessary signature was missing from the application form.

Federal and some state wage laws require a prevailing local pay rate as determined by the DOL to be paid by contractors performing government projects. In 2012, the DOL collected $430,000 in back wages for employees when a contractor paid a lesser but competitive rate for some projects in Minnesota. The *prevailing rate* is commonly the rate under union contracts, although 86 percent of construction workers are non-union. Those who accept work for government bodies should know the obligations under the Davis-Bacon Act and Service Contract Act.

Charges of age discrimination, defined as discrimination against those over age forty under federal law, are particularly likely at a time of staff reductions. Even when the employer is able to express a *business justification* for any termination or denial of promotion that favors a younger employee, an allegation shouldn't be a surprise. Thinly veiled attempts to eliminate an employee's job only to have it be reconstituted under another title months later and occupied by a younger employee are not uncommon and create legal exposure for the employer.

Risk Reduction Actions

A Knowledge Base

To accomplish compliance with regulations and reduce legal risks requires *knowledge of the rules and regulations* and the methods available for coping with them. Important, too, is an understanding of the *consequences* for neglecting them. Newsletters from professional and employer associations provide notices of legal developments. For complex or uncertain situations, expert advice should be sought, and is typically available through an industry association in the private sector or

---

[281] *Donnellon v. Fruehauf Corp.*, 794 F.2d 598 (11th Cir. 1986).
[282] *Kasten v. Saint-Gobain Performance Plastics Corp.*, 09-834 (S. Ct. March 22, 2011).

through state bureaucratic resources. Often, certified public accountants are a source of counsel to their small-business clients. Municipalities and school districts frequently use labor contract experts for union negotiations, and outside expertise is often used in the private sector upon the receipt of any enforcement investigation notice, a threat of litigation, and for labor-relations assistance.Enforcement agencies of the federal government provide valuable resources through their websites. In terms of regulations that presently exist, OSHA, EEOC, DOL and the DOT provide extensive information.

Management Direction

Management must declare its position on compliance matters at least as clearly as it does in regard to other priorities, such as high quality or customer service. That should be followed by designating responsibility for oversight, preparing supervisors for fulfilling their responsibilities and educating management on appropriate conduct.

Implementation Tools

Communicated and applied *policies* on crucial matters can make expectations clear. Such policies serve as "standing orders" and give notice of the way things are to be handled. Well-drafted and implemented policy can prevent erroneous decisions and inconsistency and keep matters on the intended path.

Standard procedures and programs establish considered and intended practices in order to achieve uniform and consistent application within settled operational routine. Protocols in staffing, such as trained interviewers using patterned formats and thorough background investigations, prevent untold numbers of undesirable incidents. Established regimen reduces the likelihood of missteps.

> **Actions necessary to ensure compliance and avoid missteps should be designed into forms, programs, meeting agendas and routine daily activities whenever practical.**

Informed supervisors fulfill a principal role in avoiding legal issues. They must know of management priorities and expectations, legal hazards, and desirable practices for giving directions, training and discipline. The application and implementation of continuous management education will keep the subjects on the screen. The earlier chapter on training suggests specific subject matter.

Written materials should represent desired intentions and principles in a consistent manner. Personnel management activity is often verbal, but there are administrative forms, postings and materials that might be subject to ill-intended criticism and inquiry, so clarity and accuracy is necessary. Application forms, handbooks, personnel transaction forms, policies and materials distributed to employees should all be free of inadvisable wording or inquiries. Any key points and disclaimers in written materials can benefit from being conspicuous with bold or large letters.[283]

---

[283] *Silchia v. MCI Telecommunications Corp.,* 942 F. Supp. 1369 (D. CO. 1996).

The use of appropriate defensive caveats and disclaimers reduces liability. Checklists can provide administrative accuracy and help prevent overlooking an important matter. There are protocol checklists for several crucial areas herein, including interviewing, candidate evaluation, and employee separation and dismissal.

An *employee information program* consisting of policies, expectations, standards and matters of employee interest should be applied, as well as a system for feedback. A management that is receptive and effective in their listening will intercept and deflect legal issues. Employees who are adequately informed of expectations and standards are more comfortable in the environment and are less able to seek, or win, legal relief in a conflict. Behavioral standards should be presented at the time of hire, preferably acknowledged in writing, and then periodically repeated through other media. That which is communicated should be subject to some measure of monitoring and control. An employee's signature on a statement is an *acknowledgment of receipt, but not agreement*. Therefore, signatures of those reluctant to sign forms can be qualified by a *notation of their refusal* on the document.

> **The failure to monitor regulatory compliance matters and points of risk can result in legal disputes and extraneous costs.**

Recordkeeping

Legal issues and questions are impacted significantly by the absence, presence or content of records and notes. *Documentation* about departures and absences, incident memos, personnel transactions and disciplinary warnings can be crucial in litigation. In contrast, credit and consumer report information about an employee, once used, is not to be retained. Evidence of completing required *notifications* requires notation. Providing for the collection and reporting of crucial information as part of routine helps prevent valuable record information from being overlooked.

Stewardship

There are insurance policies an employer can purchase to help defray some after-the-fact costs of compliance failures and other claims, but an investment in attending to education, policy, procedure and practices is good stewardship.

Imposed regulations and benefit plans demand cost oversight. The expenses attributable to workers' compensation and unemployment benefit claims can involve substantial unnecessary expense. Specifying when vacation is actually earned can avoid issues as well as unintended expenditures. Employers frequently undertake political action to prevent costly regulations; a rule in Wisconsin requires a minimum of ten rings of the telephone when calling someone in to work overtime. If the rings are not completed, the employee is to be paid for the hours of work missed because the employer failed to give proper notice of the opportunity.

Compliance and Risk Audit

A periodic examination of legal compliance and points of risk serves as a means of measuring legal compliance and correcting wayward practices. Remote locations or small units in large locations are more likely to lose their way. Data should be examined to learn the diversity situation in the isolated locations. Pay practices should be examined for traveling technical service representatives. In small firms, the relative pay of males and females doing similar work requires just a minute to determine. Audits will surface problematic deficiencies or oversights.

> **Misrepresentations and misunderstandings are legal landmines. An expert should draft or examine all written agreements and general employee communications.**

Such reviews are sometimes carried out by outside specialists to ensure unbiased evaluations of practices and to avoid potential management conflicts. The subjects displayed in this chart are less complete with benefit matters than would be the case if conducted by a law firm. The audit records are subject to subpoena and so should *not* be retained.[284]

AN AUDIT CHECKLIST

FAIR EMPLOYMENT

- The recruiting of applicants reaches a wide scope of population sectors.
- A standard process for personnel selection exists in each unit.
- The basis of personnel choices is job-related essential functions.
- Each qualifying test used in making choices has a valid basis.
- Provisions for the assistance of applicants with disabilities are in readiness.
- Valid and essential job-related qualifications are used in filling job vacancies.
- Policies about sexual harassment and medical leave are publicized.
- Management applies a clear prohibition of disrespect or bullying of employees.
- All employees understand and comply with harassment policy.
- Pay for female employees is in compliance with law.
- Department practices dealing with time off and discipline are uniform and consistent.
- Pregnancies are considered a disability.
- Contracted third-party providers fulfill regulatory requirements.

RECORDS AND INFORMATION

- A routine and secure system of handling personnel information is in place.
- There is clear policy on the use of electronic communication devices.
- Candidates for employment are subject to diligent background investigations.
- Signed application forms are free of marks and notations.
- Payroll and overtime records are accurate.
- Guidelines for record retention are available for reference.
- Little or no private information is available on an electronic database.
- Confidential record information is suitably secured and access limited.
- An I-9 form is filed for each employee.
- Employee handouts are reviewed by subject experts.*

---

[284] The practice of HRM auditing isn't new. One early initiative was "Auditing the Personnel Function in a Decentralized, Multi-unit Organization," *Personnel Journal* 47, no. 3 (March 1968), by this author.

Records and Information (continued)

- Record content, such as appraisals and incident reports, are valid.
- Training records regarding employee safety and harassment are complete and filed.
- Supervisor training records are complete and filed.
- Personnel medical information and any contracts are under extraordinary security.
- Personnel files are devoid of references to legal shortcomings and résumés.
- The files of people younger than eighteen at the time of hire contain age certification.
- Each personnel file contains receipts for handbooks and any loaned equipment.*
- There are no employees treated as independent contractors.
- Applicable state laws are on file.
- Employer communications (applications, handbooks) use caveats and disclaimers effectively.
- Benefit plan documents are accessible to employees upon request.
- FMLA and harassment policies and other required posters are conspicuously displayed.
- Benefit plan notices to employees are available and satisfy regulations.
- Management is periodically informed of the status of employee diversity.*
- Compensation, tax and compliance reports are professionally prepared and submitted in a timely manner.
- Employee agreements are in accord with legal advice.
- An effective system for collecting and resolving complaints is in use.

EMPLOYEE SAFETY

- Supervisors accept their responsibility to negate hazards.
- First-aid equipment is in readiness.
- Medical care facilities are nearby or a first-aider is trained.
- Hazards are identified and documented.
- Evacuation procedures are in readiness and diagrams posted.
- Injuries are logged and posted (if required).
- Required material safety data sheets are used by employees.
- Applicable safety standards are satisfied and the accompanying documents available.
- Required safety training is fulfilled.
- Injury reports indicate an analysis was made to determine cause.

MANAGEMENT PRACTICES

- Management adopts and broadcasts an at-will employment condition.
- Management expectation about compliance matters is clearly understood by supervisors.*
- Supervisors know the standard procedures and complaint-handling protocol.*
- Employees can express essential standards of conduct and performance.*
- Positions and standards for performance and conduct are applied.*
- Oversight of legal requirements is assigned and fulfilled.*
- Information about legal matters is routinely collected and disseminated.*
- A legal expert has been designated for contact if necessary.*
- Complaints with legal implications are transmitted and acted upon expeditiously.
- Supervisors who interview have been instructed in appropriate processes.
- Unemployment and workers' compensation programs are administered in a cost-effective manner and in accord with regulations.
- Supervisors are knowledgeable about legal matters such as retaliation, defamation and safety compliance.
- Pay is reviewed for equal pay compliance.
- Positions requiring employment agreements are flagged.*
- Dismissals are carried out in accord with approved procedures.
- Copies of state employment, privacy and compensation laws are readily accessible.*
- The organization has an able and diverse complement of personnel.
- The uniformity and consistency of discipline and other practices is monitored.

*These indicators identify those matters that are defensive in nature rather than having imminent risk or necessity for legal compliance.

Summary Remarks

Managing compliance and legal risks is a major function of contemporary HRM. Owners, customers, employees and the public have interest in an organization functioning within the law. Government regulators have a specific duty to ensure compliance and respond to employee and citizen complaints. Management should consider the array of eyes they have upon them, the multitude of points at which they are vulnerable, and steps they can take to keep them within social parameters.

This chapter enumerates scores of federal and state legal obligations of public and private employers, principal among them federal statutes about illegal discrimination, employee health, pay practices, child labor and collective bargaining. It identifies state and federal court actions that make employers financially vulnerable. It goes on to suggest programs (EEO), activities (education) and resources (legal information) that managements can use to satisfy the law and reduce legal exposure. HRM is the normal channel through which personnel regulatory matters become implemented in organizations.

Common issues involve illegal discrimination, including harassment, faulty discharge, unpaid wages and failures to fulfill FMLA requirements. Key situations where outside expertise is recommended are the organization of unions, the monitoring of published written materials, and group benefit plan design and compliance. Additional areas to monitor include:[285]

- Workplace harassment. (Management must prohibit.)
- Interview policies and procedures. (Relate qualifications to job specifications.)
- Staffing alternatives. (Use contingent worker sources.)
- Handbooks and manuals. (Use caveats.)
- Vacation and leave-of-absence policy. (Consider eligibility questions.)
- Business communication equipment issues. (Use, abuse and misuse.)

Several conditions indicate success in meeting legal standards: 1) the absence of any agency enforcement visits or litigation, 2) all safety hazards are abated, 3) a diversity of personnel at different levels of hierarchy and in different units compatible with community characteristics and 4) the obligations of accommodation and employee notifications are duly satisfied.

The defenses an employer can apply include staying current on legal matters, assigning responsibility for compliance and risk reduction, applying obligatory policies, administering desirable procedures, using job content in personnel choices, applying uniform and consistent practices, announcing and implementing a culture of legal compliance, and encouraging employees to complain to management before they contact government officials.

---

[285] Bruce Kasten, "Common HR Headaches and their Remedies," *Law Office Management and Administration Report* 5, no. 1 (January 2005): 3–5.

Applicable Competencies

Knowledge of internal and external HRM regulations and the points of the organization at which exposure exists; skills and authority with which to accomplish management education and practices; a willingness to identify and confront neglect of policy and procedures.

Applicable Resources

Access to information and legal expertise; useful policies, programs and procedures; the support of management to monitor and implement desirable actions.

Review Materials

Content Exercises

1. List five situations or conditions that represent legal exposure of employers.
2. Explain a compliance or risk role (exposure or defense) for each of the following: job analysis, application form, interview, background examination, complaint procedure.
3. Name an employee protection, benefit or accommodation from each of the following statutes: OSHA, NLRA, FLSA, USERRA, FEP.
4. Describe the general obligation of an employer under the following statutes: ADA, ERISA, FMLA, COBRA.
5. List several tactics available to management to satisfy necessary legal obligations.
6. List several steps management can take to prevent legal transgressions.
7. Why and how do general employment and termination practices differ between public and private institutions?
8. Know what the following acronyms mean:
   Federal agencies: OPM, ICE, DOL, DOT, FEPC, NLRB
   Laws: CRA, CSRA, ADEA, IRCA, HIPAA
   Other: BFOQ, ADR, CDL, MBO, MSDS, ROI, OJT

Practical Applications

1. Determine if your employer is subject to FMLA, ADA, FEP or COBRA. If so, what is the smallest size of employer subject to that particular state regulation?
2. What are any unique classes protected under your state EEO or FEP law?
3. Early in this chapter, a program of fair employment standards is set forth. In your experience, which seem to suffer neglect, and which have you observed to be well established?
4. Research the content of an affirmative action plan and be prepared to explain its construction and use.

Case-Study Discussions

Case 11.1

In 2008, 900 ICE agents arrested 400 illegal employees at Agriprocessors Inc. in Iowa. The next year, eighteen illegal immigrants were arrested in a San Diego bakery and several Peruvian nationals were arrested in an Idaho coffee shop.

1. What do you think is at issue in these situations?
2. Why were laws likely neglected or ignored?
3. Why would these conditions develop?
4. What are the current political views and/or controversies regarding immigration law?

Case 11.2

With a few years' experience as a department supervisor, an acquaintance has asked to meet with you to discuss a new start-up venture in the gaming industry, for which she will soon have an initial interview as a personnel manager. She has been working as a payroll/records/interview administrator and wants a career improvement, but is a newcomer to the gaming industry. The enterprise is a small casino that seeks an HR manager. The owners are transferring in experienced executives to manage finance, gaming, security, and food and beverage. Their established stature, and presumably preferred way of doing things, is of some concern to your acquaintance. It's been explained that the State Gaming Commission requires assurances of able management, felony-free employees and the implementation of an aggressive affirmative action plan.

1. Develop five inquiries that your acquaintance should use in the interview about employment law that can demonstrate knowledge of legal considerations and/or a start-up situation.
2. What other subject matter, questions and issues for the start-up phase would you suggest the applicant be prepared to discuss or question? List four.
3. At what point should the employer put an HR staff position to work? Why?

LIST OF ACRONYMS

AAP	Affirmative Action Plan
ADA	Americans with Disabilities Act
ADEA	Age Discrimination in Employment Act
ADR	Alternative Dispute Resolution
AFL–CIO	American Federation of Labor and Congress of Industrial Organizations
ASTD	American Society for Training and Development
BFOQ	Bona Fide Occupational Qualifications
BLS	Bureau of Labor Statistics
BMCS	Bureau of Motor Carrier Safety
CDC	Centers for Disease Control and Prevention
CDL	Commercial Driver's License
CFR	Code of Federal Regulations
CMV	Commercial Motor Vehicle
CMVSA	Commercial Motor Vehicle Safety Act
COBRA	Consolidated Omnibus Budget Reconciliation Act
CRA	Civil Rights Act
CSRA	Civil Service Reform Act
DHHS	Department of Health and Human Services
DHS	Department of Homeland Security
DOJ	Department of Justice
DOL	Department of Labor
DOT	Department of Transportation
EAP	Employee Assistance Program
EEO	Equal Employment Opportunity
EEOC	Equal Employment Opportunity Commission
EOE	Equal Opportunity Employer
EPA	Equal Pay Act
EPLI	Employment Practices Liability Insurance
EPPA	Employee Polygraph Protection Act
ERISA	Employment Retirement Income Security Act
ERP	Emergency Response Plan
ESA	Employment Standards Administration
ESOP	Employee Stock Ownership Plan
FAA	Federal Aviation Administration
FCRA	Fair Credit Reporting Act
FEPC	Fair Employment Practices Commission

FHWA	Federal Highway Administration
FICA	Federal Insurance Contributions Act
FLRA	Federal Labor Relations Authority
FLSA	Fair Labor Standards Act
FMCS	Federal Mediation and Conciliation Service
FMLA	Family and Medical Leave Act
FOIA	Freedom of Information Act
FRSA	Federal Railroad and Safety Act
FTE	Full-Time Equivalency
FUTA	Federal Unemployment Tax Act
HAZCOM	Hazardous Communication Program
HAZMAT	Hazardous Material Notification Program
HCW	Health Care Worker
HHC	Highly Hazardous Chemicals
HIPAA	Health Insurance Portability and Accountability Act
HMO	Health Maintenance Organization
HRA	Health Reimbursement Account
ICE	Immigration and Customs Enforcement
ICMA	International City/County Management Association
IRA	Individual Retirement Account
IRCA	Immigration Reform and Control Act
IRS	Internal Revenue Service
ISO	International Organization for Standardization
LMRA	Labor Management Relations Act
MBO	Management by Objectives
MSDS	Material Safety Data Sheet
MSHA	Mine Safety and Health Administration
NASPE	National Association of State Personnel Executives
NIOSH	National Institute for Occupational and Safety Health
NLRA	National Labor Relations Act
NLRB	National Labor Relations Board
OFCCP	Office of Federal Contract Compliance Programs
OJT	On-the-Job Training
OPIM	Other Potentially Infectious Materials
OPM	Office of Personnel Management
OSHA	Occupational and Safety Health Act
OWBPA	Older Workers Benefit Protection Act
PDA	Pregnancy Discrimination Act
PERA	Public Employees Retirement Association
PHI	Protected Health Information
PPE	Personal Protection Equipment

LIST OF ACRONYMS

QMCSO	Qualified Medical Child Support Orders
QWL	Quality of Work Life
RIF	Reduction in Force
ROI	Return on Investment
RSI	Repetitive Stress Injury
SEP	Simplified Employee Pension Plan
SHRM	Society for Human Resource Management
SPD	Summary Plan Description
SSA	Social Security Act
TPA	Third-Party Administrator
TPD	Total and Permanent Disability
TQM	Total Quality Management
TTD	Temporary Total Disability
UIFSA	Uniform Interstate Family Support Act
USERRA	Uniformed Services Employment and Reemployment Rights Act
WARN	Worker Adjustment and Retraining Notification Act
WHD	Wage and Hour Division

GLOSSARY

One hallmark of an established field of study or vocation is a common body of language. This glossary provides many of the terms used in human resource management. These definitions are conceptual in nature and are not to be used for legal purposes.

Ability: The potential capabilities of an individual.

Accidental Death and Dismemberment Insurance (AD&D): Insurance providing benefits in the event of loss of life, limbs or eyesight as the result of an accident.

Accommodation to disabilities: An adjustment made by an employer to facilitate employment of a disabled employee by altering a job or modifying equipment.

Accountability: Being answerable for an assignment.

Administer: To execute an established matter (policy, law).

Adverse impact: In employment, when a selection practice or technique results in a lower proportion of minorities being selected than from other groups.

Affirmative action: Proactive measures taken to correct the effects of past discrimination in hiring and promotion.

Applicant: An individual demonstrating desire for employment.

Arbitration: Method of deciding a controversy under which parties to the controversy have agreed in advance to accept the award of a third party.

Archives: Records stored for a long period.

Area rate differentials: Pay differences resulting from geographical patterns (Keokuk vs. NYC).

Attrition: A normal reduction in the number of employees due to resignation or retirement.

Audit: An organized, documented inspection and verification of records and procedures.

Authority: The power of a position.

Authorization card: A card to be signed by employees to indicate interest in having a union-organizing election. Management should never look to see who has signed such cards.

Background check: To gather information about people of interest.

Bargaining unit: A group of employees officially designated to be a union.

Base rate: The hourly rate or salary paid for a job performed; does not include shift differentials, benefits, overtime, incentive premiums or any other pay element other than the base pay rate.

Benchmark: A point of reference sufficiently defined and common that other units can be compared to it. In compensation, a benchmark refers to the specific job and is used for making pay comparisons either within the organization or to comparable jobs outside the organization.

Beneficiary: The person designated to receive a benefit resulting from the death of an employee, such as benefits from a pension plan or the proceeds of a life insurance policy.

Benefits: Non-cash compensation programs often provided by the employer that are not job related but are common to employees of the organization in general.

Blacklisting: An illegal step to prevent a former employee from obtaining other employment.

Blood-borne pathogens: Microorganisms that are present in human blood and can cause disease in humans. These bacteria include the hepatitis B virus (HBV) and the human immunodeficiency virus (HIV).

Bodily fluids: Fluids that have been recognized by OSHA and the CDC as linked to the transmission of HIV and/or HBV: blood, semen, blood products and vaginal secretions.

Bona fide occupational qualifications (BFOQ): An essential job-related requirement for a position, such as a specific gender for the role of restroom attendant.

Bonus: Usually an annual lump sum payment made in addition to an employee's normal salary or wage; ostensibly based on personal or group performance.

Boycott: To avoid dealing with or buying the products of a business as a means of exerting pressure in a labor dispute.

Break in service: A separation from the payroll requiring an employee to "start over" as new; an event ending the period of qualifying for compensation.

Broadbanding: Reducing the number of salary grades with corresponding increases in the number of jobs included in grades.

Buddy system: The assignment of experienced employees to train newcomers.

Budget: A plan for spending.

Bumping: An act of replacing another worker by virtue of a longer period of employment.

Business agent: A paid representative of a local union who handles its grievance actions, negotiates with employers, enrolls new members and manages other business affairs.

Cafeteria (flexible) plan: A program in which an employee allocates pre-tax dollars for a choice of benefits.

Callback pay: A pay guarantee to employees called in to work for unscheduled hours; a normal union contract provision.

Candidate: Someone who satisfies qualifications and is to be considered for employment.

Career: The vocations and jobs held by an individual during their work life.

Case law: Court interpretations that form a legal pattern.

Cash compensation: The monies paid to a worker.

Chain-of-custody protocol: Procedures for ensuring accurate specimen identification and handling in drug testing.

Checkoff: A union security provision whereby the employer agrees to deduct dues from employee paychecks and remit them to the union.

Civil law: Concerned with the constitutional rights of private persons; a victim would have a right to a civil action for redress in money damages. In contrast, criminal law is concerned with public rights and public authorization of punishment through fines or imprisonment.

Civil rights: In the U.S., rights protected by the U.S. Constitution and various statutes by which an individual may not be discriminated against in education, housing, voting, employment, public accommodations and other matters based on their minority status, age, sex or other specified characteristics.

Class (collective) action: A legal action often filed by one person but extended on behalf of all individuals who are "similarly situated"; potentially a costly action against employers.

Climate: In an organization, the nature of a group of people (e.g., friendly, businesslike, suspicious).

Coaching: Providing goals, feedback and guidance.

Coinsurance: An insurance provision whereby the carrier and claimant share the cost at a set percentage.

Collective bargaining: A process whereby representatives of employees and an employer negotiate an agreement.

Commercial motor vehicle: A motor vehicle used in commerce to transport passengers or property if the motor vehicle (1) has a gross combination weight rating of 26,001 or more pounds inclusive of a towed unit with a gross vehicle weight rating of more than 10,000 pounds; or (2) has a gross vehicle weight rating of 26,001 or more pounds; or (3) is designed to transport sixteen or more passengers, including the driver; or (4) is of any size and is used in the transportation of hazardous materials.

Commissions: Pay for units sold. Similar to production piece rates, commissions are often a percentage of the revenue.

Comparable worth: A doctrine that men and women who perform work of the same value should receive the same pay except for specific differences, such as seniority, merit or a different location.

Compensation: The amount of earned income an individual receives from services rendered as a result of employment, including money, benefits, services, in-kind payments and psychological benefits.

Compensatory time off: "Comp time" is time off in exchange for an excess of work hours in a period, balancing weekly hours to avoid premium pay. Time off in one workweek cannot be used to offset extra hours in a different week. There is an exception in the health care industry.

Competitive pay: The pay rates of the organization compared to those paid by competitors.

Complaint: In a non-legal context, an employee's disagreement with management.

Complete staff work: Full and accurate work of the highest quality.

Compression: In pay, a condition when the pay of one position becomes undesirably close to the next higher or lower position in the job hierarchy.

Concerted activity: Actions undertaken by a group of employees verses an employer.

Conflict resolution: A process of addressing a problem or issue through compromise or other techniques.

Consortium: A group or association of employers or contractors that collaborate to provide a service, such as trucking employers providing controlled substance testing services.

Contract: A mutually binding agreement agreed to by participating parties.

Constructive discharge: When an employer creates conditions that a person cannot endure so that the employee quits, this is treated by courts as a discharge.

Consultant: A knowledge or skill specialist.

Consumer price index (CPI): An index published monthly by the federal government that is intended to reflect changes in the cost of living of a "market basket" of U.S. goods and services.

Contingent employees: Personnel on call by an employer.

Contributory benefit plan: A benefit plan in which the employee contributes part (or all) of the cost.

Controlled substances: Includes alcohol, marijuana, amphetamines, opiates, phencyclidine (PCP) and cocaine.

Core hours: Those hours during which employees are required to be at their place of work.

Cost-to-benefit ratio: The value (benefit) of something relative to the cost.

Cost-of-living adjustment: Increase or decrease in wages according to the rise or fall of the consumer price index (CPI). Actual job market indices vary to a different degree than the consumer market basket.

Credit bureau: A company that compiles and maintains information on consumer credit and provides the information for a fee.

Criteria: Key dimensions of a matter, such as crucial hiring needs.

Cronyism: Unfair awarding of jobs, contracts and favors to friends by persons in authority.

Culture: Prevailing perceptible and established pattern of themes, attitudes and values in a society of people.

Data: Factual material for later application.

Defamation of character: The result of a written or oral statement initiated or permitted to circulate based on false and/or potentially damaging information about a person.

Deferred compensation: Compensation payments that accrue to the employee to be received at some time in the future.

Defined benefit plan: A retirement option with a benefit formula requiring an employer to contribute enough to satisfy an estimated benefit.

Delegation: Assigning work and accountability to another person or unit.

Direct compensation: All forms of compensation that involve direct and immediate payment to the worker; generally paycheck monies.

Disability: A physical or mental impairment that substantially limits one or more of the major life activities. This is often a permanent condition under the ADA but is often classified as temporary in workers' compensation situations.

Discharge: An employer action that indicates a worker's services are no longer wanted; an involuntary removal from the payroll.

Discipline: A condition relative to desired standards; a technique used to correct behavior.

Disclaimer: A denial of responsibility. An example is an employee handbook stating that the handbook is not a legal contract.

Discrimination: To differentiate. Illegal discrimination is where there is different treatment in violation of a statute; for example, treating an employee differently on the basis of a protected characteristic such as age or sex.

Dismissal: Involuntary terminated, discharged, fired.

Disparate impact: The result of an employer's action, negatively affecting a protected class of employees.

Diversity: Differences of gender, age, religion, race and so on in a group of people.

Downsizing: Reducing the number of employees in a workplace.

Drug and alcohol testing: Analysis of a body sample for the purpose of measuring the presence or absence of drugs or alcohol in the sample tested.

Due diligence: Acquiring full knowledge of characteristics, weaknesses and risks.

Due process: Procedures used to pursue justice that provides for a defense and a fair decision.

Early retirement age: The age when an employee is first permitted to retire and elect a retirement plan payment option.

Earnings: Total wages or compensation received by an employee, including all overtime, premium pay and bonuses.

EEO Report: An annual report to the EEOC by employers of 100 or more employees showing the percentage representation of women, veterans and minorities in job categories.

Employee assistance plan: Programs to help employees with problems that interfere with work performance.

Employee benefit: Something of monetary value to an employee that is not related to work performed and is paid for either partially or wholly by the employer.

Employee health program: An available and self-directed program of education, exercise and health promotion to improve employee health.

Employee relations: The level of allegiance of employees to the employer or the composite of practices affecting the relationship.

Employee stock ownership plan (ESOP): A stock bonus plan with awards of an employer's stock.

Employer: An entity that employs one or more employees, or a person who has the power to hire or fire.

Employment at will: A common law doctrine whereby an employee can be terminated for good cause or no cause.

Employment contract: A contract that provides an employee and employer with a guarantee of certain considerations.

Employment law: The body of law dealing with the employee-employer relationship.

Engagement: A condition of mental or emotional involvement by an employee with an employer.

Engineering controls: In safety, physical steps that isolate or remove blood-borne bacteria from the workplace.

Equal Employment Opportunity (EEO): An employment condition in which neither intentional nor unintentional illegal discrimination is present.

Equal Employment Opportunity Commission (EEOC): A commission of the federal government charged with enforcing the provisions of the Civil Rights Act of 1964 and the Equal Pay Act as it pertains to gender discrimination in pay.

Ergonomics: The study of workers interacting with job demands, equipment and conditions to prevent injuries such as repetitive stress injuries or cumulative trauma disorder.

Essential functions: The fundamental, not marginal, duties of a job.

Ethnic group: A group of a particular race, religion or national origin.

Evaluation: To appraise or judge in a thoughtful, deliberate manner.

Executive: A principal manager of an organization who allocates resources and sets objectives that will influence results.

Executive compensation: Any of a variety of methods for rewarding executives of an organization (e.g., bonus payments, stock plans, incentives and perquisites).

Executive order: A regulation by the president of the United States, or the chief executive of a state, which has the effect of law in the governmental jurisdiction with which it deals.

Exempt job: A job not subject to the provisions of the Fair Labor Standards Act with respect to minimum wage and overtime. Exempt employees include most professionals, administrators, executives and outside sales representatives.

Expatriate: A U.S. citizen who works in foreign countries.

Exposure: Herein this refers to conditions that open the possibility of adverse legal action or injury.

Exposure incident: A situation in safety when an employee's skin has been penetrated by a contaminated object, or when mucous membranes or injured skin has come in contact with potentially infectious material.

External equity: A fairness criterion of wages that corresponds to rates prevailing in external markets of an employee's occupation.

Face validity: An expression applied to a test that logically appears valid but may be without statistical proof.

Factor comparison: A job evaluation plan in which relative values for each of a number of factors of a job are established by comparing them with the values established for the same factors on other jobs.

Fair employment practices: Usually state and local laws prohibiting illegal discrimination.

Family of jobs: Refers to a grouping of positions, such as levels of accounting or engineering competency.

Fiduciary: One who is trusted with someone else's money; the entity responsible for the judicious administration of funds.

Flexible benefits: An individualized plan that accommodates individual preferences for benefits.

Flextime: Flexible hour arrangements in which employees are allowed to set their own schedules, usually around a core time.

Fringe benefits: A term first used around 1943 by the National War Labor Board to describe benefits such as vacation, holidays and pensions, which were thought to be "on the fringe of wages"; the term is now considered obsolete and inappropriate by compensation and benefit professionals.

Full-time equivalency: A method of measuring time allotments. The number of work hours divided by that available and expressed with a decimal. Hence, 1.0 FTE is representing a full day's work of eight hours, and .5 FTE indicates the work requires only half (four hours) of the normal eight-hour schedule.

Gainsharing: A cost savings plan benefiting production employees.

Garnishment: A court order requiring the employer to deduct a portion of the debtor's pay.

Garrity warning: A necessary notification to an employee that questions are part of an official investigation, it provides legal protection in order to engender honest answers.

General duty clause: Refers to the general duty clause of the OSH Act, Section 5(a)(1), which states that "[e]ach employer . . . shall furnish to each of his employees employment and a place of employment which are free from recognized hazards that are causing or are likely to cause death or serious physical harm to his employees."

Glass ceiling: A perceived barrier that prevents women from advancing in management.

Golden parachute: A special financial protection plan (including cash payments and future income) for key executives in the event of an unfriendly takeover by another firm.

Good faith and fair dealing: Acting with an honest, sincere and reasonable basis.

Good-faith bargaining: The type of bargaining in which an employer and union must engage in order to meet their bargaining obligations under the Taft-Hartley Act.

Grandfathered: An exception to the norm based on prior conditions or agreements; a fixed rate of pay for an individual or group.

Grievance: A complaint under a labor agreement where the employee alleges a violation. The established procedure normally involves a number of steps in search of resolution.

Group benefits: A bundling of employees whereby benefits are made available at a pricing advantage and often on a tax-free basis.

Group term life insurance: Annual renewable term life insurance covering a group of employees in accord with a stipulated schedule of benefits.

Hard copy: Information recorded on paper.

Hazardous substance: Dangerous matter as determined by the Resource Conservation and Recovery Act.

Headhunter: A firm or individual engaged in the recruitment of executive-level management and professional personnel who are normally presently employed.

Health care provider: Those who are paid for delivering health services.

Health maintenance organization (HMO): Defined in the Health Maintenance Organization Act of 1973 as "an organized system for the delivery of comprehensive health maintenance and treatment services to voluntarily enrolled members for a pre-negotiated, fixed, periodic payment." HMOs must be offered to participants in group health plans as an alternative choice for coverage.

Health reimbursement accounts: A type of defined contribution health plan. This plan design allows participants to use an account to reimburse current medical expenses and carry over unused amounts to subsequent years.

Hiring rate: As a matter of pay practice, the beginning rate at which people are hired into a job.

Holidays: Specific days when most employees do not work but are often paid as if they did. Employees who do work on such days typically receive premium pay or compensable time.

Hostile environment: Conduct unwisely tolerated by the employer that is offensive and abusive to a reasonable person; often true in sexual harassment situations but applicable to age, national origin and other protected categories of employees.

Human resource function: A function devoted to the effective acquisition, maintenance and utilization of an organization's employees for the purpose of achieving its goals.

Human Resource Information System (HRIS): A computer system for gathering, storing, analyzing, retrieving and distributing accurate human resource data and information.

Implied contract: A perceived agreement that is suggested by the behavior of the parties of an employment relationship but is not in writing.

Incentives: The encouragement of output with pay for targets achieved.

Incumbent: The person occupying a position.

Indirect compensation: Compensation beyond the salary or wage being paid, such as paid vacation and employer insurance contributions.

Individual pay rate: The rate of pay assigned to a given individual; individual pay rates may vary on the same job as a function of time in grade or performance.

Individual retirement account (IRA): A form of defined contribution plan for individuals; an employee may make tax-deductible contributions to their own retirement account and to their spouse's if the spouse is not employed; contributions are limited.

Industry: A group of organizations with similar products. The term can be used broadly ("food products") or more narrowly (" cheese").

Inflation: A term commonly used in reference to the increase in price of a constant basket of goods.

Insubordination: When an employee refuses to comply with a reasonable order of an employer.

Intellectual property: The patents, trademarks, copyrights, designs and trade secrets of a company.

Internal equity: A fairness criterion whereby an employer sets pay rates that correspond logically to the relative value of other jobs in the organization.

Internal Revenue Service (IRS): The agency of the federal government responsible for collection of income tax and the enforcement of the Internal Revenue Code; IRS rules are important in the design of benefit programs and executive compensation.

Investigative consumer reports: Provides information through personal interviews of others.

Involuntary termination: A termination initiated by the company.

Job: A cluster of work tasks. A position is a collection of tasks assigned to a specific individual.

Job analysis: A study of the tasks constituting a job, the skills required, time factors, technology use, physical aspects, information flows and interpersonal interactions to provide the information needed to define jobs and determine job values.

Job description: A concise and accurate summary of work performed, specific responsibilities and employee knowledge, and the skills required to accomplish a job.

Job design: Constructing duties, methods and relationships of a job to achieve an objective effectively and efficiently.

Job evaluation: A systematic process by which management determines the relative value of various jobs within the organization. The end result of job evaluation is usually a hierarchy of pay grades to enable the fair pay of jobs.

Job evaluation committee: A committee that carries out the process of job evaluations, normally with variable membership.

Job function: A composition of related activities formed as a unit of a larger system, directed to a common purpose.

Job preview: Exposing a job prospect to working conditions.

Job pricing: The practice of establishing wage rates for jobs, usually based primarily on competitive pay data but referencing internal job relationships.

Job qualifications: Education, experience and other competencies determined to be requirements for job success.

Job title: A label for a job that may or may not accurately reflect the actual content of the job.

Just cause: A nebulous standard that claims an action is for sufficient reason.

Key jobs: Jobs that are used either in wage surveys or in job evaluation for making comparisons with other jobs; a position critical to the success of an organization.

Layoff: A temporary release from work when recall to the same employer is expected; an interim status.

Leadership: Skills in influencing the thinking and behavior of others to follow in course of action.

Lead person: The member of a work group who works along with the group and assists the supervisor as requested.

Leave of absence: An authorized absence for a period of three days or more, usually expressed in writing; without an understanding, an absence is simply an absence.

Line management: Makes operational decisions and directs product or service production.

Litigation: An engagement in a lawsuit.

Lockout: Closing a business to employees as a form of economic pressure to force acceptance of an employer's bargaining terms.

Long-term care: Services to help with the living routines of the handicapped for an extended period of time.

Long-term income protection: Plans based on income level that provide financial assistance to workers when they incur permanent disabilities that limit or prohibit future employment.

Major medical insurance: Protection for costly surgical, hospital or other medical expenses and services. Benefits are paid once a specific deductible is met and are then generally subject to coinsurance.

Malice: An intentional act done for the purpose of causing harm to another.

Managed care: Medical care provided with cost parameters.

Management: The function of a position that involves planning, organizing and controlling the resources and activities of an organization towards its objectives.

Management development: To provide learning experiences expected to be helpful for present or future managers.

Management malpractices: An employer's conduct toward employees beyond society's boundaries.

Management rights: Prerogatives of an employer to direct and control operations.

Management rights clause: Collective bargaining contract clause that expressly reserves to management certain rights not subject to the grievance procedure or arbitration.

Manager: An employee with command authority who directs activity to achieve some result.

Market pricing: A pay-setting practice that sets job rates to be paid based on the going wage rate in the competitive marketplace for that job.

Material safety data sheet (MSDS): A technical safety document provided by the manufacturer about chemical hazards.

Median: The value in the middle of data; half the data is greater and half is less than that point.

Mediation: An informal negotiation of an agreement through a third party.

Medical savings account (MSA): An account established by an employee to help cover the expense of a high-deductible health plan (at least $1500); tax-free contributions can be made by either the employee or employer.

Medicare: Federal health insurance for basic hospital and medical care for those ages sixty-five and older.

Mentor: An advisor.

Merit increase: An adjustment to individual salary, theoretically based on performance.

Midpoint: The salary midway between the minimum and maximum rates of a pay range.

Minimum wage: A minimum wage level for American workers established by Congress as part of the Fair Labor Standards Act; also established by state legislators for intrastate commerce.

Minor: Someone younger than eighteen years of age.

Minority: A group of lesser number than the majority; often associated with affirmative action policies.

Mission: A concise statement of direction for an organization.

Negligence: The failure to use a reasonable amount of care.

Negligent hiring: The liability of an employer when the employer knew or should have known of an employee's dangerous tendencies that caused injury to others.

Nepotism: Patronage bestowed upon a family member.

Non-contributory benefit plan: A plan in which the employer pays the total cost of providing the benefit.

Nonexempt: A reference to employees subject to the FLSA, requiring time-and-a-half pay for work over forty hours per week.

Nonprofit firms: Tax-advantaged organizations that do not have owners or distribute profits, often providing services; education, health care, social services, arts and foundations that have appropriate pursuits.

Non-qualified pension plans: Plans that provide excessive benefits or for other reasons do not meet IRS requirements, and thereby do not qualify for favorable tax treatment.

Objective: A statement in writing expressing a desired end result to be achieved within a certain cost and time frame.

Occupation: A generalized job or family of jobs, such as accounting or nursing.

Occupational exposure: Circumstances open to a dangerous incident, such as the presence of blood-borne pathogens.

Occupational injury: An injury such as a cut, fracture or sprain that results from a work incident or from an exposure involving a single incident in the workplace.

Ombudsman: An appointed official who hears and seeks the resolution of issues.

Open-door policy: A system that theoretically permits an employee to visit with management about any concerns.

Opinion survey: A technique to collect worker views.

Organization: An arrangement of resources under direction that is dedicated to a desired result.

Organization development: A planned process of intervention and change to an organization or its culture (norms, standards, rules, authority structure, values, beliefs).

Orientation: Basic education about new circumstances.

Outplacement: A program to help released employees find other employment through help with materials preparation, tactics and interview training.

Outsourcing: Contracting with another provider to perform some work of the organization.

Overtime: Under the Fair Labor Standards Act, nonexempt employees subject to the law must be paid one and a half times their normal wage rates for all hours worked in excess of forty in any workweek; state statutes also exist with different regulations.

Pathogen: An agent such as bacteria or a virus that causes a disease.

Pay grade: One of the pay levels into which jobs of the same or similar value may be grouped for compensation purposes; all jobs in a pay grade have the same pay parameters.

Pay range: The range of pay rates from minimum to maximum set for a pay grade; used as a guideline for setting individual employee pay rates.

Pay structure: A hierarchy of pay rates for jobs in an organization.

Pay survey: The collection of wage and salary data from other employers from which a pay structure can be developed.

Pay-trend line: A line fitted to a scatter plot that treats pay as a function of job values; the most common technique for fitting a pay-trend line is regression analysis.

Pension: Established by an employer for deferred payments to eligible retired employees.

Pension Benefit Guaranty Corporation (PBGC): An employer-financed insurance fund to guarantee defined retirement plan benefits, similar to FDIC insurance for bank accounts.

Pension trust fund: A fund consisting of money contributed by the employer and, in some cases, the employee, which is granted to a trustee who invests the money, collects the interest and earnings, and disperses the benefits under the terms of the plan.

Performance appraisal: A system intended to determine how well an employee has performed during a period of time.

Performance management: Activities intended to improve personal and unit performance.

Performance standards: Task or behavioral standards established that provide the basis for judging performance.

Perks: A term used for perquisites or extraordinary privileges (e.g., club memberships, parking places).

Permanent partial disability: A disability that cannot be mended.

Personnel documents: All information kept by an employer about an employee in the course of employment.

Physical impairment: Any physiological disorder or condition affecting one or more body systems.

Piece rate: Payment based on production by a worker; a payment made for each piece or other quantitative unit of work produced by an employee.

Placement: In employment, selecting a position for someone out of various options.

Plaintiff: A person who brings suit before a court of law; a complainant.

Plan administrator: As defined by the Employee Retirement Income Security Act (ERISA) of 1974, the organization designated by the terms of the instrument under which a pension or welfare plan operates.

Point factor method of job evaluation: A commonly employed job evaluation technique used by large employers.

Policies: Written management pronouncements that establish intentions and guidelines for decision making throughout an organization.

Portability: The transfer of a benefit from one employer to another.

Position: A construct of duties to be occupied by an employee; if an organization has a need for twenty people performing those same duties, it has twenty people in common positions, or a job.

Prevailing rate: Ostensibly the common amount paid for similar work by other employers in the labor market. The Davis-Bacon Act of 1931 requires most federal contractors of construction or related contracts to pay wage rates and fringe benefits prevailing in the area (normally at levels of union pay).

Principle: An accepted truth.

Privacy: The protection of one's personal affairs.

Procedure: The customary method of accomplishing an objective.

Process: A chain of interrelated actions to achieve a particular end.

Productivity: The level of production (output), such as the number of gadgets or reports produced.

Profit sharing: A discretionary benefit plan in which employees are granted a share of profits in cash or stock.

Program: A body of provisions and actions assembled to accomplish a purpose.

Project: Coordinated actions to accomplish a one-time end within a time frame.

Promotion increase: An increase in pay that accrues to a person because of a promotion to a job of greater difficulty.

Protected activity: An activity by an employee that is protected by law and from employer retaliation.

Protected group/class: Any group specifically protected by EEO laws; this includes sex, race, color, religion, national origin, age and disabilities, among others.

Protocol: Prescribed rules and guidelines.

Public policy: Generally refers to standards for behavior formed by law in support of the common good of our society; it is reflected through statutes, court decisions and the Constitution.

Punitive damages: Damages that compensate above actual loss and are punishment for evil behavior.

Qualifications: A term for attributes necessary for job success, often used interchangeably with *hiring specifications*.

Qualified plan: A tax-favored instrument meeting rigid specifications, such as pension, profit sharing, or stock bonus plans, which permit the employer to deduct contributions and the employee to pay no taxes until funds are withdrawn.

Quality management: A collection of policies, standards and procedures to accomplish a product or service quality function.

Quality of work life: The level of satisfaction available to an organization's workforce.

Quit: To voluntarily terminate employment.

Random selection basis: A mechanism for selecting employees for drug testing that does not give an employer discretion in the decision.

Range: A dollar spread with a minimum and maximum within which a position is to be paid.

Ranking method of job classification: A job-to-job comparison of jobs, resulting in an ordering of jobs from highest to lowest based on perceived difficulty.

Reasonable accommodation: An effort on the part of the employer to alter methods or conditions to enable a worker.

Red-circle rates: Rates that are above the maximum rate for a job or pay range for a specific reason.

Regulations: Enforceable rules established by legal bodies.

Release: The relinquishing of a claim or a right, usually by a written document, as a part of a settlement or compromise agreement.

Resignation: A voluntary, permanent separation initiated by the employee.

Responsibilities: Those matters that a position is expected to accomplish.

Retaliation: An adverse action by an employer against an employee for exercising a legal right.

Reverse discrimination: Not defined in statute, the term is commonly used in reference to the exclusion of whites or males in favor of racial minorities or women resulting from affirmative action efforts.

Reward: To compensate after the fact.

Risk: Uncertainty due to the potential occurrence of an event.

Risk management: Making and carrying out actions that will minimize accidental losses to an organization.

Rules: Guidelines that regulate and restrict behavior.

Sabotage: Malicious damage done to equipment or other property.

Safety-sensitive function: Work performed in the employ or service of a common, contract or private transportation entity, including servicing or inspecting equipment, driving, and loading or unloading equipment that might have public safety consequences.

Safety-sensitive position: A job, including any supervisory or management position, in which error or misbehavior might threaten the health or safety of others.

Salary: Compensation paid by the week, month or year (rather than by the hour); generally applies to non-production, non-routine or supervisory jobs exempt from the provisions of the Fair Labor Standards Act.

Salary schedule: A structure of pay ranges, each with a dollar value.

Sampling: Taking selected items from a total population of items.

Savings (thrift) plan: A plan established and maintained by an employer to systematically provide for the accumulation of capital in accord with contributions from employees and/or the employer.

Scattergram: A mathematical technique designed to display data related to a relationship between two variables, such as pay levels and job point values, a scattergram shows plotting of coordinates simultaneously representing x and y scores for a number of observations.

Selection (hiring) process: The steps involved in arriving at a decision of whether to choose a given individual to fill a vacancy.

Self-funded: An employer accepts the risks of financing and does not insure against losses.

Seniority: The length of service an employer has gained in a unit.

Sexual discrimination: Discriminatory actions based on gender distinctions rather than legitimate considerations, or different treatment of an employee based on gender.

Sexual harassment: Sexual advances or requests for sexual favors as well as other verbal or physical conduct of a sexual nature if submission to such conduct is (1) made either a term or condition of an individual's employment, (2) is used as the basis for employment decisions, (3) has the purpose or effect of unreasonably interfering with an individual's work performance or (4) creates an intimidating, hostile or offensive working environment.

Severance pay: Money paid, usually at the employer's option, when a person leaves an organization. In some cases, severance pay formulas may be employed to create incentives for a person to leave prior to normal retirement.

Sharps: Anything that can penetrate the skin, including needles or broken glass.

Shift differentials: Extra pay, usually expressed as a percent or cents per hour, made for employees who work hours deemed undesirable by most.

Sick leave: Paid time when not working due to illness or injury.

Single-rate system: A compensation policy under which all employees in a given job are paid at the same rate instead of being placed in a pay range; generally applies in situations where there is little room for variation in job performance, such as an assembly line.

Skill-based pay: Rewarding workers for a mastered set of skills and knowledge, used or unused.

Slotting: The act of assigning a job ranking relative to others on a list based on an educated guess.

Span of control: The number of people directly supervised.

Specialist: One whose attention is devoted to a particular aspect within a larger function.

Staff: A unit, or position, not directly involved in operating the business; staff units include personnel, legal or accounting that contribute support, expertise or advice. Used in the broadest scope, the total group of personnel.

Staffing: A system of matching people with daily, temporary or contracted labor needs.

Stakeholder: Those who have an interest in an enterprise, such as workers, suppliers, customers, shareholders and government.

Standard: The condition that exists when accountability is suitably satisfied.

Standard operating procedures: Written instructions, usually developed from trial and error.

Status: The condition of an employee relative to the employer; working, inactive, absent.

Statute: A law passed by a legislative body and set forth in a formal document.

Stock: In corporate finance, the form in which an owner's interest is represented, distributed in units known as shares.

Stock option: A form of executive compensation; a right to purchase stock at a stated price.

Stock option plan: A savings plan under which an employee can save and invest money with which the employer's stock is purchased.

Stock purchase plan (qualified): A program under which employees acquire shares in a company's stock.

Strategic planning: Developing action steps that will move the organization or a unit in a desirable direction.

Strategy: An activated plan applying a variety of resources and methods to achieve an ultimate goal.

Strike: The withdrawal of labor by workers.

Structured interview: Thoughtfully constructed standard questions used to gather information about candidates for a position.

Subpoena: A court order directing action or testimony on a specific matter.

Substance abuse: The misuse of drugs or alcohol.

Suggestion system: A formal program that typically includes definite procedures and reward formulas for encouraging employee suggestions.

Summary plan description (SPD): A required description of the rights and benefits provided to each participant and beneficiary of a benefit plan covered under ERISA.

Supervisor: A person who directs others and can normally hire, fire or assign work; the first level of management.

Survivors insurance: Paid upon the death of the employee for the benefit of survivors.

System: A number of interrelated parts used to accomplish a predictable outcome.

Tactic: A relatively small-scale action serving a larger purpose.

Take-home pay: An employee's earnings less taxes, Social Security and other deductions, both voluntary and involuntary, paid by the employer.

Task: A component of work.

Team: A group of people organized to undertake certain work.

Teambuilding: A process to form effective work units of people.

Telecommuting: When an employee works off-site, perhaps at home.

Temporary partial disability: An incapacitating condition precluding an employee from normal duties for a limited period.

Temporary total disability: An incapacitation preventing any work for a period of time.

Termination (separation): A cessation of a relationship with an employer. These terms are more neutral than *dismissal* or *quit*.

Test: Any qualification, question or tool used to differentiate an individual's knowledge or abilities in order to make an employment-related decision. In EEO, a test includes application forms, interviews, performance appraisals, written or skills tests, references, etc., all of which are expected to be valid.

Third-party administration (TPA): A firm whose business is processing claims and fulfilling administrative duties for client employers.

Time study: Determining a standard of performance based on the time necessary to perform the task, often including method analysis and improvement.

Turnover: Voluntary and involuntary addition and termination of people.

Undue hardship: A potentially controversial point of accommodation by an employer at which accommodation costs are beyond that necessary for compliance.

Unemployment insurance: State-administered program that provides financial protection for workers during periods of joblessness.

Unfair labor practice: Actions such as retaliation or threats taken by one of the parties that are prohibited by labor relations statutes.

Uniform Guidelines on Employee Selection Procedures: A voluminous set of federal recommendations and practices published in 1978.

Validity: In employment, if a test is valid, it predicts to some degree what was intended to be measured.

Variable pay: Pay normally related to performance; distinct from fixed or base pay.

Vesting: A provision granting rights for benefits after a specified number of years or service.

Wage: Compensation usually in the form of an hourly rate and typically for only hours worked.

Wage rate: The money rate expressed in dollars and cents paid to an employee per hour.

Wage survey: A survey of a labor market to determine the going rates for benchmark jobs.

Waiver: The relinquishment of a right or claim.

Warning: A verbal or written expression delivered to an employee that denotes the potential of dire consequences.

Welfare plan: Defined under ERISA as health, disability and life insurance as distinct from pension (retirement) plans.

Whistle-blower: One who reports alleged illegal conduct by his or her employer.

Wrongful discharge: Discharge from employment for reasons that are, or might prove, illegal.

Workers' compensation insurance: A means of providing employees who have been injured on the job with cash payments, medical care and rehabilitation service to restore workers to their fullest economic capacity. All benefits are financed by the employer.

Workstation: A location at which work is performed; sometimes mobile.

INDEX

A

Abbreviated Job Content Recording Form, 14
absences, unpaid, 177-179
abusive treatment, 262-263
accident reports, 196-197
Accidental Death and Dismemberment Insurance (AD&D), 182
accommodations, 55-57, 266-267
accounting, 249
acronyms list, 279-281
action word examples, 17
administrative assistants, 100
administrative positions, job descriptions, 17
administrative work, defined, 7
advertising job vacancies, 38-40
affirmative action, 37, 261, 267
Affordable Care Act (ACA), 170, 180
age discrimination, 269
alarms, 203
alcohol testing, 49
alternative dispute resolution (ADR), 224-225
Americans with Disabilities Act (ADA)
    alternative dispute resolution, 224-225
    equal employment opportunity, 29, 31
    family and medical leave, 178
    medical exams, 49
    medical information in personnel file, 247
    working conditions and job duties, 18-19, 63
applicants and application forms, 34-37, 41-43, 52-53. *See also* interviewing applicants
appraisals, 76-79
arbitration, 120-121, 224-225
Argyris, Chris, 118
attitude surveys, 136
at-will doctrine, 227-228
audit checklist, 272-273
audits, 256, 263, 266, 272-273
authority, 34-35, 72, 98, 100, 107-108, 110

B

background checks, 35, 52-55
bargaining units, 4. *See also* unions
benefits
    administration, 187-188
    ancillary benefits, 184-185
    communicating value, 186-187
    competitive patterns, 172-173
    costs, 172
    deferred income plans, 182-184
    defined benefit plans, 258
    free time, 173-179
    fringe, 185
    government influence, 170-171
    group benefits, 266

health care, 180-182, 190
history of, 170
influence on performance, 124
non-financial benefits, 186
pension, 182-184
perks, 94, 126
planning considerations, 169-173
purpose of, 169-170
retirement, 182-184
summary plan descriptions, 186-187
survivors insurance, 182
time off, 124, 173-176
unemployment, 175-176
workforce character, 171-172
review materials, 189-190
blacklisting, 264
blood-borne pathogens, 207
bona fide occupational qualification (BFOQ), 57
bonuses, 147, 149-150
broadbanding, 165, 284. *See also* pay
bumping, 30-31, 222
buy-out agreements, 234

C
campus alarms, 203
Capelli, Peter, 47
career training, 65-66. *See also* training
categories of jobs, 2-8
change within organizations, 105-106
charitable organizations, 94
chemical safety, 205-208
child labor safety, 201
Civil Service Commission, 225
civil service jobs. *See* government entities
Civil Service Reform Act of 1978, 120
Claffey, Doug, 126
Classification Act of 1923, 8
clerical positions, job descriptions, 17
coaching workers, 76
collective bargaining. *See* unions
commercial drivers, 4, 54-55, 198, 201-202, 248
communications
about pay, 163
command structure of organization, 98-100
geographically remote connections, 135
management messages, 132
methods, 134-136
new employees, 87
principal subject matter, 133-134
providing paths, 142
transmissions from employees, 137-138
community, sense of, 127-128
company, defined, xvii
comparable worth, 163, 286
compensation. *See* pay
compensatory time off, 265, 267
competitive testing, 32
computer expert, defined, 7
conduct standards, 72-73
confidentiality agreements, 57
consultants, 3-4, 25-26
continuing education. *See* training

contractors, 3-4, 25-26
cooperative enterprises, 94
core thinking, 139
corporate culture, 104-105, 115, 122, 142
cost-of-living adjustment (COLA), 147, 162

D
defamation of character, 231-232, 244, 268, 273
deferred compensation, 182-184
Deming, W. Edwards, 21, 135
disabled workers, 56, 266. *See also* Americans with Disabilities Act (ADA)
discharge of workers. *See* separations
discipline, 131, 135, 226-227
disclaimers, 35, 74, 187, 224, 259, 270-273
discrimination
    affirmative action, 37
    age, 269
    illegal, 29-30, 260-263
    legal, 57, 261
    racial, 5, 29-30, 37
    unfair labor practices, 264
dismissal. *See* separations
diversity, 260-262
documentation, 18-19, 34-35, 60-61, 130-131, 222-226, 233. *See also* records and recordkeeping
downsizing, 106, 219, 226. *See also* separations
Driver Conduct Training Information Sheet, 198
drug testing, 49, 200-202, 247
due process, 226

E
early retirement, 220
earnings. *See* pay
education. *See* training
educational support programs, 185
electronic communication devices, 268
emergency evacuation plans, 205
employ, defined, xvii
employee appraisals, 76-79
employee assistance plans (EAPs), 184-185
employee information program, 271
Employee Polygraph Protection Act of 1988 (EPPA), 48
employee rights, 263
employee stock ownership plans (ESOPs), 185
employees. *See* workers
employer, defined, xvii
employment at will, 5, 59, 130
employment compliance, 65. *See also* interviewing applicants; staffing practices and oversight
employment stability, 123
employment verification, 244
enculturation, 72
English-language workplaces, 56-57
enrollment of new employees, 59-62
enterprise, defined, xvii
environment. *See* work environment
equal employment, 260-263
ergonomics, 204
ethics, 130
E-Verify, 61, 263

executive compensation, 150

exempt jobs, 6-7, 148, 157-159, 162, 177

exit interviews, 135, 220

expatriate workers, 33, 97

F

fabrication of applicant qualifications, 52-53

factor comparison, 153-156, 290

fair employment practices, 29-30, 260-263. See also racial matters

Fair Labor Standards Act, xvi, 201

family and medical leave, 177-179

federal government. See government entities

fire prevention, 205

firm, defined, xvii

First Report of Injury (FROI), 196

fixed rate pay, 147-148

flexible spending accounts (FSAs), 181

flextime, 173-179

focus groups, 136

foreign workers, 37, 56-57, 61, 276

forged documents, 61

Forrest, J., 127

Fox, James, 223

free time, 173-179

fringe benefits, 185

full time equivalency, 222, 290

function, defined, xviii

functional hierarchy diagrams, 98-100

furloughs, 219

G

gainsharing, 149-150

gender pay inequity, 163

general duty clause, 193, 195, 204, 290

generalist, defined, xvii

glossary, 283-303

golden parachutes, 234

Goodpaster, Kenneth, 110

government entities
    affirmative action, 37
    as employers, 32, 34
    legal compliance, 258
    performance management, 101-102
    supervisors, expectations of, 79-81
    training, 68-69
    as workplace organizations, 92-94

grievances, 138

group benefits, 266

guiding statements, 101

H

handbook for workers, 72-74. See also communications

harassment, 262-263

hazardous substances, 205-207

headhunters, 32, 38

health care benefits, 180-182

health concerns in the workplace. See occupational safety and health

Health Information Technology for Economic and Clinical Health Act (HITECH), 181

Health Insurance and Portability and Accountability Act (HIPAA), 181
health savings plans, 181
health threats. See occupational safety and health
Herzberg, Frederick, 122
hierarchy of needs, 121-122
hire, defined, xvii
hiring. See staffing practices and oversight
holidays, 175
home-based workers, 56
honesty tests, 48
hostile environment, 262
human resource management
    defining, xvii-xviii
    function of, 107-108
    history of, xv-xvii
    practitioners and specialists, 108-111
human resources information systems (HRIS), 245, 255-256

I
I-9 forms, 61, 241-242, 245, 248-250, 263, 266
Immigration and Customs Enforcement (ICE), 61, 276
Immigration Reform and Control Act (IRCA), 29
incentives, 148
income. See pay
independent contractors, 3-4, 25-26
individual retirement accounts (IRAs), 184
industry groups, 82
injury prevention, 193-200
input/output schemes, 9

inspections, 198, 210-211, 265-266
insurance, 180-182. See also benefits
international staffing, 32-34
Internet job postings, 38
interviewing applicants
    appearance of applicant, 55
    inadvisable inquiries, 43-44
    interviewers, 36
    outline for initial interview, 46
    personal interviews, 44-46
    reception of applicant, 44
    telephone interviews, 44-45
    worksite previews, 52

J
job, defined, xvii
job analysis
    case studies, 25
    collecting information, 10-12
    essential vs. non-essential functions, 19
    job ranking data, 21, 152-156, 166-168
    job study techniques, 9-10
    learning about work, 1-2
    position formation, 13
    production schemes, 9
    productivity standards, 20-21
    qualifications, determining, 19-20
    work knowledge, using, 8-9
Job Content Recording Form, 14
job descriptions
    development process, 10

essential *vs.* nonessential functions, 19
program administration, 21
samples, 22-23, 253-254
writing, 13-18
job design, 13
job evaluations, 153-156
job instruction training (JIT), 76
job loss notification, 223
job placement inventories, 48-49
job ranking, 21, 152-156, 166-168
job rights, 225-226
job security, 116
Job Study Interview Pattern, 11
Job Study Questionnaire Content, Sample, 12
jury duty, 177
just cause, 226-227

K
knowledge base, 269-270

L
language competency, 33, 56-57
laws. *See* legal compliance and risks
layoffs, 219-220, 222
learning organizations, 68
leasing workers, 31
legal compliance and risks. *See also* records and recordkeeping; separations
accommodations, 266-267
compensation matters, 265-266
discrimination, 260-263
fair employment practices, 260-263
group benefits, 266
harassment and abuse, 262-263
implementation rules, 270-271
misrepresentations, 273
notifications to employees, 263
regulations, sources of, 259
risk minimization, 268-273
role of laws and regulations, 257-260
standards, 260
state laws, 267-269
unions and collective action, 264-265
wage and hour investigations, 265-266
review materials, 275-276
legal entitlement to work in the U.S., 59-61
legal statements, paraphrasing, 103
lie detector tests, 48
life insurance, 182
local government. *See* government entities
long-term disability (LTD) plans, 174
Ludlow Massacre, xv
lying about applicant qualifications, 52-53

M
MacDougall, M.P., 234
management
definitions, 7
job descriptions, 17
rights, 107, 109
standards of conduct, 72
structure, 98-100
styles, 101-103, 128-132, 138-139

management by objectives (MBO), 102
mandates, 71-72, 132, 134, 202, 247-248, 263
Maslow, Abraham, 121-122, 126
material safety data sheets (MSDS), 206-207
matrix management, 98
McLean, Gary, 78
medical care on site, 198, 204
medical information in personnel files, 247
medical leave, 177-179
Medical Testing Agreement, 202
meeting management, 83-84, 86
mental health assistance, 184-185
merit increases, 147
merit-based employment, 93-94
military duty, 57, 59, 177, 266
minors in the workplace, 55
mission statements, 100-101, 100-107
Myers-Briggs Type Indicator (MBTI), 48

N
National Labor Relations Act, xvi
needs, hierarchy, 121-122
negligent hiring, 53, 268
nepotism, 31
non-compete agreements, 57
nonprofit firms, 94-95

O
occupational safety and health
    accident investigation reports, 197
    background, 191-193
    blood-borne pathogens, 213-214
    catch-all clause, 214
    chemical safety, 205-208
    child labor, 201
    code of conduct newcomer checklist, 199
    consultation assistance, 211
    injury prevention, 193-200
    material safety data sheets, 206-207
    program structure, 195-200
    regulations, 200-208
    resources for advice, 200
    review materials, 212-215
offers of employment, 58-59
organization charts, 98-100
organization development (OD), 106
organizations
    change within, 105-106
    command structure, 98-100
    congruency, 103-104
    culture and character, 104-105
    defined, xviii
    direction, 101
    economic sector differences, 91-97
    framework and processes, 97-100
    human resource management, 107-111
    improvement, 68
    international, 96-97
    management styles, 101-103
    policies and procedures, 103-105
    principles of organization, 106-107
    purpose, 100-101

       rights of workers and managers, 107, 109

       work process, 97-98

       review materials, 112-114

orientation, 62, 70-77

OSHA (Occupational Safety and Health Administration), 204-211, 229

output requirements, 21

outsourcing, 30

overseas workers, 96-97

overtime, 6-8, 56, 100, 147, 163

P

paid time off, 124, 173-176

pay

       administration, 161-163

       bonuses, 147, 149-150

       broadbanding, 165, 284

       common methods, 147-150

       communications about, 163

       comparable worth, 163, 286

       compensatory time off, 265, 267

       compression, 163

       decisions, 160-161

       executive, 150

       fixed rate, 147-148

       grades and schedules, 157-159

       guideline construction, 157-159

       income replacement programs, 176

       job ranking, 166-168

       legal compliance, 163, 265-266

       levels, developing, 152-156

       market surveys, 156-157

       negotiations, 161

       for output, 148

       overtime, 147, 163

       planning for, 145-147

       programs and practices, 150-152

       salary surveys, 156-157

       sales incentives, 148-149

       severance, 234

       skill-based, 147-148

       team-based, 148

       variable, 149-150

       wage laws, 265-266, 269

       review materials, 165-168

Pendleton Civil Service Reform Act, xv

pensions, 182-184

performance

       action programming, 138-139

       appraisals, 76-79

       communications, role of, 132-138

       compensation, influence on, 124

       corporate culture, 115

       effective systems, 130-132

       employee-employer relationships, 115-121

       employment and job security, 123

       engagement and affiliation, 127-128

       ethics, 130

       fairness, 127

       influences on, 122-128

       job design and placement, 125-126

       management, 101-102

       management styles, influence of, 128-132, 138-139

opportunity and growth, 128
psychology of workers, 121-122
recognition, 127
rewards, 149-150
social relationships, 126
social responsibility, 129
standards, 20-21, 139, 271
supervisors' role, 131-132
tests, 47
working conditions, 124-125
review materials, 141-142
perks, 94, 126
personal information. *See* records and recordkeeping
personal needs, accommodating, 125
personal protective equipment (PPE), 208
personality tests, 48
personnel change notification, 246
personnel changes, 117
personnel development. *See* training
personnel files. *See* records and recordkeeping
personnel management, 108-111, 116, 270-271
policies and procedures, 103-105
policy statements, 74, 262-263
position, defined, xvii
Position Description, Sample, 22-23
position titles, 98
posters, required, 133
Powell, Colin, 128
practitioner, defined, xvii
preferential hiring, 57, 261
premium pay. *See* overtime

principles, xvii, 55, 101, 139. *See also* names of specific topics
privacy, 181-182, 241-244, 269
privacy officers, 242
private sector organizations, 94-96
probationary periods, 47, 59
process management, 102-103
production positions, job descriptions, 17
production schemes, 9
productivity standards, 20-21
professional work, defined, 7
profit sharing, 149-150, 185
promotion increase, 50
protected class, 231, 267. *See also* affirmative action; discrimination
psychological contracts, 118
psychology, xvi-xvii
public personnel selection systems, 32
public sector organizations. *See also* government entities
generally, 92-96
dismissals, 225-230
employment security, 116
group benefits, 266
public transportation jobs, 4, 49, 55-56

Q

qualifications. *See* job analysis; job descriptions
quotas, 21

R

racial matters, 5, 29-30, 37

ranking, 21, 152-156, 166-168
recognition of performance, 127
records and recordkeeping
    access to information, 242-243
    accounting, 249
    administration of information, 244-251
    authorizations, 247
    contents of files, 239-241
    disclosures to the outside, 244
    disposal, 249-251
    drug-testing data, 247
    forms, 246
    high-security files, 247
    human resources information systems, 245, 255-256
    legal compliance, 269, 271
    mandated information, 247-248
    medical information, 247
    multiple depositories, 247
    precautions, 248-249
    privacy protection, 241-244
    reports, 251-252
    requirements, 240
    retention, 249-251
    schematic of record system, 245
    review materials, 255-256
recruiting, 32, 38. *See also* benefits
reductions in force (RIF), 222
references for hiring, 52-55
regulations. *See* legal compliance and risks
religious accommodation, 55, 57, 266
relocation of worker, 57-58
reporting relationships, 98-100
residency requirements for workers, 56
retaliation, 269
retention, 124, 268. *See also* benefits
retirement plans, 182-184
return on investment (ROI), 150
rights of workers, 164
risk management, 272-273
Robinson, Ken, 126
Roosevelt Administration, xvi

S

safety. *See* occupational safety and health
safety-sensitive function, 4
salary. *See* pay
salary surveys, 156-157
sales incentives, 148-149
sales work, defined, 7
sanitation, 204
satisfiers and dissatisfiers, 122
savings (thrift) plans, 183-184
Schön, Donald, 118
search professionals, 32, 38
seniority, 50
separations
    administrative (without fault), 220-221
    checklist, 221
    constructive discharge, 220
    definitions, 219
    discharges, monitoring, 231
    dismissals, 223-230

involuntary, 222-223
meeting plan, 233
notification meeting, 232-233
overview, 219
recovery from, 234
voluntary, 219-220
review materials, 236-237
severance pay, 234
sexual harassment, 262-263
sick leave, 174
skill-based pay, 147-148
small employers, defined, 95
smoke-free regulations, 202
social media, use in background checks, 54
social responsibility, 129
social security, 184
Social Security Act of 1935, xvi
special accommodations, 56
specialist, defined, xvii
staffing practices and oversight.
See also interviewing applicants
authorization by management, 34
background checks, 52-55
broadcasting job vacancies, 38-40
candidate considerations checklist, 51
categories of work and workers, 2-8
choosing among candidates, 49-55
compatibility, 50
conditions, documenting, 18-19
confidentiality agreements, 57
definitions, 27-28
disabled workers, 56
discrimination, legal, 57, 261
employment compliance case study, 65
English-language workplaces, 56-57
enrollment of new employees, 59-62
fairness, 29-30, 260-263
forms and documentation, 34-35
government entities, 32, 34
integration into workplace, 62
international, 32-34
job descriptions, writing, 13-18
learning about the work, 1-2
methods, 27-28, 30-32
military obligations, 57
non-compete agreements, 57
offers of employment, 58-59
position formation, 13
preferential hiring, 57, 261
preparation and tools, 34-40
program administration, 21-23
qualifications of applicants, 35-36
religious accommodations, 57
relocation, 57-58
residency requirements, 56
screening applicants, 41-43
selection process, 40-49
seniority, 50
sourcing applicants, 36-37
studying work, 9-12
testing, 47-49
training. See training
transportation workers, 55-56

uncommon situations, 55-58
work knowledge, using, 8-9
work-at-home arrangements, 56
young workers, 55
review materials, 24-26, 64-66
standard employment process, defined, 29
standards. *See* job analysis; job descriptions; legal compliance and risks; performance
standards of conduct, 72-73
state government. *See* government entities
stewardship, 271
Strong Interest Inventory, 48-49
supervisors. *See also* management
communication, 134-135
discipline of workers, 131, 135, 226-227
documentation, 130-131, 222-226, 233
expectations of, 79-81
pay decisions, 160-161
performance appraisals of workers, 76-79
role in avoiding legal issues, 270
role in worker performance, 131-132
training, 75-79, 79-82
survivors insurance, 182

T

team-based pay, 148
telecommuting, 173
telephone interviews, 44-45
termination. *See* separations
tests, 32, 47-49. *See also* drug testing
thrift plans, 183-184
Thrift Savings Plans (TSPs), 184

time off, 124, 173-176
titles, 17-18, 98
training
generally, 67-69
career training case study, 65-66
coaching improvement, 76
in dismissal procedures, 230
Driver Conduct Training Information Sheet, 198
educational support programs, 185
enculturation, 72
government entities, 68-69
government mandated, 71
hazardous chemical training, 205-207
job skill straining, 76
management development, 69, 82, 230
newcomers, 70-77
occupational education, 82
preparatory training, 75
resources, 69-70
safety, 196, 205-207
for supervisors, 79-82
supervisors' role, 75-79
tools and instruments, 83-84
written materials, 72-74
review materials, 86-87
transition assistance, 234
transportation workers, 4, 49, 55-56
turnover, 117

U

unauthorized workers, 59-61

underage workers, 269
undocumented workers, 61, 276
unemployment benefits, 175-176
unfair labor practices, 120, 264
uniformity, 81, 108, 130, 273
unions
    blacklisting, 264
    "bumping" into vacant positions, 30-31, 222
    communication with, 138
    contracts, 120
    grievance procedures, 138
    history, xv-xvi
    influence of, 118-121
    legal compliance, 264-265
    public *vs.* private sector, 96
unit cost reduction, 148
unpaid personal absences, 177-179

V

vacations, 175
validity of measures, 153-155, 302
variable pay, 149-150
verification of worker status, 59-61
veterans, 59, 266
violence in the workplace, 53, 203-204
vision statements, 101
volunteers, 40

W

wage and hour investigations, 265-266
wages. *See* pay
walk-around visits, 136
Walker, James W., 8
Whistleblower Protection for Railroad Workers, 229
women, 18, 123, 163, 171, 262. *See also* discrimination; harassment
work conditions, documenting, 18-19
work environment, 104-105, 115, 122, 142, 262
work-at-home arrangements, 56
worker, defined, xvii
Worker Adjustment and Retraining Notification (WARN) Act, 223
workers. *See also* performance; staffing practices and oversight
    categories, 2-8
    files. *See* records and recordkeeping
    health of, 199. *See also* occupational safety and health
    performance standards. *See* performance
    personal relationships between, 262
    recruiting, 32, 38
    rights, 107, 109, 164, 263
    turnover, 117
    underage workers, 269
    undocumented, 61, 276
workers' compensation, 176
working conditions, 124-125. *See also* occupational safety and health
workplace history, xv-xvii
workplace inspections, 198, 210-211
workplace organizations. *See* organizations
worksite previews, 52

wrongful discharge, 227-229.
　　See also separations

Y
young workers, 55

Z
zero-tolerance policies, 103
Zuckerman, Mortimer, 160